The Social Psychology
of Bargaining

Also by Dr Stephenson
THE DEVELOPMENT OF CONSCIENCE
(*London, Routledge and Kegan Paul, 1965*)

The Social Psychology of Bargaining

Ian E. Morley
Lecturer in Psychology
Department of Psychology, University of Warwick

Geoffrey M. Stephenson
Reader in Psychology
Department of Psychology, University of Nottingham

London
George Allen & Unwin Ltd
RUSKIN HOUSE   MUSEUM STREET

© George Allen & Unwin (Publishers) Ltd. 1977

ISBN 0 04 301081 4

Printed in Great Britain by
Willmer Brothers Limited, Birkenhead,

Preface

This book deals with some of the social psychological factors which influence the process of bargaining, defined as negotiation for agreement. A concern with structure in that process is its central theme. We have focused upon collective bargaining between representatives of groups, and our approach derives in part from Ann Douglas's (1957) suggestion that negotiations can be characterised according to change in the balance between the interpersonal and interparty forces involved.

Douglas's ideas were immediately appealing: intuitively they seemed to make sense of the case material described, and they provided a theoretical framework which might be used to guide future research. In 1968 we therefore began a programme of investigation, funded by the Social Science Research Council,[1,2] which was designed to throw light on industrial bargaining at plant level. Our basic strategy was to develop an objective technique (Conference Process Analysis or CPA) for describing what goes on in negotiation groups and to use the technique to describe the process of both simulated (laboratory) and real life negotiations.

Laboratory simulations of plant level negotiations were designed in order experimentally to manipulate the balance between the interpersonal and interparty 'climates' identified by Douglas. At the same time we began to collect tape recordings and transcripts of real life negotiations. It was hoped that 'insights' gained from the laboratory data could be used to guide the search for stages in the case material obtained.

Our first observations of negotiations (at 'Demy Ltd' and 'B. M. Workshops') provided a contrast between controlled orderly debate on the one hand and spontaneous discussion on the other. This led us to attempt to change the balance between interpersonal and interparty forces in experimental work in a fairly straightforward way: using communication systems which varied along a dimension of formality–informality. But the choice of an experimental task posed more serious problems. The psychological literature was dominated by laboratory tasks which were described as bargaining games simply because the players were assumed to have motives both to co-operate and to compete. Dissatisfaction with this (continuing) state of affairs led us to consider in some detail the logic which guides experimental research.

[1]Social Science Research Council Grant, Ref. No. HR.506/1, 'Social psychological factors in union–management negotiating behaviour at the plant level', awarded to Geoffrey M. Stephenson, 1968–69.
[2]Social Science Research Council Grant, Ref. No. HR.1546/1, 'The experimental development of a training programme in negotiating skills', awarded to Geoffrey M. Stephenson, 1972–75.

Experimental studies of bargaining involve laboratory simulations of real states of affairs. As such, they must deal with three sorts of problem: (a) the investigator must define the behaviour he is trying to simulate; (b) he must identify certain key components of that behaviour; and (c) he must translate those components into components of a laboratory task. These problems are discussed in the first three chapters of this book. Chapter 3 identifies different experimental paradigms for the study of negotiation and provides a preliminary classification of experimental tasks. Chapters 4, 5 and 6 provide a critical and comprehensive review of laboratory studies of bargaining.

Part One of our book provides for the first time a systematic review of social psychological approaches to the study of bargaining (negotiation for agreement). It will, we hope, establish guidelines for the conduct of research besides making explicit to both psychologists and practitioners the extent of our knowledge and the nature of the issues to which social psychologists may legitimately address themselves. Part Two presents the results of our own programme of research. Chapters 7 to 9 deal with the effects of more or less formal systems of communication upon the outcomes of simulated (laboratory) negotiations. Chapters 10 to 12 deal with the process of negotiation, which is described by means of a set of categories provided by CPA. Analyses of both simulated and real life negotiations are presented, and the results are used to put forward an extended version of Douglas's theory of stages in the process of negotiation. We hope that this part of the book will be of some practical use to those involved in negotiation.

We have not set out to produce a manual detailing the applications of social science research. We eschewed such a policy partly because in our judgement the time was not right to undertake such a task. By and large, authors must choose between an emphasis upon applications or an emphasis upon 'internal analysis' (Golombiewski 1962). Here we have chosen the latter, in the hope that we can make a contribution to social psychological research. We thought that to choose the former would have required simplification and exaggeration of too many points. In other words, while we hope that practitioners will appreciate our having made evident the importance of social psychological factors in bargaining, we would direct their attention in particular to the final chapters whose practical usefulness is clear-cut. For the most part the text is written at an advanced undergraduate or postgraduate level, and we hope it will appeal to students from a variety of disciplines within the general area of social science research.

We gratefully acknowledge all those who have helped us. In particular we wish to thank: the Social Science Research Council for their financial support; 'Demy Ltd', 'B. M. Workshops' and other firms who have allowed us to observe their committees; and Sandra Ward for her encouragement and expert preparation of the typescript.

Contents

PART ONE

Social Psychological Approaches to Bargaining and Negotiation

A
Definitions and Methods of Study

Introduction

While the experimental study of negotiation groups is of comparatively recent origin, interest in bargaining, negotiation, diplomacy and related processes is long-standing. In the first chapter we shall examine the traditional usage of these terms in the field of international relations and their more recent usage by students of conflict research. In the most general sense, *'bargaining'*, *'negotiation'* and *'diplomacy'* have all been employed to indicate the process whereby parties with conflicting aims establish on what terms they will co-operate. Reliable distinctions between the three concepts are difficult to discern. However, we suggest that to qualify as a negotiation a conference must (a) be a decision-making group, (b) contain members with differing views about what is an acceptable decision, (c) permit a battle of wits between opposing strategists, and (d) undertake discussion before action is taken. Additionally, it is appropriate to distinguish between negotiation and quasijudicial means of determining decisions, like arbitration. Negotiation is ultimately defined as 'any form of verbal communication, direct or indirect, whereby parties to a conflict of interest discuss, without resource to arbitration or other judicial processes, the form of any joint action which they might take to manage a dispute between them'. When negotiators are intent on securing agreement, we suggest that the term 'bargaining' is appropriately used.

Chapter 2 describes four major approaches to bargaining, two of which – those of Joseph McGrath and Ann Douglas – have been seriously neglected in the past. McGrath's *tripolar model of collective bargaining* distinguishes between three sets of forces acting on collective bargainers: those directed towards his *own party*, those directed towards the position of the *opposing party*, and those directed towards the position of the *'community'* (the 'third party'). Forces towards own party are essentially divisive and are expected to exert the greatest influences on outcomes. They are predicted to be inversely related to outcomes, measured as the degree to which a given settlement point satisfies leaders of the three 'parties'. Like Douglas before him, McGrath was interested in the possibility that successful negotiations possess characteristics that distinguish them from unsuccessful negotiations. More importantly he has suggested that forces towards own party are the critical determinants of group process and hence of the success of the negotiation.

Another approach to bargaining emphasises that a negotiator may bargain very differently on behalf of others from how he would on merely his own behalf and that as a representative he faces two additional problems: his *role obligations* to the party he represents, and his *personal commitment to the group* whose position he expresses. Some work on the *psychology of intergroup relations* suggests that these forces independently exert a systematic influence on the conduct of negotiators: (a) both may influence a negotiator's willingness to compromise, and (b) both may affect adversely a negotiator's accurate perception of his own and his opponent's positions.

Third, Walton and McKersie's theory of *bargaining subprocesses* highlights the complexity of relationships in collective bargaining. In collective bargaining, negotiators are not merely dividing the available profits between their respective parties (the subprocess called *distributive bargaining*); they are attempting to increase future profits (*integrative bargaining*), maintain unity each within his own camp (*intra-organisational bargaining*), and as well sustain a relationship each with his opponent which is in line with previous expectations and adequate for present purposes (*attitudinal structuring*). Needless to say, there is considerable conflict between the tactics appropriate to each of these four subprocesses, and Walton and McKersie's work skilfully elucidates the dilemmas involved.

In another approach, Douglas has formulated what amounts to a *prescriptive* or at least *normative account of successful negotiation* in collective bargaining. There are three stages in successful negotiations. In the first stage, *establishing the negotiating range*, negotiators undertake an exhaustive explanation of the differences between their respective party positions; in this their role as representatives is uppermost. In the second stage, *reconnoitering the negotiating range*, negotiators explore the range of possible outcomes but do not commit themselves; they act more as individuals, and their behaviour does not so readily reveal their particular party allegiance. In the final stage, *precipitating the decision-making crisis*, the representative aspect reasserts itself; decisions are made and verified with respective principals before agreement is concluded. A number of investigators have examined negotiations in terms of the process of concession making. In all cases the opening stages are seen to be crucial, as Douglas suggests. In particular, the extent to which the two sides initially differentiate their positions is likely to influence the magnitude of subsequent concessions and the rate at which they are exchanged.

Chapter 3 examines the *form of experimental studies* of negotiation groups. The bulk of work in the so-called psychology of 'bargaining' has required subjects to play abstract *matrix games*. A leading proponent of the approach (Deutsch) believes that key psychological and social psychological issues in union–management and other relationships may be studied meaningfully using abstract versions of the Prisoner's Dilemma and other games in laboratory situations. We argue against the view that the process of bargaining may be studied meaningfully in this way: most importantly, matrix games are not an exercise in group decision making; in addition, subjects have complete knowledge of the results that certain actions will produce; also, these results are trivial and are determined in the absence of a social relationship between the participants. Another variety of game legitimately examines one important aspect of the process of negotiation: the distribution of outcomes. However, *distribution games* have limited communication possibilities and ignore what is customarily a vital part of negotiation: the argument stemming from the differences of belief, attitude and interpretation of information that negotiators bring to the situation. It was economists who first studied bargaining experimentally. Buyers and sellers have to agree on price and quantity of goods exchanged, and bargaining constitutes an exchange of bids between the players. However, the same criticisms as apply to distribution games apply also to such *games of economic exchange*. On the other hand, both *role-playing debates* and *substitute debates* aim to provide realistic simulations. Subjects act as representatives of groups, communicate freely and argue over 'inputs' as well as outcomes. In a substitute debate, subjects are actually selected on the basis of their membership of groups whose interests conflict.

The structure of issues varies from one bargaining situation to another; for example, in management–union negotiations there are frequently many issues at stake, permitting an exchange of concessions of different items in the negotiation of a complex 'package deal'. *Three types of task* are distinguished within each type of game: complex one-dimensional issues, simple one-dimensional issues and multidimensional issues. It is evident that the process of negotiation may vary according to which type of task is employed.

Chapter 1

Definition of Bargaining and Related Terms

Traditional Usage

BARGAINING: THE ECONOMIC CONTEXT

Consider the following passage from P. G. Wodehouse's *Aunts Aren't Gentlemen* (1974):

'"How much do I want, sir?"
"Yes. Give it a name. We won't haggle."
He pursed his lips.
"I'm afraid", he said, having unpursed them, "I couldn't do it as cheap as I'd like, sir . . . I'd have to make it twenty pounds."
I was relieved. I had been expecting something higher. He, too, seemed to feel that he had erred on the side of moderation, for he immediately added:
"Or, rather, thirty."
"Thirty!"
"Thirty, sir."
"Let's haggle." I said.
But when I suggested twenty-five, a nicer looking sort of number than thirty, he shook his grey head regretfully, and he haggled better than me, so that eventually we settled on thirty-five. It wasn't one of my better haggling days.' (pp. 100–1)

According to the OED, to bargain is 'to haggle over terms of give and take'. Economic theories of the bargaining process refer to bargaining in just this sense. P. G. Wodehouse's splendid prose illustrates both the economic connotations of the term 'bargaining' and its somewhat lower status than the related terms 'negotiation' and 'diplomacy'. One feels that Bertie Wooster regards bargaining as the last resort. The economic context is also emphasised by the use of the term 'collective bargaining', introduced late in the nineteenth century in Britain. 'Collective bargaining' was and is used to refer to the arrangement whereby employees agree to have the terms of their individual contracts with employers determined by elected representatives in discussion with employers or employers' representatives.

NEGOTIATION AND DIPLOMACY: THE CONTEXT OF INTERNATIONAL RELATIONS

Despite diverse usages in everyday English, the term 'negotiation' generally refers to the process of conferring with another with the purpose of securing agreement on some matter of common interest. In addition one may of course 'negotiate an affair', 'negotiate a cheque' or 'negotiate a fence', the only similarity between these usages being the surmounting of obstacles or difficulties. In the language of the social sciences the term has been employed in the first general sense and traditionally located in the field of international relations. It there refers to formal discussions between representatives of states, whether public or secret, designed to secure agreement on matters of mutual concern. It is important to note that initial division of opinion between the two parties to a negotiation is not necessarily involved. Increasingly, conferences are arranged in international affairs because the desirability of concerted action on some matter of common interest between two or more states has become apparent, not because there has been or will necessarily be disagreement over what that action should be. Negotiation is, however, typically distinguished from a number of alternative means of securing a solution to conflicts between states, such as resorting to armed force, an international court or arbitration. Moreover, negotiation has traditionally been distinguished from diplomacy, which may also involve discussions between representatives of states.

In its most general sense the term 'diplomacy' has been used to refer to the carrying on of relations between states; thus it comprehends negotiation. In addition to the formal discussions in negotiations, however, a diplomatic 'exchange of views' may occur which is different from negotiation, being designed more to clarify respective positions than to secure agreement. Nevertheless Neal (1964) has proposed that according to prevalent usage diplomacy may be regarded as 'synonymous with negotiation. Since negotiation aims at agreement, and agreement invariably means compromise, *diplomacy* may be defined as the art of making compromises in international political matters which promote rather than jeopardize the basic interests and security of a nation' (p. 201).

'Bargaining' is not a term commonly employed by students of international relations, although its usage in other fields suggests that it could just as well be employed to describe the behaviour observed in many international negotiations. As Brown (1964) has said, '*Bargaining* denotes . . . the process of argument, persuasion, threat, proposal and counter-proposal by which the potential parties to a transaction discuss its terms and possibly reach agreement on them' (p. 50). In other words, bargaining may almost be said to denote the *manner* in which agreement is negotiated.

TERMINOLOGY IN CONFLICT RESEARCH

The growth of interest in social conflict as a specialist field in its own right has further confused the distinctions to be drawn between 'negotiation' and related terms. As our discussion has already indicated, and as Iklé (1964, p. 1) has pointed out, certain concepts 'appear to be well understood until we wish to define them'. This is perhaps especially true in the literature which deals with social conflicts, where 'A finite number of conflict relevant terms is related to a finite (but probably larger) number of conflict relevant concepts. But the relations among these are not invariant' (Fink 1968, p. 430). Indeed, according to Fink, the literature on social conflicts contains both conceptual diversity (i.e. different definitions for the same term) and terminological diversity (i.e. different labels for the same concept). Not surprisingly, this can generate a great deal of semantic confusion: 'Sometimes a given pair of terms may be synonymous; in other contexts they may refer to sharply distinguished, coordinate categories; and in still other contexts, the first may denote a special case of the second, or vice versa' (p. 430). It will be useful to consider further the use of the terms 'negotiation', 'bargaining' and 'diplomacy' in the light of Fink's comments.

Broad definitions

Each term has been used in a very general sense to refer to the processes by which two or more parties relate common interests to conflicting interests. However, although negotiation and diplomacy necessarily involve verbal communication, bargaining may or may not.

(a) Negotiation. It is in this general sense that Pruitt (1969) has defined negotiation as 'verbal communication between two or more parties which is at least ostensibly aimed at reaching joint agreement on some course of action or verbal formulation' (p. 2). Similarly, Nicholson (1970) has defined negotiation as explicit verbal communication 'whereby two contending parties decide between themselves what action to take, when some are better for one than for the other' (p. 67). Thus, in its most general sense, negotiation includes both 'the stiff, solemn deliberations of an international trade conference' and 'emotional outpourings of two small boys arguing over possession of a toy' (Pruitt 1969, p. 2); that is, it includes *all forms of discussion in which parties to a conflict exchange information relevant to the issues which divide them.* The discussion may involve either a direct exchange of views between the interested parties or the transmission of information via a third party. In the latter case, negotiation need not involve a dialogue at all.

Negotiation may have the primary objective of reaching an agreement, or it may have objectives which are primarily propagandistic in nature. Nogee (1963), for instance, has commented that 'It is hardly deniable . . . that propaganda has been an integral feature of much of the disarmament negotiations since 1946' (p. 510). Many would agree with him (e.g. Spanier and Nogee 1962; Strachey 1962); 'they regard the negotiations primarily as parallel monologues in which basic appeals are made to the galleries of world public opinion rather than across the table to the opposition' (Jensen 1963, p. 522). As Stagner (1967) has said, negotiation is sometimes like 'the dialogue of the deaf' (p. 157).

While some commentators would disagree with this analysis of the postwar disarmament negotiations (e.g. Jensen 1963), few would argue that the negotiations served no useful purpose. Negotiation may be justified because it functions either to maintain contact between the parties or to gather intelligence about an opponent (Iklé 1964). In short, negotiation may be justified because it serves a *diplomatic* function.

(b) Diplomacy. Diplomacy is of course usually regarded as a political process which occurs within an international environment (Plischke 1972; Simpson 1972). But in a wider sense diplomacy may be taken to refer to

'the art and science of (1) establishing and maintaining by due and personal process, cooperation between individuals and groups of varying purpose and interest, (2) carefully analyzing and articulating the issues involved in relationships, (3) conciliating through informed competent and responsible discourse and negotiation emergent conflicts between the parties, and (4) identifying and utilizing relevant strategies and tactics for the achievement of desired objectives' (Flack 1972, p. 80).

To the extent that diplomacy is a 'due and personal process' involving an exchange of views between the parties, the concept of diplomacy is similar to the concept of negotiation. Moreover, to the extent that both these concepts involve verbal communication between the parties, both are *bargaining* processes in Kelley and Schenitzki's (1972) sense. As they have put it, 'the essence of bargaining' is that it allows the participants to state their preferences and 'to talk about their relationship before *doing* anything about it' (p. 305).

(c) Bargaining. In the most general sense bargaining refers to any activity whereby parties with conflicting and common interests determine the terms of their interdependence. It is in this sense that Schelling (1960) has used the term when pointing out that 'The subject includes both explicit bargaining and the tacit kind in which adversaries watch and interpret each other's behaviour, each aware that his own actions are being interpreted and anticipated, each acting with a view to the expectations he creates' (p. 21). From this point of view bargaining situations are simply situations involving strategic interdependence of the participants, i.e. 'situations in which the ability of one

participant to gain his ends is dependent to an important degree on the choices or decisions that the other participant will make' (p. 25). In Schelling's view, therefore, any game of strategy which involves both conflicting and common interests is to be defined as a bargaining game (p. 89).

Narrow definitions

The terms 'negotiation', 'diplomacy' and 'bargaining' each have been given a more restricted range of application than that considered so far.

From one point of view, *negotiation* involves more than a decision to confer: 'there must be an operative desire to clarify, ameliorate, adjust or settle the dispute or situation. In short, there must be a will to move from the status quo. If this is absent there cannot be a negotiation' (Lall 1966, p. 31). Accordingly, it might be said that the postwar disarmament conferences have involved gamesmanship rather than negotiation.

From another point of view, negotiation is distinguished from tacit bargaining and other conflict-relevant behaviour. It is in this sense a process 'in which *explicit proposals* are put forward ostensibly for the purpose of reaching agreement on an exchange or on the realization of a common interest where conflicting interests are present' (Iklé 1964, pp. 4–5).

Some authors have defined negotiation to exclude arbitration or other judicial processes but to include all other forms of information exchange between the interested parties (e.g. Lall 1966); others have defined it to exclude 'enquiry, mediation, conciliation, arbitration, judicial settlement, resort to regional agencies or arrangements, or other peaceful means' (Article 33 of the United Nations' Charter).

There is also a sense in which *diplomacy* is defined as being essentially the art of negotiation (Hartmann 1952; Hill 1954; Nicholson 1954). In this sense the distinguishing feature of negotiation or diplomacy is 'that it is an intentional activity carried out between representatives whose role is legitimized by those who they represent' (Brown 1973, p. 25). It is in this sense also that negotiation is identified with *collective bargaining* (Walton and McKersie 1965; Flanders 1968). This has the advantage that collective bargaining is rightly distinguished from bargaining in the marketplace. Negotiation or collective bargaining is seen as a rule-making process involving a power relationship between organisations. This distinguishes it from bargaining defined as a market process which culminates in an act of exchange. In that sense a so-called 'collective bargain' is not really a bargain at all (Flanders 1968, pp. 13–14). However, while the identification of negotiation with collective bargaining has a certain heuristic value (because it emphasises that collective bargaining is not the same as other forms of bargaining), it is not entirely accurate. As Brown's (1973) analysis shows, there are collective bargaining processes which are in this sense non-negotiated: 'their most obvious source is fragmented piecework bargaining. They also arise from the fiddles, windfalls and increases in productivity of individual pieceworkers, from bargaining over merit rates and condition money and the like, and, in certain circumstances, from bargaining over "institutionalized" overtime' (p. 26).

Negotiation as bargaining and bargaining as negotiation

Negotiation may denote a special case of bargaining, or vice versa. In general, psychologists seem to have adopted the widest possible definition of bargaining 'as any activity in which each party is guided mainly by his expectations of what the other will accept' (Schelling 1960, p. 21). Unfortunately, this means that the reader interested in negotiation will rarely find what he is looking for if he turns to the social psychological literature on 'bargaining'. Any mixed motive game will be defined as a bargaining game in this sense, and any form of strategic decision making will be defined as a form of bargaining. It is clear that, given this definition of bargaining, the study of negotiation will be part of the study of bargaining behaviour, however negotiation is defined.

But bargaining need not be defined in this way, and many authors would define it as part of negotiating behaviour. In fact most formal theories of bargaining behaviour (e.g. Zeuthen 1930; Siegel and Fouraker 1960; Foldes 1964; Bishop 1964; Cross 1965; Kelley, Beckman and Fischer 1967; Coddington 1968) confine themselves to a consideration of bargaining behaviour in this narrow sense (Patchen 1970) of arranging an exchange of goods in a given market.

SOME DEFINING CHARACTERISTICS OF NEGOTIATION

If the term 'negotiation' is to be used meaningfully for others, it is (more than ever) important precisely to define just what behaviour it is we wish to study. Fortunately, despite the semantic confusion evident in the literature our review does indicate a certain amount of common ground.

1 All the definitions of negotiation are agreed that negotiators must engage in a process of *joint decision making*. Consequently, while negotiation may include all forms of discussion in which parties to a conflict exchange conflict-relevant information, it may not include just any form of verbal disagreement. There will of course frequently be verbal disagreement between the parties, but if this is to constitute negotiation the disagreement must be concerned with the form of the joint action to be taken. Negotiation involves more than just a conflict of opinion.
2 Negotiators have different preferences concerning the set of joint actions which may be taken. Sometimes these are completely opposed; sometimes they are not, in which case there are clear-cut motives for both co-operation

and competition. However, if, as implied by (1), each party would like to reach agreement, it is necessarily the case that negotiation invokes *mixed motives*. As Nemeth (1972) has said, each party has 'a motive for cooperation in order to reach a mutually agreeable solution and, simultaneously, a motive for competition in order to gain at the other's expense' (p. 210). In other words, the relationship between the parties is one of 'precarious partnership' or 'incomplete antagonism' (Schelling 1960). Negotiation situations are mixed motive situations.

3 Negotiation involves *strategic decision making* of one sort or another. This effectively follows from (2) for it is dictated by the existence of conflicts of interest between the negotiators. Necessarily if interests are to be defended, attempts will be made to outwit, or at least to match in wit, the opponent. Effective 'ploys' must be selected and pursued, subject of course to moderation from the motives dictating a degree of co-operation between the contestants.

4 Negotiation involves *talking* about a relationship before doing anything about it. At one extreme this may involve a thoroughgoing discussion-to-consensus; at the other it may simply involve a change of bids.

Summarising: there is general agreement that negotiation involves verbal communication of one sort or another and that the communication concerns the possibility of a joint agreement on some form of action or verbal formulation. There is also implicit the assumption that each party may try to misrepresent its own position in one way or another (e.g. Jervis 1970; Bartos 1970). As Jervis has put it, 'rational actors try to project desired images, whether accurate or not, and skeptically view the images projected by others' (p. 15). Negotiation may be conducted as a collaboration in which the participants attempt to solve a common problem, or it may be conducted as a strategic confrontation in which each attempts to outwit the other and maximise his own gains (Walton and McKersie 1966; Dutton and Walton 1966; Druckman 1967). The possibility of deception is inherent in the nature of the task.

Towards a More Formal Definition of Negotiation

Two outstanding problems already broached need to be decided before a formal definition of negotiation can be given. In the first place, there are a number of other processes by which parties may settle their differences, and the relationship of these to negotiation is unclear. Are *discussion, inquiry, mediation, conciliation, arbitration, judicial settlement, etc.* different types of negotiation, or is negotiation different in kind from some or all of these?

There would seem to be an important psychological difference between the processes involved in direct discussion, inquiry, conciliation and mediation, on the one hand, and in arbitration and other forms of judicial or semijudicial settlement, on the other. In the latter full responsibility for the outcome is withdrawn from the main protagonists, whereas in the former, even in inquiry, mediation and conciliation, it is the principals who determine the settlement. Accordingly, we shall follow Lall (1966) in excluding the latter group from the domain of negotiating behaviour.

It does not, however, seem desirable to make a sharp distinction between direct discussion and discussion involving third parties (i.e. inquiry, conciliation and mediation). From a psychological point of view, the similarities may be more important than the differences (Kerr 1954; Landsberger 1955a; Peters 1955; Douglas 1957, 1962; Walton 1969). As Douglas (1957) has put it, 'the mediator's functions in rehabilitating a deteriorating situation cannot be understood apart from the main trunk of . . . interaction onto which they are grafted' (p. 70). Similarly, Walton has argued that 'By understanding the ingredients which third parties bring to a conflict and the functions they may perform, a participant may in effect simulate a third party, performing the same functions' (p. 4). It remains to be seen whether the similarities between direct and indirect communication processes are in fact more important than the differences; there is no systematic body of empirical research to guide us (McGrath and Julian 1963; Rehmus 1965; Sawyer and Guetzkow 1965; McGrath 1966). Consequently, while the arguments of Douglas and Walton are by no means conclusive, we are forced to take them seriously. There does not now seem to be any compelling reason to mark the distinction between direct and indirect forms of communication by applying the label 'negotiation' to the former but not to the latter. Negotiation will therefore be defined to include both direct and indirect forms of communication.

The above characteristics may obtain – disagreement, strategic discussion and so on – but the discussants have still to decide whether or not actively to search for agreement. Is the decision to confer sufficiently different from *the decision to search for agreement* that it needs to be marked in some way? We feel it should, but not necessarily by ruling the 'decision to confer' outside the domain of negotiation. Iklé (1964) has allowed negotiation to have different objectives and, in particular, distinguished negotiation 'for agreements' from negotiation 'for side-effects'. Jensen (1963) has also used 'negotiation' as a generic term and distinguished between types according to whether or not a bargaining model would apply. Bargaining involves a process of give and take, 'a willingness to make concessions in order to enhance agreement' (p. 522), or, as Nemeth (1972) has put it, 'a series of communication exchanges and compromises' (p. 208). In this sense negotiation for agreements involves bargaining whereas negotiation for side effects does not. Lall (1966) has made the same point in a different way. From his point of view, negotiation *is* negotiation for agreements; negotiation for side effects is not really negotiation at all. The decision to adopt one form of labelling rather than another seems to be almost entirely arbitrary. However, since it is difficult to find a satisfactory label to replace 'negotiation for side-effects' (Lall has made no suggestion), the terminology of Iklé (1964) and Jensen (1963) will be preferred.

Hence, negotiation is defined formally as *any form of verbal communication, direct or indirect, whereby parties to a conflict of interest discuss, without resort to arbitration or other judicial processes, the form of any joint action which they might take to manage a dispute between them.* Bargaining is defined simply as *the process of negotiating for agreement.*

Chapter 2

Approaches to Collective Bargaining

So far negotiation and bargaining have been treated as pervasive social processes, involving dyads, small groups, organisations or governments in an attempt 'to define or redefine the terms of their interdependence' (Walton and McKersie 1965, p. 3). However, different bargaining situations differ in detail and may lead to different kinds of bargaining behaviour. In particular, different bargaining situations may be distinguished according to:

1 The nature of the decision makers involved (McGrath 1966; Vidmar and McGrath 1967; Flanders 1968; Stephenson 1971a; Frey and Adams 1972).
2 The nature of the decision (Iklé 1964; Walton and McKersie 1965; Wilcox 1971).
3 The relationship between the decision makers or the parties they represent (Walton and McKersie 1965; Dutton and Walton 1966; Pondy 1967).
4 The nature of the context within which the interaction occurs (Pruitt 1969; Nicholson 1970; Chalmers and Cormick 1971).

Distinguishing between different bargaining situations according to the nature of the decision makers involved amounts to distinguishing between *collective bargaining*, which involves representatives of groups, and *interpersonal bargaining*, which does not. This is similar to McGrath's (1966) distinction between formal negotiation and informal negotiation, according to which 'a *formal* negotiation situation refers to an occasion where one or more *representatives* of two or more *parties* interact in an *explicit attempt* to reach a jointly acceptable position on one or more *issues* about which they are in disagreement' (p. 101). Formal negotiation, in McGrath's sense, therefore corresponds to collective bargaining. However, McGrath's definition of informal negotiation does not correspond to the definition of interpersonal bargaining in Chapter 1. It eliminates the representative role and, in addition, does not require an intent to resolve differences. In his own words, informal negotiation 'relaxes the representative requirement and requirement for explicit awareness of and intent to resolve differences' (p. 101). We shall avoid this confusion and take the difference between formal and informal negotiations to be equivalent to the distinction between collective bargaining and interpersonal bargaining, while negotiations refer always to negotiation for agreement.

Very many psychological studies have in fact involved interpersonal bargaining rather than collective bargaining (Swingle 1970a; Wrightsman *et al.* 1972). Frey and Adams (1972) have commented that 'Most studies in bargaining ... place the subject in a decision-making situation where he has to interact only with his opponent. His choices are made mainly on the basis of his individual strategy and reactions to his opponent's strategy'. As these comments aptly continue, 'While this is, of course, an important question in its own right, the findings of such studies cannot readily be generalized to a large class of conflict situations which occur quite often in real life' (p. 331). It is therefore important to consider the differences between interpersonal bargaining and collective bargaining in more detail.

There have been four psychological approaches to the theory of collective bargaining which merit particular attention. Of these, that of Walton and McKersie and that represented by the tradition of research in the psychology of intergroup relations are relatively well-known, but the other two have been neglected. McGrath and his associates in the 1960s developed a model of the collective bargaining process which yielded many interesting data. Earlier still Douglas developed a theory of 'successful negotiation' which is well grounded in observational data and capable of empirical test. All these theories emphasise the distinctive character of the collective bargaining process in different ways and ways which complement one another. As the more comprehensive theory, we shall start with a discussion of McGrath's tripolar model of collective bargaining.

McGrath's Tripolar Model of Collective Bargaining

STATEMENT OF THE MODEL

The tripolar model was first presented by McGrath and Julian (1962) but subsequently elaborated by Vidmar and McGrath (1965, 1967, 1970), Vidmar (1971) and McGrath (1966). It is called the tripolar model because it assumes that each spokesman is subject to forces towards three conflicting 'party' positions: *R-forces*, directed towards the position of the party the negotiator represents; *A-forces*, directed towards the position of the opposing party; and *C-forces*, directed towards the position of 'the broader organization or social system in which all parties participate' (McGrath 1966, p. 110).

R-forces are of at least two types: those arising from a negotiator's ideological or *attitudinal identification* with his reference group, and those arising from his role obligations as a *representative* of that party (Vidmar and McGrath 1967; Vidmar 1971; McGrath 1966). A-forces include such components as the attraction a negotiator has for his opponent as a person, any sympathy he has for the goals of the other party, and his perception of whether his opponent is bargaining 'in good faith' or not. The C-force 'pressure' on a negotiator is 'analogous to the "pull" toward the position of a generic or universalistic reference group' (McGrath 1966, p. 112) and is constituted in the 'desire to set forth a solution which would be good for the general community' (Vidmar and McGrath 1965, p. 40).

It is assumed that the success of a solution must be judged from the viewpoint of each of the parties to the conflict. The 'totally successful solution' would maximally satisfy all three parties (i.e. own party, opponent's party and the 'community'). The degree of success actually obtained is in consequence likely to be determined by the balance between the three sets of forces towards those three parties. As Vidmar and McGrath (1965) have said,

'The ability to achieve *any* solution depends upon some effective degree of A-force pressure on both negotiation teams. However, when the negotiation task is (or is perceived as) one in which the groups are contriently opposed, the R-force pressure acts against the A-force pressure. Hence, the success of a negotiation session is contingent upon the balance of pressures acting on the individuals (or teams) making up the negotiation group' (p. 40).

R-forces are, however, regarded as more important determinants of task success than either A- or C-forces, and R-force pressure is assumed to be inversely related to task success. 'Task success' in McGrath's work and that of his associates is invariably assessed in terms of some 'multipartisan' criterion. Ideally, ratings of the success of an outcome would be obtained from leaders of the three respective main parties, and the product of these would be taken to define the degree of success. Strong R-forces prevail against successful negotiation because they are the major source of divisiveness and conflict within the group. As Vidmar and McGrath (1967) have said, 'Conflict arises not as a result of the task *per se*, but rather from a conflict-producing role structure derived from member commitments to reference groups outside the actual negotiation situation and from perception of a contrient reward situation' (p. 6).

Conflict in formal negotiation groups is thus regarded as a function of: the task itself, the attitudinal commitments of a negotiator to a party position, and the role obligation of a negotiator to represent a party. To quote from Vidmar and McGrath (1967) again 'it is not just the task or conflicting member attitudes *per se* that causes performance decrement, but also the effects of a representational role structure' (p. 65).

EVALUATION OF THE MODEL

Importance of the representative role structure

Vidmar and McGrath (1967) have laid considerable emphasis on the importance of the representative role structure, to such an extent that, as we shall see, the portrayal of their experimental work is in one instance grossly distorted. In their view group members may be attitudinally identified with (or 'committed to') a reference group (or reference group position), but R-forces will *not be generated* and performance will not be impaired *until this commitment is made explicit and salient* (p. 7). Apparently R-forces are only generated when the negotiators are given explicit role obligations as representatives of groups; 'when a representational role is not explicit, R-forces do not exist' (p. 7). In operational terms this amounts to saying that 'the attitudinal measures used as indicants of R-, A-, and C- forces are efficacious in predicting performance only in conjunction with representational role structures' (p. 44).

Vidmar and McGrath (1967) have cited experimental evidence for this somewhat provocative and extreme viewpoint. They have suggested that in the sphere of *interpersonal* bargaining attitudinal commitment does not impair the performance of bargainers, whereas in *collective* bargaining it has a deleterious effect. In the experimental work quoted their aim was to compare groups 'with and without a representational role structure while holding task and member attitudes constant' (p. 65). What they did in fact was to compare the performance of subjects in formal negotiation groups with that of matched subjects in problem-solving groups. In the first case, subjects acted as representatives of organisations to which they belonged and could win 'contrient-type' prizes for fulfilling their role obligations (each subject was 'to make sure his organizations' viewpoints were represented in the final written group solution'); in the second case, subjects were 'given information from a conflicting position merely to make them an expert on this position' and could win 'promotive-type' prizes for setting forth 'a fair and constructive solution' (pp. 20–3). Consequently, although subjects in the two conditions used the same experimental materials they were, nevertheless, given different tasks. It is not surprising that subjects in the former groups performed 'less well' than subjects in the latter groups, because (a) the former were given a negotiation task and the latter a problem-solving task, and (b) subjects given competitive instructions undoubtedly will perform less co-operatively than subjects given instructions to co-operate!

The task was not identical in the two situations, making it invalid to impute differences in the outcomes to the fact that subjects were representatives in one condition but not in the other. R-, A- and C-forces predicted 'success' more effectively in the negotiation task than in the problem-solving task. However, it is not legitimate to conclude, as Vidmar and McGrath have done, that 'Representational role demands on the negotiators can by themselves account for the performance decrement in negotiation groups' (pp. 65–6). R-, A- and C-forces are essentially measures of subjects' 'attitudes' (or opinions), and presumably these will be made 'explicit and salient' when subjects are engaged in a negotiation task rather than, say, a problem-solving task. However, it is likely that measures of R-, A- and C-forces will predict task success in *any* negotiation group (whether group members are representatives or not).

Timing in negotiation groups

There is a certain vagueness in the tripolar model. R-forces are said to be inversely related to success, but the way in which R-forces prevail against effective negotiation is not made explicit. However, McGrath and his colleagues have at least attempted to characterise the process of successful negotiation by analysing the transcripts of successful and unsuccessful experimental groups.

It is the conclusion of McGrath and Julian (1963) and McGrath (1966) that the timing or phasing of activities in successful groups is distinctive. In McGrath and Julian's (1963) experimental work negotiation 'success' was defined in terms of ratings (made by members of the research team) of 'how well each group's proposal reflected a constructive, creative solution to the socio-political problem under consideration' (p. 123). Apparently, successful groups resolved an internal crisis of control in time to write out and endorse an agreed set of proposals, whereas unsuccessful groups did not. More precisely, McGrath and Julian have concluded that

'successful groups resolve their internal structuring problems and attain diminished negative affect sufficiently early in the session to permit time for adequate formulation of the group's final product under *favourable* social-emotional conditions. Unsuccessful groups, however, do not come sufficiently to grips with the control problem until late in the session, so that the group's final product is produced under unfavourable conditions of high negative affect' (p. 134).

How do these findings relate to the tripolar model? It is assumed that R-force 'pressure' is greater in unsuccessful than in successful groups. The greater pressure towards own group results in a characteristically inappropriate process of bargaining, which in turn diminishes the prospects of a successful outcome to the debate. More generally, it is asserted that differences in R-force pressure lead to different patterns of bargaining behaviour and that different patterns of bargaining behaviour lead to different outcomes. While this is not unlikely, it is perhaps important to consider whether any differences in the performances of successful and unsuccessful groups are specific to the particular negotiation task employed, and for this reason we shall describe McGrath and Julian's experimental procedures in rather more detail.

Members of each of three campus religious organisations were asked to formulate group positions on a number of issues, such as the granting of federal aid to parochial and other private schools. Each negotiation group was composed of a representative from each organisation and a graduate student chairman. Subjects were instructed to get as much as possible of their reference group's position embodied in the written proposals put forward by the negotiation group. They were also offered the opportunity to win prize money of up to $25 according to what might be called the 'combined merit score' assigned to the proposals they endorsed. Thus each subject expected that his negotiation group's product would be rated (from 0 to 5) by officials of each organisation in terms of 'acceptability' to that organisation and also by neutral judges in terms of 'constructiveness as an approach to the underlying issue'. Each subject was to receive as his prize the dollar equivalent of the product of the average rating made by officials of his own organisation and that made by the team of neutral judges. (In fact all ratings were made by associates of the experimenters.) Negotiation sessions were divided into two main parts: the first lasted twenty-five minutes and constituted the main discussion task; the second lasted five minutes and constituted time to write out the final group proposals.

Given a negotiation task of this type, it is perhaps not surprising that successful groups were those which resolved their problems of content structuring by the end of the discussion phases of the negotiation, whereas unsuccessful groups were those which did not. Content structuring, defined as 'attempts to delimit the area of discourse, or to guide the discussion in a particular direction', includes such statements as: 'It seems to me that we are not concerned with the issue of Church and State, but rather we should. . .' and 'Can we agree that the real problem here is one of deciding whether the Bible is a good reading text?' (p. 10). This result is both interesting and important, but different negotiation tasks differed in detail, and the timing of such structuring activity may not be so important when different tasks are involved.

In fact there is another, more serious, difficulty in interpreting McGrath and Julian's results. Timely resolution of the 'control crisis' depends very much upon the behaviour of the chairmen involved. From one point of view, the R-force pressures may be different in successful and unsuccessful groups and lead to different behaviours from the discussion chairmen (which in turn may lead to different outcomes); from another, the difference between successful and unsuccessful groups may simply reflect differences between effective and ineffective chairmen, which are not related to differences in the R-forces acting upon individual negotiators. Unfortunately, this issue cannot be investigated directly since McGrath and Julian took no independent measures of the R-forces involved. What evidence there was tended not to support the latter interpretation, since 'chairmen showed only marginal consistency in tending to have either successful or unsuccessful groups' (McGrath and Julian 1963, p. 135; McGrath 1966, p. 125). However, this is clearly not conclusive, and it would be wise to look elsewhere for indications of the mechanism which underlies the tripolar model.

The Psychology of Intergroup Relations

McGrath (1966) has posited two types of R-force pressure: that arising from a negotiator's *role obligation* to represent a group, and that arising from his *attitudinal identification* with a reference group position. There is a certain amount of experimental evidence that both types may seriously affect an individual's judgement of the essential elements in a competitive intergroup situation. Judgements of the intentions of own and other side, of their abilities and goals, will be biased in accordance with own group interests. McGrath has rather neglected the importance of such perceptual influences, whereas we would argue that each type of R-force pressure may affect bargaining behaviour either *directly*, via negotiators' willingness to compromise, or *indirectly*, via negotiators' perceptions of party positions (which will in turn affect negotiators' willingness to compromise). The differences between interpersonal bargaining and collective bargaining will be elaborated in terms of these mechanisms.

ROLE OBLIGATIONS AND NEGOTIATORS' WILLINGNESS TO COMPROMISE

First of all, it is clear that representatives face problems of *intra-organisational bargaining* which individuals do not (Walton and McKersie 1965; Frey and Adams 1972). The result may be, as Blake and Mouton (1961e) have claimed, that 'representatives act on loyalty, and are motivated to win, or at least to avoid defeat, even though a judgement which would resolve an intergroup problem is sacrificed in the process' (p. 183). Certainly the representatives studied by Blake and Mouton possessed considerable 'intellectual' and 'procedural' skills relevant to the creative solution of their in-group task. They were, for instance, rated as 'offering more original ideas' than other members and as 'helping others to express their ideas' (Blake and Mouton 1961c, 1961d). However, they manifestly did not regard representing their group as an intellectual exercise of this type. In contrast to their behaviour within their own groups, their behaviour as representatives was rigid and intransigent and took little or no account of the *quality* of the solution proposed by the other side (Blake and Mouton 1961d, 1961e).

Even in the 'Human Relations Training Laboratory' representatives could hardly afford to behave in any other way. During intergroup negotiations Blake and Mouton allowed each group to communicate by note with its elected representative. Most groups were concerned with destruction of the other group's proposals rather than with elucidating similarities and differences between the group positions (Sherif and Sherif 1969, p. 263). The typical reaction to 'defeat' was one of disorganisation and dismay. Members of 'losing' groups saw their representatives as being less intelligent, less mature and less well-intentioned than before, and in some cases representatives were forced to accept new and less influential roles within their groups.

Oppenheim and Bayley's (1970) description of the union district organiser emphasises the importance of such considerations:

'he needs great flexibility, a capacity for thinking himself into the role and problems of management, and a sure touch for the possible and the impossible. His own role is highly ambiguous; sometimes he acts strictly as a representative, stating his members' demands and apparently acting purely as a mouthpiece; at other times he acts as a negotiator with a good deal of latitude to settle for as much as he thinks he can get; occasionally he acts more as a mediator, going back to the men time and again to persuade them of the correctness of a given course of action. This latter requires a great deal of moral authority, courage and farsightedness' (p. 106).

The studies of Hermann and Kogan (1968) and Frey and Adams (1972) provide further examples of how the problem of representing a group may affect subsequent compromise behaviour. Let it suffice to say that, so far as compromise behaviour is concerned, the processes of collective bargaining cannot be understood simply in terms of the processes of interpersonal bargaining.

ROLE OBLIGATIONS AND PERCEPTIONS OF PARTY POSITIONS

It has also been suggested that representatives, by virtue of their role, may find it difficult to avoid errors in perception of one sort or another. For example, Stagner (1967) has argued that

'When a man first takes on a job he is conscious of the distinction between his personal values and the rules he must follow. As a consequence of repeated behaviour within this framework, he becomes accustomed to disregarding some considerations whilst paying close attention to others. He knows well the kind of evidence he must use as a guide to action in his role as agent. Soon he fails to see conflicting evidence at all. The learning process operates to make him selectively sensitive to facts bearing on his social role while he becomes blind to contradictory material' (p. 115).

ATTITUDINAL COMMITMENT AND WILLINGNESS TO COMPROMISE

Representatives are, however, often selected precisely because they are attitudinally committed to the groups they are to represent (Shurtleff 1949), and it is therefore important to separate the effects of an obligation to represent a group from the effects of an attitudinal commitment to a group position. Certainly, attitudinal commitment does have effects over and above the effects of the obligation to represent a group, as Druckman and Zechmeister (1970) have shown. When party positions are explicitly related to a negotiator's own belief system (i.e. when there is an 'ideological link'), compromise is unlikely and negotiations will tend to result in either deadlock or capitulation. Presumably, the mechanism involved can be either direct (i.e.

attitudinal commitment affects negotiators' willingness to accept a compromise 'solution') or indirect (i.e. attitudinal commitment affects the perception of party positions). Most psychologists would regard these propositions as self-evident, but it may nevertheless be instructive to examine some of the research findings in more detail.

ATTITUDINAL COMMITMENT AND PERCEPTION OF PARTY POSITIONS

Many authors would maintain that it is the *relationship between different groups* which largely determines how their members perceive and act towards each other (Sherif and Sherif 1953; Sherif *et al.* 1961; Sherif 1967; Campbell 1965; Frank 1968; Harvey 1956). Apparently, 'extended competition' between groups often leads *to an increase in attraction to the in-group (or in-group position) and to a decrease in attraction to the out-group (or out-group position)*, although the precise nature of the effects may depend upon how the competition is characterised by the members of the group (Rabbie and Wilkens 1971).

Such attraction to the in-group is reflected in (a) more positive ratings of the in-group and its members than of the out-group and its members (Sherif 1967; Sherif and Sherif 1969; Rabbie and Horwitz 1969), and (b) a higher estimate of the performance of the in-group than of the out-group (Bass and Dunteman 1963; Blake and Mouton 1961d, 1962; Sherif *et al.* 1961). Similarly, to a very large extent opposed nations 'attribute the same virtues to themselves and the same vices to each other' (Frank 1968, p. 117), so that one nation sees itself as a 'mirror image' of its 'opponent' (Bronfenbrenner 1961; Angell, Dunham and Singer 1964; White 1970). If this analysis is correct, the result may be negotiators who are 'not able to understand and appreciate the problems of the other side' (Campbell 1960), who come to see Right on one side and Wrong on the other (Stagner 1948), who perceive more substantive conflict than actually exists (Blake and Mouton, 1961a, 1961d, 1962; Walker, 1962; Niemela *et al.* 1969), and who fall into the errors of 'possibilistic thinking' (Frank 1968) or the 'zero-sum trap' (Rapoport, 1964, 1968). Blake and Mouton (1962) have even reported one summary made by management of a set of union proposals, which listed 62 areas of disagreement but failed to list 182 areas of agreement.

It is interesting to consider Janis's (1972) study of foreign policy decision and 'fiascoes' in the light of what has been said so far. Janis has presented four case studies of crisis situations in which government advisers made 'incredibly gross miscalculations about both the practical and moral consequences of their decisions' (p. iv) and two case studies of crisis situations in which members of similar groups made realistic appraisals of the consequences of their actions. The former case studies were of the Bay of Pigs invasion in 1961, the decision to invade North Korea in 1950, the failure to be prepared for the attack on Pearl Harbour in 1941, and the various decisions to escalate the

Vietnam War during 1964–67. The latter case studies were of the Cuban Missile Crisis in 1962 and the making of the Marshall Plan in 1947–48. According to Janis,

'a group whose members have properly defined roles, with traditions and standard operating procedures that facilitate critical inquiry, is probably capable of making better decisions than any individual in the group who works on the problem alone. And yet the advantages of having decisions made by groups are often lost because of psychological pressures that arise when the members work closely together, *share the same values, and above all face a crisis situation* [our italics] in which everyone is subject to stresses that generate a strong need for affiliation . . . *The more amiability and esprit de corps among the members of a policy-making in-group, the greater is the danger that independent critical thinking will be replaced by groupthink, which is likely to result in irrational and dehumanizing actions directed against out-groups*' (p. 13).

The symptoms of 'groupthink' identified by Janis include: a 'shared illusion of being invulnerable to the main dangers that might arise from a risky action in which the group is strongly tempted to engage' (p. 36); an unquestioned belief in the inherent morality of the group; and stereotyped perceptions of enemy leaders 'as too weak to warrant genuine attempts to negotiate, or as too weak and stupid to counter whatever risky attempts are made to defeat their purposes' (p. 198).

We are tempted to agree with Boulding (1964, 1968) that the images of the 'international system', which largely determine the behaviour of its decision makers, are 'literary' in character. In his opinion they are derived from 'a melange of narrative history, memories of past events, stories and conversations, etc., plus an enormous amount of usually ill-digested and carelessly collected "current information"' (Boulding 1968, p. 9). Furthermore, he has argued that 'when we add to this fact that the system produces strong hates, loves, loyalties, disloyalties, and so on, it would be surprising if any images were formed that even remotely resembled the most loosely defined realities of the case' (Boulding, 1968, p. 9).

While this may be unduly pessimistic there is no reason to restrict this sort of comment to the discipline of international relations. Perceptions are likely to be selective and parochial in any system which is uncertain, complex and open (Hoffmann 1968). In other words, attitudinal commitments are likely to play an important part in determining the behaviour of any negotiation group, especially when negotiators face severe problems of information overload (Frank 1968; Janis 1972).

Walton and McKersie's Subprocesses of Collective Bargaining

Walton and McKersie (1965, 1966) have done much to illustrate the sheer complexity of the decisions facing collective bargainers. Dilemmas abound in collective bargaining because the negotiator, by virtue of his role, finds himself subject to sets of incompatible expectations. For example, according to Pruitt (1969) all negotiation behaviour can be classified under four headings: (a) struggle behaviour, i.e. attempts to move the other party in a direction favourable to one's own; (b) accommodative behaviour, i.e. attempts to reach agreement on a single alternative; (c) integrative behaviour, i.e. efforts to discover new alternatives and to increase the joint gains available to the parties; and (d) image manipulation, i.e. attempts to structure the images of oneself in the eyes of one's constituents, the other party or third parties. Similarly, Walton and McKersie (1965) have distinguished between four sub-processes: *distributive bargaining, integrative bargaining, attitudinal structuring* and *intra-organisational bargaining*.

Whatever terminology is used, it is apparent that the behaviours fulfil different functions and that the conflicting demands of the subprocesses may pose dilemmas for the negotiators involved. Thus Walton and McKersie (1966) have pointed out that the processes of distributive bargaining and integrative bargaining are 'manifestly dissimilar in form': integrative bargaining is 'tentative, exploratory, and involves open communication processes', whereas distributive bargaining is just the opposite and involves 'adamant, directive, and controlled information processes' (p. 381). Consequently, each negotiator has to decide whether or not to engage in (or attempt to engage in) integrative bargaining. If such a problem-solving strategy is in fact chosen it may allow the negotiators to increase the size of the cake to be divided between them, but it may mean that one party (the one that initiates the problem-solving activities) will get a very small slice.

Other dilemmas can be readily identified. For example, integrative bargaining may demand concessionary orientation towards the opponent which is deemed inconsistent with the need to keep faith with those the negotiator represents, i.e. with demands of intra-organisational bargaining. The problems of attitudinal structuring – i.e. of keeping the personal relationship appropriately consistent with past expectations – may evoke behaviours which are radically at variance with that conduct which in the negotiator's considered view is demanded by the present circumstances of the dispute.

Walton and McKersie's (1965) 'subjectively expected utility' (SEU) framework is also useful for characterising the negotiation process. In their view, 'certain points on the total conceivable spectrum of outcomes attain unique distinction and prominence in the thinking of the negotiator and provide a guide to his decisions' (p. 25). In particular, each negotiator is assumed to identify a *resistance point* or minimum goal corresponding to the level of value at which he would rather break off negotiations than settle. Such minimum goals may actually be quite vague, involving a range of outcomes rather than a single point (Iklé and Leites 1962), and may be formulated at the bargaining table (Iklé and Leites 1962; Iklé 1964; Walton and McKersie 1965). They may be either compatible (defining a *positive settlement range*) or incompatible (defining a *negative settlement range*).

When resistance points are incompatible no agreement can be reached unless 'circumstances or the tactics employed by one or both negotiators change their location' (Pruitt 1969, p. 5). In such cases a negotiator cannot hope to achieve a settlement above his minimum goal. However, when resistance points are compatible each negotiator is also assumed to identify, at any given time, a *target point* or forward goal to which he is currently aspiring (Iklé and Leites' (1962) 'estimated probable outcome').

A negotiator's SEU is not linear between his target and resistance points. As Walton and McKersie (1965) have pointed out, to a negotiator with a resistance point of ten cents 'a concession from 15 to 11 cents means more than one from 30 to 15 cents' (p. 88).

Douglas's Delineation of Stages in Successful Negotiations

The three approaches so far considered have each been concerned to identify the main tasks faced by negotiators and to list the behaviour, tactics, perceptions and misperceptions, pressures and dilemmas to which these give rise. In this final section we wish to outline some attempts – principally those of Douglas – to say how the different tasks should be ordered in negotiations. The idea is that successful negotiations may go through a sequence of stages which unsuccessful negotiations do not.

THREE STAGES OF NEGOTIATION

Douglas (1957, 1962) has presented what amounts to a normative theory of the bargaining process. All productive negotiations, she has said, go through three stages. Furthermore, she has apparently regarded it as essential that there be an orderly progression through these stages and that the appropriate behaviours be displayed in each.

The first stage (*establishing the negotiating range*) consists of 'a thorough and exhaustive determination' of the range within which the parties will have to do business with each other (Douglas 1957, p. 73). The behaviours of the negotiators emphasise the representative role they have to play: speeches are exceptionally long in contrast to those which follow, and the negotiators 'strive for a convincing demonstration that they are impossibly at loggerheads' (p. 73). Interparty conflict is brought to the fore, emphasising areas of substantive disagreement. Indeed, Douglas has gone so far as to say that 'To the extent that the contenders can intrench their seeming disparity in this period, the more they enhance their chances for a good and stable settlement in the end' (p. 73). It is, however, extremely important that negotiators do not confuse conflict between the parties with antagonism between persons at this stage (Landsberger 1955a; Julian and McGrath 1963; McGrath and Julian 1963; Walton and McKersie 1965, esp. pp. 246–8). In Douglas's words, 'Antagonism between parties is the lifeblood of this stage: antagonism between individuals at this stage would be highly detrimental as a precursor to the psychological activity which is to come to the fore in the next phase' (p. 75). What is required is that negotiators 'fight the antagonism, not the antagonist' (Walton and McKersie 1965, p. 247). Consequently, a great deal of image manipulation may be involved in insuring that interparty conflict is not 'transformed to a depreciation of the whole person', as Galtung (1959, p. 78) has put it.

In the second stage (*reconnoitering the negotiating range*) negotiators attempt, in the words of one novelist, to 'convey without commitment' (Haggard 1970, p. 114). As Douglas (1957) herself has put it, negotiators 'search earnestly in the background for signs of tacit agreement, long before in their public exchange they can afford to profess anything but continued strong disagreement' (p. 77).

In the third and final stage (*precipitating the decision-making crisis*) a decision-making crisis is reached, in which negotiators must consult with their respective parties and, if possible, conclude an agreement.

Similarly, Stevens (1963) has identified a *negotiation cycle* in labour negotiations in which the emphasis shifts from interparty conflict towards problems of 'cooperation and coordination' (p. 97). And in the context of third-party interventions in disputes, Walton (1969) has argued:

'At least two phases of an effective conflict dialogue can be identified – a differentiation phase and an integration phase . . . A conflict resolution episode does not necessarily include just one differentiation and one integration phase. It may be composed of a series of these two phases, but the potential for integration at any one point in time is no greater than the adequacy of the differentiation already achieved' (p. 105).

The extent to which party initially differentiates self from opponent may affect how concessions are subsequently exchanged between the two sides. Pruitt (1969), for instance, has argued that negotiators must in some sense 'reach an agreement about the exchange rate for their concessions before they can move toward agreement' (p. 44); that is, they must know what sized concessions from party should be exchanged for what sized concessions from opponent (as being equivalent to it). It might be said that negotiations are initially 'virtually unhampered by any norm of fairness' and that 'typical opening speeches are examples of unrestrained individualism' (Bartos 1970, p. 64); later speeches tend to be an 'exact opposite' and to 'emphasise the need to subordinate individual interests to the broader need for a fair agreement'. Presumably, this shift occurs as a result of increased information, obtained from a satisfactory determination of the settlement range in the first stage of negotiation.

THE CONCESSION DILEMMA

According to Pruitt (1969) and Walton and McKersie (1965), negotiators often find themselves in a mutual and 'progressively deepening *concession dilemma*' (Pruitt 1969, p. 16). At any given point in time a negotiator may consider whether or not to make a concession, whether only to indicate flexibility or whether further to commit himself to a position. Various cost considerations are involved whether he makes a concession or not.

If he makes a concession a negotiator suffers both position loss and image loss (Pruitt 1969, p. 11). *Position loss* occurs because once a concession has been made it is extremely difficult to go back on it, whereas if party had held out opponent might have accepted his demands in full. Some movement is required by the 'rules of play' or negotiation mores if a representative is to be seen as negotiating 'in good faith' (Stevens 1963; Iklé 1964). However, a negotiator who 'magnanimously moves to his resistant point at an early stage' may fail to reach an agreement because he has nothing left to trade (Pruitt 1969, p. 18; Douglas 1962; Stevens 1963). It is to party's advantage to withhold concessions at an early stage, not only in anticipation of an eventual exchange but also in order that his final concession be 'large enough . . . to be dramatic and symbolic of closure' (Walton and McKersie 1965, p. 92). *Image loss* occurs because making a concession implies flexibility where previously there may have been commitment. However firmly party may have seemed committed to a position, that position was (demonstrably) subject to modification. Indeed, occasionally a concession may make party look so flexible that opponent's target is upgraded and he adopts new and more ambitious commitment tactics (Pruitt 1969, p. 12). On the other hand, if a negotiator does not make a concession he may become committed to an unviable position or risk antagonising his opponent, thus 'losing what goodwill remains in the relationship with him' (Pruitt 1969, p. 9).

As time goes by, arguments both for and against making concession become more convincing (Pruitt 1969, p. 15), and negotiators may fail to resolve their respective dilemmas even when they have goals which are compatible. Many authors believe that a game-theoretical format is useful in highlighting the nature of this situation and view it as analogous to either the Prisoner's Dilemma Game (PDG) (Pruitt 1969; Sawyer and Guetzkow 1965) or the Chicken game (Walton and McKersie 1965). These views are not necessarily incompatible; rather the dilemma may approximate the one reward structure or the other, depending upon the time elapsed and the perceived costs of mutual inflexibility (Pruitt 1969, p. 19).

Unless one side capitulates, typically each will engage in various integrative and/or accommodative behaviours. The goal of each is to convey flexibility in ways which reduce fears of position loss and of image loss. Consequently, attempts to resolve the deepening concession dilemma mark the transition from the first stage of negotiation to the second (Pruitt 1969, p. 17). Integrative bargaining may arise since, if the parties can agree on some new alternative, each may to a large extent avoid both position and image loss. However, since the processes of integrative bargaining and distributive bargaining involve opposing tactics and since integrative solutions may be extremely hard to find, negotiators may prefer to attempt to co-ordinate an exchange of concessions. Party may, for example, explicitly propose such an exchange or even make a small unilateral concession. Further concessions could then be made conditional upon similar concessions being made by the other side (Osgood 1960a; 1960b; Crow 1963). Of course, in some cases negotiators may deem the problems of image loss (particularly in the eyes of their constituents) as too severe to allow any explicit move of this sort. For this reason many authors have stressed the importance of tacit communications in both indicating a readiness to move and co-ordinating specific exchanges (Peters 1955; Schelling 1960; Douglas 1962; Walton and McKersie 1965).

To summarise: this discussion of stages in the negotiation process serves two purposes: (a) it emphasises the range of behaviours involved in negotiation and reiterates the potential importance of integrative bargaining; and (b) it introduces the idea that negotiators face concession dilemmas which have the reward structures of certain matrix games (e.g. PDG or Chicken), an important point because certain abstract simulations of negotiating behaviour attempt to translate the concession dilemma into experimental terms.

Chapter 3

Experimental Approaches to the Study of Negotiation Groups

There are several good reasons for studying negotiation groups experimentally. Although, as we have seen, there are behavioural theories of the negotiation process, there is a dearth of reliable observation against which the theories may be evaluated. Moreover, the prospects for rectifying this situation are poor, given the many difficulties encountered by field researchers in their quest for reliable data. However, the laboratory researcher will be encouraged by the moderate successes of previous experimental researchers. Sufficient at least has been done to ensure that economists will in future pay respect to behavioural as well as economic principles in their future accounts of bargaining processes (cf. Walton and McKersie 1965). In this chapter we aim to provide a comprehensive description of the approaches adopted in previous experiments and to provide a framework for our own studies which we shall subsequently describe. Terms like 'experiment', 'game' and 'simulation' have been used freely and vaguely by research workers, but rarely have the characteristics of the chosen method been made formally explicit or its limitations been discussed. Having formally defined our terms and described some principal characteristics of the process of negotiation in Chapters 1 and 2, we are well set for an examination of the methods by which negotiation may be further studied.

Definition of Gaming Simulation

The methods we shall discuss involve the gaming simulation of negotiation situations under controlled (laboratory) conditions. The term *'gaming'* indicates that the study of subjects engaged in laboratory tasks has been substituted for the study of decision makers in the real world and that the games the subjects play are games of strategy. Outcomes are formally determined by the choices of the participants (who may of course be representatives of parties), and typically each participant is attempting to gain an advantage that only he (or his party) can fully achieve. Each will act in accordance with his expectations of how the other will respond to what *he* does (Parsons 1951; Coddington 1968).

The term *'simulation'* has been used in at least two senses by psychologists and other behavioural scientists. Simulations of the first type require the investigator *to make quite explicit and precise assumptions about the processes involved in the system to be simulated.* The object of the exercise is to determine whether or not, given certain input statements, the process model embodied in the simulation is able to generate the output statements which have already been observed in the referent system. The simulation should therefore be regarded as a demonstration of plausibility or a test of sufficiency (Bem 1972). A successful simulation would imply that the process model was 'functionally equivalent to the process being simulated and, further, that the selection of the input statements was not in error' (Bem 1972, p. 29). It would not imply that the model was unique in being able to generate the appropriate output statements, nor that the model was correct or true. Examples of this type of simulation include the computer simulation of a variety of cognitive processes (Feigenbaum and Feldman 1963; Newell, Shaw and Simon 1963; Tomkins and Messick 1963; Abelson 1968) and the interpersonal simulation of 'dissonance' phenomena (Bem 1965, 1967, 1968, 1972).

Simulation of the second type does not require the investigator to have a well-specified dynamic model of the processes involved in the referent system. Instead the investigator attempts *to identify the essential aspects of the task situation and to translate as many as possible of these into experimental terms.* The simulation thus provides a simple experimental analogue of a more complex real-life task. The value of the simulation will depend upon the extent to which the simulate and referent systems are 'isometric in substantive theoretical terms' (Etzioni 1969, p. 562). It is hoped that the behaviour observed in the simulate system will replicate behaviour which it is harder to observe in the referent system, so that the study of the former can to some extent be substituted for the study of the latter.

The gaming simulation of negotiation behaviour involves simulation in this second sense. As Bartos (1970) has put it, 'we must address ourselves to a relatively simple process that, hopefully, resembles real life negotiations well enough to permit application of the conclusions to the real world' (p. 46). General discussions of this sort of simulation are given in a variety of sources (e.g. Benson 1962; Coplin 1966; Guetzkow 1962, 1968; Guetzkow *et al.* 1963; Hermann 1967; Hoggatt and Balderston 1963; Rapoport 1963; Singer 1965; Snyder 1963; Zinnes 1966). To use the term 'gaming simulation' is to emphasise that 'A game is a simple model of the world', as Wiener has put it. But 'to start gaming, you have to have a simple model' (Wiener, cited in Wilson 1970, p. 113). More precisely, all simulation studies of this sort must deal with three sorts of problem:

1 The investigator must *define the behaviour* he is trying to simulate. In this case it is necessary to define what is meant by negotiating behaviour, and to distinguish 'negotiation' from other related terms such as 'bargaining', 'debate', 'diplomacy' and so on. This task has been undertaken in Chapter 1. The games of strategy now to be described involve simulations of

bargaining behaviour, understood as the process of negotiating for agreement (see p. 26).

2 The investigator must *identify certain key components* of the behaviour he is attempting to simulate. This is not a simple matter. As Brody (1969) has pointed out, 'whether a phenomenon, palpable in the reality being simulated, must be represented in the simulate is a matter settled on the basis of theory and the level of explanation sought' (p. 121). The investigator is therefore required to consider a number of different approaches to the study of negotiations. This task has been undertaken in Chapter 2.

3 It is necessary to *translate the key components* of the real life behaviour into the components of an experimental task. Chapter 3 is concerned with this process of translation.

Experimental Paradigms

We may distinguish (at least) five sorts of game which have been put forward as experimental paradigms for the study of bargaining behaviour. There is, however, no agreed terminology for referring to these games, and we propose to label them as *matrix games, distribution games, games of economic exchange, role-playing debates* and *substitute debates*. The essential features of each paradigm are summarised in Figure 3.1. The different paradigms involve different types of simulation, allow different communication possibilities, involve different decision procedures, and define different bargaining situations in different ways. Each will now be considered in more detail.

MATRIX GAMES

Despite the immense popularity of matrix games as a research tool (more than one journal has a regular section devoted to 'gaming'), there are good reasons for doubting the relevance of gaming research to the bargaining process. This is not to deny their usefulness for the study of aspects of social behaviour; it is merely to exercise rather more critical caution than is customary when assessing the relevance of such studies to conflict resolution in real settings (cf. Deutsch 1973).

The use of matrix games of one sort or another may be traced to the work of Deutsch (1958) and Scodel *et al.* (1959). Figure 3.2 gives a general representative example of a two-person two-choice matrix game. Each player (X and Y) is required independently to choose one response (C or D) from a set of alternatives (C and D). No other choices are possible, and each player's payoff is jointly determined by his own choice, his opponent's choice, and the values of X and Y in the payoff matrix defining the game. For example, when X chooses C and Y chooses D, X gets a payoff of X2 units and Y a payoff of Y2 units. The game may be played once or many times in succession. When

Essential Features	Matrix Game	Distribution Game	Game of Economic Exchange	Role-playing Debate	Substitute Debate
1 Type of simulation	Abstract	Abstract	Realistic	Realistic	Realistic
2 Communication possibilities	Extremely restricted	Restricted	Restricted	Unrestricted	Unrestricted
3 Amount of information about other's profits	Complete	Typically incomplete	Typically incomplete	Typically incomplete	Typically incomplete
4 Sequence of choice	Simultaneous	Sequential	Sequential	Sequential	Sequential
5 Identification of different bargaining situations	According to characteristics of payoff matrix	According to characteristics of profit tables	According to characteristics of profit tables and 'scenario'	According to characteristics of profit tables and 'scenario'	According to characteristics of profit tables and 'scenario'

Figure 3.1 Essential features of five experimental paradigms

	Y	
	C	D
C	X1,Y1	X2,Y2
D	X3,Y3	X4,Y4

(X to the left, spanning C and D rows)

Figure 3.2 General form of a two-person two-choice matrix game

each (X,Y) entry in the payoff matrix sums to zero, the game is called a zero-sum game and defines a pure conflict of interest in which what X wins Y (necessarily) loses, and vice versa. Mixed motive games are those in which the interests of the players are partially coincident and partially conflicting and thus form a subclass of non-zero-sum games.

The so-called Prisoner's Dilemma Game is one type of mixed motive game and has the reward structure set out in Figure 3.3. (The reward structure of Chicken is also shown.) The game derives from a problem formulated by the mathematician A. W. Tucker but is, with rare exceptions (e.g. Orwant and Orwant 1970), presented to subjects in a completely abstract form.

A great deal of research has involved repeated plays of games such as the PDG and Chicken, and reasons for the popularity of such games are not hard to find. In the first place they are exceedingly easy to establish experimentally. When they are played abstractly there is little need to consider the background characteristics of the population and no problems are encountered of the construction of an appropriate 'scenario'.

	Y		where
	C	D	
C	R,R	S,T	$X1 = Y1 = R$
			$X2 = Y3 = S$
			$X3 = Y2 = T$
			$X4 = Y4 = P$
D	T,S	P,P	

Payoffs satisfy the following inequalities:

	PDG		*Chicken*
1.	$T>R>P>S$	1.	$T>R>S>P$
2.	$2R>S+T$	2.	$2R>S+T$

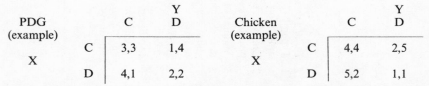

PDG (example)		Y			Chicken (example)		Y	
		C	D				C	D
	C	3,3	1,4			C	4,4	2,5
X	D	4,1	2,2		X	D	5,2	1,1

Figure 3.3 Reward structures of Prisoner's Dilemma Game and Chicken

More justifiably, the existence of 'game theory' encourages the use of matrix games. Game theory was designed to give precise meaning to the notion of rational decision making (Morgenstern 1949; Luce and Raiffa 1957). This is possible within the context of a zero-sum game, where it is rational for each player pessimistically to assume that the other knows his plans and to assess each choice by the payoff it will guarantee to him whatever the other's choice. However, this notion of rationality cannot be extended to the context of the non-zero-sum game (Luce and Raiffa 1957; Peston and Coddington 1967; Rapoport 1970). In the PDG, for example, strategy D dominates strategy C for both players, and 'rational' play by both X and Y would lead to the outcome (D,D) which is worse for both than the outcome (C,C). Nevertheless there are often strong psychological pressures on decision makers to conceptualise bargaining situations as if they were zero-sum games, and, as Rapoport (1968) has pointed out, 'In such situations, if each actor tries to minimize his losses (or maximize his gains), the two may not get as much as they could get otherwise' (p. 74).

A final reason for the continuing popularity of matrix games is the possibility of providing an operational definition of co-operative and competitive responses and hence of examining experimentally the conditions in which co-operation will be elicited and competition discouraged. Many authors have viewed the C response in games like the PDG as 'co-operative' and the D response as 'competitive'. For example, Oskamp and Perlman (1965) have pointed out that the C response is co-operative because 'it allows the other player to obtain a relatively high payoff, and, if reciprocated, it produces the maximum joint payoff' (p. 359) and that the D response is to be regarded as competitive because 'it prevents the other player from earning very much and may produce high payoffs for oneself at the expense of the other player' (pp. 359–60). Similarly, the game has been regarded as offering the players the opportunity to demonstrate either complete trust or complete suspicion of their opponents. This is oversimple. Each player can infer the other's intentions only from his choices, and the outcomes of the game provide information which is inherently ambiguous (McClintock and McNeel 1966; Messick and McClintock 1968; McClintock 1972; Kelley and Stahelski 1970).

The principal value of matrix games for students of bargaining derives from the possibility that they can provide abstract formulations of the concession dilemma faced by negotiators in the course of their bargaining behaviour (Walton and McKersie 1965). The paradigm arises as soon as the C response is labelled 'concede' and the D response 'not concede'. However, there are very serious objections to a translation of this sort.

1 One major focus of research using the PDG has been to identify sequences of play which increase the probability that subjects will develop a stable pattern of interaction characterised by a series of mutually rewarding CC responses (Rapoport and Chammah 1965; Pilisuk *et al.* 1965; Oskamp

1971). But making a series of CC responses is not at all like making a series
of concessions in order to reach an agreement (Nemeth 1972). The PDG is
not a simulation of a bargaining situation, even a very minimal one, because
playing the PDG is *not an exercise in joint decision making at all.* Subjects do
not have to reach some agreement before they can carry through an action.
Thus, while the PDG involves 'joint determination of outcomes' (i.e. while
payment is contingent upon combinations of choices made), it does not
involve 'joint determination of action' (Daniels 1967, pp. 50–1). There is
therefore no joint decision which has to be made. The only communication
possibilities are those inherent in the outcomes of the game.

2 Subjects are given *complete knowledge* of the payoff matrix involved,
   whereas in reality a negotiator often does not know how his opponent feels
   about the alternatives involved (Pruitt 1969; Iklé and Leites 1962) and may
   even be quite vague about his own preferences (Iklé and Leites 1962; Iklé
   1964).

3 The payoffs involved are often *trivial in value.*

4 *No social relationship* exists between the players. As Nemeth (1972) has put
   it, 'With no information about the other individual, how can one decide to
   develop a relationship? A subject does not know and cannot see or hear the
   other individual; nor can he *get* to *know* him since information is limited to
   a game choice between two alternatives, information that . . . is highly
   ambiguous. There is no real past, no real present, and no future between the
   participants in a Prisoner's Dilemma Game' (p. 215).

There would seem to be at least two important consequences of these
restrictions: (a) 'elements of uncertainty and surprise' may enhance the appeal
of such games as 'tests of wit and games of skill' (Sermat 1970); and (b)
subjects may even wonder what the point of the game really is (Alexander and
Weil 1969; Nemeth 1972). As Alexander and Weil (1969) have stated, 'we may
imagine subjects wondering why they are asked to make replicative forced
choices for meaningless points with unclear objectives under conditions
enforcing non-communication. Such a situation virtually begs for explanation
of the broader purpose of play in terms of "hidden" experimenter interests'
(pp. 127–8). Subjects' subsequent play may therefore become an attempt 'to
create and express an appropriate situated identity' in terms of the in-
terpretive conclusions they reach about the real purposes of the experiment
(p. 128).

Similar arguments would apply to many of the mechanical (or
electromechanical) games extant in the literature (e.g. Deutsch and Krauss
1960, 1962; Shure, Meeker and Hansford 1965; Swingle 1967, 1970a; Sermat
1970). Accordingly, such games will not be given separate treatments in this
chapter. The general point is sufficiently clear: *abstract games of this sort
(whether matrix games or mechanical games) do not simulate bargaining
situations at all, even very simple ones.*

Matrix games with preplay communication

Some investigators have introduced possibilities for preplay communication into matrix games of one sort or another. In some cases the communication simply allows subjects to deliver threats and/or to state which choice they intend to make (e.g. Horai and Tedeschi 1969; Schlenker *et al.* 1970; Tedeschi 1970); in other cases subjects are able tentatively to agree how to co-ordinate their choices (e.g. Deutsch 1958; Thibaut and Faucheux 1965; Murdoch 1967; Kahan 1968; Thibaut 1968; Thibaut and Gruder 1969; Gruder 1970). However, in neither group of cases are subjects' payoffs decided by the verbal communication between them, and in neither is negotiation involved.

Similar comments would apply to the preplay communication involved in mechanical games of the type used by Deutsch and Krauss (Deutsch and Krauss 1962; Krauss and Deutsch 1966). As Morley and Stephenson (1970b) have pointed out, negotiation is not pregame communication of this sort; what is required is a paradigm in which negotiation *is* the game.

DISTRIBUTION GAMES

Unlike matrix games, distribution games do provide abstract formulations of negotiation tasks. Subjects are given minimum necessary share (MNS) values (i.e. assigned minimum goals) and asked to negotiate the division of a specified number of points or a given sum of money. Those who succeed in obtaining outcomes above their MNS values are paid accordingly. Typically, subjects bargain in ignorance of their opponent's MNS value. In some cases bargaining is restricted to an exchange of bids (e.g. Morgan and Sawyer 1967; Froman and Cohen 1969); in other cases it is not (e.g. Kelley, Beckman and Fischer 1967; Fischer 1970). Subjects may act as individuals or as representatives of teams.

Kelley, Beckman and Fischer (1967) have provided what is perhaps the best-known example of a task of this type, and this will now be described for the case in which subjects X and Y negotiated. On any one play of the game X and Y were asked to negotiate the division of 9 points such that each subject received a whole number of points. There were thus eight possible contracts for X and Y to consider: X1/Y8, X2/Y7, X3/Y6, X4/Y5, X5/Y4, X6/Y3, X7/Y2 and X8/Y1. Each subject was given an MNS value and paid, in points, a sum equal to the difference between the value of the contract he agreed and the MNS value he was given. For example, if X was given an MNS value of 4 and Y an MNS value of 1, a contract at X5/Y4 would have been worth 1 point to X and 3 points to Y. Subjects were not allowed to negotiate contracts below their MNS values and were penalised severely for taking too long to reach an agreement. Subjects played a number of games with the same opponent (each involving different combinations of MNS values) and were given cash prizes according to the total number of points they obtained.

Kelley, Beckman and Fischer could, of course, have paid subjects after a single game, and it is important to distinguish between: (a) a game played once (e.g. Morgan and Sawyer 1967; Froman and Cohen 1969), (b) repeated play of the same game with the same opponent (as in most experiments involving matrix games), (c) repeated play of the same type of game with the same opponent (e.g. Kelley, Beckman and Fischer 1967; Kelley *et al.* 1970; Fischer, 1970), and (d) repeated play of the same type of game with different opponents (e.g. Kelley 1966).

Two features of distribution games may limit the generality of any results obtained by their use:

1 Some experiments place subjects under very considerable *time pressure* (e.g. Kelley, Beckman and Fischer 1967; Fischer 1970), whereas others do not (e.g. Kelley 1966; Kelley *et al.* 1970; Morgan and Sawyer 1967). For example, in one experiment (Experiment II) Kelley, Beckman and Fischer (1967) set a deadline of ninety seconds per game; in another (Experiment I) they subtracted 1 point from each subject's profit for each complete minute taken to reach agreement. Time pressures of this sort may mean that subjects care more about reaching an agreement than about what sort of agreement is reached. In particular, subjects may exchange very few communications and learn very little about the MNS values of their opponents during the course of their interactions (Kelley, Beckman and Fischer 1967, p. 365).

2 Distribution games involve *communication of a rather restricted sort*. Even when experimental procedures place no constraints on the nature of the communication between subjects, bargaining is, in principle, limited to moves such as bidding, threatening, exaggerating one's MNS value, appealing to common interests and offering to trade concessions on different plays of the game. There is nothing else to argue about. In other words, distribution games simulate those comparatively rare situations in which communication focuses primarily upon *outcomes*; they do not simulate situations which also contain the potential for disagreement over *inputs*. The latter situations are of course extremely common (Iklé 1964; Messé 1971).

GAMES OF ECONOMIC EXCHANGE

Games of economic exchange provide what Rapoport (1963) has called 'realistic simulations' of a variety of trading situations involving buyers and sellers.

The best-known examples of games of economic exchange are perhaps those in which a single (unique) buyer confronts a single (unique) seller, thus simulating the market situation known as *bilateral monopoly* (e.g. Siegel and Fouraker 1960; Johnson and Cohen 1967; Holmes, Throop and Strickland

Seller's Profit Table					Buyer's Profit Table			
	Quantity					Quantity		
Price	8	9	10	11	Price	8	9	10	11
240	1190	1350	1430	1430	240				
230	1120	1260	1320	1300	230				
220	1050	1170	1210	1170	220				
210	980	1080	1100	1040	210	50	0		
200	910	990	990	910	200	120	90	33	
190	840	900	880	780	190	190	180	143	91
180	770	810	770	650	180	260	270	253	221
170	700	720	660	520	170	330	360	363	351
160	630	630	550	390	160	400	450	473	481
150	560	540	440	260	150	470	540	583	611
140	490	450	330	130	140	540	630	693	741
130	420	360	220	0	130	610	720	803	871
120	350	270	110		120	680	810	913	1001
110	280	180	0		110	750	900	1023	1131
100	210	90			100	820	990	1133	1261

| A | B | C | D | | A′ | B′ | C′ | D′ |

$$A + A' = 1030$$
$$B + B' = 1080 = \text{maximum joint profit (MJP)}$$
$$C + C' = 1023$$
$$D + D' = 871$$

Figure 3.4 Example of profit tables used in bilateral monopoly games (adapted from Kelley and Schenitzki 1972)

1971; Kelley and Schenitzki 1972). In such cases subjects are given profit tables and asked to agree upon a price/quantity combination at which goods are to be exchanged. Typically, the bargaining involves only an exchange of bids, and subjects are paid the value (e.g. in cents) of the contract they have negotiated. Examples of the sort of profit table used are given in Figure 3.4.

Two features of the profit tables are worthy of further comment:

1 Subjects are able to offer a variety of possible contracts at a given level of profit. Two contracts which are of equal (or almost equal) value to one subject may differ considerably in their value to the other. For example, contracts at 8/160 and 9/160 are of equal value to the seller (630 cents) but differ by 50 cents in their value to the buyer (400 cents *v.* 450 cents); similarly, contracts at 11/140 and 8/110 are of almost equal value to the buyer (741 cents *v.* 750 cents) but differ by 150 cents in their value to the seller (130 cents *v.* 280 cents).
2 Some agreements are Pareto Optimal in the sense that they maximise the joint gain available to the subjects, whereas others are not. In the example given, the buyer and seller attain their maximum joint profit (MJP) when 9

items are exchanged (whatever the price). Measures of joint profit are often used as indices of bargaining efficiency.

The generality of results obtained using games of this sort may also be limited by features such as excessive time pressure and focus on outcomes to the exclusion of inputs, as in the case of distribution games.

ROLE-PLAYING DEBATES

Debates are intended to provide realistic simulations of rather complex collective bargaining tasks. They allow conflict over inputs as well as conflict over outcomes and require subjects to act as representatives of groups. Different types of debate are distinguished by the methods they use to incorporate a representational role structure into the experimental task.

Subjects in a role-playing debate are required actually to learn the details of a particular dispute (from materials provided by the experimenter) and to bargain as if they were representing a party to that dispute. Consequently, while the role-playing paradigm allows different subjects to use the same experimental materials it makes very considerable demands upon the actors involved.

Perhaps the best-known task of this type is that used by Campbell (1960), Bass (1966) and Druckman (1967, 1968) and described by Bass (1967) and Bass, Vaughan and Cox (1968). Subjects were assigned to union or management roles and each given experimental materials consisting of background information about the company involved, a statement of nine issues to be negotiated, details of settlements in other local firms, and a one-page memorandum explaining their party's position in more detail. Each issue (e.g. 'night shift differential') was presented in the form of a bargaining range, as shown in Figure 3.5. The company position defined one end of the range

Night Shift Differential

Past contract: an extra 5 cents per hour is paid for nightwork.
Union: demanded a 5 cent increase to 10 cents per hour.
Company: rejected.

	0	1	2	3	4	5	
Company	———————————————————————————						Union
Total	1000	2000	3000	4000	5000	6000	

Money value per 2 years.

Figure 3.5 Presentation of an issue in Exercise Negotiations (from Bass, Vaughan and Cox 1968)

and the union position the other. A number of possible settlement points and the corresponding costs to the company for the period of the contract were marked on the bargaining range. Subjects were asked to reach agreement on as many of these issues as possible in the given time. Sometimes a deadline was set; sometimes it was not. Sometimes subjects incurred time costs; sometimes they did not.

As a general comment on the logical status of such techniques we can do no better than to extend Nicholson's (1970) evaluation of the gaming simulation of various international systems: 'Not all aspects of behaviour are, at present, well reproduced, nor are we sure which ones are well reproduced and which are not' (p. 152). In particular, we do not know to what extent subjects do act as if they are representatives of groups. Consequently, we do not know to what extent the paradigm succeeds in simulating a collective bargaining situation rather than an interpersonal one. This does not mean that the paradigm cannot be used for purposes of testing research hypotheses, but it does mean that results should be interpreted with a great deal of caution (Etzioni 1969; Nicholson 1970).

SUBSTITUTE DEBATES

McGrath (1966) and Vidmar and McGrath (1967) have argued that a paradigm for experimental research on collective bargaining should fulfil four requirements:

1 Subjects are genuine representatives of a party to the negotiation.
2 There is a 'discussion-type' task.
3 The issues being debated are realistic, important to the parties and sufficiently complex for a genuine debate to take place.
4 The conflict of interest between the parties occurs independently of the experimental setting.

The object of a substitute debate is thus to substitute an encounter which occurs under laboratory conditions for one which might in any case occur elsewhere. In McGrath's (1966) words, 'we wish to study the negotiation of issues which are *actually* divisive issues for the people involved and the groups they represent. What is non-real, artificially created, is the actual negotiation – the confrontation of the opposed parties in an attempt to resolve the issue' (p. 118).

In practice, it is necessary to ensure that all subjects are given the same task (since the conflict of interest between the parties may involve more than one issue), and each negotiator is therefore given a position paper to use as a guideline for representing his group.

One study of this sort has already been described in Chapter 2, namely that by McGrath and Julian (1963), and it should therefore be clear that, while the substitute debate paradigm faces few problems of external validity, it places considerable constraints upon the nature of the subject populations available to an experimenter. It is in fact extremely difficult to find subjects in sufficient numbers to conduct an experiment at all. Furthermore, the background material is specific to the subject population used (since it refers to the position of the particular groups to which the subjects belong). Each new experiment is likely to require new subjects and the preparation of new experimental materials.

Formal Classification of Experimental Tasks

Four types of bargaining game have been identified: distribution games, games of economic exchange, role-playing debates and substitute debates. In principle, (at least) three types of experimental task can be distinguished within each of these paradigms according to the structure of the issues involved:

1 Tasks of Type 1, in which subjects negotiate a single (complex) issue requiring agreement on two dimensions, such as price and quantity (e.g. Siegel and Fouraker 1960; Kelley and Schenitzki 1972).
2 Tasks of Type 2, in which subjects negotiate a single (one-dimensional) issue involving either the exchange of a single item (e.g. Chertkoff and Conley 1967; Pruitt and Johnson 1970) or the division of a single sum of money (Morgan and Sawyer 1967; Messé 1971).
3 Tasks of Type 3, in which subjects negotiate a number of issues, each involving the exchange of a single item or the division of a single sum of money (e.g. Kelley 1966; Froman and Cohen 1969).

Consequently, as shown in Figure 3.6, experimental tasks may be distinguished according to a 4×3 classification scheme which identifies both the type of paradigm and the type of issue involved.

GENERAL DISCUSSION

It is of course an empirical question whether results obtained with one type of task will be obtained with another, but *a priori* two dimensions of difference would seem to be especially important: one concerning the amount of information subjects can exchange in their bargaining, the other concerning the number of contracts subjects can offer at a given level of profit.

Distribution games and games of economic exchange involve more limited communication possibilities than do debates. Sometimes bargaining is restricted to an exchange of bids (e.g. Kelley, Beckman and Fischer 1967; Chertkoff and Conley 1967; Pruitt and Drews 1969), but even when it is not

Structure of issues	Distribution game	Game of Economic Exchange	Role-playing Debate	Substitute Debate
Single multi-dimensional issue (Type 1)	DG1	GEE1	RPD1	SD1
Single one-dimensional issue (Type 2)	DG2	GEE2	RPD2	SD2
Several one-dimensional issues (Type 3)	DG3	GEE3	RPD3	SD3

Figure 3.6 Formal classification of bargaining tasks

(e.g. Kelley 1966; Fischer 1970) it is inherent in the nature of games of this sort that disagreement focuses primarily upon outcomes to the exclusion of disagreement over inputs. But, as Messé (1971) has pointed out, in other situations 'inputs are also an important dimension of the bargaining process. That is, persons do not only conflict over which outcome they want, but also over the relative contributions of their own and the other's inputs' (p. 290); moreover, in certain cases it may be relatively easy to reach an agreement on outcomes if an agreement on inputs can first be obtained (p. 290).

Tasks of Type 1 and Type 3 allow subjects to offer more than one contract at a given level of profit, whereas tasks of Type 2 do not. Two points would therefore seem to be worthy of note:

1 As far as tasks of Type 3 are concerned, exploration of alternative contracts at a given level of profit is possible only if subjects negotiate all issues simultaneously ('logrolling') rather than sequentially, one at a time ('compromise'). Since some authors have stressed the benefits of the former strategy (e.g. Kelley 1966; Froman 1967; Froman and Cohen 1970) and others the benefits of the latter (e.g. Fisher 1964, 1969), it is of considerable theoretical interest to determine when 'logrolling' is more efficient than 'compromise' and when it is not (Kelley and Schenitzki 1972).

2 When communication is restricted to an exchange of bids, task of Types DG2 and GEE2 simulate extremely simple negotiation situations. Thus, as Pruitt and Drews (1969) have pointed out, their own task [GEE2][1] 'greatly simplifies the usual negotiation situation. Because there is only one commodity, alternatives involving packages or trades are not possible. New alternatives cannot be developed. Of the myriads of strategies that are possible in most negotiations (e.g. persuasive communication and threat) the only ones possible here involve manipulating one's own demand' (p. 47). This may place very considerable restrictions on the generality of results obtained using tasks of these types.

The 4×3 classification scheme we have introduced is of course a simplification introduced for analytic purposes. It is possible to identify more than four paradigms and more than three types of task. For instance, some experimenters have used hypothetical issues but asked subjects to represent experimental groups (e.g. Johnson 1967; Johnson and Dustin 1970); others have given subjects extended experience in laboratory groups and studied the negotiation of disputes between competing groups (e.g. Blake and Mouton 1961d). In some cases contracts may increase in value after a sequence of agreements (Kelley *et al.* 1970); in others subjects may be allowed to introduce

---

[1] The letters and figures in square brackets used hereafter in the book indicate the precise nature of the task used, in the terminology of Figure 3.6. Thus Pruitt and Drews's (1969) study was of the game of economic exchange (GEE) type and involved the negotiation of a single one-dimensional issue (Type 2).

issues not specified by the experimental materials (Morley and Stephenson 1969, 1970a). However, in general these leads have not been followed (Stephenson 1971a), and it is not necessary to do more than indicate that such variants do exist.

EVALUATION OF OUTCOMES

Negotiation may be regarded as successful when agreements are reached and those agreements are of high quality. However, while it is easy to measure number of deadlocks, time to agreement, etc. it is not always easy to say when an agreement is of high quality and when it is not. In fact different measures of quality may be appropriate in different situations.

First, consider those studies in which the task focused upon outcomes rather than inputs (i.e. distribution games and games of economic exchange). Two questions may be of interest, as Siegel and Fouraker (1960) have pointed out: (a) whether or not subjects attained MJP outcomes, and (b) the difference in the profits attained by each subject. When the tasks were of Type 1 or Type 3 interest was focused on bargaining *efficiency*, as measured by subjects' joint profits (e.g. Johnson and Cohen 1967; Froman and Cohen 1969); when the tasks were of Type 2 interest was focused on the nature of the compromise involved (e.g. Morgan and Sawyer 1967; Liebert *et al.* 1968). In principle, one might ask questions like: Did one subject dominate another? Did settlements reflect principles of equity or equality? How satisfied were the subjects with the agreements reached?

Second, consider those studies in which the task focused upon inputs as well as outcomes (i.e. role-playing debates and substitute debates). Several measures of quality of agreement are available. For example, McGrath and Julian (1963) used the product of experimenter ratings to provide a combined merit score; Campbell (1960) and Bass (1966) measured absolute and algebraic deviations from a 'going rate'; and Evan and MacDougall (1967) rated each item of an agreement as 'reflecting domination, compromise, or integration elements'. None of these measures takes account of the fact that negotiators' SEU functions are likely to be nonlinear (Chapter 2), and it is not at all obvious which measure is to be preferred.

B

A Critical Review of
Experimental Studies

Introduction

The experimental study of negotiation groups is a relatively recent enterprise, dating only from Siegel and Fouraker's (1960) investigations of bilateral monopoly (introducing the game of economic exchange paradigm) and Campbell's (1960) investigation of the effects of partisan commitment (introducing the role-playing debate paradigm). Consequently, while there is an extensive literature dealing with problems of social conflict (Bernard 1965; Fink 1968; Patchen 1970, Levine and Campbell 1972), there is not as yet a substantial body of experimental research dealing with the process of negotiation *per se* (Sawyer and Guetzkow 1965; McGrath 1966; Stephenson 1971b). Most psychologists have in fact devoted their attention to the study of those forms of strategic decision making which do not involve bargaining, as evidenced by the very large number of experiments using a matrix game or equivalent type (Rapoport and Orwant 1962; Gallo and McClintock 1965; Rapoport and Chammah 1965, 1966; Rapoport 1968; Terhune 1968, 1970; Wyer 1969; Swingle 1970a; Oskamp 1971; Nemeth 1972; McClintock 1972; Wrightsman, O'Connor and Baker 1972). The major implications of this research for the study of bargaining behaviour would seem to be as follows:

1 Whether subjects 'co-operate' or 'compete' depends upon the reward structure of the game (Rapoport and Chammah 1965, 1966; Oskamp 1971) and the way that structure is displayed to them (Evans and Crumbaugh 1966; Messick and McClintock 1968; Pruitt 1967, 1970). Apparently an extreme competitor and an extreme co-operator may 'show striking behavioural differences' in one game but act 'almost indistinguishably alike' in another (Sermat 1970, p. 101).
2 The more complex the game is (i.e. the greater the number of trials and choice alternatives), the smaller the influence of personality variables upon overall levels of co-operation and competition, and the greater the influence of the form of the interaction between the players (Rapoport and Chammah 1965, 1966; Pilisuk *et al.* 1965; Terhune 1968, 1970). Consequently, one would not expect to find personality variables to have a large effect upon the outcomes of experimental negotiations of the debate type (see also McGrath 1966; Stephenson 1973).

In Chapters 4 to 6 we shall attempt to provide a detailed and critical review of those experimental studies of negotiation which are available, distinguishing between the twelve types of task identified in Figure 3.6. As far as we know, such a review has not previously been attempted, although beginnings have been made by Sawyer and Guetzkow (1965) and Stephenson

(1971b). We shall, however, deal only with those studies in which subjects actually complete a negotiation task, and a great deal of social psychological research which is potentially relevant to the study of negotiation will therefore not be considered. We shall not, for example, discuss the many experimental studies of 'intergroup discrimination' (reviewed in Blake and Mouton 1961d; Stephenson 1971b; Rabbie and Wilkens 1971; Turner 1972), nor the research into 'cognitive conflicts' conducted by Hammond and his associates (Hammond *et al.* 1966: Brown and Hammond 1968; Miller 1972; Hammond and Boyle 1971; Hammond and Summers 1972; Balke, Hammond and Meyer 1972).

Psychologists have made two distinctive contributions to the study of negotiation groups.

1 They have emphasised the importance of a negotiator's relationship to the group (or groups) for whom he acts. This may affect the way issues are perceived, the choice of strategy, and the method of preparation for negotiation. Such variables will be considered in Chapter 4.
2 They have examined the process of negotiation in some detail. This research will be outlined in Chapters 5 and 6, Chapter 5 dealing with the process of bid and counterbid in distribution games and games of economic exchange and Chapter 6 with the process of negotiation in experimental debates.

Chapter 4

Intergroup Relations and Bargaining Behaviour

Traditionally, study of the psychological factors involved in group performance has concentrated upon individual performance in a group context (Golombiewski 1962; Davis 1969). This emphasis has been transferred to the study of negotiation groups. Experimental studies have demonstrated the importance of a negotiator's relationship to the group or groups he represents.

Initially we shall consider the psychological 'pressures' acting upon individual negotiators as they go about their daily work. McGrath and his associates have tried to predict negotiation success from knowledge of the participants' level of commitment or obligation towards their respective parties (measured by R- or 'role' forces). R-forces are assumed to be of greater importance than pressures arising from C-forces (directed towards the community) or A-forces (directed towards opponent's party). We shall argue that McGrath's model underemphasises the role of A- and C-force pressures.

In Chapter 2 we have argued that R-force pressure may affect bargaining behaviour either directly, via negotiators' willingness to compromise, or indirectly, via negotiators' perceptions of party position. When R-force pressures acting on negotiators are directed towards different issues, misunderstanding of 'tougher' bargaining positions may mean that agreements have less chance of being obtained. We shall examine this problem via Bonham's (1971) research on international relations and shall argue that his findings are of general interest.

Generally, R-force pressure is assumed to be detrimental to performance in negotiation groups. Consequently, some attention has been paid to the question of whether such effects can be modified by appropriate experimental treatments. In practice, of course, mediators often intervene in disputes when negotiations break down. But what is their effect? And what might they achieve if employed from the outset? Psychologists have examined both these questions and produced results which once again highlight the distinctive character of negotiation groups.

One supposed virtue of the mediator is the responsibility he takes for the agreement. This enables negotiators who must abandon party positions to 'save face' and perhaps to avoid charges of ineptitude and 'betrayal'. Consequently, we shall return to the link between the individual and the group, since the need to save face will be determined by the extent of the commitment to represent a party position. Here we shall emphasise structural and organisational variables to complement our earlier concern with individual 'forces'. Two themes predominate: how negotiators prepare for negotiation and how their behaviour is monitored once negotiation has begun.

We shall also consider the role of individual differences in the selection of negotiators. Can one predict who will be an effective negotiator from knowledge of his personality traits? Some people may be consistently better negotiators than others, but do they possess any distinguishing characteristics?

We shall argue that, while there have been some positive findings, the search for paper-and-pencil measures which predict negotiation outcomes has met with only very limited success. Evidence will also be presented which shows the predictive power of 'negotiator trait scores' derived from management ratings.

Most research in this area comes from the USA, and it is of some interest therefore to examine whether or not the style of negotiating involved varies according to cultural background. The value placed on different objectives may vary from one country to another and lead to different patterns of behaviour. Several experimental studies have examined such possibilities. These will be discussed, and we shall conclude the chapter with an examination of what constitutes a 'fair' exchange between different groups and individuals.

Predicting Negotiation Effectiveness from McGrath's Tri-polar Model

Vidmar and McGrath (1965) [SD3] examined the effects of R-forces on the outcomes of negotiation groups composed of members of competing housing organisations at the University of Illinois. Subjects were informed that the dyad which achieved the highest combined merit score would receive $20 in prize money from the experimenters ($10 for each negotiator). Measures of the R-forces (directed towards own party position) acting upon each negotiator were derived from his answer to a housing issue questionnaire (measure R1) and from his perception of how that questionnaire would be answered from the point of view of his party 'as a whole' (measure R2). These measures were in general negatively correlated with judges' ratings and together yielded highly significant multiple correlations with neutral ($R = \cdot76$, $p < \cdot01$) and product ($R = \cdot87, p < \cdot001$) criteria for negotiation effectiveness.

These findings were replicated in the negotiation (N) condition of Vidmar and McGrath's (1967) [RPD3] study. Subjects represented hypothetical organisations with different views about the purpose of a university education ('an orientation favouring a broad, general education' *v.* 'an orientation favouring specialized, career-oriented education') and were assigned to roles consonant with their own attitudes and beliefs. The task was in two parts. Subjects were required to recommend to the 'President's Council on Planning' what changes the University of Illinois should make in its selection procedures (Part I) and what types of curriculum change there should be to attain educational objectives (Part II). R-force measures again were inversely correlated with judges' ratings and together yielded significant multiple correlations with neutral (Part I: $R = \cdot52, p < \cdot05$; Part II: $R = \cdot52, p < \cdot05$) and product (Part I: $R = \cdot53, p < \cdot05$; Part II: $R = \cdot27$, n.s.) criteria for task success. However, in contrast to the earlier study, measures of C-forces (directed towards community) were also obtained. In general, these were positively correlated with judges' ratings and together yielded highly significant multiple correlations with neutral (Part I: $R = \cdot63, p < \cdot01$; Part II: $R = \cdot62, p < \cdot01$) and product (Part I: $R = \cdot77, p < \cdot01$; Part II: $R = \cdot70, p < \cdot01$) criteria for task success. Consequently, while these findings provide general support for McGrath and Julian's (1962) tripolar model, they also suggested that R-force pressure may not always be more important than A- (directed towards opponent's party) and C-force pressure in determining the quality of the agreement obtained.

A study by Druckman and Zechmeister (1970) [RPD3] also is relevant to the tripolar conceptualisation. Subjects were asked to take the role of political decision makers empowered to divide an $8 million government budget among eight proposed methods of dealing with urban racial problems. Each subject championed four of the proposals and was assigned to a role consonant with his own attitudes and beliefs. In an 'ideological link' (IL) condition, one set of proposals was explicitly derived from an ideology of 'social change' and the other set from an ideology of 'system maintenance'. In a 'no ideological link' (NIL) condition, the additional ideological information was excluded. Subjects in the IL condition found it harder to reach agreement than subjects in the NIL condition (4/8 dyads in the NIL condition reached agreement before a thirty-minute deadline, whereas 0/7 dyads in the IL condition did so). Consequently, the number of pairs who maximised their joint profit (by apportioning the entire $8 million) was greater in the NIL condition than in the IL condition (7/8 dyads in the NIL condition reached MJP agreements, whereas only 2/7 dyads in the IL condition did so). Furthermore, compromise was unlikely in the IL condition, and conflict tended to result in either deadlock or capitulation.

Two further studies have manipulated the R-force pressure operating upon negotiators (or teams of negotiators). Vidmar and McGrath (1965) [RPD3] compared the effectiveness of 'standard' negotiation groups (in which a member of party A represents party A and a member of party B represents party B) and of 'cross-assigned' negotiation groups (in which a member of party A represents party A and another member of party A represents party B). The tripolar model of course implies that the latter groups would have produced higher quality settlements than the former. However, while the

c

difference between the experimental conditions was in the predicted direction, it reached only a marginal level of statistical significance ($p < \cdot 10$). Campbell (1960) [RPD3] compared the effectiveness of standard and cross-assigned negotiation teams. In each group two subjects negotiated as a team for the union and two as a team for the management in a hypothetical union–management dispute. Three levels of R-force pressure were involved: 'low identification' (LI) groups, in which team members had no clear party affiliations; 'high identification' (HI) groups, in which members of each team identified strongly with the party they were to represent; and 'high identification, cross-assigned' (HI/C) groups, in which each team was made up of one subject who identified strongly with the party he represented and one who identified strongly with the opposing party. The tripolar model suggests that the contracts negotiated by LI groups would have been of higher quality than those negotiated by HI/C groups, which would in turn have been of higher quality than those negotiated by HI groups. Quality of settlement was measured in terms of (both absolute and algebraic) deviations from the 'going rate' in other local firms. The hypothesis derived from the tripolar model was not supported. HI, HI/C and LI groups did not reliably produce contracts which had different absolute deviations from the going rate. Furthermore, while HI/C groups produced 'more impartial' settlements than LI groups in terms of algebraic deviation from the going rate, LI groups did not produce 'more impartial' settlements than HI groups. The results of these studies therefore provided only limited support for the tripolar model and (again) suggested that the emphasis upon R-forces to the exclusion of A- and C-forces may be rather premature.

Stephenson, Skinner and Brotherton (1976) [SD3] examined the effect of prenegotiation participation in group preparation on subsequent debate, in either standard or role-reversed conditions. Full role reversal brought about fewer deadlocks and more varied settlements, but participation had no discernible effects. To our knowledge, there are no other published studies which have included such a role reversal condition, in which team A consists entirely of representatives who identify with party B and team B of representatives who identify with party A.

The Effects of Issue Emphasis

Negotiations may be harder to conclude (and may possibly lead to lower quality agreements) when R-force pressures are focused upon *different issues* for the parties concerned, as Bonham (1971) [RPD3] has shown. This excellent study used a laboratory task in an attempt to simulate the disarmament negotiations which took place between 1946 and 1961. Bonham has discussed in detail the problems involved in such a simulation and made a serious attempt to compare and contrast the laboratory findings with those obtained from a detailed examination of the case material concerned.

The experiment consisted of eleven 4-hour sessions in which three 'chief negotiators' took the roles of representatives of the United States (US), Soviet Union (SU) and United Kingdom (UK). Each session was structured as follows:

1 Each negotiator received sealed instructions from the 'leader' of his nation.
2 Negotiators were given a 45-minute briefing by the experimenter to familiarise them with the rules and procedures involved in the game.
3 Each negotiator engaged in a 20-minute conference with a team mate ('Agency Director') responsible for formulating and implementing national policy.
4 Five 30-minute 'move periods' then followed, each consisting of 20 minutes of written negotiations, 5 minutes of conference with the appropriate Agency Director and 5 minutes to complete a questionnaire.

Issue emphasis was manipulated by means of the initial instructions given to subjects. In six of the sessions (the experimental groups) each negotiator received different sealed instructions: one negotiator was instructed to give priority to reducing arms; a second was instructed to give priority to problems of inspection; a third received instructions which were neutral in these respects. (A different combination of instruction was assigned to the chief negotiators concerned in each session of the game, thus providing a counterbalanced design.) In five of the sessions (the control groups) all subjects received neutral instructions.

COMPARISONS BETWEEN EXPERIMENTAL GROUPS AND CONTROL GROUPS

Apparently, 'when negotiators disagree with respect to the importance of the issues, they deal with the discrepancy either by interacting less to avoid the problem, or by interacting more to resolve the problem' (p. 306). US and UK negotiators exchanged fewer messages in experimental sessions than in control sessions (thus exemplifying the former trend), whereas US and SU negotiators exchanged more messages (thus exemplifying the latter trend) (p. 306). However, if this increased interaction is to be taken as evidence of an attempt to resolve the issues concerned, we must conclude that the attempt was not a success. There was in experimental sessions a greater likelihood that US and SU messages were used to exchange hostility ('operationally defined as attacks on the motives of others') than there was in control sessions. Furthermore, there was also some evidence that concessions were generally less likely to be reciprocated in experimental sessions ($R = -\cdot23$) than in control sessions ($R = \cdot54$). Bonham has concluded that 'differences between negotiating nations in the relative saliency of the issues may lead to misunderstanding, negative attitudes, hostile interaction, fewer concessions and a lower probability of eventual agreement' (p. 313).

COMPARISONS BETWEEN SIMULATION RESULTS AND ANALYSES OF
TRANSCRIPTS

Written messages were analysed in terms of Jensen's (1962) categories of
insecurity propaganda and hostility. Three sorts of analyses are presented:

1 *Relative amounts of insecurity etc. expressed in experimental sessions and in
   meetings 22–49 of the 1955 Disarmament Sub-Committee.* In each case the
   US negotiators made significantly more statements coded as insecurity
   than propaganda. However, the relatively low frequency of hostility in the
   simulation was in marked contrast to the relatively high frequency of
   hostility coded in the Sub-Committee transcripts. Bonham has therefore
   concluded that 'Two negotiation processes were replicated successfully by
   American teams in the simulation runs' (p. 310). The pattern of behaviour
   shown by SU negotiators in the Sub-Committee was, however, exactly the
   reverse of that exhibited in the simulation, 'suggesting that the absence of
   cultural variation in the simulation decreased its ability to replicate
   negotiation processes' (p. 310).
2 *Comparisons of correlations between US and SU behaviours in experimental
   sessions, Disarmament Sub-Committee meetings, and major disarmament
   negotiations.* The relevant correlations are reported in Table 7 (p. 311) of
   Bonham's paper and may be interpreted as 'reflecting the degree to which
   expressions of insecurity, propaganda, and hostility were reciprocated by
   the two sides' (pp. 311–12). In general, the data from the simulation were
   more like the data from the Sub-Committee meetings (coded by Bonham)
   than like the data from the major disarmament negotiations (coded by
   Jensen 1962). US and SU expressions of insecurity and propaganda were
   reciprocated to the same extent in experimental sessions of the simulation
   and in Sub-Committee meetings. However, the correlation between US
   and SU hostility was equally high in experimental sessions ($R = \cdot65, p <
   \cdot01$) and major negotiations ($R = \cdot61, p < \cdot01$) but not significantly
   different from zero in the Sub-Committee sessions ($R = \cdot28$, n.s.).
3 *Comparisons of concession behaviour in experimental sessions and major
   disarmament negotiations.* In both cases US negotiators tended to make
   concessions earlier in a round of negotiations than did SU negotiators.
   Furthermore, here Bonham found some evidence (p. 312) that the type of
   concessions made was similar in the two cases (although the specific
   content of the concessions differed considerably in detail).

This is an important paper. 'Until researchers have more access to important
negotiations, the study of negotiation may have to be conducted in laboratory
settings similar to the one described here' (p. 313). It is therefore as well to give
very serious consideration to any study which allows the comparison of
experimental and real life findings.

Introducing a Mediator

One way of modifying the detrimental effects of R-force pressure may be to introduce a mediator into a negotiation group. Thus, Vidmar and McGrath (1967) [RPD3] found that, while measures of R-, A- and C-forces were powerful predictors of task success in negotiation groups (for unmediated groups, neutral criterion gave Part I: $R = \cdot69$, $p < \cdot01$; Part II: $R = \cdot69$, $p < \cdot01$; while product criterion gave Part I: $R = \cdot77$, $p < \cdot01$; Part II: $R = \cdot70$, $p < \cdot01$), they were much less powerful predictors of task success in negotiation groups containing a discussion chairman (for mediated groups, neutral criterion gave Part I: $R = \cdot51$, n.s.; Part II: $R = \cdot65$, $p < \cdot05$; while product criterion gave Part I: $R = \cdot33$, n.s.; Part II: $R = \cdot60$, n.s.). While mediated groups produced higher quality settlements than unmediated groups (in terms of both neutral and product criteria) on both parts of the task, in general these differences did not reach acceptable levels of statistical significance. Even so, the groups containing chairmen were more like the problem-solving (or discussion) groups used by Vidmar and McGrath than were the standard negotiation groups.

This is an interesting finding, since Landsberger (1955a) has also suggested that successful mediation sessions resemble problem-solving discussions of the type studied by Bales and Strodtbeck (1951). More precisely, Landsberger used Bales's (1950) 'Interaction Process Analysis' (IPA) categories to analyse negotiations arising from twelve disputes referred to a US Government Mediation Agency and found that participants were more likely to be satisfied with outcomes when negotiations conformed to Bales and Strodtbeck's idealised phase movement than when they did not. Landsberger has also reported the association between Bales's social-emotional behaviours and negotiation success. In particular, it seems that the more negotiators showed antagonism (category 12) in the early stages of their interaction, the smaller was the likelihood that the interaction would be judged as successful at its close. These findings need to be interpreted with caution. For instance, a single session with the mediator produced a return to work in all twelve cases. Such a result is not unusual, but industrial disputes are almost inevitably concluded at some stage (because of economic pressures), and the tactics used to terminate a long hard struggle may not be the most effective tactics to use in other circumstances. Nevertheless the findings are consonant with Douglas's (1957) suggestion that, to be successful, negotiators must convey disagreement between the parties without inducing dislike between the delegates.

In the opinion of at least one commentator mediation is, however, 'perhaps the least studied subject in the field of industrial relations' (Rehmus 1965, p. 118). What literature there is is largely anecdotal in nature and concerns the possibilities for 'strategic' rather than 'tactical' mediation (Kerr 1954). Very few studies have investigated the impact of a mediator in an immediate negotiation situation, and those that have have indicated both the potential value of mediation (Podell and Knapp 1969; Pruitt and Johnson 1970) and the difficulty of the task facing the mediator (Vidmar and McGrath 1967; Vidmar 1971).

Once a deadlock has been obtained concessions are more likely to be made in mediated than in unmediated groups. Thus Pruitt and Johnson (1970) [GEE2] found a main effect of mediation upon the percentage of subjects who made concessions and upon the relative size of the concessions made (measured by the ratio of the distance moved to the distance required to reach agreement). Furthermore, while subjects in general felt weaker in mediated groups than in unmediated groups, in two studies perceived personal strength was unrelated to the size of the concessions made ($r_1 = \cdot08$; $r_2 = \cdot06$). Since perceived personal strength was inversely related to the size of the concessions made in standard negotiation groups ($r_1 = -\cdot43$; $r_2 = \cdot53$), Pruitt and Johnson (1970) have argued that 'The absence of such a relationship in the mediation condition supports the . . . contention that after intervention by a mediator, people are able to make concessions without viewing themselves as weak. In other words, mediation provides the negotiator with a face-saving device whereby he can retreat without feeling that he has capitulated' (p. 246).

A similar mechanism may underlie Podell and Knapp's (1969) [RPD3] finding that subjects made less ambitious revisions of their opponents' target points when concessions were made through a mediator than when concessions of the same absolute size were made over the bargaining table. However, the consequences of certain points of procedure in their study detract from the value of this work. Subjects were given MNS values of about 38 cents on each of two issues and bargained against a programmed management opponent (PMN) in a simulated industrial dispute. All negotiations ended in deadlock, with final offers from the PMN of 20 cents and 14 cents respectively. Subjects accepted an offer from the experimenter to mediate one issue (chosen at random) but not the other. Consequently, while subjects received concessions of the same absolute size, these were made from different positions on different issues. The precise effects of such procedures are extremely difficult to assess, and we cannot help feeling that a simpler design would have been more appropriate.

Mediators incur costs. As they become more active they face increasing hostility from other members of the negotiation group (Landsberger 1955b) and themselves become more anxious and tense (Landsberger 1955b; Vidmar and McGrath 1967). Chairmen of negotiation groups are seen as more disagreeable and less satisfactory as co-workers than are chairmen of problem-solving groups who discuss the same experimental materials (Vidmar and McGrath 1967). Other members of the negotiation group also incur costs. Vidmar and McGrath (1967) found that subjects' esteem for their opponents was lower in groups containing a chairman than in standard negotiation groups. This may, however, simply reflect the fact that discussion chairmen help negotiators to reach better-quality agreements. Thus Vidmar and McGrath (1965) found that, while members of cross-assigned groups tended to produce better-quality agreements than members of standard negotiation groups, 'their activity . . . had concomitant results of increased strain, devaluation of partner, and a generally negative perception of the negotiation session' (p. 37).

Negotiators as Representatives of Groups

THE COMMITMENT TO REPRESENT A GROUP

Four studies have attempted to demonstrate the effects of being given a role obligation to represent a group by comparing the performance of representatives and nonrepresentatives on the same negotiation task. Three of the studies have reported differences of one sort or another (Druckman, Solomon and Zechmeister 1972; Benton and Druckman 1974; Lamm 1975); only one has not (Druckman 1967). Since this latter study [RPD3] contains a number of methodological flaws (Vidmar 1971; Morley 1974), it is fairly clear that the commitment to represent a group sometimes does affect a negotiator's behaviour in isolation from other variables.

Druckman, Solomon and Zechmeister (1972) [DG2] found that the commitment to represent a group affected the ease with which agreements were obtained (measured by the total number of offers exchanged and percentage of offers rejected) rather than the *discrepancy in outcomes* after three plays of a board game. Benton and Druckman (1974) [DG2] confirmed these findings but showed that the precise effects obtained depended upon the perceived 'bargaining orientation' (minimum goal) of the reference group concerned. In both studies subjects played three games with the same opponent and each received zero payoff in the event of nonagreement. It is not clear whether the variables concerned affected the probability of reaching an agreement, but Lamm's (1975) (preliminary) results indicate that this is the case when a different DG2 task (adapted from Kelley, Beckman and Fischer 1967) is used.

Other studies have attempted to show how bargaining behaviour depends upon the role a negotiator plays within his own group.

REPRESENTATIVES ARE ACCOUNTABLE TO THEIR CONSTITUENTS

Negotiators are accountable to their constituents for their actions as representatives of groups. But their behaviour may be monitored in different ways. At one extreme there are 'open covenants openly arrived at' (Klimoski and Ash 1974; Katz 1959); at the other, private negotiations in which judgements may be suspended until long after settlements have been obtained. Experimental studies have investigated the effects of both 'continuous' and 'terminal' accountability to one's constituents (Klimoski and Ash 1974). Not surprisingly, subjects sometimes take longer to reach agreements and make smaller concessions when they expect to defend their behaviour than when they do not (Gruder and Rosen 1971 [DG2]), but sometimes the effects are confined to the first concessions made (Gruder 1971 [DG2]). Once again the precise effects obtained are likely to depend upon other variables, as shown by Klimoski and Ash (1974) [RPD3]. In the latter study, despite the time costs involved, subjects who expected to report to their groups took reliably longer to reach agreement than subjects who did not. This effect was entirely due to subjects accountable to 'highly cohesive' groups, as shown by inspection of the statistically significant accountability/attraction interaction which was also obtained. It is also important to note that these effects may be obtained only when negotiators are (randomly) assigned to representative roles rather than elected to them as Klimoski and Ash (1974) have shown.

NEGOTIATORS AS 'LEADERS' OR 'DELEGATES'

Hermann and Kogan (1968) [RPD3] demonstrated that the way in which out-group conflict is managed depends upon the role a negotiator plays within the in-group. Subjects were assigned to *leader* or *delegate* roles, according to their 'class status' in the University of Princeton. Prior to negotiations, leader–delegate pairs were given one hour to reach consensus on the twelve problems presented in the Wallach and Kogan (1959) 'Choice Dilemmas Questionnaire'. Leaders directed the discussions and had the final responsibility for determining the dyad's decision in the event that agreement could be reached in no other way. Once consensus had been obtained, subjects were reassembled into (four-person or five-person) all-leader and all-delegate groups and again asked to reach consensus on the choice dilemmas. Each subject was, however, instructed to represent the position of his dyad, and 'to emphasize their representative function, the delegates were told that they would report back to their leaders concerning the results of the intergroup negotiations' (pp. 335–6). A seven-minute time limit was imposed on the discussion of each item. On average, both leader and delegate groups deadlocked on two of the twelve problems. Delegates, however, tended to compromise more than leaders, especially when initial positions were highly discrepant. Leaders, in contrast to delegates, typically resolved their initial discrepancy by shifting to the position of one of the parties and compromised only when initial positions were highly similar.

Subsequent research has shown that deadlocks are more likely in leader than subordinate groups, at least when status is randomly ascribed, and when negotiations are conducted under conditions of continuous accountability (Kogan, Lamm and Trommsdorff 1972 [RPD3]). It is interesting to note that, relative to their prenegotiation dyadic positions, leader delegates in Hermann and Kogan's (1968) study, unlike delegate groups, exhibited a statistically reliable shift to risk. Delegate groups also moved in the direction of risk but their shift was not statistically reliable. Lamm and Kogan's (1970) results suggest that these effects may be reversed when subjects are elected as 'principal bargaining agents' rather than designated as leaders by the experimenter. In other words, the effects of a negotiator's status may depend upon how that status is obtained (Lamm 1973).

These findings have demonstrated very clearly how the problems of representing a group position may affect subsequent negotiation. Delegates have to champion a group position and, if they capitulate, must convince their parties that they had good reasons for doing so. Leaders, on the other hand, presumably do not face such severe problems of intra-organisational bargaining and are more likely to be persuaded to move by other negotiators. In this context it is interesting to note that the *nature* of a delegate's prenegotiation experience affected his subsequent behaviour in Hermann and Kogan's (1968) experiment. The greater the influence that delegates perceived they had exerted upon their leaders in the earlier dyadic negotiation, the greater their movement in subsequent intergroup negotiations. As Hermann and Kogan have pointed out, 'a delegate who has succeeded in influencing his leader in the dyadic negotiation might feel quite confident in his ability to justify a change following intergroup negotiation' (p. 340). If delegates who were most committed to in-group positions were those who exerted the most influence upon their leaders, this would explain the otherwise surprising finding that, the more committed delegates were to their in-group position, the more often capitulation to one party's position occurred in the subsequent negotiations and the more quickly the issues were resolved.

This sort of analysis is also suggested by the simulation of union–management wage negotiations made by Frey and Adams (1972) [RPD2]. All subjects were assigned to management roles, and negotiation consisted of an exchange of ten written communications (selected from a set of seventeen possible communications) with a simulated opponent. Three dependent variables – subjects' final offers, subjects' mean levels of demand, and subjects' mean levels of resistance to their constituents – were jointly subjected to a multivariate analysis of variance. Briefly, subjects' mean levels of demand were higher when the union tactics were 'exploitative' (i.e. messages were 'demanding and threatening' and 'frequently emphasized the harm that a strike would do to the company') than when they were 'co-operative' (i.e. messages were 'conciliatory and emphasized the mutual gain which an agreement would bring about'). However, within a condition of constituent distrust, subjects who received exploitative messages from union negotiators made smaller last offers, made smaller mean concessions and showed greater resistance to suggestions from their constituents than did subjects who received co-operative messages from the union. In other words, subjects' bargaining behaviour was jointly determined by 'an internal conflict factor' (constituent trust *v.* constituent distrust) and 'an external conflict factor' (received co-operation *v.* received exploitation). Consequently, as Frey and Adams have pointed out, 'In such a context, a negotiator's behaviour cannot be adequately explained by the variables of the dyadic bargaining process alone' (p. 345).

This is not to say that bargainers who represent groups always behave differently to those who bargain only for themselves. However, much more research is needed before we can say exactly when such differences occur and when they do not. At present we can do little more than speculate.

Preparing for Negotiation

It is clear that the provision of certain sorts of prenegotiation experience facilitates agreement. In experimental studies subjects have been asked to prepare for negotiation either alone or in groups, and have been given either 'strategy' or 'study' orientations. Generally, strategy orientation requires subjects to prepare for concessions and to decide on which issues they will stand firm, whereas study orientation requires subjects only to try to gain an understanding of the issues involved.

Bass (1966) [RPD3] conducted three experiments dealing with the effects of

Time Pressure Manipulation	Type of Preparation	Strategy	Study
Experiment One	Alone	No	No
Deadline plus time costs	Unilateral groups	Yes	Yes
	Bilateral groups*	×	Yes
Experiment Two	Alone	No	No
Time costs	Unilateral groups	Yes	Yes
	Bilateral groups*	×	No
Experiment Three	Alone	Yes	Yes
Deadline	Unilateral groups	Yes	Yes
	Bilateral groups*	×	No

*Bilateral strategy groups are almost a contradiction in terms and cannot be formed.

Figure 4.1 Block diagram of Bass's (1966) experimental design

preparation of this sort upon subsequent dyadic negotiations, using a modified version of Campbell's (1960) collective bargaining game. Time pressure was manipulated by imposing a deadline of seventy minutes (Experiments One and Three) and deducting $6,000 in wages or profits for each five minutes of negotiation time (Experiments One and Two). Consequently, *all* subjects negotiated under time pressure of one sort or another: Experiment One involved a deadline and time costs; Experiment Two involved time costs alone; and Experiment Three involved a deadline alone. Such differences in procedure mean that, in general, statistical comparisons can be made only between treatments within the same experiment, and Bass's findings must therefore be interpreted with care. A block diagram of his design is shown in Figure 4.1, and the major findings are detailed in Figure 4.2.

Only one comparison can be made in all three of Bass's experiments: that between strategy and study preparation in unilateral (eight- or nine-man) groups. Briefly, strategy *v.* study preparation affected the *ease* with which agreements were reached in Experiments One and Three but not in Experiment Two. In general, when a deadline was imposed (Experiments One and Three) subjects given strategy orientations found it harder to reach agreements (in terms of number of deadlocks and harmonic mean times to agreement) than those given study orientations; when no deadline was imposed (Experiment Two) there were no differential effects of strategy *v.* study preparation. (In fact, Figure 4.2 shows that agreements were very slightly quicker when subjects prepared for negotiation in strategy groups than when they prepared in study groups.) More precisely, it seems that

'If deadlines were imposed and if the strategists had non-overlapping strategies, deadlocks were very likely. On the other hand, if the opposing strategists had highly overlapping strategies, very speedy resolution was possible . . . In short, the effects of strategic thinking could produce deadlocks on the one hand or faster than average resolutions on the other. Where deadlines were imposed, the overall effect on the calculated harmonic means was to yield slower speeds of negotiating for strategists than for those who studied the issues' (p. 9).

However, the fact that agreements may be hard to achieve says nothing about the *quality* of those which are obtained, and, if we accept Campbell's (1960) criterion of algebraic deviation from the going rate, it can be seen that in each case the speed of agreement was inversely related to quality of agreement. That is, when a deadline was imposed subjects given strategy orientations reached more impartial settlements than those given study orientations; when a deadline was not imposed subjects given strategy orientations reached less impartial settlements than those given study orientations. (Similar results were obtained in Experiments Two and Three

	Percentage Deadlocks		Harmonic Mean Time		Absolute Deviation From Going Rate		Algebraic Deviation From Going Rate	
	Strategy	Study	Strategy	Study	Strategy	Study	Strategy	Study
Experiment One								
Alone	—	—	—	—	—	—	—	—
Unilateral Groups	55·6	12·5	163·0	24·5	230·5	171·9	−49·0	−78·2
Bilateral Groups	×	6·3	×	23·5	×	177·8	×	−72·2
Experiment Two								
Alone	0·0	0·0	38·0	41·3	264·1	245·1	−116·4	−40·2
Unilateral Groups	×	—	×	—	×	—	×	—
Bilateral Groups								
Experiment Three								
Alone	0·0	0·0	44·8	36·3	235·2	265·3	−63·7	−125·0
Unilateral Groups	25·0	20·0	56·2	51·9	337·2	288·0	−0·4	−91·8
Bilateral Groups	×	—	×	—	×	—	×	—

Figure 4.2 Effects of prior experience of negotiators on contracts they negotiated subsequently (adapted from Bass 1966, p. 10)

using a measure of absolute deviation from the going rate. However, in Experiment One subjects given strategy orientations produced settlements with greater absolute deviations from the going rate than those given study orientations.)

Two further results seem worthy of note:

1 There seem to have been no reliable differences in the behaviour of subjects given study orientations in the unilateral and bilateral groups of Experiment One. In other words, when subjects incur time costs and negotiate to a deadline, type of orientation (strategy *v.* study) seems to be a very much more important determinant of bargaining behaviour than type of group (unilateral *v.* bilateral).

2 In Experiment Three settlements were (a) easier to obtain but (b) less impartial in terms of algebraic deviation from the going rate, when subjects prepared alone rather than when they prepared in unilateral groups and when subjects were given study orientations rather than when they were given strategy orientations. In other words, when subjects negotiate to a deadline but do not incur time costs, their bargaining behaviour is jointly determined by the type of orientation they are given (strategy *v.* study) and the social context in which they are placed (individuals *v.* unilateral groups).

However, a great deal of systematic research needs to be done before we can confirm and extend speculation of this sort.

Druckman (1967, 1968) [RPD3] replicated and extended some of the findings obtained in Bass's (1966) first experiment. Subjects were assigned to three-man union or management teams and given forty minutes of preparation time in unilateral strategy, unilateral study or bilateral study groups. Subjects in a control condition (Druckman 1968) were given ten minutes by themselves to read the background information provided and therefore had no time for extended preparation of any sort. Subsequently, pairs of subjects were given thirty minutes to negotiate a new wage agreement and incurred time costs of $5,000 for each five minutes of negotiation time taken.

Again, even bearing in mind some procedural differences between the studies of Bass and Druckman, what is immediately apparent in the data is the contrast between study preparation on the one hand, whether in unilateral or bilateral groups, and strategy preparation on the other. In Druckman's (1968) words, 'informal discussion before debate that is concentrated on the issues is a technique for inducing cooperation. Whether the informal discussion consists of unilateral focus with teammates or bilateral focus with opponents seems to make little difference in bargaining outcomes' (p. 380). Two comments, however, seem appropriate:

1 Druckman was concerned only with ease of negotiation, not with quality of negotiation.
2 In terms of speed of resolution, average distance apart and average yielding, outcomes attained by subjects given forty minutes of strategy preparation in unilateral groups were not significantly different from outcomes attained by control subjects given ten minutes to read the experimental materials presented to them.

It may be that subjects' perceptions of negotiations as 'win/lose' rather than 'problem-solving' situations, and the degree of their commitment team positions, acted as intervening variables relating prenegotiation experience to subsequent behaviour in negotiations (Druckman 1968, pp. 377–8), although postnegotiation questionnaires are notoriously difficult to interpret. Subjects given strategy orientations saw the situation as more of a win/lose confrontation, and felt more committed to their assigned positions, than did those given study orientations. Similarly, subjects from unilateral groups saw the situation as more of a win/lose confrontation, and felt more committed to their assigned positions, than did those from bilateral groups. Subjects from control groups perceived the situation as win/lose in much the same way as subjects given strategy orientations, but they felt committed to their assigned positions in much the same way as those given study orientations.

It may, however, be the case, as Kahn and Kohls (1972) [GEE1] have suggested, that 'the discussion groups may have brought forth more relevant information than the strategy formation groups, and this information rather than strategy *per se* produced the differences in toughness of bargaining' (p. 307). Kahn and Kohls therefore gave subjects five minutes, either alone or in three-man groups, to study the profit tables to be used in a modified version of Siegel and Fouraker's (1960) dyadic bargaining game: some subjects saw both sets of profit tables ('high information') while others saw only their own ('low information'); some subjects went on to plan a negotiation strategy while others began negotiation straight away. In other words, all subjects received study orientations, and some went on to plan strategies (strategy plus study) while others did not (study only). The findings 'strongly support the predictions that both a lack of task relevant information and group preparation lead to toughness in bargaining, while strategy formation alone does not' (p. 313). Whether these findings may generalise to other tasks, however, remains to be seen.

It is also important to note that the effects of preparation in position formation *v.* study groups may disappear when only one negotiator is selected (at random) to represent his group (Klimoski 1972 [RPD3]).

Personal Characteristics of Members of Negotiation Groups

One way of reducing the detrimental effects of R-force pressure upon negotiation success is, of course, to select negotiators who are best equipped to deal with those pressures. However, a precondition for any individual difference variable to be predictive of negotiation success is that certain individuals are systematically associated with certain sorts of outcomes. This seems unlikely to be the case in subject populations with little experience of negotiation tasks (McGrath and Julian 1963 [SD2]; Julian and McGrath 1963 [SD2]; McGrath 1966). Certainly the search for personality correlates of successful negotiation has met with only very limited success (Sawyer and Guetzkow 1965; McGrath 1966; Bass 1966 [RPD3]; Lifshitz 1971 [RPD2]). While there have been some positive findings (Bass 1966 [RPD3]; Lamm 1973 [RPD3]) the overall picture is quite clear (Stephenson 1971b). Personality may become more important as information decreases and stress increases (Sawyer and Guetzkow 1965), but as far as self-report measures are concerned it seems that attention should rather be given to the nature of the group task and the precise conditions under which groups perform (McGregor 1967; Janis 1972; Stephenson 1973).

Karass (1970) [RPD2] obtained 'negotiator trait scores' from management ratings of professional negotiators employed in the American aerospace industry as 'buyers, subcontract administrators, contract managers, and termination specialists' (p. 14); 120 negotiators subsequently took part in a task involving a legal damages case. Negotiations were conducted under conditions of 'equal power' or 'plaintiff power', manipulated by changing the number of court decisions used as precedents and 'adding a degree of uncertainty to the equal power variation' (p. 15). 'Unskilled' negotiators (i.e. those who obtained trait scores below the sample median) obtained more favourable settlements when given higher power than did their opponents. The performance of 'skilled' negotiators (i.e. those who obtained trait scores above the sample median) was unaffected by variations of this sort.

Cultural Differences Between Negotiators

There are of course important cultural differences between negotiators. Porat (1969) [RPD3] studied the bargaining behaviour of 54 managers from the United Kingdom and 118 managers from the United States, using the data collected by members of the International Research Groups on Management (IRGOM) within the context of Bass's (1967) 'Exercise Negotiations'. All subjects prepared for negotiation in five- or six-man unilateral groups and were given a strategy orientation. The UK and US samples chose different primary goals and planned to negotiate the issues in different ways. Porat has concluded briefly that 'settling close to the community average was a goal sought by British union representatives and American union and management but not by the British managers' (pp. 10–11). UK negotiators were less likely than US negotiators to begin negotiations by trying to find out their opponent's goals, more likely to set maximum and minimum limits for negotiating each issue, and less likely to describe their approach as 'trading off items'. The average UK pair took less time to reach agreement than the average US pair and consequently negotiated more profitable contracts (i.e. with smaller costs to the company and larger profits to the union).

Porat (1970) [RPD3] conducted a similar study comparing the bargaining behaviour of managers from five European countries: Denmark, Spain, Sweden, Switzerland and the United Kingdom. For present purposes two comments will suffice, without going into the results in detail:

1 Differences between samples were sufficiently large to 'advise against collapsing of samples of geographic proximity or assumed cultural similarities' (p. 441).
2 The study replicated Porat's (1969) finding that, within the UK sample, the primary union goal was to negotiate a settlement close to the community average, whereas the primary management goal was to minimise company expenses. Taken together, Porat's (1969, 1970) results suggest that the 'impartiality' of a contract may appropriately be assessed by measures of deviation from the going rate within a US sample but not within a UK sample.

Kelley *et al.* (1970) [DG2] studied sequential plays of a single-issue abstract bargaining game at eight universities in France, Belgium, the Netherlands and the United States. Subjects were male university students, and each pair of subjects negotiated a sequence of thirty problems. Once subjects had negotiated five consecutive agreements contracts were approximately doubled in value (and remained so until an agreement was not obtained, at which point they reverted to their original values). After the game had been explained subjects rated how they expected themselves to behave. Factor analyses were made of these pregame ratings. Perhaps the most important finding was that 'cooperation/competition' was defined in different ways by subjects at different research sites: 'In some instances, the situation seems to be defined in moral terms, and in this case to be cooperative is to be good (moral, honest). In other instances, the situation seems to be defined more in task or achievement terms, and to be cooperative is to be weak or passive' (p. 435). For example subjects at Paris, Leuven and Dartmouth (USA) defined co-operation in 'evaluative' terms (as moral and honest) and took longer to reach agreements than subjects at Columbia, North Carolina and Los Angeles, who defined co-operation in 'dynamism' terms (as weak and passive). When co-operation/competition was defined in dynamism terms, pairs of subjects who described themselves as co-operative produced significantly more agreements than pairs who described themselves as competitive. This difference between co-operative and competitive pairs disappeared when co-operation/competition was defined in evaluative terms.

The findings of Kelley *et al.* are both interesting and important and bring to mind Sampson's (1969) distinction between considerations of *mastery* and *justice*. Negotiations are of course attempts to control the behaviour of other people and so necessarily involve considerations of mastery. But if the issues of mastery and justice are both involved in any social relationship, as Sampson has suggested, negotiators, like other people, have to strike 'a *balance* between the forces seeking resolution of the issue of mastery and those seeking resolution of the issue of justice' (p. 265). Consequently, it is important to consider the ways in which negotiations may be constrained by issues of justice.

Considerations of Equity and Equality

In fact, to talk about justice is oversimple, since there are at least two separable concepts of justice extant in the psychological literature: justice as equity and justice as equality. *Equity* obtains when participants are allocated resources commensurate with their investments and costs. To be precise, Homans's (1961) principle of 'distributive justice' amounts to the rule that an equitable relationship is one in which (A's rewards − A's costs)/A's investments = (B's rewards − B's costs)/B's investments; similarly, Adams's (1965) formulation amounts to the rule that an equitable relationship is one in which A's outcomes/A's inputs = B's outcomes/B's inputs. *Equality* obtains when participants are allocated resources equally, regardless of their investments and costs (Gouldner 1960), and is thus distinguished from the equity which obtains when participants have equal profits and equal investments (Sampson 1969).

While the precise statement of equity theory is somewhat controversial (Weick 1966; Weick and Nesset 1968; Stephenson and White 1970; Wiener 1970), both sorts of principle seem to be necessary: to define justice as only equity or only equality 'appears to be both too limiting and not to encompass adequately several bodies of empirical data' (Sampson 1969, p. 264). Unfortunately, while a number of studies (Adams 1965; Lawler 1968; Pritchard 1969; Kahn 1972) have investigated the consequences of A's being overpaid or underpaid by some third party in comparison to B, only two studies (Morgan and Sawyer 1967; Messé 1971) have investigated whether equitable or equal outcomes will be negotiated when A and B are in a direct exchange relationship. In each of these two studies two subjects faced each other across a 'bargaining board' which gave one a much greater reward potential than the other. When subjects had equal investments, considerations of equity and equality combined to promote agreements which gave subjects equal payoffs (Morgan and Sawyer 1967 [DG2]); when subjects had different investments, considerations of equity seemed more important than those of equality, and in general agreements were reached which gave subjects payoffs proportional to their investments (Messé 1971 [DG2]).

Messé manipulated subjects' investments by varying the amounts of time they spent completing a 'moral conflict questionnaire' before negotiations began. However, both the nature of the initial task and its relationship to the bargaining game may limit the generality of Messé's results.

1 Writing short essays dealing with moral conflicts might have increased the salience of considerations of equity, and different results may be found if subjects' investments are manipulated in different ways (although see Messé 1971, p. 288).
2 Subjects were not bargaining *about* the importance of their investments nor about the terms of their future relationship, and different results may be found if different experimental tasks are used.

Chapter 5

The Process of Bid and Counterbid

This chapter and Chapter 6 are concerned with what happens in negotiations. Most of the studies reported in Chapter 4 have looked at the effect of a variety of factors on the settlements achieved by negotiators. It may reasonably be suggested that understanding of these effects may be enhanced if the *process* by which various agreements are achieved is examined in detail. In this chapter we shall examine the results of experiments which by and large *exclude* the possibility of discussion between the participants, i.e. games of economic exchange and distribution games. Such games allow a detailed examination of the process of bid and counterbid.

Toughness in bargaining is a concept familiar enough to practitioners and has been the subject of some attention from laboratory researchers. In experimental work, '*toughness*' has referred to the way in which bargainers have made concessions to their opponents, whether sparingly or generously. Toughness is not, however, a simple concept, and for purposes of accurate description certain varieties of toughness are distinguished, within the context of studies of distribution games. A bargainer may be tough by demanding a high return initially or maintaining a high level of demand throughout the bargaining encounter, by making few concessions or only small concessions, or by maintaining an optimistic minimum goal, whatever his way of working towards it.

Maintaining a high level of demand has a powerful effect on outcomes when complex issues are being negotiated, although there is some evidence that the relationship between the sides may influence the extent to which the tougher party achieves the greater share of the available profit. Where a number of issues are up for debate at the same time, there is some evidence that 'logrolling', whereby issues are negotiated simultaneously, is more efficient than 'compromise', whereby issues are negotiated sequentially. In such negotiations there is good evidence that a tough strategy will induce 'softness' in one's opponent. However, there is also evidence that the probability of agreement may be adversely affected by the adoption of a tough strategy. Whereas a moderately tough strategy is of benefit, excessive toughness may be counterproductive. When issues are 'simple' there is some evidence that negotiators may enhance their prospects by adopting a strategy which prescribes a set pattern of responses to the concessions made by opponents.

The results are not, however, very consistent, although there is evidence that subjects with a high level of expectation are more reluctant to make concessions than those with lower ambitions. This does not necessarily result in the achievement of greater profits.

The use of *threat* in negotiation is a more or less legitimate tactic in management–union bargaining, but its effectiveness is a matter for debate in the academic literature. Some would maintain that the availability of threat promotes an accelerating decline into profitless competitiveness, while others would assert that the use of threat may indeed profit the user. It is not as yet clear precisely under what circumstances either of these viewpoints will be substantiated. However, it is clear that the type of threat and its magnitude will systematically determine the advisability of its use in negotiation.

Investigating the Negotiation Process

Several authors have called attention to the tendency among social psychologists to disregard the specific influence and communication processes which mediate the effects of independent variables upon final outcomes (Dashiell 1935; Kelley and Thibaut 1954; Julian and McGrath 1963; McGrath and Julian 1963; Morley 1973). Many have felt that this general neglect is reflected in studies of negotiation and that our knowledge of negotiation is severely limited by inadequate analysis of the process of interaction *per se* (McGrath and Julian 1963; Stephenson 1971a, 1971b; Morley 1973). Certainly, the studies reported in Chapter 4 include very few attempts to consider the process by which outcomes are obtained. We are tempted to reiterate the comments made by McGrath and Julian (1963) that

'One major limitation in nearly all studies of negotiation . . . has been a failure to investigate directly the negotiation process itself . . . investigations implicitly assume that the effects of . . . individual, group, and task conditions are mediated through the interactive process by which participants accomplish the assigned task. However, direct measurement of that interaction process, which could permit a tracing of these mediating effects, is seldom attempted' (p. 119).

However, over thirty experimental studies explicitly dealing with interaction in negotiation groups have been published in the last ten years. These will be reviewed in this chapter and Chapter 6.

Of course, direct measurement of the interaction process (i.e. defining 'strategy' as a dependent variable) is only one way of investigating the process of negotiation. Another way is to programme a participant (or participants) to behave in some specified manner (i.e. defining 'strategy' as an independent variable) and to observe the effects of the intervention. Or a combination of the two techniques may be used (i.e. programme one participant to adopt a given 'strategy' and observe the 'strategy' adopted by the other). Each experiment reviewed here will be described in sufficient detail to indicate the nature of the technique involved.

Concession Making in Distribution Games and Games of Economic Exchange

THEORIES OF THE BARGAINING PROCESS

A number of formal models of negotiation have been put forward to deal with the process of bid and counterbid by which agreements are obtained. These have been reviewed elsewhere by Coddington (1968) and Patchen (1970), and our intention is not to repeat what they have said. Coddington's review deals only with theories put forward by economists (i.e. Edgeworth 1881; Zeuthen 1930; Harsanyi 1956; Nash 1950; Pen 1952; Foldes 1964; Bishop 1964; Cross 1965; Coddington 1968) and mathematicians (Von Neumann and Morgenstern 1964). Patchen has dealt with theories put forward by psychologists, but his major objective was to contrast 'negotiation' models with 'cognitive', 'learning' and 'reaction process' models. Rather, we wish to indicate the contrast between models which involve the mutual adjustment of the expectations of the parties involved (e.g. Siegel and Fouraker 1960; Cross 1965) and models which do not (e.g. Kelley, Beckman and Fischer 1967; Kelley and Schenitzki 1972).

Models of the first sort involve Harsanyi's Mechanism II and emphasise that negotiators *change their expectations about their opponent's behaviour 'during* the bargaining process itself, as a result of their testing out each other's attitudes by means of tentative bids and counterbids' (Harsanyi 1962, p. 37). Thus, Siegel and Fouraker (1960) have suggested a model in which the initial level of aspiration of a negotiator is predicted to increase when an opponent makes concessions and to decrease when he does not. Similarly, Cross's (1965) theory implies that 'even when a contract zone exists, the bargainers may or may not reach some agreement within the contract zone depending on the relationship between parameters representing their learning and discounting behaviour' (Coddington 1969, p. 47). (Here it is interesting to note that Karass's (1970) skilled and unskilled negotiators were *equally bad* at estimating their opponent's minimum goals.)

Models of the second sort involve what Kelley and Thibaut (1969) have called 'extrasystemic modes of attaining "solutions"', specifically 'the adoption or emergence of various types of rules specifying response sequences' (p. 48). The point is that, when faced with a difficult task and uncertain of the other's response, a negotiator may *follow a simple rule which will guide his bargaining behaviour* 'without respect of what the other will do meantime' (p. 49). The process by which subjects attain maximum joint profit (MJP) in Siegel and Fouraker's (1960) bilateral monopoly games seems to involve 'simple behavioural "adjustments"' of this type, since MJP contracts will be generated provided only that one negotiator makes systematic concessions (explores contracts at a given level of profit before offering contracts at a lower level) and that the other accepts the highest offer available to him (Kelley 1964; Kelley and Schenitzki 1972). Kelley, Beckman and Fischer's (1967) nonparametric model may perhaps also be regarded as involving simple behavioural adjustments of this sort, since it postulates a resistance (R) to making further concessions which depends only upon a negotiator's own MNS and last offer (pp. 382–93, 396–7).

While it seems important to emphasise the contrast between models involving mutual changes in expectations and models involving simple behavioural adjustments, it is also important to emphasise that *only three theories have been put forward to explain observed patterns of bargaining behaviour*: those of Siegel and Fouraker (1960); Kelley (1964) and Kelley and Schenitzki (1972); and Kelley, Beckman and Fischer (1967). *Most formal theories have been put forward as general solutions to 'the bargaining problem' and have not been subjected to empirical tests* (Coddington 1968). Indeed, according to Coddington it is doubtful whether such theories can in fact be seriously tested 'within the context of existing institutions and research techniques' (p. xix), since 'sufficiently rich data for this purpose can most likely be obtained only under the highly artificial circumstances involved in gaming experiments' (p. 97). But what is much more serious is that very few of the theories reviewed by Coddington allow the identification of key components of the bargaining which an experimenter is trying to simulate under laboratory conditions. The decision rules that negotiators are expected to follow are specified simply in terms of the utility functions of each of the participants. These utilities are assumed to be known. Consequently, these theories not only have not been subject to empirical tests but also do not have any obvious behavioural implications. They do not illuminate the changes in expectations which occur during the process of bid and counterbid. Nor do they identify simple response sequences which allow a negotiator to obtain satisfactory outcomes 'without a rational analysis of information' and 'without understanding of the relationship' (Kelley and Thibaut 1969, pp. 48–9).

TASKS OF TYPE 1: STUDIES OF BILATERAL MONOPOLY

It is perhaps appropriate to begin with a discussion of Siegel and Fouraker's (1960) [GEE1] classic investigations of bargaining under conditions of bilateral monopoly. Briefly, they found that, when subjects did not incur bargaining costs, they tended to negotiate MJP contracts even though they had no information about the other's profits and could negotiate only by an exchange of written bids. This tendency was increased when subjects were given information about the other's profit tables (cf. Johnson and Cohen 1967) and when there was a large difference in value between contracts at Q_m, the quantity which maximises joint payoff, and contracts at quantities other than Q_m. Siegel and Fouraker have described the bargaining behaviour of their subjects as follows:

'In general . . . the subjects opened the negotiations by requesting a high level of profit (frequently the maximum amount shown on the iso-profit tables they used). This payoff level might be maintained for a few bids, or concessions might begin immediately. Quite often the subject would drop to a new payoff level and give several bids associated with this level. Then another break to a lower payoff plateau would follow. Typically the concessions were larger and the plateaus were shorter in the early stages of the negotiations. As more bids and offers were exchanged, the rate of concession diminished and the length of the plateaus increased. Thus, the negotiation pattern tended to approach some payoff figure asymptotically' (pp. 76–7).

This description corresponds almost exactly with the systematic concessions model proposed by Kelley (1964) and Kelley and Schenitzki (1972) to explain the process by which MJP contracts are attained. In fact, MJP contracts will be generated provided only that 'one individual behaves systematically and that the other one terminates the process by accepting the highest offer available to him' (Kelley and Schenitzki 1972, p. 323). If bargainers do not make their concessions in a systematic manner they will be less likely to attain MJP outcomes. Indeed, Schenitzki (1962) [GEE1] has shown that subjects given a 'group goal' (whereby each gains half of the total profit made by the pair) make less systematic concessions than subjects given an 'individual goal' (whereby each is instructed to maximise his own profits) and are less likely to attain MJP outcomes. As Kelley and Schenitzki (1972) have pointed out, 'These results show a paradoxical situation, in which even though *explicitly* trying to obtain MJP, the cooperative bargainers did so less often than the individualistically oriented ones who . . . attain it *implicitly*' (p. 325). Certainly, the poor performance of the co-operative bargainers 'makes one wonder how often it happens in real interpersonal negotiations that the implicitly generated consequences of selfishly oriented parties are superior to the more socially conscious actions of cooperatively oriented persons' (p. 325).

Subjects negotiating in bilateral monopoly games of the Siegel and Fouraker type generally achieve MJP outcomes, but there is considerable variation in the share of MJP allocated to each member of a pair (Siegel and Fouraker 1960; Kelley 1964; Kelley and Schenitzki 1972). According to Siegel and Fouraker, when subjects negotiate under conditions of complete-complete information 'the result is almost invariably a fifty-fifty split of the joint payoff' (p. 70), but when subjects negotiate under conditions of incomplete-incomplete information 'the larger share of the joint payoff will go to the bargainer with the higher level of aspiration' (p. 62).

In one of Siegel and Fouraker's experiments subjects were told that they would be given an opportunity to double their earnings provided that they obtained a given level of profit in the current negotiations. For subjects given a high level of aspiration (LOA) the required level of profit was \$6·10; for those given a low level of aspiration it was \$2·10. (Note that LOA is not the same as MNS. Subjects could still make a profit in the first part of the study even if they received payoffs lower than the \$6·10 or \$2·10 necessary for them to go on to the second part of the study.) Negotiators given high LOA values always bargained against negotiators given low LOA values. They made larger initial demands, maintained higher mean levels of demand, made fewer concessions, and obtained very much larger shares of the MJP than their low LOA opponents (MJP = \$9·60; mean profit for negotiators given high LOA values = \$6·25; mean profit for negotiators given low LOA values = \$3·35). In terms of Siegel and Fouraker's model, the behaviour of the low LOA negotiators would confirm the high LOA values of their opponents, and vice versa, leading to an unequal distribution of the joint profit between the members of the pairs.

'TOUGHNESS' IN BARGAINING

It is tempting to say that negotiators given high levels of aspiration adopt tougher bargaining strategies than negotiators given low levels of aspiration, but this would be oversimple. A negotiator's behaviour may vary along dimensions such as level of initial demand (i.d.), mean level of demand (l.d.), number of concessions (n.c.), size of concessions (s.c.) or level of minimum goal (m.g.). Apparently an independent variable (e.g. time pressure) which affects a given dependent variable (e.g. mean level of demand) in one way need not affect another (e.g. level of minimum goal) in the same way (Pruitt and Drews 1969). Consequently, to say that A's behaviour is tougher than B's is simply to use a shorthand method of indicating that A's behaviour is ranked as more demanding than B's along a dimension (e.g. mean level of demand) which has already been specified (Bartos 1966, 1970).

It is convenient to use subscripts to identify the dimension involved: (i.d.), (l.d.), (n.c.), (s.c.) or (m.g.). Thus, when we say that A's behaviour is tougher$_{(i.d.)}$ than B's we mean that A makes larger initial demands than B; tougher$_{(l.d.)}$ indicates a higher mean level of demand; tougher$_{(n.c.)}$ indicates fewer concessions; tougher$_{(s.c.)}$ indicates smaller concessions; and tougher$_{(m.g.)}$ indicates a higher level of minimum goals. When we say that A's behaviour is tougher$_{(i.d.)(l.d.)}$ than B's we mean that A makes larger initial demands than B and maintains a higher mean level of demand; and so on.

Siegel and Fouraker's (1960) results may now be described by saying that negotiators given high levels of aspiration adopt tougher$_{(i.d.)(l.d.)(n.c.)}$ strategies than negotiators given low levels of aspiration and obtain larger shares of the available 'cake'. Other investigators have confirmed that negotiators given high LOA values in general adopt tougher$_{(i.d.)(l.d.)}$ strategies than negotiators given low LOA values but have not confirmed that they adopt tougher$_{(n.c.)}$ strategies. Holmes, Throop and Strickland (1971) [GEE1] had subjects given high LOA values (47 points) bargain with subjects given low LOA values (34 points) in a version of Siegel and Fouraker's game which involved time costs, strike costs and expanded communication possibilities. A deadline of twenty minutes was set. Some negotiators were given high MNS values (30 points); others were given low MNS values (22 points). There were four sorts of dyad: high LOA low MNS–low LOA low MNS; high LOA high MNS–low LOA low MNS; high LOA low MNS–low LOA high MNS; and high LOA high MNS–low LOA high MNS. Subjects given high LOA values adopted tougher$_{(i.d.)(l.d.)}$ strategies than those given low LOA values, except in high LOA high MNS–low LOA high MNS dyads when the subject with the lower LOA adopted the tougher$_{(i.d.)(l.d.)}$ approach.

Neither Siegel and Fouraker nor Holmes, Throop and Strickland systematically explored the relationship between strategy and profit within their experimental treatments, but their results are consistent with the hypothesis that toughness$_{(l.d.)}$ is an important determinant of the price at which goods are to be exchanged in bargaining under conditions of bilateral monopoly. Apparently, nearly all pairs reached agreements at $Q = Q_m$, but the greater the extent to which A's mean level of demand exceeded that of B the greater A's share of the joint profit obtained by A and B.

Toughness$_{(l.d.)}$ does not, however, always pay, as Hatton's (1967) [GEE1] research has demonstrated. His subjects were negro high school girls who obtained high scores on Kelley, Ferson and Holtzman's (1958) Desegregation Scale. They believed that in general whites were likely to be highly prejudiced against negroes. Some of them bargained against a negro girl opponent, some against a white girl opponent. Hatton investigated the effects of toughness$_{(l.d.)(n.c.)(s.c.)}$ by having confederates follow either a 'yielding' or 'demanding' programme of offers. In his own words,

'The yielding schedule provided for rather large and rapid concessions in the opening phase of the bargaining and smaller but generally consistent concessions as the bargaining progressed. Under the demanding schedule, concessions were small and were made slowly throughout the bargaining . . . Several offers were made repeatedly. In addition, concessions were not made uniformly; that is, successive offers occasionally reduced the profit of the subject, usually by a considerable amount. Both schedules terminated at a point which yielded the subject a profit of $1·70. If this point were reached, the same offer was made by the confederate until it was accepted. This point of maximum profit for the subject was reached by the yielding schedule at Trial 28 and by the demanding schedule at Trial 59' (p. 303).

The schedules followed by Hatton's confederates 'tended to follow the systematic concessions pattern', and 'apparently as a consequence of this' all subjects reached agreements at quantity $Q = Q_m$ (Kelley and Schenitzki 1972, p. 328). However, the price at which goods were exchanged depended upon both the schedule followed and the race of the confederate who followed it. Negro confederates sold goods at higher prices when they followed the yielding schedule than when they followed the demanding schedule, but white confederates sold goods at higher prices when they followed the demanding schedule than when they followed the yielding schedule. In other words, toughness$_{(l.d.)(n.c.)(s.c.)}$ paid for one type of confederate (whites) but not for the other (negroes).

Hatton has also reported that if his subject sample is considered as a whole there was a large negative correlation ($r = -·85$, $p < ·005$) between the number of 'zero profit offers' a subject made (i.e. those offers which if accepted would lead to zero profit for the confederate) and the price at which she was able to buy goods. Given that all subjects reached agreements at $Q = Q_m$, this means that (in general) the larger the number of zero profit offers a subject made, the smaller the price she had to pay and the larger the profit she made. It is, however, unfortunate that Hatton has not given a detailed description of how his subjects responded to each type of confederate and each programme of bids – since, if we assume that the above correlation obtained in each cell of Hatton's design and that the number of zero profit offers a subject made was positively correlated with her mean level of demand, we are led to the paradoxical conclusion that toughness$_{(l.d.)}$ was productive for negro *subjects* but counterproductive for negro *confederates*.

These assumptions may of course be incorrect (indeed they probably are), but what has been said does demonstrate how little we know about the process of bid and counterbid and indicates the value of a detailed analysis of the behaviour of each member of a negotiation group.

Let us summarise what has been said so far.

1 MJP contracts (at $Q \times Q_m$) will be attained provided that only one negotiator makes simple behavioural adjustments of the type described by Kelley and Thibaut (1969) and Kelley and Schenitzki (1972).
2 The share of the joint profit attained by each negotiator will depend upon the strategy he adopts, the strategy his opponent adopts, and the nature of the relationship between the two. Each of the experiments described has been concerned with the effects of toughness of one sort or another and, in particular, with the hypothesis that the tougher$_{(l.d.)}$ a subject's behaviour the larger his share of the available cake. It seems that in some situations toughness$_{(l.d.)}$ pays but in others does not. The problem of course is to know when toughness$_{(l.d.)}$ pays and when it does not. We do not yet have the answers.

These two issues will be reconsidered in the context of tasks of Type 3.

'LOGROLLING' AND 'COMPROMISE' IN TASKS OF TYPE 3

To recapitulate: tasks of Type 3 (in which subjects negotiate a number of one-dimensional issues) are like tasks of Type 1 (in which subjects negotiate a single complex issue requiring agreement on two dimensions such as price and quantity) in so far as they allow subjects to offer more than one contract at a given level of profit.

Fractionating disputes

Kelley (1966) [DG3] has reported that undergraduate students faced with 'classroom dilemmas' learned that it was advantageous to negotiate 'package deals' of some sort. Similarly, Froman has argued that 'logrolling' (whereby issues are negotiated simultaneously) is a more efficient strategy than 'compromise' (whereby issues are negotiated sequentially, one at a time), in both experimental games (Froman and Cohen 1970 [DG3]) and a variety of real life contexts (Froman 1967). In fact, Kelley's subjects learned that it was worthwhile to explore various contracts at a given level of profit before moving on to contracts at a lower level, and it may be that one advantage of logrolling is the opportunity it provides for subjects to make simple behavioural adjustments of this type. Froman and Cohen had subjects negotiate four separate issues, each with four alternatives. They have reported that logrolling was more 'efficient' than compromise in terms of the number of MJP contracts obtained, the amount of joint profit obtained and the number of moves to agreement.

Nevertheless, under certain circumstances there may be considerable gains to be made from 'fractionating' a dispute into smaller issues which can be dealt with one at a time (Fisher 1964; Iklé 1964). Perhaps, as Kelley and Schenitzki (1972) have suggested, it may be of benefit to negotiate 'more political' disputes (involving 'questions of principle, power, prestige, and ideology') by dealing with issues one at a time, 'split away from the principles and settled on more pragmatic terms', and to negotiate 'strict economic' disputes by dealing with all the issues at the same time (p. 328). But at present this remains speculation, and it is unfortunate that such an important hypothesis has not been submitted to experimental test.

THE EFFECTS OF MEAN LEVEL OF DEMAND

So far as the effects of toughness$_{(l.d.)}$ are concerned, two fairly comprehensive research reports are available (Bartos 1966, 1970). Each presents data from a series of thirty or more experiments of the distribution game type, conducted at the University of Hawaii between 1960 and 1967. Bartos has called these 'abstract' experiments. Subjects negotiated under incomplete information and were given one hour in which to endorse one of a set of thirty-one proposals. Negotiation was restricted to an exchange of bids of the type 'I endorse proposal X,' delivered in a fixed sequence. If agreement was not obtained within the given time all subjects received zero profit. Most of the experiments involved groups of five participants, each acting independently, but some included dyads. The major findings were as follows:

1 *Relation between toughness$_{(l.d.)}$ of subject and opponent.* There was a large negative correlation ($r = -\cdot71$, $p < \cdot005$) between a subject's own toughness$_{(l.d.)}$ and the toughness$_{(l.d.)}$ of his opponent in a two-person group (Bartos 1970, p. 57). In other words, toughness$_{(l.d.)}$ tended to generate softness$_{(l.d.)}$ in two-person groups, and vice versa. This is of course consistent with Siegel and Fouraker's (1960) model of the bargaining behaviour of pairs of subjects faced with tasks of Type 1. However, the demands made by subjects in the five-person groups depended very little upon the offers made to them (Bartos 1966, p. 16). Consequently, when subjects from five-person groups were included in the analysis the correlation between a subject's toughness$_{(l.d.)}$ and his opponent's toughness$_{(l.d.)}$ dropped to a value of $- \cdot4$, which was not significantly different from zero (Bartos 1970, p. 57). This implies that we cannot expect the process of negotiation to be very similar in two-party and *n*-party cases.

2 *Relation between toughness$_{(l.d.)}$ and probability of reaching agreement.* Toughness$_{(l.d.)}$ made it slightly less likely in general that an agreement would be reached at all, as shown by a correlation of $- \cdot18$ ($p < \cdot001$) between a subject's own toughness$_{(l.d.)}$ and the probability of reaching an agreement (Bartos 1970, p. 62). However, this correlation was based upon the combined data from two-person and *n*-person groups and explained only about 3% of the total variation in the probability of reaching an agreement. This may mean that the relationship between toughness$_{(l.d.)}$ and reaching an agreement is nonlinear or that toughness$_{(l.d.)}$ is simply not an important determinant of whether or not an agreement is obtained. Alternatively, it may mean that the relationship between toughness$_{(l.d.)}$ and the probability of reaching an agreement is different in two-person and *n*-person groups.

Bartos (1966) has presented correlations based upon data from five-person groups involved in experiments of the distribution game and role-playing debate types. He has called the latter 'spoken' experiments, since subjects were permitted to say almost anything they wished (except to reveal their own payoffs). Subjects were given the roles of political decision makers (Heads of State or US Senators) meeting to deal with an agenda containing five separate issues. They could reach any one of thirty-one distinct agreements, and they were given a number of possible arguments to use in defending proposals which gave them high payoffs and attacking proposals which gave them low payoffs. A deadline of two hours was set. Taking the data as a whole, Bartos has reported a correlation of $- \cdot16$ ($p < \cdot001$) between a subject's own toughness$_{(l.d.)}$ and the probability of reaching an agreement (p. 18). Furthermore, if a negotiator's mean level of demand is expressed in terms of standard deviations from the grand mean demand of negotiators given the same role and using the same profit tables, it can be seen that 'the probability of agreement remains at ·75 until the Z score of $+1\cdot00$ or more is reached; at that point it drops to ·45' (p. 19). That is, in five-person groups the probability of reaching an agreement was independent of a subject's own toughness$_{(l.d.)}$ unless he persisted in maintaining a level of demand which was very much higher ($Z+ < 1\cdot00$) than would usually be found.

This conclusion has been modified, however, by Bartos's (1970) presentation of the combined data from two-person groups, n-person groups and n-team groups. The basic design of the 'team' experiments was the same as that of the 'spoken' experiments. There were, however, three important differences in procedure: (a) after each negotiator had delivered three speeches each team was given an opportunity privately to reconsider its strategy; (b) agreement had to be reached within five negotiation sessions; and (c) each team consisted of two members who took turns in speaking for their team. Some subjects participated in experiments of the distribution game type, others in experiments of the role-playing debate type. Once again subjects were classified in terms of the Z score associated with their mean demand; a subject was classified as 'moderate' if he was given a Z score with an absolute value between ·30 and 1·00 and as 'extreme' if this value exceeded 1·00. The relationship between a subject's own toughness$_{(l.d.)}$ and the probability of reaching an agreement (p_a) was found to be an inverted U-shaped function. The maximum value of p_a (·8) corresponded to 'average' and 'moderately soft' strategies; both 'extremely soft' and 'moderately tough' strategies lowered p_a to ·7; and p_a reached its minimum value (·6) when an 'extremely tough' strategy was used. Given a curvilinear relationship of this sort, it is of course not surprising that the linear correlation between p_a and toughness$_{(l.d.)}$ was very small ($r = -·16$, $p < ·001$) and accounted for less than 3% of the variation in Bartos's data. What is surprising is that p_a was independent of toughness$_{(l.d.)}$ in Bartos's team experiments, since all teams reached agreements ($p_a = 1$).

Clearly, any interpretation of these data must be viewed with caution and regarded as speculation which remains to be subjected to rigorous experimental testing. Nevertheless, both the size of Bartos's correlations and the graphical data he has presented are consistent with the assumption that the relationship between p_a and toughness$_{(l.d.)}$ is often nonlinear, and the following hypotheses seem to be worthy of further investigation:

Hypothesis 1: Extreme toughness$_{(l.d.)}$ will increase the probability that an agreement will not be reached in two-person and n-person negotiations of the DG3 and RPD3 types.

Hypothesis 2: p_a will be independent of toughness$_{(l.d.)}$ within the extremely soft to moderately tough strategy range in five-person negotiations of the DG3 and RPD3 types.

Hypothesis 3: The smaller the size of the group, the greater the likelihood that extreme softness of strategy will lead to a breakdown in negotiations of the DG3 and RPD3 types. This would be expected to obtain only when a deadline was set, the assumption being that A's softness raises B's level of aspiration to such an extent that B is unable to get what he wants within the given time. (Taken together, Hypotheses 1 and 3 suggest that the smaller the size of the group the greater the likelihood that the relationship between p_a and toughness$_{(l.d.)}$ will be an inverted U-shaped function in negotiations of the DG3 and RPD3 types.)

3 Relation between toughness$_{(l.d.)}$ and profit. Provided an agreement is in fact obtained, toughness$_{(l.d.)}$ made it more likely that a subject would achieve a slightly higher profit, as shown by the correlation of $\cdot 22$ ($p < \cdot 001$) between a subject's own toughness$_{(l.d.)}$ and his final payoff in Bartos's (1970) abstract groups.

4 Relation between toughness$_{(l.d.)}$ and size of concessions. The frequency with which a negotiator made concessions was independent of his mean level of demand, but tough$_{(l.d.)}$ and soft$_{(l.d.)}$ negotiators tended to exchange concessions of a different size. Thus Bartos (1970) has reported that

'While the fact of a concession was reciprocated, the *size* of a concession was not. To put it differently, the data suggest that, by and large, subjects tended to make a concession when the opponent made one. But there was a difference between those who ended up being tough (with a high mean demand) and those who ended up being soft (with a low mean demand) in that *the tough negotiators tended to make smaller* concessions, trading a chicken for a cow, so to speak' (p. 59).

In fact, Bartos's conclusion was based upon two separate findings: that toughness$_{(l.d.)}$ tended to be met with softness$_{(l.d.)}$ (p. 57), and that negotiators were more likely to make concessions when an opponent had conceded than when he had not (p. 58). Neither tendency was very marked, and it is evident that the correlation between toughness$_{(l.d.)}$ and toughness$_{(s.c.)}$ is therefore unlikely to be very large.

Bartos (1966, 1970) has presented findings based upon data aggregated from a very large number of separate experiments. Consequently, we can be very confident about the reliability of what he found. However, statistical significance is not at all the same as psychological significance. Bartos has demonstrated that a subject's own toughness$_{(l.d.)}$ is related to the toughness$_{(l.d.)}$ of his opponent, the probability of reaching an agreement, and the profit he will obtain if an agreement is reached, but in general his findings have little predictive power. The strongest relationship reported is that between a subject's own toughness$_{(l.d.)}$ and the toughness$_{(l.d.)}$ of his opponent in a two-person 'abstract' game ($r = -·71$). However, a relationship of this size explains only about 50% of the total variance and suggests that, while toughness$_{(l.d.)}$ often generates softness$_{(l.d.)}$ (and vice versa), other relationships between the toughness$_{(l.d.)}$ of two negotiators will also be found: toughness$_{(l.d.)}$ on the part of A may generate toughness$_{(l.d.)}$ on the part of B; softness$_{(l.d.)}$ on the part of A may generate softness$_{(l.d.)}$ on the part of B; or toughness$_{(l.d.)}$ on the part of A may be unrelated to toughness$_{(l.d.)}$ on the part of B.

'SINGLE' ISSUES IN TASKS OF TYPE 2: THE EFFECTS OF DIFFERENT SCHEDULES OF BIDS

The relationship between toughness on the part of two negotiators has also been explored in seven studies using tasks of Type 2. Each used 'simulated opponents' to examine the effects of a given schedule (programme) of bids. In some cases the schedules used were made contingent upon the subject's own behaviour (Komorita and Brenner 1968; Komorita and Barnes 1969; Druckman, Zechmeister and Solomon 1972); in others they were not (Chertkoff and Conley 1967; Liebert *et al.* 1968; Pruitt and Drews 1969; Pruitt and Johnson, 1970). Two of these seven studies used schedules of both types (Komorita and Brenner 1968; Druckman, Zechmeister and Solomon 1972).

The studies of Komorita and Brenner, and Komorita and Barnes

Komorita and Brenner (1968) [GEE2] and Komorita and Barnes (1969) [GEE2] used schedules which responded to toughness$_{(i.d.)(l.d.)(n.c.)(s.c.)}$ with similar toughness and to softness$_{(i.d.)(l.d.)(n.c.)(s.c.)}$ with similar softness. In each case a 'simulated opponent' made a concession whenever the subject made a concession, but the relative size of the concessions varied between schedules. Komorita and his associates identified different strategies by the value of a single variable (c) indicating the ratio of the amount conceded by the schedule to the amount conceded by the subject. One schedule ($c = ·10$) made concessions one-tenth as large as those made by the subjects; another ($c = ·50$) made concessions half as large; a third ($c = 1·00$) made concessions equal in size. Subjects were assigned to roles as buyers and could win between 50 cents and $5 depending upon the location of the final agreement within the price range $50–100. However, information about profits was 'deliberately vague', and subjects knew neither the profits made by their opponents nor the exact value of a particular agreement to themselves. Although informed that a 'conversion scale' would be used at the end of each experiment to determine how much they had won, details of the conversions were not given to them. A deadline of twelve trials was set, and the major dependent variable was the subject's offer on the first trial.

Taken together, the two studies demonstrated that subject's final offers depended upon an interaction between the schedule they faced and the costs they incurred in bargaining. When subjects incurred bargaining costs of $2 per trial they made *higher* final offers in response to the strategy of $c = 1\cdot00$ than in response to the strategy of $c = \cdot50$ (Komorita and Barnes 1969), but when subjects incurred zero costs they made *lower* final offers in response to the former strategy than in response to the latter (Komorita and Brenner 1968).

Data relevant to the comparison between strategies $c = \cdot10$ and $c = \cdot50$ are available only from Komorita and Brenner's experiments, which did not involve bargaining costs. In their Experiment I subjects made higher final offers in response to a strategy of $c = \cdot10$ than in response to a strategy of $c = \cdot50$, but in Experiment II they did not.

In general, the findings for subjects who incurred zero costs are consistent with Siegel and Fouraker's (1960) [GEE1] model, but the other findings are not. Since bargaining is always initiated by the buyer, suppose that subject's initial offers were much the same in each of the experimental treatments used by Komorita and his associates; subjects who initiated concessions would have found their concessions matched when $c = 1\cdot00$ but not when $c = \cdot50$ or $c = \cdot10$. The fact that subjects who incurred zero costs made higher offers when $c = \cdot10$ than when $c = \cdot50$, and when $c = \cdot50$ than when $c = 1\cdot00$, is consistent with Siegel and Fouraker's suggestion that concession making on the part of an opponent raises a negotiator's level of aspiration. The finding that subjects who incurred costs of $2 made higher final offers when $c = 1\cdot00$ than when $c = \cdot50$ is not consistent with this suggestion, reinforcing Cross's (1969) arguments that Siegel and Fouraker's model may have only limited application.

Komorita and Brenner also used one fixed (noncontingent) schedule of bids which began with an offer of $75 and made no further concessions beyond that point. This strategy was notably unsuccessful, despite the fact that almost all the subjects initially thought that $75 would be a fair price. In fact, evidence from other sources suggests that 'final offer first' strategies are rarely successful, presumably because of the 'rule' that concessions will be made if the parties are bargaining in good faith (Stevens 1963; Iklé 1964).

The studies of Chertkoff and Conley, and Pruitt and Johnson

Chertkoff and Conley (1967) [GEE2] manipulated toughness$_{(i.d.)}$ and toughness$_{(n.c.)}$ in a 2×2 factorial design in which subjects were given roles as buyers (MNS = $1,500) or sellers (MNS = $1,000) negotiating the purchase of a used car. Some subjects bargained against a programme which opened with an 'extreme' initial offer ($2,000 when the subject was a buyer, $500 when he was a seller), others against a programme which opened with a 'moderate' initial offer ($1,000 when the subject was a buyer, $1,500 when he was a seller). Some subjects bargained against a programme which made 'moderately frequent' concessions (five concessions of $10 each every ten trials), others against a programme which made 'infrequent' concessions (one concession of $50 every ten trials). Subjects did not incur bargaining costs and a time limit was not set.

Subjects made more frequent concessions ($F = 34 \cdot 06, p < \cdot 01, d.f. = 1,232$) in response to a moderate concession rate from the programme (mean $= 2 \cdot 28$ concessions per ten trials) than in response to an infrequent concession rate (mean $= 1 \cdot 38$ concessions per ten trials). But in this case, getting the subject to concede more frequently was something of an empty gain, since the total amount a subject conceded was smaller in response to the former strategy (mean $=$ $369) than in response to the latter (mean $=$ $456) (although this difference was not statistically significant).

Subjects moved more in response to an extreme opening offer from the programme than in response to a moderate opening offer ($F = 51 \cdot 52, p < \cdot 01$, $d.f. = 1,232$). (This latter result has been confirmed by Karass (1970) [RPD2] in the context of a legal damages case. 'Losers' were also likely to come from dyads in which they, rather than their opponents, made the largest single concession.)

Pruitt and Johnson (1970) [GEE2] manipulated the 'speed' with which the simulated opponent (seller) moved towards agreement in the first ('pre-intervention') phase of their study on mediation. The schedule always began with the same offer and made only two concessions before the point of intervention. The 'fast' schedule consisted of five trials, and concessions of $25 were made on trials three and four; the 'slow' schedule consisted of twenty trials and concessions of $25 were made on trials four and eleven. In the second ('post-intervention') phase of the experiment subjects bargained under high or low time pressure and participated in mediated or unmediated groups.

Considering only the post-intervention data from Pruitt and Johnson's unmediated groups we can see that, when time pressure was low, differences between the effects of fast and slow strategies were negligible, but that, when time pressure was high, more subjects made concessions and subjects made larger concessions in response to the fast strategy (mean percentage concession $= \cdot 833$, mean ratio concession $= \cdot 228$) than in response to the slow strategy (mean percentage concession $= \cdot 333$, mean ratio concession $= \cdot 078$).

Chertkoff and Conley, and Pruitt and Johnson, have demonstrated the importance of an opponent's concession rate (CR) in determining a subject's own bargaining behaviour, although they have reached very different conclusions about the effects of fast *v.* slow schedules: (a) Chertkoff and Conley found that larger concessions resulted in response to a *slow* CR than in response to a fast CR; whereas (b) Pruitt and Johnson found that larger concessions resulted in response to a *fast* CR than in response to a *slow* CR.

There are, however, several methodological differences between the two studies and therefore several different ways of attempting to reconcile the apparent contradiction between the findings of Chertkoff and Conley and

D

those of Pruitt and Johnson. Perhaps the most obvious possibility is that a slow CR generates a greater amount of movement than a fast CR *in the absence of a deadline* (as in the Chertkoff and Conley study), and that a fast CR generates a greater amount of movement than a slow CR *when any sort of time pressure is involved* (as in the Pruitt and Johnson study). Another possibility is that result (a) obtains when the average amount conceded per trial is identical for the fast and slow schedules (as in the Chertkoff and Conley study) and that result (b) obtains when the average amount conceded per trial is greater when a fast schedule is used than when a slow schedule is used (as in the Pruitt and Johnson study).

The studies of Liebert et al., and Pruitt and Drews

The results of studies by Liebert *et al.* (1968) and Pruitt and Drews (1969) suggest that, when concessions are made on every trial, differences in toughness$_{(i.d.)}$ are important determinants of subjects' bargaining behaviour but differences in toughness$_{(s.c.)}$ are not.

Liebert *et al.* (1968) [GEE2] manipulated toughness$_{(i.d.)}$ by using programmes which began with relatively favourable or unfavourable offers and thereafter conceded 10% of the simulated opponent's profit on every trial. However, when the programme began with an offer which was relatively favourable to the subject the concessions were smaller in (absolute) size than when it began with an offer which was relatively unfavourable. As Liebert *et al.* have pointed out, 'the effects of first bid of the opponent and his absolute concessions should act antagonistically' (p. 440).

Some subjects negotiated under conditions of complete information, others under conditions of incomplete information. Liebert *et al.* found a statistically significant interaction between information and opponent's initial offer in the determination of a subject's opening bid ($p < \cdot 05$), the mean number of trials to reach agreement ($p < \cdot 01$), and the value of the final agreement ($p < \cdot 005$). In each case there was a simple main effect of information for subjects who received a favourable initial offer, and in two of the three cases there was a simple main effect of initial offer for subjects given incomplete information. Given a favourable initial offer, informed subjects made smaller initial demands ($p < \cdot 05$), took fewer trials to reach agreement ($p < \cdot 05$) and obtained smaller profits ($p < \cdot 05$) than incompletely informed subjects. (Smith (1971) [RPD2] found that knowledge of an opponent's minimum goal did not affect the value of settlements obtained in a legal damages case.) Given incomplete information, subjects who received favourable first offers made larger demands ($p < \cdot 05$), took more trials to reach agreement ($p = $ n.s.) and obtained larger profits than subjects who received unfavourable initial offers. However, while subjects given different experimental treatments started bargaining from different positions and persisted for different numbers of trials, there were no significant differences between treatments in the amount of profit subjects gave up from bid to bid.

Similarly, Pruitt and Drews (1969) [GEE2] have reported that they found their subjects 'apparently reacting rather mechanically after the first trial' (p. 58). They used programmmes which began with the same offer but thereafter made relatively large or small concessions on every trial. (They have described their programmes as 'high CR' and 'low CR'. The fact that some authors have used 'CR' to mean the relative frequency with which concessions are made (e.g. Chertkoff and Conley 1967; Pruitt and Johnson 1970) while others have used 'CR' to mean the average amount given up from bid to bid (e.g. Liebert *et al.* 1968; Pruitt and Drews 1969) has often led to confusion.) On the basis of their subjects' behaviour in later trials, Pruitt and Drews described them as 'automatons', 'tuning out external stimuli and new ideas, and moving mechanically a standard distance from the position adopted on the first trial' (p. 57). They also found that subjects who bargained under 'acute' time pressure set higher minimum goals, engaged in a greater amount of bluffing and maintained higher mean levels of demand than subjects who bargained under 'mild' time pressure.

The study of Druckman, Zechmeister and Solomon

The most ambitious study to date is that of Druckman, Zechmeister and Solomon (1972) [GEE2], who used a $2 \times 2 \times 4$ factorial design to manipulate the 'relative defensibility' of the seller's asking price ('high' *v.* 'low'), the size of the concession made on trial one ('large' *v.* 'small') and the schedule of bids followed thereafter. In their view, 'most of the variance in subjects' concession making is accounted for by other situational variables which sometimes interact with opponent's concession rate' (p. 515). They have noted, however, that other investigators have used schedules in which the relationship between the behaviour of the subject and that of the schedule remained *constant* throughout (i.e. a 'linear' schedule). As they say, it is quite possible that the relative importance of an opponent's strategy in determining a subject's behaviour would be much greater when this relationship *changed* (i.e. a 'nonlinear' schedule). Four different schedules were therefore used: two linear and two nonlinear. One of the linear schedules was identical to the reciprocating ($c = 1 \cdot 00$) schedule used earlier by Komorita and Brenner (1968) and Komorita and Barnes (1969); the other made the same (moderate) concession on every trial. One of the nonlinear schedules was positively accelerating ($c = \cdot 1$ on trial two, $\cdot 2$ on trial three, $\cdot 3$ on trial four, etc.); the other was negatively accelerating ($c = 1 \cdot 1$ on trial two, $1 \cdot 0$ on trial three, $\cdot 9$ on trial four, etc.). Subjects were boys at a summer camp, aged between 8 and 15 years. There were no time costs and a maximum of twelve sequential offers could be made.

Analysis of variance of subjects' final offers demonstrated a main effect of opponent's strategy ($p < \cdot001$), but no other significant results were obtained. Buyers made significantly higher final offers ($p < \cdot05$) in response to the positively accelerating schedule (mean $= 80\cdot3$ cents) than in response to the reciprocatintg (mean $= 73\cdot8$ cents) or noncontingent (mean $= 70\cdot3$ cents) schedules. Although the highest offers were obtained in response to the negatively accelerating schedule (mean $= 82\cdot8$ cents), the comparison with the noncontingent schedule was the only one found to be statistically reliable ($p < \cdot05$). Analysis of changes in subjects' behaviour over time showed that the difference between schedules was primarily a function of subjects' behaviour in the final phase of negotiations, when large concessions were made, except in response to the noncontingent schedule. It is, however, important to note that subjects received no payment unless agreements were obtained. Different trends may therefore be obtained when 'the costs of failing to agree are not so severe' (p. 528). The effects of nonlinear schedules are, however, well worth further investigation.

To summarise: there is good evidence that the strategy adopted by an opponent can affect a subject's concession behaviour in games of the GEE2 type. Some authors have found main effects of initial offer (Chertkoff and Conley 1967), whereas others have not (Liebert *et al.* 1968; Druckman, Zechmeister and Solomon 1972). Some authors have found main effects of the opponent's schedule of bids (Komorita and Brenner 1968; Komorita and Barnes 1969; Druckman, Zechmeister and Solomon 1972). Sometimes the two variables interact (Liebert *et al.* 1968), and it is clear that a number of other variables such as time pressure, bargaining costs, etc. are likely to affect the precise results obtained. These results are in marked contrast to some of the findings reported in studies of the DG2 type.

A NONPARAMETRIC MODEL OF THE BARGAINING PROCESS

Kelley, Beckman and Fischer (1967) have identified certain regularities in the bargaining behaviour of subjects playing games of the DG2 type and have constructed a 'nonparametric model' to explain them. It seems that certain rather general features of subjects' bargaining behaviour are consistent with the assumption that each subject's current demand is independent of the previous demands made by his opponent. Rather than deal with all their findings we shall concentrate upon those which seem to have been crucial in the development of that model.

The most crucial findings relate to the concession curves showing the variation in mean demand with time for subjects given each MNS value. In Kelley, Beckman and Fischer's words. 'A comparison of curves for different MNS values shows that persons with large values begin higher and reach agreement at higher values . . . However, it will also be noted that at any given point in time, the rate of decline of the concession curve tends to be smaller for the higher MNS values. Persons with low values typically have to come down further from their starting point to the point of agreement' (p. 371). They also found that subjects given low MNS values typically obtained greater profit than subjects given high MNS values.

In order to explain these findings, Kelley, Beckman and Fischer have postulated the existence of a resistance (R) to making further concessions (e.g. from X5/Y4 to X4/Y5), such that the greater the value of R the greater the pressure that must be exerted upon the party concerned (by persuasion or the passage of time) before he will make a further concession. It is assumed in the model that agreement will be obtained when the sums of the resistances overcome by each negotiator are approximately equal and when the offers they make sum to the value of the 'total reward' available. The formal model is completed by a set of assumptions specifying the distribution of R 'over the domain of locations (defined in terms of MNS values and offers) reached by the parties in the course of the bargaining process' (p. 382).

Three major assumptions are made about the distribution of R:

1 R increases as a subject approaches his MNS value. This was suggested by the finding that the time required for a further concession to be made increased as a negotiator was forced closer to his own MNS value.
2 R increases with increasing MNS. This was suggested by the finding that any given concession required more time the larger the MNS value which was assigned.
3 For a given level of profit, R is higher the lower the MNS value which is assigned. This was suggested by the finding that subjects given low MNS values typically obtained greater profits than those given high MNS values.

Other subsidiary assumptions are also made, but in each case Kelley, Beckman and Fischer 'have proceeded from assumptions that relate R for a given party only to his own MNS value and last offer' (p. 383). This is a very considerable simplification, but it is also a very powerful one since it allowed these authors to explain a number of other aspects of their data. However, in view of the restricted nature of the task used (Chapter 3, p. 54) it is of particular interest to note that Holmes, Throop and Strickland (1971) [GEE1] have been able to confirm the major findings of Kelley, Beckman and Fischer for negotiators given *low* levels of aspiration but not for negotiators given *high* levels of aspiration.

The Use of Threat

A great deal of research has been concerned with the relationship between power, the use of power, and the efficiency with which conflicts of interest are managed, and, as Brotherton and Stephenson (1975) have pointed out, 'these studies merit attention because equivalent effects of power may occur in negotiations' (p. 48).

EFFECT OF THREAT ON PROFIT

Probably the best-known work dealing with threat is that of Deutsch and Krauss (1960, 1962), who have argued that the availability of a threat option results in a decrease in the joint profit obtained by the protagonists concerned. More precisely, their theory amounts to the following propositions:

1 If threats are available they will tend to be used. (Raven and Kruglanski (1970) have suggested some of the reasons why this may be so: in particular, that actors tend to infer their opponents' intentions from their opponents' capabilities.)
2 This tendency will be stronger the more irreconcilable the conflict is perceived to be.
3 In an equal status relationship the subject who is threatened will feel intimidated, his motivation will change from individualistic to competitive, and he will respond to threat with a threat of his own. Consequently, it will be harder for the subjects to reach an agreement.

Deutsch and Krauss had individualistically oriented subjects play twenty 'trials' of a two-person trucking game (see Figure 5.1) with the same opponent and for imaginary rewards. Each subject accumulated profits in direct

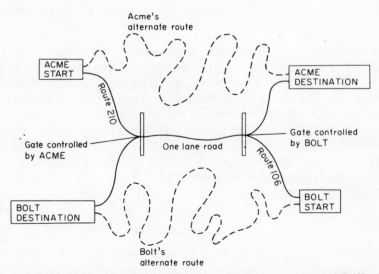

Figure 5.1 Deutsch and Krauss's (1960) trucking game (from Baron, Byrne and Griffitt 1974, p. 390)

proportion to the time taken to reach his goal and could only learn his opponent's position when they met head-on in the common path. In unilateral threat groups one player could prevent his opponent from taking the common path by closing a gate; in bilateral threat groups both players were provided with gates. The efficiency with which the conflict was managed (measured by the mean joint profits of the players) was highest in the no-threat condition and progressively lower in unilateral and bilateral threat conditions respectively. Furthermore, the bilateral threat condition was unique in showing no increase in efficiency over trials.

The most efficient strategy in this game is for the two players to adopt a pattern of alternate first access to the common path. Deutsch and Krauss have argued that the provision of gates, with their subsequent use, changes the subjects' motivation from individualistic (in which they are concerned only to maximise their own profits) to competitive (in which they are concerned to maximise their gains *relative* to the other). This reduces the possibility that subjects will reach agreement about the use of the common path and thereby reduces the joint profit that they can make (since in this game time means money, albeit imaginary money).

The line of investigation (and analysis) begun by Deutsch and Krauss has been extended by others (e.g. Borah 1963; Kelley 1965; Gallo 1966; Shomer, Davis and Kelley 1965; Schelling 1966; Rapoport 1967; Shure and Meeker 1968). Even so, according to Smith and Leginski (1970), 'the status of the Deutsch and Krauss hypothesis is uncertain, and an understanding of the role of threat . . . has not been achieved' (p. 58). What has been achieved is a clear critique of certain methodological aspects of Deutsch and Krauss's studies.

1 Deutsch and Krauss's use of 'threat' amounted to the use of a gate preventing the other player from taking the shorter and more profitable route. Thus closing a gate was necessarily a damaging act in the game, whereas a threat should be a conditional expression of hostile intent which is not in itself harmful. To use a gate in the trucking game was to employ some sanction, not to indicate that sanctions would follow if and only if certain unwanted behaviours were performed. The current tendency to talk about 'noncontingent threats' is exceedingly unhelpful (e.g. see Tedeschi 1970; Schlenker *et al.* 1970).

2 Subjects playing mechanical games of the type used by Deutsch and Krauss may not be individualistically motivated anyway: they may 'invent' their own game which depends on beating their opponent rather than maximising their own score. This may be especially true when payoffs are trivial in value.

3 The game itself suffered from providing only *one* real 'solution', i.e. alternation, so that little communication was necessary and little occurred.

4 Deutsch and Krauss have suggested that the effect of the gates was to change the subject's motivation from individualistic to competitive but

provided no direct evidence to support their view. Rather, the level of competition was simply inferred from the joint profits obtained by the pairs. If the amount of time spent in confrontation on the short path is taken as an index of competitiveness, it seems that subjects were equally competitive in all conditions (Borah 1963). Both Kelley (1965) and Gallo (1966) have argued that this competitiveness would show itself in different ways in the different conditions, thus producing the pattern of averages observed by Deutsch and Krauss.

OTHER METHODOLOGICAL CONSIDERATIONS

Tedeschi (1970) has pointed out some of the advantages of considering the effects of threat messages within the more general context of literature dealing with persuasion, attitude change and conformity. It is important 'who (source) says *what* (message) to *whom* (recipients) through which *medium* (channel) with what *effect*' (Rosnow and Robinson 1967, p. xvii), and at the very least Tedeschi's writing emphasises the potential importance of source, message and target characteristics which have been neglected by theorists such as Deutsch and Krauss (1960, 1962).

Tedeschi's major contribution is the suggestion that compliance to threats is directly related to the degree of negative utility of the message, where negative utility equals the probability that sanctions will follow if the target fails to comply multiplied by the magnitude of the sanctions (Horai and Tedeschi 1969; Tedeschi 1970; Schlenker *et al.* 1970). In other words, a threat's credibility and its magnitude both need to be manipulated in experimental studies.

It is also important to realise that more than one sort of threat can be made and to be clear which sort of threat is being studied. Schelling (1966) has distinguished between *compellence* threats, which specify what must be done ('Unless you do X, I will do Y'), and *deterrence* threats, which specify what must not be done ('If you do X, I will do Y'). Given that the decision situation involves more than just two alternatives, a compellence threat may be perceived as more hostile in intent than a deterrence threat, since it restricts the target's freedom of action to a single alternative (X) rather than a number of alternatives (anything but X). Consequently, results which obtain when a compellence threat is used may not obtain when a deterrence threat is used.

If a threat does have to be enforced there is a clear distinction to be made between precise and imprecise power. As Smith and Leginski (1970) have put it, 'If A's power is such that he has available the potential for delivering a number of different outcomes to B, fairly evenly spread across the range which defines amount of power, A may be said to have precise power. If A has few responses, e.g. he can either deliver his most severe punishment or not punish at all, he may be said to have imprecise power' (p. 60). This distinction may be of considerable theoretical interest. For instance, Smith and Leginski themselves predicted an interaction between magnitude and precision of power such that 'threats and punishments would increase in frequency and strength with increasing magnitude of power where power was precise; and that threats and punishments would decrease in frequency and strength with increasing magnitude of imprecise power' (p. 60). Deutsch and Krauss studied the possession (and use) of imprecise power only.

THREATS AND BARGAINING EFFICIENCY

Six studies have investigated various aspects of the relationship between the use of threat and bargaining efficiency (Kelley 1965; Hornstein 1965; Froman and Cohen 1969; Fischer 1970; Smith and Leginski 1970; Tjosvold 1974), but unfortunately only the three by Hornstein, Smith and Leginski, and Tjosvold have been described in sufficient detail to determine which type of threat (i.e. deterrence or compellence) was involved.

The study of Hornstein

Hornstein (1965) [GEE1] gave his subjects 'threat potentials' which allowed them to reduce their opponent's profits by 90%, 50%, 20% and 10% in different experimental conditions. Bidding proceeded through the exchange of offer slips and notice slips, the latter constituting 'a threat which told its receiver that unless he accepted a certain offer, which was indicated thereon, the sender might reduce his profits' (p. 284). All subjects played eight games with the same opponent, with a time limit of six minutes for each game.

Two sets of data are most relevant to Deutsch and Krauss's (1960, 1962) general theoretical position. We shall consider: (a) the data relating the use of threat (and fine) to the probability of reaching agreement (p_a) in the first game; and (b) the relationship between magnitude of power, use of power, and bargaining efficiency in treatments which gave subjects threat potentials that were equal in size (i.e. 90%–90%, 50%–50%, 10%–10%).

1 Of 48 pairs of subjects: (a) in 15/48 pairs neither subject threatened his opponent, and all 15/15 pairs reached an agreement ($p_a = 1.00$); and (b) in 33/48 pairs one or both of the subjects made a threat, and only 12/33 pairs reached an agreement ($p_a = .36$). Of these 33 cases where a threat was made: (a) in 20/33 pairs neither subject went on to enforce his threat, and 11/20 pairs reached an agreement ($p_a = .55$); and (b) in 13/33 pairs one or both of the subjects did go on to enforce his threat, but only 1/13 pairs reached an agreement ($p_a = .08$). These data are of course consistent with Deutsch and Krauss's position.

2 Presumably, Deutsch and Krauss would expect the use of threat to increase as the capacity to threaten was increased. Consequently, if subjects had

equal capacities to threaten one another, it might be expected that subjects given high threat potentials would use more threats and make larger threats, but reach fewer agreements and obtain smaller profits, than subjects given low threat potentials. Hornstein's data, however, do not support this analysis, since (a) no statistically reliable differences were obtained between treatments along the dimensions indicated, and (b) subjects' mean profits were largest in 90%–90% pairs and smallest in 50%–50% pairs.

The study of Smith and Leginski

Smith and Leginski (1970) [DG3] manipulated both the size and precision of the power available to subjects who played a distribution game of the type used by Kelley (1966) against simulated opponents. Subjects could send deterrence threats by means of warning slips which 'stated that if the other negotiator did not offer the subject a better deal, the subject would take some specified number of points from him' (p. 66). The subjects were, however, given greater coercive power than their simulated opponents (and knew that they had the greater power). Whereas subjects could only be fined 10 points if they ignored a warning from their opponents, they were themselves given the potential to deliver fines of 20, 50, 90 or 140 points depending upon the experimental treatment concerned.

Subjects given high threat potentials (90 or 140 points) obtained more profitable contracts than those given low threat potentials (20 or 50 points). However, subjects' bargaining behaviour depended upon both the magnitude of the power at their disposal and the precision with which that power could be used. When power was precise, subjects given high threat potentials included threats in a greater proportion of their bids than did subjects given low threat potentials (and the threats were larger in size); but when the power was imprecise, subjects given high threat potentials included threats in a smaller proportion of their bids than did subjects given low threat potentials.

The data most relevant to Deutsch and Krauss's (1960, 1962) theory are, however, those relating subjects' threats (and fines) to the threats (and fines) received from their opponents. Subjects were more likely to follow a threat with a fine when given precise power than when given imprecise power ($p < \cdot 05$), and inspection of their reported results suggests that this tendency might have been particularly marked in the high power conditions. But subjects in high power conditions and subjects in precise power conditions were more likely to receive threats (and fines) from their opponents than subjects in low power conditions and subjects in imprecise power conditions respectively. Consequently, a subject might have used his threat capacity to prevent further threats from being made by his opponent. However, if counterthreat is defined as threat which is made immediately (i.e. one bid) after a threat has been received, it seems that relatively little counterthreat occurred (p. 74).

The studies of Froman and Cohen, and Kelley

Two studies have compared the bargaining efficiency of subjects in no-threat, unilateral threat and bilateral threat groups. One study by Froman and Cohen, which gave subjects imprecise power, has provided considerable support for Deutsch and Krauss's (1960, 1962) position; the other, by Kelley, which gave subjects precise power, has failed to support that position.

Froman and Cohen (1969) [DG3] found that bargaining efficiency (as measured by time to agreement, frequency of MJP contracts and mean joint profit) was lowest in bilateral threat groups and progressively higher in unilateral threat groups and no-threat groups respectively, as predicted by Deutsch and Krauss's theory. Furthermore, within the bilateral threat groups, the frequency with which threats were made correlated negatively ($r = -·44, p < ·005$) with the frequency with which MJP contracts were obtained. Froman and Cohen have therefore concluded that 'not only is bargaining more efficient in the absence of an ability to threaten, but it is also more efficient when the ability to threaten is present but exercised less often' (p. 151). Kelley (1965) [GEE1], however, failed to find differences between the threat conditions in terms of time taken and the number of MJP agreements obtained, when subjects were given precise power.

The study of Fischer

Fischer (1970) [DG2] has conducted what is in many ways the most comprehensive test of Deutsch and Krauss's (1960, 1962) hypotheses. Apparently, subjects could make either deterrence or compellence threats, since threats were defined 'as an initial occurrence or any repetition of a statement, direct or indirect, making reference to a punishment to be imposed if the other party would not concede to a demand' (p. 305). The game involved was adapted from Kelley, Beckman and Fischer (1967), and subjects were given a threat potential which was 'high' in some conditions and 'low' in others (amounting to 8% and 1% respectively of the joint profit a pair could make). 'Low–low', 'high–high' and 'low–high' conditions were created 'as analogues of the Deutsch and Krauss No-threat, Bilateral Threat, and Unilateral Threat conditions' (p. 303). All subjects were given imprecise power, as in Deutsch and Krauss's original studies.

An interesting methodological problem is raised by Fischer's design. Studies such as those of Deutsch and Krauss, Kelley (1965) and Froman and Cohen (1969) forced the experimenter to give different instructions to subjects who were given a threat potential and those who were not. As Fischer has pointed out, the experimenter might therefore inadvertently have suggested the use of threat in those conditions in which he provided power and have instructed in its use. Fischer's design had the advantage that the same instructions could be used in each experimental treatment but the disadvantage that, strictly speaking, each subject was given a threat potential of one sort or another. The alleged similarity between the low–low condition used by Fischer and the no-threat condition used by Deutsch and Krauss rests upon the 'relatively insignificant' threat potential given to subjects in the low–low groups. It is, however, unfortunate that Fischer did not include an additional no-threat condition in his design.

If we assume that Fischer's low–low condition is analogous to Deutsch and Krauss's no-threat condition, we can see that Fischer's study has provided very little support for Deutsch and Krauss's theories.

1 There were no statistically significant differences between low–low and high–high conditions in terms either of mean times to agreement or of mean gross profits.
2 Although subjects in high–high groups made more threats and imposed more fines than subjects in low–low groups, again these differences were not statistically significant.
3 The use of threat was not associated with increased competitiveness. However, Fischer did find some evidence that, when threats were followed with fines, the use of *fines* increased the possibility of a 'spiral of competitiveness' similar to that suggested by Deutsch and Krauss.

DISCUSSION

Let us review what has been said so far. There is no evidence from experimental games that the use of threat leads to a change in motivation of the sort suggested by Deutsch and Krauss (1960, 1962), although the use of fines may sometimes have that effect. It is clear that the use of threat sometimes leads to a decrease in bargaining efficiency and sometimes does not. It is, however, not clear when the use of threat will be productive (from the point of view of the user) and when it will be counterproductive. Among other variables which seem important in determining the universe of discourse of Deutsch and Krauss's theory are (a) the magnitude and precision of the power available to subjects, and (b) the type of threat (compellence or deterrence) they choose to send. Tjosvold's (1974) [GEE2] results suggest that the use of threat will lead to a spiral of competitiveness only when an opponent is 'affronted' by its use.

It is also important that the threat 'be placed in context among a set of conflict strategies' (Fischer 1970, p. 313). In particular, it is important to distinguish between tactics involving the use of *power* and those involving the use of *information*. Fischer found that (a) subjects given high threat potentials made relatively greater use of coercive tactics than those given low threat potentials, and (b) conversely, subjects given low threat potentials made relatively greater use of informational tactics than those given high threat potentials. While subjects given high threat potentials made more threats and imposed more fines than those given low threat potentials, subjects given low threat potentials made higher initial demands and more often misrepresented the value of the MNS they had been assigned than those given high threat potentials. Given that lies, if revealed as such, are likely to be just as disruptive as threats, it is easy to see why Fischer failed to find differences in the bargaining efficiency of the high–high and low–low pairs in his study. (The availability of information manipulation in the form of lies may also help to explain the (otherwise) surprising finding that 'low' subjects obtained larger profits than 'high' subjects in low–high pairs.) In Fischer's own words,

'One immediate implication of this study is that experiments which narrow the behavioural alternatives of the subjects may create artifactual results. For instance, assuming a constant amount of competition in an average dyad, to restrict personal interaction to little more than mutual threats will channel competition through that means. A wider repertoire of possible behaviours, ranging in their subtleties, allows this competition to be expressed in various ways and degrees' (p. 313).

In our opinion, Fischer's 'alternative strategies' hypothesis will not by itself allow us to reconcile the findings of the studies we have considered, but there can be little doubt about the importance of his general line of argument. It was in recognition of this fact that we have made (in Chapter 3) a major distinction between (a) games which involve limited communication possibilities and focus disagreement primarily upon outcomes (i.e. distribution games and games of economic exchange), and (b) games which involve much wider communication possibilities and focus disagreement upon inputs as well as outcomes (i.e. role-playing debates and substitute debates). There are in fact no experimental studies of the use of threat in formal negotiations. This may be quite a serious limitation, since it is clear that subjects do make use of the increased communication possibilities available in the context of experimental debates. We shall now move on to consider experiments of this type.

Chapter 6

The Process of Formal Negotiation

The studies reviewed in Chapter 5 have been of experimental situations which excluded the possibility of free communication between the participants. In that event, the 'process of bid and counterbid' is the only material available to describe behaviour in negotiations. If the possibilities for free communication were increased, we would expect the outcomes of a negotiation to differ from those obtained in situations of restricted communication. Communication may elicit a variety of alternative approaches to the issues, besides enhancing the salience of the personal relationship between the negotiators. In fact there is evidence that the outcomes of negotiations are systematically affected by the introduction of communication possibilities. A great deal more communication occurs in formal negotiations than the mere exchange of bids and counterbids. The possibilities for both distributive bargaining and attitudinal structuring are greatly increased.

Distributive bargaining may be directly affected by the opportunity to initiate complex strategies requiring high level communication skills. Walton and McKersie's (1965) discussion of commitment tactics provides some excellent examples of the sorts of skill we have in mind. Here our analysis will focus upon strategies designed to reduce tension in international relations. Apparently, it is sometimes possible to induce co-operation by means of small unilateral moves. We are not able to say when this is possible and when it is not, although it seems likely that techniques of image manipulation or attitudinal structuring may have an important part to play. Experimental evidence relating to such techniques will be discussed in some detail.

There are unfortunately few detailed analyses of the behaviour of participants in formal negotiation groups. Those in existence confirm the view that negotiation groups have characteristics of their own which set them apart from the task-oriented groups which have received most attention in the past. Both experimental and field studies will be discussed.

Finally, we shall attempt to evaluate the contribution of the experimental research reviewed in this chapter and Chapters 4 and 5. Three 'cautionary' themes will be introduced, concerning (a) the reliability (replication) of the existing data, (b) the generality of the data across different negotiation tasks, and (c) the generality of the data across different subject populations. It is concluded that investigators have preferred to initiate new lines of research rather than to consolidate existing findings. Consequently, there is a great deal of uncertainty involved in judgements of the value of particular experimental results.

Opportunity to Communicate

Smith (1969) [RPD2] compared the effects of a 'restricted' and an 'unrestricted' channel of communication upon negotiations in which subjects took roles as counsel in a legal damages case (concerning the effects of an experimental drug). Subjects in the restricted communication condition negotiated via an exchange of written bids, while subjects in the unrestricted communication condition were free to talk to each other and had no constraints placed upon the nature of the messages they could exchange. Restricting the range of communication allowed reduced the probability that an agreement would be obtained at all and limited the range of the agreements which were. In Smith's words, 'The apparent effect of the greater opportunity to communicate is to allow one party or the other to push the settlement further in his preferred direction' (p. 254). Exactly how this push is obtained is a matter for further investigation.

The view that communication variables are of considerable importance in the study of experimental debates is also suggested by Bartos's (1966) analyses. Bartos constructed a simple mathematical model of the process of concession making in experimental negotiations, by assuming that a negotiator's current demand (Y) would depend upon his own previous demand (X) and upon the previous offer (Z_i) made by each of his opponents ($i = 1, 2, \ldots n$). This may be written as

$$Y = a + bX + c_1Z_1 + c_2Z_2 + \ldots + c_nZ_n$$

By using this equation Bartos was able to explain 31% of the variance in his 'abstract' [DG3] experiments but only 18% of the variance in his 'spoken' [RPD3] ones. Formal negotiation involves a great deal more than just a process of bid and counterbid.

An experiment by Crow (1963) [RPD3] serves to illustrate this point. Crow used Guetzkow's (see Guetzkow *et al.* 1963) 'Inter-Nation Simulation' (INS) to create a fictitious world of five nations: Omne, allied with Erga, and Utro, allied with Algo and Ingo. Subjects were told that Omne and Utro, the two most powerful nations, had once been at war and still remained hostile to one another; at the beginning of the exercise each possessed nuclear weapons capable of destroying the other. Each nation had three decision makers who decided how 'basic capability units' were to be used and who attempted to arrange trade agreements with the decision makers of other nations. Omne,

Erga, Utro and Algo were members of an 'International Organization' which Ingo was attempting to join. The central decision maker (CDM) of Omne was a confederate of the experimenter who 'was told that from time to time he would be required to take special actions that no one else was to know about'. He was instructed to begin 'with a policy maintaining the "status quo" ' and to respond to disarmament proposals or suggestions that Ingo be admitted to the International Organization with statements of 'not now, later'. He was also required to 'engage in a gradual buildup of force capability units and to solidify his alliance with Erga through favourable trade and aid agreements' (p. 587). There followed a gradual increase in tension (shown by perceptions 'of the likelihood that war would occur, of the trust being shown among nations, etc.') which was sharply accelerated when Omne gave nuclear capability units to Erga, its ally. Utro responded with a massive increase in force capability units of its own, and at this point of 'crisis' Crow instructed the CDM of Omne to initiate a GRIT strategy of the type proposed by Osgood (1960a, 1960b) (where GRIT stands for 'Graduated Reciprocation in Tension Reduction'). Here, the CDM of Omne stated that his country 'intended to take specific steps designed to reduce world tension, that it would announce these steps in advance, and that while the steps may seem small individually, one would add to another and become more important if and when they were matched by other nations' (p. 588). One such step was to invite Ingo to attend meetings of the International Organization as a nonvoting member; another (subsequent) step was to stop its arms buildup altogether. Apparently, these moves 'were initially met with suspicion and hostility by Utro' but were 'finally reciprocated' (p. 588).

Crow's experiment has been described in some detail, partly because of the practical importance of Osgood's proposals and partly because of the complexity of the interventions involved. Other investigators interested in Osgoods' ideas have either used more artificial tasks – specifically expanded versions of the Prisoner's Dilemma Game (e.g. Pilisuk and Rapoport 1964; Pilisuk *et al.* 1965; Pilisuk *et al.* 1967; Pilisuk and Skolnick 1968) – or seriously misrepresented the statement of the interventions concerned (e.g. Bartos 1966; Komorita and Brenner 1968; Komorita and Barnes 1969). Osgood's work does *not* imply that concessions made by one negotiator will typically be reciprocated by his opponent. It is likely to be extremely difficult to induce co-operation by means of small unilateral moves (Singer 1958), and it is therefore important to pay particular attention to the details of any intervention which has been successful. A great deal of further research will be needed before we can specify when a GRIT strategy will lead to a reduction in tension and when it will not.

Other studies have programmed confederates to use techniques of image manipulation (Pruitt 1969) or attitudinal structuring (Walton and McKersie 1965) but left them free to make concessions whenever they pleased. These will now be reviewed.

Image Manipulation and Attitudinal Structuring in Experimental Debates

One problem involved in implementing a GRIT strategy is that a small co-operative gesture is particularly likely to be viewed as part of a more general competitive orientation. So, apparently, is any attempt to introduce certain forms of superordinate goal. Johnson and Lewicki (1969) [RPD3] asked subjects (belonging to two- or three-man teams) to negotiate terms for dealing with a racial integration problem in a hypothetical community. At some point during the negotiations one of the teams, chosen at random, introduced the information that if the two teams could reach a mutually acceptable agreement 'the National Government would award the city a large poverty grant which would include enough to meet the needs of both groups' (p. 13). The introduction of the superordinate goal, however, led to a 'pathology' involving 'an intensification of the conflict, increased misunderstanding, and a refusal to compromise' (p. 23).

One technique which may facilitate the attribution of 'co-operative' or 'exploitative' intentions is the form of 'role reversal' advocated by Cohen (1951), Rapoport (1960) and Deutsch (1962), whereby a negotiator repeats the other's position (to the other's satisfaction) before he presents his own. This may be viewed as a form of image manipulation in which a negotiator attempts to demonstrate that he really is concerned with what the other has to say. But it seems that the technique affects the actor as well as the audience. Johnson (1967) [RPD2] found that role reversal led to greater understanding of the other's position in a legal damages case than did 'self presentation' but that this increase in understanding was communicated to the other only when goals were compatible. Furthermore, when goals were compatible and role reversal was skilfully performed, agreement was more likely to be obtained when role reversal was employed than when it was not. This was not the case when goals were incompatible. When genuine differences are accurately perceived conflict may of course be harder to resolve than when they are not.

Johnson's (1967) study involved the intervention of a third party (the experimenter) whereby both members of a pair were instructed to employ the technique of role reversal in their negotiation. A subsequent investigation by Johnson and Dustin (1970) [RPD2] considered role reversal as a technique which might be introduced at the bargaining table by only one of the participants. It seems that individualistically oriented subjects and competitively oriented subjects differed in their response to the skilful use of role reversal by a trained confederate. In particular, 'subjects in the individualistic conditions compromised their positions more, perceived themselves as being more willing to compromise, and made more agreements in a shorter period of time than did the subjects in the competitive conditions' (p. 201). This result is not at all surprising, and it is a very great pity that Johnson and Dustin did not go on to compare the effects of role reversal with the effects of self presentation in their different experimental conditions. As it stands it is difficult to see why their paper was thought worth publishing.

Evan and MacDougall (1967) [RPD3] investigated the consequences of intraparty conflict perceived by one's opponents at the bargaining table. Subjects were formed into two-man teams and asked to negotiate the settlement of a union–management dispute involving the introduction of automated equipment. In some cases subjects were given roles which required them to adopt a 'moderate' negotiating position; in others they were given roles which required an 'extreme' negotiating position. Whenever two 'extremists' were assigned to the same team their bargaining behaviour was guided by a 'principle of unanimity', according to which 'each party must in its own best interest, present a united front to the opposition' (p. 399). Whenever a 'moderate' and an 'extremist' were assigned to the same team their bargaining behaviour was guided by a 'principle of dissent', according to which 'each party airs its internal differences in the course of negotiations with its adversary, (p. 399). Three types of negotiation group were employed: *bilateral consensus*, in which each team consisted of two extremists; *bilateral dissensus*, in which each team consisted of one moderate and one extremist; and *unilateral dissensus*, in which one moderate and one extremist negotiated against two extremists.

Three major hypotheses were tested: (a) that a condition of bilateral dissensus would more frequently promote agreement than a condition of bilateral consensus; (b) that these agreements would be more likely to be 'integrative' and reflect 'mutual satisfaction'; and (c) that a team adopting a strategy of dissensus in opposition to a strategy of consensus would tend to be dominated (have to capitulate). The first hypothesis was not confirmed. There were no differences between the three sorts of group in 'number of terms of agreement', and 'even the rank order turned out differently from what had been expected' (with bilateral consensus groups and not bilateral dissensus groups achieving the most success). To test the second hypothesis, each term of agreement was judged as reflecting *domination* (i.e. 'unilateral satisfaction for one side and unilateral dissatisfaction for the other'), *compromise* (i.e. 'both bilateral satisfaction and bilateral dissatisfaction') or *integration* (i.e. 'bilateral satisfaction'). Bilateral dissensus groups yielded a greater number of terms of agreement which reflected integration than did unilateral dissensus groups, but there were no differences between bilateral dissensus and bilateral consensus groups in this respect. Consequently, the second hypothesis was partially confirmed. The third hypothesis was not confirmed.

Thus, bilateral consensus groups were not reliably differentiated from bilateral dissensus groups with respect to either amount or quality of agreement. It may be true, as Evan and MacDougall have said, that 'Negotiations governed entirely by the principle of dissent tend to approximate what Rapoport (1960, pp. 5–12, 245–309) conceptualizes as a "debate" in which an exchange of genuinely held views occurs, rather than as a "game" in which such views may be deliberately camouflaged' (p. 399). But the result of such 'debate' was no more (mutually) acceptable to the participants than the result of the 'game'. This is particularly interesting in the light of what has been said (in Chapter 2) about the importance of an 'interparty' or 'differentiation' phase in negotiations. Logically, the first dilemma negotiators face is whether to adopt a 'problem-solving' or 'status-quo' strategy (Walton and McKersie 1966). In Douglas's (1957, 1962) studies negotiations had previously broken down and a mediator had been called in. Under such circumstances, groups which settled their differences seemed to Douglas to be those in which both parties initially adopted a 'hard' distributive approach. Under other circumstances it seems that different approaches may be equally effective.

Process Analysis of Experimental Debates

One method of providing a more detailed specification of what is going on in negotiations of this type is to use a category system as complex as Bales's (1950) 'Interaction Process Analysis' (IPA). So far as distribution games and games of economic exchange are concerned, analysis of the process of negotiation consists (very largely) of analysis of the process of bid and counterbid. So far as experimental debates are concerned, detailed analysis of the process of negotiation must involve not only analysis of the *process* of bid and counterbid but also analysis of the *arguments* involved. Only four studies have attempted to carry out this sort of task: Manheim has used Bales's IPA categories; Morris has used categories similar to those used by Bales; and Julian and McGrath in two studies have used category systems developed by themselves.

Manheim (1960) formed sixteen all-male triads from junior, senior and graduate students who had each attained an average scholastic grade of C or above (although the precise composition of each triad has not been made clear). Triads were differentiated according to relative status (high *v*. low) and type of leader (appointed *v*. emergent), ostensibly on the basis of members' scores on an Otis IQ and a Thurstone Temperament Schedule. Consequently, there were four types of triad: high status, appointed leader; high status, emergent leader; low status, appointed leader; and low status, emergent leader. Groups were situated in separate rooms and negotiated via written notes. Manheim found that Bales's index of 'Expressive-Malintegrative Behaviour' (the ratio of the number of positive social-emotional acts to the total number of social-emotional acts) increased consistently and reliably with the number of dimensions (zero, one or two) along which the triads differed. In other words, as Williams (1947, pp. 51–8) has pointed out, the greater the differentiation between groups the greater the (likelihood of) conflict between them.

Strictly speaking, both Manheim (1960) and Morris (1970) used 'standard' groups rather than 'negotiation' groups (see Vidmar and McGrath 1967).

Their work is included in this review because of its theoretical interest and because standard groups can take on many of the characteristics of negotiation groups (Stephenson 1971a). Morris in fact has described his experiment as involving a 'negotiation' (or 'proposal') task and a 'group creativity' (or 'fable') task. In each case he was able to confirm Bales and Strodtbeck's (1951) phase hypothesis, but there were also important differences between the two tasks. Negotiation tasks are *not* the same as group creativity tasks. Whereas most planning activity in the negotiation task consisted of *orientation* (i.e. attempts to 'structure or delimit problem, objectives, eventual solution; propose generic solutions') rather than *information* (i.e. attempts to 'give factual information relevant to the problem area'), most planning activity in the group creativity task consisted of information rather than orientation. Furthermore, while *clarification* (i.e. attempts to 'clarify, explain, or defend without further developing') was the most frequently used activity in the negotiation task, *proposal* (i.e. attempts to 'propose or develop specific solutions; reword or revise solutions; choose from among alternatives; make a compromise') was the most frequently used activity in the group creativity task. In fact, surprisingly few proposals were put forward in the negotiation ('proposal') task. This might have been due to the precise nature of the task involved or to the fact that Morris's category system, like Bales's, was essentially designed for use with problem-solving groups.

Only two studies have used category systems specifically designed for use with negotiation groups. McGrath and Julian's (1963) [SD2] study has already been discussed in some detail (see Chapter 2, pp. 31–2, and Chapter 3, pp. 53–4). Julian and McGrath (1963) [SD2] found some evidence that low LPC chairmen spoke more often and at greater length than high LPC chairmen and, in addition, communicated 'negative interpersonal feeling' more frequently and 'positive interpersonal feeling' less frequently – LPC being a score derived from a subject's description of his 'least preferred co-worker' (see Fiedler 1967). Despite these differences the LPC scores of the chairmen were not related to the quality of the negotiated settlements obtained, when all groups were included in the analysis: for three separate topics Julian and McGrath's correlations were $r_1 = -\cdot01$, $r_2 = -\cdot03$, $r_3 = \cdot09$. However, Fiedler (1967) has reported additional analyses which suggested that 'somewhat more systematic results appeared when the authors took into consideration the Group Atmosphere score of the moderator' (p. 232), where Group Atmosphere 'indicates the degree to which the leader feels accepted by the group and relaxed and at ease in his role' (p. 32). Apparently, when the chairman's Group Atmosphere score was low (below the median) the correlations were all positive ($r_1 = \cdot44$, $r_2 = \cdot27$, $r_3 = \cdot18$), but when his score was high (above the median) two of the three correlations were negative ($r_1 = -\cdot56$, $r_2 = -\cdot39$, $r_3 = \cdot46$). It must be admitted, however, that the interpretation of these figures is not at all straightforward. Fiedler has presented overall values of r (namely $r_1 = \cdot02$, $r_2 = -\cdot12$, $r_3 = \cdot03$) which are not quite the same as those given by Julian and McGrath, and the analyses based on chairmen's Group Atmosphere scores are presented only in his book. It is not yet possible to say how these findings relate to Fiedler's 'contingency model' of leadership effectiveness in interacting groups (Fiedler 1967; Foa, Mitchell and Fiedler 1971). Julian and McGrath themselves have simply commented that

'The behavioural differences associated with LPC differences apparently conflicted in their contributions to negotiation performance. Low LPC chairmen, while active and dominant in the discussion, were more prone to contribute to hostility, rather than control and diminish it. On the other hand, psychologically close, accepting chairmen remained too passive to direct group members toward superior solutions, even though they contributed less to the interpersonal antagonism among group members' (p. 24).

Discussion

McGrath and Julian (1963) felt able to say that one major limitation in nearly all studies of negotiation was that they focused upon outcomes to the exclusion of the process by which those outcomes were obtained. However, very few experimental studies were available for them to review. Very many more findings have now been reported, and it seems useful to reconsider their conclusion, distinguishing between different types of experimental task.

THE USE OF DIFFERENT NEGOTIATION TASKS

Figure 6.1 lists sixty-nine experimental studies of negotiation groups which have now been published (or are readily available in the form of mimeographed reports). Slightly less than half of these studies have involved distribution games or games of economic exchange; slightly more than half have involved games of the role-playing debate or substitute debate type. A more detailed breakdown of experiment types is shown in Figure 6.2.

Only forty-nine of the studies listed supply any details of the process by which agreements were obtained. Thirty of them are studies of the DG or GEE types, and McGrath and Julian's (1963) conclusion would no longer apply to games of this sort. It would, however, still apply to studies of the RPD and SD types since eighteen of the studies listed have little or nothing to say about the process by which agreements were obtained. Only four studies used category systems such as Bales's (1950) IPA, and in two of these no attempt was made to relate the process variables involved to the outcomes of negotiations. Five studies of the RPD type instructed one or both parties to follow programmed strategies of one sort or another (e.g. Crow 1963; Evan and MacDougall 1967). Programmed strategies do not determine exactly what subjects will do, but rather constrain their behaviour in certain ways. The success of a given strategy may therefore depend upon how it is implemented in detail, and it is a pity that none of the studies have been supplemented by a description of the other communications involved. The

DISTRIBUTION GAMES

Tasks of Type 2
Kelley, Beckman and Fischer (1967)
Morgan and Sawyer (1967)
Fischer (1970)
Messé (1971)
Gruder (1971)
Gruder and Rosen (1971)
Druckman, Solomon and Zechmeister (1972)
Benton and Druckman (1974)
Lamm (1975)

Tasks of Type 3
Kelley (1966)
Froman and Cohen (1969)
Froman and Cohen (1970)
Smith and Leginski (1970)

GAMES OF ECONOMIC EXCHANGE

Tasks of Type 1
Siegel and Fouraker (1960)
Kelley (1964)
Hornstein (1965)
Kelley (1965)
Hatton (1967)
Johnson and Cohen (1967)
Holmes, Throop and Strickland (1971)
Kelley and Schenitzki (1972)
Kahn and Kohls (1972)

Tasks of Type 2
Chertkoff and Conley (1967)
Komorita and Brenner (1968)
Liebert *et al.* (1968)
Komorita and Barnes (1969)
Pruitt and Drews (1969)
Pruitt and Johnson (1970)
Druckman, Zechmeister and Solomon (1972)
Tjosvold (1974)

DISTRIBUTION GAMES + ROLE-PLAYING DEBATES

Tasks of Type 3
Bartos (1966)
Bartos (1967, 1970)

ROLE-PLAYING DEBATES

Tasks of Type 2
Johnson (1967)
Morley and Stephenson (1969)
Smith (1969)
Johnson and Dustin (1970)
Karass (1970)
Morley and Stephenson (1970a, 1970b)
Lifshitz (1971)
Short (1971a)
Short (1971b)
Short (1971c, 1974)
Smith (1971)
Frey and Adams (1972)
Short (1973)

Tasks of Type 3
Campbell (1960)
Manheim (1960)
Crow (1963)
Bass (1966)
Druckman (1967)
Evan and MacDougall (1967)
Vidmar and McGrath (1967); Vidmar (1971)
Druckman (1968)
Hermann and Kogan (1968)
Johnson and Lewicki (1969)
Porat (1969)
Podell and Knapp (1969)
Druckman and Zechmeister (1970)
Lamm and Kogan (1970)
Morris (1970)
Porat (1970)
Bonham (1971)
Klimoski (1972)
Kogan, Lamm and Trommsdorff (1972)
Lamm (1973)
Klimoski and Ash (1974)

SUBSTITUTE DEBATES

Tasks of Type 2
Julian and McGrath (1963); Fiedler (1967)
McGrath and Julian (1963)

Tasks of Type 3
Vidmar and McGrath (1965)

Figure 6.1 Experimental studies of negotiation groups

potential value of such analysis has, however, been confirmed by a number of observational studies (e.g. Guetzkow and Gyr 1954; Landsberger 1955a; Grace and Tandy 1957).

Task Type	DG	GEE	RPD	SD	DG+RPD
1	—	9	—	—	—
2	9	8	13	2	—
3	4	—	21	1	2

Figure 6.2 Frequency of use of different experimental tasks in sixty-nine studies of negotiation groups

Guetzkow and Gyr found that substantive conflict ended in a high degree of consensus when there was relatively little expression of 'self-oriented needs'; when the group's problem-solving activity was 'understandable, orderly, and focused on one issue at a time'; and when there was a 'genuinely pleasant atmosphere and the participants recognised the need for unified action' (pp. 373–81). Landsberger used Bales's IPA categories to analyse twelve labour–management negotiations settled with the help of a Government Mediation Agency (as described in Chapter 4). Apparently, the more successful the group the more closely it conformed to an idealised problem-solving sequence conceptualised in terms of IPA. Grace and Tandy used Bales's categories to analyse changes in the behaviour of the Soviet Delegation in the two years following the admission of the Soviet Union to the League of Nations (using English translations of speeches made to the General Assembly of the League). They concluded that 'changes in the tension of a group may be determined by analysing the communication of its representatives' (p. 97).

The category systems used in these studies were of course designed primarily for use with *problem-solving* groups. But negotiation groups are not problem-solving groups. As McGrath and Julian (1963) have pointed out, 'A negotiation task does not so much require the solving of a problem as it requires the resolving of conflicting goals. Thus, it would seem that the central problem in a negotiation session would not be so much the exchange and evaluation of problem-relevant information, as the flow of interpersonal influence and accompanying affect' (pp. 120–1). Moreover, since a number of the studies cited have used Bales's IPA categories, it is important to realise that IPA was originally conceived as 'a general purpose *supplement* to various other instruments and procedures that will be required for particular groups' (Bales 1950, p. v). At present the only other instruments specifically developed for use with negotiation groups are those due to Osterberg (1950), Julian and McGrath (1963) and Rackham (1972). These will be considered in more detail in Chapter 7.

SOME CAUTIONARY REMARKS

In Chapters 4, 5 and 6 we have attempted to provide a detailed review of experimental studies of bargaining (i.e. negotiation for agreement), distinguishing between different types of laboratory task. The length of the review is partly a reaction to the facts that, despite its importance for a genuinely *social* social psychology, basic texts have rarely dealt with the topic of negotiation at all (e.g. Insko and Schopler 1972; Stotland and Canon 1972; Wrightsman *et al.* 1972) and that when they have done so the treatment has been limited at its best (e.g. Hollander 1967; Sherif and Sherif 1969; Baron, Byrne and Griffitt 1974) and misleading at its worst (e.g. Secord and Backman 1974; Smith 1974). The length of the review also reflects the fact that it is difficult (and often misleading) to impose a simple structure upon research involving a number of different experimental tasks and a variety of experimental procedures. We have attempted to 'seek simplicity and distrust it' (Whitehead 1953), to report what has been established, and to indicate how much must remain speculation.

Three themes seem worthy of further consideration:

1 *The reliability of the research findings.* Briefly, most researchers have preferred to investigate new areas of research rather than to repeat previous studies. Indeed, given the classification of experimental tasks presented in Chapter 4, it can be seen that *only three studies have been replicated* and these only in part: some of Bass's (1966) findings (concerning preparation for negotiation) have been replicated by Druckman (1967, 1968); some of Porat's (1969) findings (concerning cultural differences) have been replicated by Porat (1970); and finally, some of Siegel and Fouraker's (1960) findings (concerning bilateral monopoly) have been replicated by Kelley (1964), Johnson and Cohen (1967) and Kelley and Schenitzki (1972).

2 *The generality of the research findings across different experimental procedures and/or different experimental tasks.* Bartos (1966, 1967, 1970) has presented data aggregated from a number of studies of the DG3 and RPD3 types. Otherwise, only four studies have attempted to establish the generality of given findings by using different experimental procedures and/or tasks (Vidmar 1971; Karass 1970; Holmes, Throop and Strickland 1971; Morley and Stephenson 1970a, 1970b). In particular, it must be noted that very few studies have involved the use of bargaining teams and that only Bartos has attempted to extend his findings beyond the two-person case.

3 *The generality of research findings across different subject populations.* Most research on bargaining has been conducted using university students as subjects, usually Americans and usually male. This may limit the generality of the experimental findings in (at least) two respects: (a) results may apply only to inexperienced and unskilled negotiators (Karass 1970); and (b)

many results may require modification to apply to UK or European populations (Porat 1969, 1970; Kelley *et al.* 1970).

Our purpose is not to decry experimental research but rather to indicate the amount of uncertainty involved. Very few studies have been replicated and very few problems have been studied in any real depth. Many conclusions emerge as the result of long and complicated arguments and, in any case, are often derived from a small range of negotiation tasks. At the moment there is a great deal of speculation about negotiation and very little evidence.

PART TWO

Interpersonal and Interparty Exchange:
A Research Programme

A

The Outcomes of Experimental Negotiations

Introduction

The second half of this book describes first an experimental programme which we initiated before having completed a comprehensive review of the literature. However, at its inception we were clearly aware of some of the limits of the experimental work that had been undertaken and, more importantly, familiar with the case study material in the work of Ann Douglas and of Walton and McKersie. In particular, that made us anxious not merely to repeat the existing experimental paradigms.

Let us be more specific. The use of simulation games seems to us a necessary and desirable feature of social psychological work in this area. The prospects of carrying out manipulative experimental work in real situations are negligible. Much can be learned from observing selected disputes, but not everything we wish to discover can be so learned. However, the acute lack of realism in much of the experimental work is obvious but apparently avoidable. Observation of negotiations in local industrial plants soon demonstrated to us that negotiation was not a mere exchange of offers, pursued until time was up and an agreement had to be hastily hatched. It was, in addition, about principles, pragmatics, personalities and the past. We realised that some such 'input' material must be included in any scenario we might use, for anything like a realistic debate to be produced.

Observation of a number of industrial disputes from the outset permitted us to devise more realistic scenarios without, we hope, swamping our subjects with too much detail to master in the time available. It also taught us a lesson that subsequently provided the basis of our experimental manipulations. It taught us that one side frequently has a stronger and more compelling case than the other and, more importantly, that the party defending that case is not always victorious. In 'B. M. Workshops', for example, the unions actively connived in the downgrading of many of their members in a way most bystanders would have judged improbable if not infamous. Reading the background material of many role-playing debates, however, gives the impression of two equally powerful antagonists destined for deadlock, straight compromise or, given weariness on one side, unjust victory for one at the other's expense. The reason for this is not hard to find. Normally, only the initial demands of the respective parties are 'given', or if more information is provided this is of a neutral factual kind such as not to prejudice the outcome one way or the other. Historical attitudinal data of the kind needed to give subjects some 'fuel' for the dispute is difficult to provide without eliciting bias. Investigators anxious to avoid such asymmetry in their exercises have therefore tended to avoid providing such information. The consequence is that no side has been able to win by persuading the opposition that its stand has been justifiable. In brief, experimental work has failed to provide information relevant to any subprocesses of collective bargaining other than that of distributive bargaining (Walton and McKersie 1965).

This failure has another important and related consequence. Besides its practical importance, negotiation claims the attention of social psychologists because it highlights a pervasive conflict between individual needs and group allegiances. Role-playing material, however, by not providing sufficient material for discussion of the issues considerably lessens the prospects of a subject's becoming creatively involved in the dispute. In Douglas's terms, he may readily 'establish' the bargaining range, but his 'reconnaissance' will be severely curtailed because of the constraints imposed by the experimental material. Hence, argument is likely to remain firmly entrenched in the first 'representative' phase of negotiation until time pressures impose a swift exchange of offers to conclusion. Alternatively, a superficial exchange may lead to a ludicrously speedy resolution of the conflict.

In the experimental work which follows, an effort was made to write scenarios which would permit argument about the merits of the parties' respective positions and allow 'creative' solutions to be devised by bargainers prepared to throw off the representative mantle. In short, our scenarios were devised to allow both interparty and interpersonal considerations some influence on outcomes.

It remained to devise a means of examining the contribution from interparty and interpersonal sources. Our decision to use medium of communication (e.g. telephone *v.* face-to-face) owed most to the contrasting styles we had observed in two local plants. In 'B. M. Workshops' (see Chapter 9) rarely did one speaker interrupt another, and speech was slow and precise, approached the articulate and was invariably addressed to the chairman. By contrast, speech in the 'Demy Ltd' negotiation (reproduced in full in Chapter 12) was rapid, frequently interrupted and at times incoherent, proving a nightmare for successive transcribers. The ethos of the two establishments differed fundamentally for a variety of reasons, but at least we hoped that our manipulations of 'formality' by varying the physical conditions of communication would have a predictable effect on the balance of interpersonal and interparty considerations and hence on the outcomes of the negotiations.

Our review of studies on the process of negotiation (see Chapter 6) highlighted the dearth of adequate studies of social exchange between participants. Douglas's studies of four mediated disputes proved more illuminating than other more systematic studies. Above all else, she threw light on the role structure of negotiation by demonstrating that the identifiability of negotiators may undergo regular change as negotiations proceed to a successful conclusion. This important suggestion clearly needed further study, but it surprisingly escaped the notice of others who, following Douglas, had access to more extensive supplies of suitable data. Partly this resulted from too great a dependence on Bales's 'Interaction Process Analysis' as a tool for describing behaviour in negotiations. Our criticisms of this procedure stem largely from Bales's inability to throw light on interpersonal and interparty processes of exchange. We believed this deficiency to be sufficiently important to develop, from the beginning, an alternative category system for describing interaction in negotiations which would do greater justice to the complexity of debate. We hoped that this would help redress some areas of ignorance noted in our review of real negotiations, as well as throw light on how the outcomes of our role-playing debates were achieved by the participants in our experimental studies.

E

Chapter 7

Strength of Case and Medium of Communication

The Balance Between Personal and Party Forces

Experimental debates are laboratory simulations of collective bargaining situations. Consequently, as Morley and Stephenson (1970b) have put it, 'Negotiators must come to terms with the demands of representing their parties on the one hand, and maintaining a personal relationship with their opposite numbers on the other' (p. 20). In this view, the outcome of a negotiation is (at least partially) determined by the *balance* between these two sets of forces.

Similarly, Douglas (1957, 1962) has argued that it is important to distinguish between 'interpersonal' and 'interparty climates' in bargaining and that most differences between effective and ineffective negotiations concern the way in which Personal and Party considerations are reconciled. (Subsequently, the terms 'Personal' and 'Party' will be used in a technical sense to distinguish between interpersonal and intergroup aspects of conflict. In particular, 'Party' is used to refer to the organisation or group that a negotiator represents.) Both the style and outcomes of negotiations between representatives of groups will be affected by (a) the more general relationship between the Parties, and (b) the (Personal) relationships between the negotiators themselves, considered as members of a small task-oriented group (Morley and Stephenson 1970b; Stephenson 1971b).

THE IMPORTANCE OF THE RELATIONSHIP BETWEEN THE PARTIES

Certain tactics characteristic of 'hard' distributive bargaining are difficult to sustain where the dominant relationship between the Parties is what Harbison and Coleman (1951) have called 'joint action' or 'working harmony'. Walton and McKersie (1965) have pointed out that, 'as parties move from the competitive end to the cooperative end of the relationship spectrum, they tend to increasingly confine distributive bargaining to the areas of inherent conflict, e.g. economic items, and to expand the number of areas in which integrative bargaining occurs' (p. 203). Moreover, they have shown how negotiators may exploit a given relationship between the Parties in order to achieve distributive gains (pp. 256–8, 270–3). Conciliatory overtures may be rejected as inappropriate when the relationship between the Parties is one of 'armed truce' (Harbison and Coleman 1951); similarly, attempts to introduce competitive tactics into a co-operative setting may be made to appear irresponsible by a skilled negotiator.

An example from a transcript (prepared by us and reproduced in full in Chapter 12) of negotiation in a co-ownership plant ('Demy Ltd') will help to illustrate this latter point:

M1:   This, this turnup: I mean it is an embarrassment to us, in fact, not to have covered. This is manifestly obvious, because somewhere there has got to be some form of coverage. Two questions I could ask. The first is: Is this merely an attempt on your part to negotiate some price for this external to the agreement . . . ?

U1:   No.

M1:   Or not to do that at all?

U1:   No, we do not. We won't accept. We don't want to do it in any case. We just want bank holidays as bank holidays. We simply want the time off. We don't, we won't accept it. We don't want to accept it for £10 a day.

M1:   ?

U1:*   We don't want money for it. We don't want money for it. We don't want to do it. We never have wanted to do it, and we thought it was about time. We've been doing it now for about five years, and we thought it was about time we made a stand.

M1:   *How would you suggest then that we deal with this now, as a company? I mean, you're part of the community in this respect.*

Later, M1 was able to forestall an adjournment by again stressing that workers and management had joint responsibility for the running of the plant:

U2:   Well, can we have a little time to stew on this, and see what we feel, really feel, among ourselves?

M1:   (interrupting) Yes.

U2:   (to own side) What do you think?

U3:   Let's discuss it, and see if . . .

U2:   What do you say?

U: ?

M1:   No, no. I don't want anybody to . . . (Interruption) What we've got is a problem. I can't solve it alone. It does, in fact, concern you. It concerns all of us. You know, if we compare this lookout with. *Well it is in fact a matter of mutual concern.* There's no agreeing . . .

U1:   (interrupting) ?

M1:   We can't pretend it isn't.

THE IMPORTANCE OF THE RELATIONSHIP BETWEEN THE NEGOTIATORS THEMSELVES

A number of authors have emphasised the role that informal conferences can play in co-ordinating exchanges of concessions in formal negotiations (e.g. Douglas 1962; Iklé 1964; Peters 1955; Walton and McKersie 1965; Pruitt 1969). Pruitt (1969) has detailed some of the norms governing meetings of this sort: e.g. that what is said should remain secret; that if an agreement is reached it should be honoured in subsequent negotiations; and that a negotiator should speak truthfully in indicating areas of flexibility in his Party's position. He has observed that 'negotiators will engage in informal conferences only if they trust their opponent to adhere to these norms. Such trust often develops through experience with the opponent, though to some extent a recognition that he is a seasoned opponent can substitute for such experience' (p. 35). Some negotiations apparently consist *only* of informal conferences in which participants scrupulously observe a norm of honesty in their dealings with one another (Pruitt 1969), but such cases are rare. More typically, agreements are reached in informal conferences and subsequently ratified in public 'negotiations'; in this way negotiators can make allowances for the problems and aspirations of their opponents while boldly acting out their representative roles (Morley and Stephenson 1970b; Stephenson 1971a). Such 'collusive' relationships function to deal with the conflict between Personal and Party expectations by separating the interpersonal and intergroup aspects of the negotiation sessions. However, any relationship short of 'collusion' permits similar influences to appear actually at the bargaining table (Morley and Stephenson 1970b, pp. 28–9).

Institutional goals are not always independent of the relationship between negotiators. Iklé and Leites (1962) have used the term 'minimum disposition' to indicate that (a) a range of outcomes may be involved in a Party's minimum goal rather than a single point, and (b) these terms may not be known at the outset but formulated (perhaps vaguely) at the bargaining table. Stephenson (1971b) has reported that, in one instance he observed, 'the management negotiator deliberately did not exploit differences of opinion in the opposing side, beyond making a light-hearted jest. To have done so would have weakened the opposing chief's position to a degree that would have jeopardised agreement between the teams, *besides undermining the close relationship between the two leaders*' (p. 359). An emphasis on distributive bargaining would have required the management chief negotiator to exploit to the full the dissensus within the union team.

Under certain circumstances a negotiator may even raise his personal problems at the bargaining table. Some examples from the 'Demy Ltd' negotiation (see Chapter 12) may help to clarify the sort of thing we have in mind:

M1:   So far as I'm concerned this is entirely something new. I didn't know this document's existence. Number one. Perhaps I ought to have done, but I haven't been here long enough for it to register.

?:   Yeah.

M1:   *And so you've got me over a barrel on this, because I didn't* ..

U1:   (interrupting) Well that's the original . . .

M1:   (continues) *know of it.*

M1:   We, we employ, we employ all kinds of people, right?

U1:   Yeah.

M1:   For certain specific functions. And from within ourselves we try to cover all the needs that we've got. I'll still have the bloody need, whatever you do.

U1:   Yeah.

M1:   *But then I'm lumbered with it. I can't find a solution.*

Medium of Communication

Factors such as seating arrangements, size of group, medium of communication, etc. may be regarded as elements in a *system of communication* by which negotiations are conducted. Some systems of communication restrict the number of social cues that one person can transmit to another; others do not. Consequently, different systems of communication may be characterised in terms of a dimension of *formality–informality*, such that by definition the smaller the number of cues available the more formal the system of communication and vice versa. Other things being equal, a telephone link between negotiators would therefore be defined as more formal than a television link between them, since a great deal of nonverbal information which can be transmitted by television (e.g. facial expression, posture, gestures) cannot be transmitted by telephone.

But in general terms, how does the system of communication influence the process and outcome of a negotiation? Elsewhere we have suggested that, as cues are reduced by the character of the system of communication used, negotiators will tend increasingly to be concerned with their role as representatives rather than with developing (or maintaining) a Personal relationship with their opponents (Morley and Stephenson 1969, 1970b; Morley 1974). In detail, a number of factors would seem to be involved (Morley and Stephenson 1970b, pp. 24–6).

1 Other things being equal, people are likely to pay *more attention* to what they are saying and what is being said the *more formal* the system of communication used (Argyle 1969a, 1969b). Sinaiko's (1963) 'Summit II' conferees were given roles as representatives of nations that had formed a military alliance. They had to decide how much support could be levied

from member nations in response to an acute external threat. Secret instructions meant that each negotiator had to give as little as possible commensurate with the emergency. Sinaiko found that participants preferred to negotiate via telephone link rather than television because they were not then distracted by nonverbal cues. Thus, as cues are reduced by the character of the communication system involved, the content of arguments will become more salient and the speaker will be better able to state his case free of his opponents' influence and control.

2 Other things being equal, people are likely to develop *more Personal* (Argyle would say more 'intimate') relationships the *more informal* the system of communication used. Consequently, institutional goals are more likely to be modified by Personal considerations. Under these conditions: (a) any distress felt by an opponent in dealing with his 'concession dilemma' (Pruitt 1969) will be more apparent and harder to gainsay; (b) negotiators are more likely to be influenced by the norm of equality and to expect equal profit (compromise) outcomes (Nemeth 1970); and (c) considerations of *equality* are more likely to be reinforced by considerations of *equity*, since the more salient the Personal relationship between the negotiators the greater the likelihood that they will perceive their investments as equal (despite any asymmetry in Party positions).

Of course, other things are *not* always equal. The presence of an audience, for instance, may be one complicating factor. Indeed, in certain extreme cases negotiators may never progress beyond the presentation of prepared statements in which they 'get on the record a turgid edition of what they wish to say about themselves and their positions' (Douglas 1957, p. 76). Harold Macmillan (1969) has given a graphic description of some of the problems posed by the setting of the Geneva Summit Conference (July 1955) which it is worth quoting at length:

'The room in which we met filled me with horror the moment we entered it. The protagonists were sitting at tables drawn up in a rectangle; the space between them was about the size of a small boxing ring. But this arena was itself surrounded by rows of benches and seats which were provided, presumably, for the advisers, but seemed to be occupied by a crowd of interested onlookers. The walls were decorated with vast, somewhat confused frescoes depicting the end of the world, or the Battle of the Titans, or the Rape of the Sabines, or a mixture of all three. *I could conceive of no arrangements less likely to lead to intimate or useful negotiations* [our italics]. It was only when Heads of Government or Foreign Ministers met in a small room outside in a restricted meeting that any serious discussion could take place' (pp. 616–17).

Strength of Case

Negotiation is seldom, if ever, a symmetrical situation for the Parties involved, as Vidmar and McGrath (1965) have pointed out. As they have said, 'Symmetry, or lack of it, in the negotiation situation is contingent upon the broad relationship between the parties and the content of the particular issues' (p. 43). In other words, we can distinguish at least two sources of asymmetry in negotiation situations: *power* and *strength of case*. However, while asymmetry of the first type has been extensively studied (e.g. Raven and Kruglanski 1970; Gruder 1970), asymmetry of the second type does not seem to have been studied at all. This is surprising. Casual observation would suggest that people are often acutely aware of difficulties in arguments that they are asked to present, and variables such as strength of case would seem to be of fairly central importance in the study of certain forms of social influence.

Strength of Case and Medium of Communication

Other things being equal, the outcome of a negotiation will be affected both by negotiators' relative strengths of case and by the formality–informality of the system of communication used. The more *formal* the system of communication the greater the emphasis that will be placed upon Party considerations, and the greater the attention that will be paid to the content of the verbal exchange. The more *informal* the system of communication the greater the extent to which Party goals will be modified by Personal considerations, and the greater the likelihood that negotiators will reach compromise outcomes. We might say that strength of case is a Party investment which is increasingly ignored as the relationship between the individual negotiators becomes more salient. Consequently, we can predict that, other things being equal, *settlements in favour of the side with the stronger case will be positively associated with formality in the system of communication used.*

We tested this hypothesis using face-to-face and telephone communication systems in two-person negotiations [RPD2].

Reliability and Generality of Findings

At the beginning of the academic year 1968–9 the management of 'Demy Ltd' (to whom we have already referred) very generously gave us access to documentary material describing the history of certain wage negotiations which had previously taken place. We decided (with their permission) to use some of this material to provide the scenario for an experimental debate [RPD2].

Our first experiments were conducted within the context of a negative settlement range under conditions of incomplete-incomplete information.

The design of subsequent experiments was guided by the following considerations:

1 The 'Demy Ltd' scenario referred to a long-standing history of 'co-operation' (Walton and McKersie 1965, pp. 188–9) and 'joint action' (Harbison and Coleman 1951) between the two Parties (each shareholders in the company). For a settlement to be biased in favour of the side with the stronger case, the other would have to modify its resistance point in the direction of a less favourable outcome. Presumably, negotiators find it relatively less difficult to justify such concessions when they are aware of a stable interparty relationship of mutual co-operation and trust. It is of course never easy to justify concessions of this type (Oppenheim and Bayley 1970; Blake and Mouton 1961b, 1961d, 1962), but such problems of 'intra-organisational bargaining' are likely to be much more severe in other situations. If subjects were given a scenario which contained references to a more conflictful relationship between the Parties, they might see their role as requiring a more rigid and inflexible approach. Consequently, it was decided to conduct some experiments in which subjects were given *background information* describing wage negotiations conducted in something like an atmosphere of 'armed truce' (Harbison and Coleman 1951). Such a scenario was prepared using materials provided by the management of 'B. M. Workshops'.

2 Initially, it was decided to conduct negotiations under conditions of incomplete-incomplete information. However, according to Walton and McKersie (1965), 'The role of information or the lack of information is of such practical importance in distributive bargaining that it needs to be handled at the outset. It affects all other tactical operations' (p. 60). In particular, the effect of information may be to increase the likelihood of equal division in negotiations (Schelling 1960; Liebert *et al.* 1968) and consequently to decrease the likelihood of an interaction between strength of case and medium of communication. In some subsequent negotiations it was therefore decided to inform subjects of the location of their *opponent's minimum goal*.

3 It was also decided to conduct some negotiations within the context of a *positive settlement range*, so that subjects needed to modify only their target points in order to reach an agreement.

A System of Categories for Describing Behaviour in Negotiation Groups

Reasons for attempting a detailed analysis of the process of negotiation in experimental debates have already been given. However, we have not yet established the necessity for developing a *new* set of categories to accomplish that task. This problem will be discussed at length in Chapter 10. At this point we shall merely stress the desirability of using a set of categories specifically designed for use with negotiation (rather than problem-solving) groups. Two such category systems were already available but were rejected, very briefly for the following reasons (there were other reasons). Osterberg's (1950) system was rejected because only eight categories are defined and because a great deal of important communication seems to fall into the 'miscellaneous' category, e.g. original statements of position, concessions and so on. Julian and McGrath's (1963) system was rejected because 'messages' are coded only as 'positive', 'negative' or 'neutral'; more explicitly, each uninterrupted speech burst is coded in terms of both its 'affective' content (positive, negative, neutral) and its structuring function (procedural structuring, content structuring).

THE PROCESS AND OUTCOMES OF NEGOTIATION

One approach to the study of negotiating skill is to compare the content of 'successful' and 'unsuccessful' negotiations. The research of Julian and McGrath (1963) and McGrath and Julian (1963) suggests that a great deal can be accomplished even with very simple analyses. These studies are, however, the only ones which have used content analyses to relate the process of negotiation to the outcomes of negotiation. We therefore decided to develop a more refined set of categories and to use these (a) to explore the effects of medium of communication in more detail, and (b) to identify parameters of 'successful' and 'unsuccessful' performance.

THE PROCESS OF REAL LIFE NEGOTIATIONS

The studies of Landsberger (1955a, 1955b) remain the sole attempt to apply a category system to real negotiations. In his case the data were twelve mediations of deadlocked disputes categorised *in vivo* using Bales's (1950) 'Interaction Process Analysis'. Landsberger discovered that the more successful mediations corresponded more exactly to the idealised phase sequence described by Bales and Strodtbeck (1951) than did unsuccessful mediations. There are, it appears, some points of similarity between the progress of negotiations and problem-solving groups. However, negotiation groups do differ in fundamental respects from problem-solving groups, and there is good reason to believe that analyses using a specially designed category system will prove considerably more informative.

Chapter 8

The Impact of Formality: 'Demy Ltd' Negotiations

The major hypothesis tested in this research was that, *other things being equal, settlements in favour of the side with the stronger case will be positively associated with formality in the communication system used.* In the simplest case of two-person negotiations it was assumed that the major contribution to the formality–informality of the *system* of communication would be made by the *medium* of communication used. In particular, it was assumed that a *telephone* 'channel' would always be more formal than a *face-to-face* 'channel' in the two-person case. Accordingly, two experiments were designed to test the hypothesis that the side with the stronger case would be more successful when negotiations were conducted by telephone than when they were conducted face-to-face.

By definition, negotiators' freedom to interrupt also contributes to the formality–informality of any system of communication. It was therefore decided to test the additional hypothesis that *the side with the stronger case will be more successful when negotiations are conducted under 'constrained' conditions* (i.e. interruption *not* allowed) *than when they are conducted under 'free' conditions* (i.e. interruption allowed). However, it was assumed that the difference in formality between constrained and free conditions would be smaller than the difference in formality between telephone and face-to-face conditions, so that the effect of the constrained *v.* free manipulation was expected to be smaller than the effect of the telephone *v.* face-to-face manipulation.

Experiment I differed from Experiment II only in terms of the scenario used. Otherwise the procedures used were identical in the two cases.

Experiments I and II

PROCEDURE

Pairs of subjects were given fifteen minutes independently to read the background information to an industrial dispute, involving the introduction of a new wage agreement in a co-ownership chemical plant ('Demy Ltd'). Some specimen arguments from each side were provided, giving an initially stronger case to either the management representative (Experiment I, also reported briefly in Morley and Stephenson 1969, 1970b) or the union representative (Experiment II, also reported briefly in Morley and Stephenson 1970a, 1970b). Subjects were (randomly) assigned to roles after five minutes' reading time, and negotiations were conducted via more or less formal systems of communication. Subjects were asked to reach an agreement within thirty minutes and given target and resistance points defining a negative settlement range; that is, there was no wage which was (initially) minimally acceptable to both Parties. There was only one issue, but subjects were perfectly free to search for 'integrative solutions' if they so desired. If a contract had not been concluded after thirty minutes subjects were told that they would be given another five minutes in which to reach an agreement if they could. If an agreement had not been reached after forty minutes of negotiation time the experiment was terminated.

The formality–informality of the communication system used was manipulated experimentally by (a) varying the medium of communication, i.e. face-to-face *v.* telephone, and (b) restricting freedom to interrupt, i.e. free conversation *v.* constrained conversation. This gave four treatments, arranged in order of increasing formality as follows: face-to-face/free; face-to-face/constrained; telephone/free; telephone/constrained.

Outcomes were assessed in terms of the following seven-point scale:

1 = settlement between the target and resistance points of the side with the weaker case.
2 = settlement at the resistance point of the side with the weaker case.
3 = compromise settlement in favour of the side with the weaker case.
4 = compromise settlement in favour of the side with the stronger case.
5 = settlement at the resistance point of the side with the stronger case.
6 = settlement between the resistance and target points of the side with the stronger case.
7 = settlement equal to or greater than the initial target of the side with the stronger case.

SUBJECTS

Five two-person all-male groups were randomly assigned to each experimental treatment in each experiment. All but four of the pairs were composed of undergraduate students from the University of Nottingham. The remaining four pairs consisted of students from Trent Polytechnic (and all participated in Experiment II). Members of a pair were generally of the same age, but care was taken to avoid matching friends or acquaintances.

INITIAL INSTRUCTIONS

Subjects made their own way to the Department of Psychology and were taken to separate rooms. The experimenter then read the following instructions to each subject in turn:

'This is an experiment in industrial relations. The handout describes the background to a dispute. Please read it thoroughly, and later you will be asked to take a role in a mock negotiation with another person who will take the opposing role. You may make notes if you wish. Please now read the handout carefully. You will have fifteen minutes for this part of the exercise.'

Paper and pencil were provided so that subjects could make notes if they wished, and a stop-clock was placed in each room to remind subjects of the time available.

STRENGTH OF CASE

Strength of case was manipulated by means of the handouts given to the subjects. Each scenario included a number of specimen arguments which could be used in the subsequent debate. However, a deliberate attempt was made to bias the available arguments in favour of one side or the other: one of the subjects (the management representative in Experiment I and the union representative in Experiment II) could easily find material with which to defend his position; the other could not. Furthermore, the arguments (readily) available to the former subject were of a high quality, whereas (in our opinion) the arguments available to the latter were not.

Because strength of case was manipulated in this way it was necessary to use different scenarios for Experiments I and II.

Experiment I

THE NEGOTIATION TASK

Briefly, subjects were given three sides of foolscap describing a dispute which had arisen over the management's introduction of a new wage agreement. One issue remained outstanding: the method of payment for weekend overtime. The management had offered to pay 60% of the value of a full attendance for *any* such callout, but this offer had been rejected by the workers who were demanding 100%. The scenario used is reprinted in full below.

SCENARIO USED IN EXPERIMENT I

Demy Ltd is a co-ownership company

A dispute has arisen over the introduction by the management of a consolidated wage agreement, whereby:

1 The minimum basic weekly wage is increased substantially, but equally across all grades, so that the percentage increase is lower on the higher grades.
2 Payment for midweek overtime is abolished, and incidental midweek overtime is consolidated within the weekly wage.
3 Uniform payments are made across all grades for weekend overtime, i.e. separated from basic pay.

Arguments in favour of the new proposals, as stated by the management

1 Overtime has many social costs and should be avoided as far as possible.
2 The proposals represent a desirable movement towards a salary structure for all employees; this enhances security and individual responsibility.
3 The new proposals make the basic rates of pay more competitive in so far as attracting good labour is concerned.
4 The 'earnings gap' between the highest and lowest paid workers is reduced.

In addition, it was generally recognised that the amount of overtime worked would be reduced dramatically, with possibly a corresponding increase in efficiency during normal working hours.

In presenting the proposals for consideration by the workers' representatives, the Personnel Manager prepared a written statement setting out the general management proposals, costs and factory wage proposals, as follows.

General management proposals

The table below outlines the wages proposals. These include a substantial increase in the minimum weekly basic rates with approximately the same increase to all rates, making the percentage increase smaller on the higher rates. Thus the value of the shift differential has not been increased. Midweek overtime payments have been abolished, and at weekends the principle is established of a uniform payment for a half or full attendance. It is claimed that the abolition of separate payments for midweek overtime will help to control the 'earnings gap' (between the lowest and highest paid members of Demy Ltd) and will place more responsibility on the individual for the organisation of his work. By these means job satisfaction is enhanced and the opportunity is provided for fuller participation in pursuit of the shared wider goals of the community as a whole.

Whereas the previous system of weekend overtime premium payments exacerbated wage differentials, the new proposals for a uniform fixed payment contribute to the control of the earnings gap. In addition, these proposals ensure the separation of overtime pay from the structure of basic pay; this means that any future percentage increase in basic pay will not be multiplied in overtime pay.

The final claim is that the proposals are the first basic step towards a salary structure for the factory as a whole. The proposals introduce uniformity of treatment, if not of salaries, in the pay of members of Demy Ltd.

Costs

The additional costs of these proposals cannot, it is claimed, be predicted with any accuracy. This is because one of the objects of the proposals is to reduce the amount of overtime worked and because the new system might be abused. The proposals involve new responsibilities for all, and these might be shirked, in which case costs might substantially increase. It is suggested that it is not meaningful to apply the proposals to the existing pattern of time worked. However, until the proposals are put into effect and it is seen how people respond to the challenges and responsibilities inherent in the new system, the only estimate of costs which *can* be made is on the basis of existing patterns of time worked. Such estimates indicate that the additional cost would involve a percentage increase of between 5% and 6% on the wages bill for the persons covered by the proposals.

FACTORY WAGE PROPOSALS

Dayworkers: basic rates

Chargehand	£19. 9. 0
Grade 1A	£18. 7. 0
Grade 1B	£17. 12. 0
Grade 2A	£17. 0. 0

Dayworkers: overtime

Present method of paying overtime replaced by:
£4. 19. 6 for one full attendance on Saturdays or Sundays.
£2. 9. 9 for one half attendance of up to 4 hours on Saturdays or Sundays.
Incidental midweek overtime consolidated within basic weekly wage.

Three-shift system: basic rates

Chargehand	£22. 14. 4
Leading hand	£21. 13. 4
Grade 1A	£20. 12. 4
Grade 1B	£19. 17. 4
Grade 2A	£18. 5. 4

Three-shift system: overtime

Present method of paying overtime replaced by:
£6. 9. 3 for one full attendance on Saturdays or Sundays.
£3. 4. 8 for one half attendance on Saturdays or Sundays.
Incidental midweek overtime consolidated within basic weekly wage.

The workers' reaction

This was generally favourable, although many points of detail had to be ironed out. There were in addition a number of jealousies between different groups over relative remuneration. These, however, culminated in an agreement to accept the new basic weekly rates but to press for a change in the method of payment for weekend overtime. The unanimous suggestion of the workers' representatives was that no distinction be made between a half and full attendance and that the full rate be paid for any attendance, no matter how long, on a Saturday or Sunday. It was argued that, by and large, any weekend attendance was equally inconvenient, whatever the length: Demy Ltd was situated five to six miles from the nearest town and was inaccessible by bus. Consequently, workers needed to provide their own transport. Craftsmen were most likely to be 'called out' at weekends, thus qualifying for overtime, and in addition to the inconvenience involved their job necessitated that they install a telephone at their own expense. Payment of the full rate for *any* overtime therefore seemed no more than adequate remuneration for the costs involved.

Furthermore, the workers generally resented the management suggestion that they might abuse the new payment scheme. This reflected a lack of trust quite incongruent with Demy Ltd's stated co-ownership principle and led to the suspicion that the management had overestimated the costs to it of the new pay structure. Moreover, the management proposals stated both (a) that one management aim was to reduce the total amount of overtime worked, and (b) that their best estimate of the costs of the scheme was based on existing overtime worked. Therefore if overtime *was* reduced, the management estimate of the costs involved, of between 5% and 6% increase, must be an exaggerated one.

The management, for their part, rejected the proposal of the workers' representatives on the grounds that it would increase the total cost of the proposals to an unacceptably high level. They suggested either (a) that the proposals as they stood be accepted, or (b) that no distinction be made between half and full payments but that a figure of 60% of the full rate be paid for each attendance; that is, dayworkers would receive their basic wage, with 60% of £4. 19. 6 (= £2. 19. 8) for every weekend overtime attendance, instead of £2. 9. 9 for a half attendance and £4. 19. 6 for a full attendance. Although it was not possible to calculate how many attendances would be half and how many full, on the basis of past weekend overtime worked it was estimated that the costs of these two alternative management proposals would be roughly the same.

The workers rejected this alternative offer, still on the grounds that a half attendance was equally inconvenient and deserved the same reward as a full attendance. They proposed that their union representative in the firm, Mr X, be allowed to discuss the matter with Mr Y, the Personnel Manager, and that any agreement reached by them be binding on both sides. This was accepted by the Board as being a satisfactory arrangement.

After five minutes of reading time subjects were assigned to roles as management or union representatives. Each management representative was given the following written instructions:

'You are to take the role of Mr Y, the Personnel Manager. You are distressed by this open disagreement. On the other hand, you fear that Mr X may take this opportunity to reassert the authority of the union, which you do not think is desirable or necessary in a co-ownership company like Demy Ltd. The Board are very anxious to avoid a settlement above the figure of 70% of the full attendance (i.e. £3. 9. 8). You will be given half an hour to reach agreement with the opposing side. First, however, will you please read again the background to the dispute at Demy Ltd, and will you please let the experimenter know when you are ready to begin negotiating.'

Each union representative was given the following written instructions:

'You are to take the role of Mr X, the union representative. The union has long been defunct in Demy Ltd, and you see this dispute as a chance to reassert the union's authority, despite the history of good relations and the co-ownership principle. The union cannot possibly afford a strike. You know that the rank and file would be happy with 80% of the full attendance rate (£4. 19. 7), but you would like to exceed that figure. You will be given half an hour to reach agreement with the opposing side. First, however, will you please read again the background to the dispute at Demy Ltd, and will you please let the experimenter know when you are ready to begin negotiating.'

Experiment II

THE NEGOTIATION TASK

Once again, subjects were given three sides of foolscap describing a dispute which had arisen over the introduction of a new wage agreement, although on this occasion the initiative for the change came from the union rather than the management. The introduction of the new scheme would mean certain financial savings for the management. Subjects were required to decide what percentage of the savings should be distributed among the workforce in the form of increases in basic pay. The union had demanded that 100% of the savings be distributed in this way; the management had offered 70%. The scenario used is given below.

SCENARIO USED IN EXPERIMENT II

Demy Ltd is a co-ownership company

There is only one union – Amalgamated Workers – at Demy Ltd. Everyone at Demy Ltd – whether they belong to the management or the union – holds shares in the company, and there is a long tradition of co-operation between the management and union in determining major aspects of company policy. Demy Ltd is a small but successful company, with a payroll of 1,500 (managers and workers) employed in the manufacture of plastics and resins for the chemical and paints industries.

A dispute has arisen over a proposal by the union to introduce a consolidated wage agreement, whereby:

1 The minimum basic weekly wage is increased substantially, but equally across all grades, so that the percentage increase is lower on the higher grades.
2 Payment for incidental midweek overtime is abolished and is instead consolidated within the weekly wage.
3 Uniform payments are made across all grades for weekend overtime, i.e. separated from basic pay.

Arguments in favour of the new proposals, as stated by the union

1 Overtime has many leisure time and family consequences and should be avoided as far as possible.
2 The proposals represent a desirable movement towards a salary structure for all employees; this enhances security and individual responsibility.
3 The 'earnings gap' between the highest and the lowest paid would be reduced (because of the effects of proposals (1), (2) and (3) above).

Initial response of the management to the union proposals

The initial management response was favourable. In accepting the union's initiative, they stressed the advantages that they would expect to accrue to the management from implementing the scheme:

1 The amount of overtime worked should be reduced dramatically, with a corresponding increase in efficiency during normal working hours (the implication being that previously overtime had been created artificially by workpeople).
2 More responsibility would be placed on the individual worker for the organisation of his own work. This should increase job satisfaction and hence his productivity.

The working party proposals

The union next initiated the establishment of a working party, comprising equal numbers of management and union representatives, to establish by how much the weekly wage should be increased to compensate workers for the loss of incidental midweek overtime.

On the basis of costs for the previous year and estimated savings from the introduction of the new scheme, the working party unanimously proposed the following increases in basic pay, given by distributing the whole (100%) of the savings among the workpeople, and a new method of standard (increased) payments for weekend overtime:

FACTORY WAGE PROPOSALS

Dayworkers: basic rates

	Old	New
Chargehand	£18. 10. 0	£21. 0. 0
Grade 1A	£17. 19. 0	£19. 19. 0
Grade 1B	£16. 14. 0	£19. 4. 0
Grade 2A	£16. 3. 0	£18. 13. 0

Dayworkers: overtime
Present method of paying overtime replaced by:
  £4. 19. 6 for one full attendance on Saturdays or Sundays.
  £2. 9. 9 for one half attendance on Saturdays or Sundays.
  Incidental midweek overtime consolidated within new basic weekly wage.

Three-shift system: basic rates

	Old	New
Chargehand	£21. 11. 0	£24. 1. 0
Leading hand	£20. 12. 0	£23. 2. 0
Grade 1A	£19. 12. 0	£22. 2. 0
Grade 1B	£18. 18. 0	£21. 8. 0
Grade 2A	£17. 8. 0	£19. 18. 0

Three-shift system: overtime
Present method of paying overtime replaced by:
  £6. 9. 3 for one full attendance on Saturdays or Sundays.
  £3. 4. 8 for one half attendance on Saturdays or Sundays.
  Incidental midweek overtime consolidated within new basic weekly wage.

The Board's response to the working party's proposals

The Board now claimed that, although the working party contained representatives of the management, the proposed increase could not be accepted without further discussion. The financial effects of the new proposals could not, they claimed, be predicted with sufficient accuracy. This was because one of the objects of the new system was to reduce the amount of overtime worked and because the workers might abuse the new system. The proposals involved new responsibilities for all, and these might be shirked, in which case costs might substantially increase. The Board went on to suggest that, until the proposals were put into effect and it was seen how people reacted to the challenges and responsibilities inherent in the new system, the increase in basic pay be limited to 70% of the savings until one year had elapsed, when the situation could be reviewed.

The union's reaction to the Board's proposal

The union objected strongly to the Board's proposal on two main grounds:

1 The arguments used by the Board indicated a shameful lack of trust in the workpeople at Demy Ltd, particularly in view of the history of co-operation in this successful co-ownership company.
2 That the union had taken the initiative in proposing the change to a more desirable system of work organisation was in itself indicative of their sense of responsibility to the firm and inconsistent with the Board's implicit charge of opportunism and calculation.

On both these grounds and the fact that the working party's proposals were unanimously agreed by both the management and union representatives, the union stated that a figure of 70% was unacceptable. However, the union agreed that their convenor, Mr X, discuss the matter with Mr Y, the Personnel Manager, and that any agreement reached by them be binding on both sides.

For your information

Translated into cash in hand, the various outcomes of this negotiation (here listed only from 70% to 100%) mean that the new basic wages of dayworkers would be:

		Dayworkers		
	Chargehand	*Grade 1A*	*Grade 1B*	*Grade 2A*
Old	18. 10. 0	17. 19. 0	16. 14. 0	16. 3. 0
New				
100%	21. 0. 0	19. 19. 0	19. 4. 0	18. 13. 0
99%	20. 19. 6	19. 18. 6	19. 3. 6	18. 12. 6
98%	20. 19. 0	19. 18. 0	19. 3. 0	18. 12. 0
97%	20. 18. 6	19. 17. 6	19. 2. 6	18. 11. 6
96%	20. 18. 0	19. 17. 0	19. 2. 0	18. 11. 0
95%	20. 17. 6	19. 16. 6	19. 1. 6	18. 10. 6
94%	20. 17. 0	19. 16. 0	19. 1. 0	18. 10. 0
93%	20. 16. 6	19. 15. 6	19. 0. 6	18. 9. 6
92%	20. 16. 0	19. 15. 0	19. 0. 0	18. 9. 0
91%	20. 15. 6	19. 14. 6	18. 19. 6	18. 8. 6
90%	20. 15. 0	19. 14. 0	18. 19. 0	18. 8. 0
89%	20. 14. 6	19. 13. 6	18. 18. 6	18. 7. 6
88%	20. 14. 0	19. 13. 0	18. 18. 0	18. 7. 0

| | Chargehand | Dayworkers | | |
		Grade 1A	Grade 1B	Grade 2A
Old	18. 10. 0	17. 19. 0	16. 14. 0	16. 3. 0
New				
87%	20. 13. 6	19. 12. 6	18. 17. 6	18. 6. 6
86%	20. 13. 0	19. 12. 0	18. 17. 0	18. 6. 0
85%	20. 12. 6	19. 11. 6	18. 16. 6	18. 5. 6
84%	20. 12. 0	19. 11. 0	18. 16. 0	18. 5. 0
83%	20. 11. 6	19. 10. 6	18. 15. 6	18. 4. 6
82%	20. 11. 0	19. 10. 0	18. 15. 0	18. 4. 0
81%	20. 10. 6	19. 9. 6	18. 14. 6	18. 3. 6
80%	20. 10. 0	19. 9. 0	18. 14. 0	18. 3. 0
79%	20. 9. 6	19. 8. 6	18. 13. 6	18. 2. 6
78%	20. 9. 0	19. 8. 0	18. 13. 0	18. 2. 0
77%	20. 8. 6	19. 7. 6	18. 12. 6	18. 1. 6
76%	20. 8. 0	19. 7. 0	18. 12. 0	18. 1. 0
75%	20. 7. 6	19. 6. 6	18. 11. 6	18. 0. 6
74%	20. 7. 0	19. 6. 0	18. 11. 0	18. 0. 0
73%	20. 6. 6	19. 5. 6	18. 10. 6	17. 19. 6
72%	20. 6. 0	19. 5. 0	18. 10. 0	17. 19. 0
71%	20. 5. 6	19. 4. 6	18. 9. 6	17. 18. 6
70%	20. 5. 0	19. 4. 0	18. 9. 0	17. 18. 0

PRENEGOTIATION INSTRUCTIONS

Again subjects were assigned to roles as management or union representatives after five minutes of reading time. Each management representative was given the following written instructions:

'You are to take the role of Mr Y, the Personnel Manager. The Board have made it quite clear that you must not permit a strike to develop. Within the limits of this constraint they would be most happy to secure an outcome of 70% and very unwilling to go above 80%.

'The accompanying document lists the cash-in-hand values of various settlement points. You have a further ten minutes before the negotiation begins.'

Each union representative was given the following written instructions:

'You are to take the role of Mr X, the union convenor, and you see your negotiating assignment as being to see that the whole (100%) of the savings are consolidated onto the basic wage. You realise that your members would be most unhappy with a figure of less than 90%. The accompanying document lists the cash-in-hand values of various settlement points.

'You have a further ten minutes before negotiation begins, and you are asked to consider the following in support of your case:

1 The management representatives on the working party agreed that the

working party could (and did) make a *conservative* estimate of the increase in productivity to be expected from the new proposals. It is only fair to let the workpeople as well as the management benefit from this.

2 Since the estimate is *agreed* to be conservative, the union is asking for the whole of the estimated savings to be consolidated onto the basic wage.

3 It should also be remembered that the union members generally live five or six miles from the factory and have to provide their own transport. Dissatisfaction with this situation is likely to be aroused if the Board does not accept the working party's proposals.

4 In view of the unanimity of the working party, one can only suspect the Board's motives in refusing to grant this increase. Should this feeling grow, productivity would almost certainly *drop* now.

5 Until the last Board meeting it had been tacitly assumed that the whole (100%) of the savings would be consolidated.'

It was hoped that these instructions would reinforce the strength of case manipulation contained in the handout.

SUBJECTS' PERCEPTIONS OF STRENGTH OF CASE

Two sorts of evidence are available:

1 Almost all subjects made some comments about the strength or weakness of their case when roles were assigned by the experimenter. These were always in line with the experimental induction.

2 Subjects were asked for their written comments about any difficulties they had encountered in taking the roles of Mr X or Mr Y. In general, these confirmed the success of the experimental induction (although subjects often confined their attention to more technical information about the adequacy of the scenarios involved). Unfortunately, no more systematic evidence was obtained.

Experiments I and II

MEDIUM OF COMMUNICATION

During negotiations, subjects in face-to-face groups sat directly opposite one another at a medium-sized table, approximately 5 × 3 feet in size. Subjects in telephone groups communicated by a microphone/headphone combination which gave reception of a quite acceptable quality.

Subjects in face-to-face/constrained groups were given the following verbal instructions:

'Mr X, this is Mr Y. Will you sit down here please? (Indicates seat.) You will each be allowed to talk without interruption, until you have had your say. When you have finished speaking you are to say, in each case, "Now it's your turn," and until you have said this the other is not allowed to make his reply. When you, Mr X, are speaking, Mr Y may not reply until you have said, "Now it's your turn," to him. And when you, Mr Y, are speaking, Mr X may not reply until you have said, "Now it's your turn," to him. Do you both understand? May I remind you that you have half an hour to reach agreement. I shall be recording the conversation in the next room. Thank you. Now you can begin.'

Subjects in telephone/constrained groups were given the following verbal instructions in Experiment I:

'When you put on these headphones you will be able to hear Mr X/Y. When you speak into the microphone he will be able to hear you. You are to begin the negotiation by calling Mr X/Y. You will each be allowed to talk without interruption until you have had your say. When you have finished speaking you are to say, in each case, "Now it's your turn," and until you have said this Mr X/Y will not be allowed to reply. Similarly, when Mr X/Y is speaking you are not to interrupt, and are not to reply until Mr X/Y has said, "Now it's your turn." Do you understand? May I remind you that you have half an hour to reach agreement. I shall be recording the conversation from the next room, so would you mind speaking with the microphone fairly close to your mouth. Thank you. Now you can begin by calling up Mr X/Y.'

Similar instructions were given to subjects in telephone/constrained groups in Experiment II. However, in this case the constraint was a mechanical one, involving a one-way channel of communication. When a subject said 'Now it's your turn,' he had to press a button giving control of the channel of communication to his opponent. Until that button was pressed anything said by his opponent would simply not be received.

ASSESSMENT OF OUTCOMES

The use of an ordinal scale of the sort described reflected two main considerations:

1 It recognised Walton and McKersie's (1965) contention that negotiators' SEU functions are nonlinear and allowed outcomes to be assessed in a way which took this into account (Chapter 2). Negotiators' target and resistance points were given special prominence in the analysis.
2 It allowed account to be taken of 'integrative' solutions. For example, in

Experiment II an outcome of 80% was clearly less favourable to the union than an outcome of 80% *plus* a review *plus* a possibility of backpayment up to a value of 90%, and it was desirable to have a scoring procedure which took this into account.

It was decided that complex agreements would be scored according to the following rules:

1 Transform the percentage concerned into the corresponding scale value, e.g. 80% = 2.
2 Increase the scale value by one point if the agreement is to be reviewed at any time in the future, e.g. 80% *plus* review = 3.
3 Increase the scale value by a further one point if the possibility of backpayment is included in the agreement, e.g. 80% *plus* review *plus* a possibility of backpayment to a value of 90% = 4.

If other complex forms of agreement were obtained it was left to the scorer intuitively to decide whether to increase the scale value obtained in (1) by one or two points.

It was also desirable to be able to include all groups in any analysis, i.e. those which ended in deadlock as well as those which ended in agreement. If no agreement had been reached after forty minutes of negotiation time, 'settlements' were determined by taking the mean of subjects' final offers and transforming this into the appropriate scale value. Subjects did not know that this procedure would be followed.

Outcomes were scored by the experimenters. Each settlement was written out fully on a single sheet of paper and assessed 'blindly' by two independent judges. One of the judges agreed with the experimenters in 39/40 cases; the other in 38/40 cases. Disagreement was resolved by assigning that scale value least favourable to the main hypothesis under test.

RESULTS

Outcomes of negotiations

Results from Experiment I (management-strong case) and Experiment II (union-strong case) are presented in Figures 8.1 and 8.2 respectively. In all analyses in this chapter Mann-Whitney U was used to test the statistical significance of trends, unless otherwise stated.

Experiment I provided partial support for the hypotheses under test. The management was more successful in telephone groups than in face-to-face groups, although this trend was not statistically reliable. The management was also more successful in constrained groups than in free groups, and this trend was statistically reliable ($p < \cdot05$). Furthermore, the effect of the

	Face-to-face/ free	Face-to-face/ constrained	Telephone/ free	Telephone/ constrained
	4	4*	6	7
	5	5	3	6
	4	3*	6	4
	4	4	2	6
	1	6	2	6
Mean	3·6	4·4	3·8	5·8

*Denotes deadlock

Figure 8.1 Outcomes of negotiations in Experiment I (in scale points)

	Face-to-face/ free	Face-to-face/ constrained	Telephone/ free	Telephone/ constrained
	1	4	6	4
	3*	4	5	7
	4	3	5	3
	4	3	5	4*
	3*	4	5	5
Mean	3·0	3·6	5·2	4·6

*Denotes deadlock

Figure 8.2 Outcomes of negotiations in Experiment II (in scale points)

constrained *v.* free manipulation was larger than the effect of the telephone *v.* face-to-face manipulation. Finally, the management was *most* successful in the most formal (telephone/constrained) condition of the experiment and *least* successful in the least formal (face-to-face/free), and the difference between these two conditions was statistically reliable ($p < ·03$).

Experiment II provided further support for the hypotheses under test. The union was more successful in telephone groups than face-to-face groups ($p < ·01$), but equally successful in constrained and free groups. Finally, the union was *more* successful in the most formal (telephone/constrained) condition of the experiment than in the least formal (face-to-face/free), and the difference between these two conditions was statistically reliable ($p < ·05$). However, the union was *most* successful in the telephone/free condition and *least* successful in the face-to-face/constrained condition.

Combining the data from the two experiments provided a less complicated picture:

1 The side with the stronger case was more successful in telephone conditions than in face-to-face conditions ($p < ·01$).
2 The side with the stronger case was more successful in constrained conditions than in free conditions ($p < ·04$).

3 The effect of the telephone *v.* face-to-face manipulation was larger than the effect of the constrained *v.* free manipulation.
4 The side with the stronger case was most successful in the most formal (telephone/constrained) condition and least successful in the least formal (face-to-face/free) condition.

It can also be seen that 17/20 face-to-face groups reached agreements at outcome level 4 *or below*, whereas 16/20 telephone groups reached agreements at outcome level 4 *or above*. Similarly, 12/20 free groups reached agreements at outcome level 4 *or below*, whereas 16/20 constrained groups reached agreements at outcome level 4 *or above*.

Times to agreement

The times required to reach agreement in Experiments I and II are presented in Figures 8.3 and 8.4 respectively. The most obvious feature of these data was the similarity of the times taken by groups of subjects using different communication systems. Between groups there were no differences approaching statistical significance in either experiment (Kruskal-Wallis one-way analyses of variance).

	Face-to-face/ free	*Face-to-face/ constrained*	*Telephone/ free*	*Telephone/ constrained*
	19	40*	31	35
	35	32	19	28
	23	40*	28	33
	33	36	30	22
	32	16	35	29
Mean	28·4	32·8	28·6	29·4

*Denotes deadlock

Figure 8.3 Time required to reach agreement in Experiment I (in minutes)

	Face-to-face/ free	*Face-to-face/ constrained*	*Telephone/ free*	*Telephone/ constrained*
	30	37	38	40
	40*	37	18	24
	19	35	37	33
	34	29	38	40*
	40*	40	36	39
Mean	32·6	35·6	33·4	35·2

*Denotes deadlock

Figure 8.4 Time required to reach agreement in Experiment II (in minutes)

Time taken and value of agreement obtained

Values of Spearman's rank correlation coefficient (r_s) were calculated for the data of Experiments I and II separately, in order to determine whether there was a linear relationship between the time taken and the value of the agreements obtained. In Experiment I the value of r_s was $-\cdot17$ ($N = 20$), and in Experiment II the value of r_s was $-\cdot03$ ($N = 20$). These values were extremely small and not significantly different from zero.

DISCUSSION

These findings provided considerable support for the hypothesis that, other things being equal, outcomes in favour of the side with the stronger case will be positively associated with formality in the system of communication used. It is, however, important to note that different systems of communication can be more or less *restricted* as well as more or less *formal*. The effect of restricting the system of communication is to limit the amount of factual information which can be transmitted in a given time, whereas the effect of increasing the formality of the system of communication is to reduce the number of social cues available to the users. Several authors have compared the effects of using 'hard copy' *v.* 'oral' systems of communication in both problem-solving groups (Sinaiko 1963; Chapanis *et al.* 1972; Chapanis 1973) and negotiation groups (Sinaiko 1963; Smith 1969; Vitz and Kite 1970), but the experiments reported in this chapter represent the first attempts to manipulate the formality of a given system of communication without simultaneously restricting the amount of factual information which can be exchanged. In fact, the telephone condition is very slightly more restricted than the face-to-face condition (e.g. documentary material cannot be exchanged). Nonetheless, the constrained *v.* free manipulation affects *when* rather than *how much* factual information can be exchanged.

One way of making this contrast is to follow Morley and Stephenson (1970b) and say that the effect of formality in the system of communication is to *depersonalise* the conditions under which negotiation takes place. This terminology has the advantage of emphasising that (a) subjects may behave in different ways when different systems of communication are used, and (b) the same behaviour may have different effects in different situations. Morley and Stephenson (1970b) have argued that 'given a strong case it is advantageous to minimize the personal aspects of the relationship by whatever means are at one's disposal. That way, the chances of achieving a deserved victory are increased. Conversely, given a less easily justified case, it is advisable to emphasize the interpersonal aspects of the relationship, in terms of which it is possible to secure an agreement more favourable than the circumstances would otherwise permit' (p. 28). Subjects given the stronger case *may* have achieved greater success in telephone groups than in face-to-face groups (etc.)

because they adopted the strategies suggested by Morley and Stephenson. Alternatively, they may have behaved in the same sorts of ways in both telephone and face-to-face groups (etc.) but found that their behaviour had different consequences in different situations. These alternatives will be explored in more detail in Chapter 11.

One possibility can be excluded at this stage. The experiments provided no evidence to suggest that victories for the side with the stronger case were achieved against 'weak' personality types who preferred to reach rapid agreements rather than to discuss the issues involved. The great majority of subjects used nearly all the time at their disposal, and time taken was unrelated to the value of the agreements obtained.

A number of other investigators have used the role-playing debate paradigm to simulate union–management negotiations of one sort or another. Nine such studies have been reviewed in Chapters 4 and 6 (Campbell 1960 [RPD3]; Bass 1966 [RPD3]; Evan and MacDougall 1967 [RPD3]; Druckman 1967, 1968 [RPD3]; Podell and Knapp 1969 [RPD3]; Porat 1969, 1970 [RPD3]; Frey and Adams 1972 [RPD2]). It is, however, instructive to consider differences between the various tasks used in rather more detail.

Each task consists of a set of *profit tables* (defining it as Type 1, 2 or 3) and a *scenario* (defining it as a role-playing debate). Consequently, two tasks of the same type (e.g. Type 3) may differ in terms of the *amount* and *nature* of the information that subjects are required to assimilate. Presumably, the smaller the amount of information presented to subjects by the scenario, the greater the similarity between distribution games and role-playing debates using 'abstract' and 'interpreted' versions of the same profit tables. Bartos (1970), whose research has been described in Chapter 5, has commented that

'The so-called "abstract" experiments were designed to overcome some of the problems encountered when using the spoken design. Foremost among these was the tendency on the part of the subjects to forego argument in favour of the proposals they were endorsing and simply stating what these proposals were. Their reason was the feeling that verbal arguments were a waste of time. What really mattered they felt, was the payoff associated with a given proposal, not the lofty arguments used to defend it' (p. 51).

But Bartos (1966, 1970) gave his subjects *very little to argue about*. In other words, despite the use of the role-playing debate paradigm, his experimental materials were such that disagreement focused primarily upon outcomes to the exclusion of disagreement over inputs. Similar comments would apply to most of the experimental tasks used in the simulation of union–management negotiations (i.e. those used by Campbell 1960; Bass 1966; Druckman 1967, 1968; Podell and Knapp 1969; Porat 1969, 1970; Frey and Adams 1972).

Disagreement over inputs was, however, the *sine qua non* of the tasks used in Experiments I and II: it was intrinsic to the manipulation of strength of case.

Consequently, subjects were required to deal with more complex issues than are ordinarily involved in laboratory simulations of union–management negotiations. They were given a great deal to argue about and spent a great deal of time in argument. The negotiations involved an exchange of bids, but they involved a great deal more besides.

The manipulation of strength of case had two further advantages besides focusing disagreement upon inputs:

1 It recognised that negotiation is rarely a symmetrical situation for the two contending sides (Vidmar and McGrath 1965). Most experimental tasks contain biases of one sort or another (Campbell 1960; Bass 1966; Vidmar and McGrath 1965), a fact which will be obvious to anyone who has ever tried to write a scenario in which both sides are given an *equal* strength of case. Yet investigators using laboratory debates have made no attempt to specify sources of asymmetry in the materials given to their subjects. Furthermore, with the exception of Druckman and Zechmeister (1970) [RPD3], no investigators have attempted to manipulate the nature of the materials given to subjects. In Experiments I and II just such a specification was given in terms of strength of case.
2 It allowed us to say that a high *quality* settlement was one which favoured the side with the stronger case. From this point of view the quality of the agreements obtained was simply measured by the use of the ordinal scale which has already been described in this chapter.

It is interesting to contrast the procedures followed here with those of Campbell (1960) and Bass (1966). Campbell and Bass used relatively simple experimental materials ('Exercise Negotiations'), gave subjects information about wages in other local firms, and assessed wage agreements in terms of departure from the going rate. They made no attempt to consider possible sources of asymmetry in the experimental materials. In contrast, the material used in Experiments I and II was extremely complex and written to make more arguments (and better arguments) available to one side than to the other. Quality of agreement was then assessed in terms of the economic benefits given to the side with the stronger case.

The practical implications of these experiments have been discussed by Morley and Stephenson (1970b), Kingston (1970) and Stephenson (1971b). However, in each case the authors (very properly) have recognised that a great deal depended upon the reliability and generality of the results obtained. These issues will be considered in detail in Chapter 9.

Chapter 9

The Impact of Formality: Replication and Extension of 'Demy Ltd' Negotiations

Five experiments are reported in this chapter, each designed to test the generality of the interaction between strength of case and formality of communication system used (along the lines mapped out in Chapter 7). A more detailed presentation of this work has been given in Morley (1974).

Experiment III

This experiment was designed to investigate the observed interaction between strength of case and medium of communication:

1 Using different experimental materials (describing a very different industrial context).
2 Within the context of a positive settlement range as well as within the context of a negative one.
3 When subjects were given knowledge of their opponent's minimum goals as well as when they were not.

It was expected (a) that the previous findings would generalise to the context of a positive settlement range but (b) that the effects of formality and strength of case would be smaller when subjects were given knowledge of their opponent's minimum goals than when they were not.

PROCEDURE

The procedure followed was basically similar to that adopted in Experiments I and II. Pairs of subjects were this time given twenty minutes independently to read the background to a complex dispute involving management's introduction of a new wage agreement in 'B. M. Workshops', a small light-engineering firm. On this occasion, after ten minutes subjects were (randomly) assigned to roles and given target and resistance points which defined either compatible (CG) or incompatible (ICG) goals. Some subjects were given full knowledge of their opponents' minimum goals (K); others were given no information at all about their opponents' minimum goals (NK). Subjects were allowed to make notes if they wished and could retain their notes throughout the negotiations (along with the scenario provided by the experimenter). Negotiations were subsequently conducted in face-to-face/free (FF) or telephone/free (T) groups. Consequently, there were eight experimental treatments to which pairs of subjects were randomly assigned, as Figure 9.1

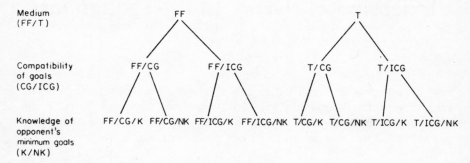

Figure 9.1 Experimental design showing details of eight conditions

shows. Subjects were given thirty minutes in which to reach an agreement, but if agreement had not been obtained in that time a further five minutes were allowed. Immediately negotiations had been completed, each representative was asked to rate his opponent in terms of thirty-six nine-point semantic differential scales. Once subjects' permission had been obtained, audio tape recordings were made of all negotiations, and face-to-face groups were filmed by video-tape recorder.

SUBJECTS

Subjects were students at the University of Nottingham. Undergraduate psychology students were excluded from participating in the experiment. Members of a pair were generally of the same age and were not previously acquainted with one another.

INITIAL INSTRUCTIONS

Subjects were taken to separate rooms in the Department of Psychology and given the following verbal instructions:

'This is an experiment in industrial relations. The handout describes the background to a dispute. Please read it thoroughly, and later you will be asked to take a role in a mock negotiation with another person who will take the opposing role. You may make notes if you wish. Please now read the handout carefully. You will have twenty minutes for this part of the exercise. You will be able to keep your notes and the handout provided throughout.'

Paper and pencil were provided, and a stop-clock was placed in each room.

THE NEGOTIATION TASK

It was intended that subjects perceive the union representative as having a stronger case than the management representative. Accordingly, the handout describing the dispute gave more and better-quality arguments to the union representative than to the management representative.

Briefly, the details of the dispute were as follows. For many years the workforce in 'B. M. Workshops' had been complaining that wages were well below those paid for similar work in other local firms (and nearly all the younger men had left to take up better-paid jobs elsewhere). Following sustained pressure by the union, the management had proposed a reorganisation of the workforce in which the supervisory structure was to be streamlined (by demoting fifty-one chargehands to the shopfloor). Basically, the dispute concerned the manner in which savings from the reorganisation were to be distributed as bonus between management and men. Management had offered to distribute 70% of the savings among the men, but this offer had been rejected by the union who were demanding 95%. Union representatives were given resistance points of 80% in CG conditions and 85% in ICG conditions. Management representatives were given resistance points of 85% in CG conditions and 80% in ICG conditions. The scenario given to subjects is shown below.

SCENARIO USED IN EXPERIMENTS III TO IV: CONTRACT NEGOTIATIONS: 'B. M. WORKSHOPS'

Background to the negotiations

B. M. Workshops form the core of B. M. Services, a government establishment (managed by civil servants) concerned to service and maintain a wide variety of public service vehicles. A production force of 300 skilled men have for many years been complaining that their wages fall well below those obtainable for similar work in 'outside industry', and indeed nearly all the younger men have left to take up better-paid jobs elsewhere. Following sustained pressure for increases in wages – from the AEF (the Amalgamated Engineering and Foundry Workers' Union, which represents over 90% of the production force) – the management have proposed a new wage agreement.

The management proposals

'That from 1 January 1970:

1 Regular overtime will *cease*, and overtime payment will be replaced by a company bonus, each man to be paid the same bonus whatever his grade.

(In those exceptional cases in which men will be asked to work overtime, they will be paid an overtime bonus at the 1969 rates: i.e. Monday to Friday $-1\frac{1}{2}$ × basic rate: weekends -2 × basic rate.)

2 The agreement will cover the period 1970–3 and be implemented in four yearly stages.

3 The supervisor force will be streamlined. At present the 300 production workers are supervised by 85 chargehands and 29 leading chargehands, so that there is approximately one supervisor for every three men. To streamline the supervisory force a single grade of supervisor will be set up at the leading chargehand level, and 63 leading chargehands will be created. The 29 men who are at present leading chargehands will keep their posts, and 34 of the 85 chargehands will be promoted. 51 chargehands will be demoted to reinforce the production force on the shopfloor but will be awarded £60 per man as a mark of their unique contribution. The savings from this reorganisation will form *part* of the company bonus (which will be calculated as set out below).

4 Standard performance times will be established for each job of work (being the time taken by a skilled operator working at *incentive* pace), and achievement will be assessed in terms of these times. One *standard hour* is one hour worked at *standard performance time*. The company bonus will be related to achievement (productivity) as follows. When the total number of *standard* hours worked in B. M. Workshops exceeds the total number of *clock* hours worked, the value of this 'excess' of production will be *added* to the value of the savings from reorganisation of the workforce. 70% of this combined total will be shared out between the production and supervisory force, each man receiving the same share regardless of his grade (as specified in (1)). Should the number of standard hours worked *not* exceed the number of clock hours worked, the value of this lost production will be *subtracted* from the savings given by reorganisation, and 70% of that total will be made available for distribution as company bonus.

5 Eighty days before the end of each stage the savings for *that* stage will be calculated and the bonus for the *next* stage paid accordingly. An *initial* bonus of £2 per man per forty-hour week will be paid during the first stage (January–December 1970).

6 Leading chargehands will be paid an additional bonus of $4\frac{1}{2}$d per hour.

7 Certain demarcation rules will be relaxed so that supervisors may be deployed in a more effective manner and their responsibility and status increased.

8 No redundancy will occur as a direct result of the agreement.'

The union's response to the management proposals

Mr X, the AEF convenor, obtained from the management a written statement to the effect that the new agreement was concerned only with *bonus* payments and would operate in conjunction with the results of national level bargaining concerning basic weekly wages. On behalf of the AEF Mr X accepted proposals (1), (2), (3), (6), (7) and (8) but *rejected* proposals (4) and (5). Mr X stated that his only aim was to secure for his members bonus payments comparable to those paid for similar work in other local firms (similarly, at a national level AEF leaders were arguing for basic weekly wages comparable to those given by private enterprise). Mr X submitted to the management a report compiled by IBC Ltd (International Business Consultants Ltd) giving details of the wages paid to skilled craftsmen in local light-engineering firms. Using data supplied by the management – at the request of the AEF – IBC Ltd also supplied a breakdown of the benefits to the management of the new agreement.

Summary of Report by IBC Ltd

1 *Weekly wage rates in local industry* (for work comparable to that done in B. M. Workshops)

	Basic	Overtime	Total
Wilson-Bell Motor Corporation			
Leading chargehand	£17. 15. 5	£4. 14. 0	£23. 9. 5
Chargehand	£17. 0. 0	£4. 5. 0	£21. 5. 0
Skilled hand	£15. 10. 8	£3. 18. 4	£19. 9. 0
Rowan-Fletcher Light Engineering Ltd			
Leading chargehand	£19. 0. 0	£5. 5. 0	£24. 5. 0
Chargehand	£18. 0. 0	£4. 11. 0	£22. 11. 0
Skilled hand	£16. 10. 0	£3. 11. 0	£20. 1. 0
B. M. Workshops			
Leading chargehand	£12. 10. 8	£3. 0. 0	£16. 10. 8
Chargehand	£13. 0. 8	£2. 15. 0	£15. 5. 8
Skilled hand	£12. 2. 0	£2. 10. 0	£14. 12. 0

2 *Analysis of new wage agreement*

(i)	Value of increase in production which will arise when the production force is reinforced by 51 men (the demoted chargehands)	£1,000. 0. 0
(ii)	Associated savings in weekly basic wage bill	£ 34. 17. 0
(iii)	Total weekly savings in overtime	£1,070. 0. 0
(1)		£2,104. 17. 0
(iv)	Cost per week of upgrading 34 chargehands	£ 63. 15. 0
(v)	Cost per week of leading chargehand bonus	£ 4. 10. 3
(2)		£ 68. 5. 3
(vi)	Total savings (1) − (2)	£2,036. 11. 9

Mr X pointed out that the bonus payments to the men were coming from *three* main sources:

(a) savings associated with the redeployment of the labour force;
(b) the elimination of overtime; and
(c) increased productivity.

He added that the contribution from (c) was likely to be small, since *standard* performance times were calculated from the performance of a skilled hand working at *incentive* pace. Mr X agreed that the bonus from (c) be shared out as suggested by the management (70% to the labour force, 30% to the management) and accepted that both management and workers could benefit from such an agreement. But the bulk of the *company bonus* would be paid for not by the savings from (c) but by the savings from (a) and (b). If the total savings listed above (i.e. £2,036. 11. 9) were shared *as proposed* (70% to the men, 30% to the management), each man would receive a bonus of £3. 3. 0 per week from that source alone. Mr X submitted the following table to the management:

Percentage of total savings available for distribution as bonus	*Bonus per man per week*
70%	£3. 3. 0
75%	£3. 7. 6
80%	£3. 12. 0
85%	£3. 16. 6
90%	£4. 1. 0
95%	£4. 5. 6
100%	£4. 10. 0

In rejecting proposals (4) and (5) Mr X noted that the men had asked for a wage increase. Even if they were given a bonus of £4. 10. 0 per week, this would not increase the management's costs at all. The increases in bonus payments would be largely accounted for by the reorganisation of the workforce; 51 chargehands would lose money in order that others might gain. The AEF accepted that the supervisory force *was* top-heavy and agreed to these changes, but argued that the management could both make their bonus payments comparable to those paid by other local firms and still decrease their present costs. In view of these considerations and in the light of the information submitted by IBC Ltd, the management proposals were quite unacceptable.

Mr X, on behalf of the AEF, proposed instead that 95% of the total savings be distributed as bonus payments and, in line with this, an initial payment of £4. 5. 6 be paid during the first year (January–December 1970).

As the union and management seemed otherwise unlikely to agree, it was accepted that Mr X should meet the Personnel Manager, Mr Y, in an attempt to break the deadlock and that any agreement reached by Mr X and Mr Y should be binding on both sides.

PRENEGOTIATION INSTRUCTIONS

After ten minutes of reading time subjects were (randomly) assigned to roles as management or union representatives. All union representatives received the following instructions:

'You are to take the role of Mr X, the AEF convenor, and you see your negotiating assignment as being to secure 95% of the total savings for distribution as bonus, and in line with this demand you would like a bonus of £4. 5. 6, to be paid during the first year (January–December 1970). You are very well aware of the fact that your members will be very dissatisfied with a settlement of less than 85%/80% (and a corresponding first-year bonus of £3. 16. 6/£3. 12. 0) and may regard you as having "sold out" to the management.'

All management representatives received the following instructions:

'You are to take the role of Mr Y, the Personnel Manager of B. M. Services. Top management have made it quite clear to you that (1) you must not permit a strike to develop; and (2) within the limits of this constraint they would be most happy to secure a settlement of 70% of the total savings' being distributed as bonus, and very unwilling to go above 80%/85%. They are very unwilling to pay a first-year bonus of more than £3. 12. 0.'

Union representatives given knowledge of their opponents' minimum goals received the additional information that:

'Mr Y has been instructed not to let a strike develop and within these limits would be most happy to secure a settlement of 70% and most unwilling to give above 80%/85%. Also, top management have indicated that they would be most unwilling to pay a first-year bonus in excess of £3. 16. 6. You have a further ten minutes before negotiation with Mr Y begins.'

Management representatives given knowledge of their opponents' minimum goals received the additional information that:

'Mr X would be most happy to secure a settlement of 95% for his members, and they may feel that he has "sold out" to management if he settles for less than 80%/85% (and a corresponding first-year bonus of £3. 12. 0/£3. 16. 6). You have a further ten minutes before negotiation with Mr X begins.'

Subjects who remained in ignorance of their opponents' minimum goals simply received the additional information that:

'You have a further ten minutes before negotiation with Mr X/Y begins.'

PERCEPTION OF STRENGTH OF CASE

How effective was the manipulation of strength of case? In order to answer this question, a total of twenty judges were given twenty minutes in which to read the scenario involved. They then rated 'the union case' and 'the management case' in terms of thirty-six semantic differential scales. Half the judges came from an *experimental* condition and half from a *classroom* condition (within each condition, half the judges began by rating the union case and half by rating the management case). In the experimental condition, ten genuine subjects were treated as if they were actually taking part in the experiment, but given twenty minutes of uninterrupted study; they were not assigned to roles and did not subsequently take part in negotiations (although they expected to do so). In the classroom condition, judges simply studied the handout for twenty minutes and then made their ratings; they neither subsequently took part in the experiment nor believed that they were acting as genuine subjects.

Figure 9.2 presents a summary of the results obtained. There were no significant differences between the experimental and classroom judges. The union case received a significantly higher score than the management case on 15/17 of the evaluative scales (A) and, furthermore, was seen as more *potent* (B) and more *active* (C) than the management case. In addition, while the union case was seen as more aggressive than the management case, it was seen as less hostile, less destructive and less obstructive than the management case (D).

By far the great majority of subjects who participated in this experiment spontaneously made comments in line with these ratings, and it seems safe to conclude that subjects perceived strength of case as intended by the experimenter.

MEDIUM OF COMMUNICATION

Subjects in face-to-face/free groups sat at adjacent sides of a medium-sized table, approximately 5×3 feet in size, facing a one-way mirror and about six feet from it. Pilot data obtained using the 'Demy Ltd' handout suggested that the change from face-to-face/opposite to face-to-face/side-by-side would not affect the outcomes of the negotiations. Outcomes in five face-to-face/opposite groups were 1, 5, 4, 4 and 4 scale points; outcomes in five face-to-face/side-by-side groups were 4, 3, 5, 4 and 4 scale points ($U = 12$, n.s.). Subjects knew that their negotiations were being filmed by a camera in the next room. Subjects in telephone/free groups negotiated via the microphone/headphone combination used for Experiments I and II.

ASSESSMENT OF OUTCOMES

Outcomes were assessed in terms of the following seven-point scale:

	Experimental		Classroom		$F(1,18)$	p
	U	M	U	M		
(A) Evaluative scales						
good–bad	7·1	4·6	7·0	4·2	28·7	<·001
like–dislike	6·0	3·5	5·7	4·0	16·4	<·001
superior–inferior	6·6	3·7	6·6	4·6	24·3	<·001
sociable–unsociable	5·4	4·7	5·7	4·7	11·8	<·01
safe–dangerous	5·4	4·5	5·5	4·8	5·1	<·05
trusting–untrusting	5·7	5·0	5·5	4·8	5·6	<·05
sweet–sour	5·2	4·4	5·2	4·6	9·8	<·025
successful–unsuccessful	6·4	4·2	6·2	4·5	24·6	<·001
pursuing–avoiding	6·6	5·5	6·4	5·6	6·4	<·025
lucid–obscure	7·4	4·7	7·4	5·8	33·0	<·001
explicit–implicit	7·3	5·7	6·8	5·6	11·0	<·025
influential–uninfluential	7·0	4·6	6·9	4·9	38·1	<·001
true–false	6·6	3·8	6·5	4·5	41·8	<·001
wise–foolish	6·7	4·1	6·5	4·3	86·4	<·001
fair–unfair	7·6	3·3	7·5	3·6	123·8	<·001
unselfish–selfish	5·0	4·0	4·6	3·8	3·1	n.s.
trustworthy–untrustworthy	5·7	5·0	5·7	5·6	1·2	n.s.
(B) Potency scales						
strong–weak	7·4	5·1	7·3	4·8	48·5	<·001
hard–soft	6·5	6·2	6·4	6·3	0·2	n.s.
large–small	5·5	5·4	5·6	5·3	1·6	n.s.
rugged–delicate	6·4	5·0	6·0	5·3	12·2	<·01
tenacious–yielding	6·5	6·0	6·6	6·4	0·8	n.s.
free–constrained	4·9	3·6	5·2	3·3	7·3	<·025
severe–lenient	5·6	6·1	5·7	6·1	1·6	n.s.
(C) Activity scales						
sharp–dull	6·9	5·1	6·6	5·3	13·2	<·01
hot–cold	4·9	3·8	5·1	3·9	13·2	<·01
active–passive	7·2	6·6	6·9	6·6	5·9	<·05
fast–slow	6·0	4·9	5·8	5·1	6·8	<·01
emotional–unemotional	5·2	4·5	5·0	4·3	1·5	n.s.
impulsive–deliberate	2·0	2·2	2·1	2·6	1·1	n.s.
(D) Other scales						
aggressive–defensive	6·5	4·0	6·0	3·9	18·8	<·001
hostile–friendly	4·3	6·3	5·2	6·0	11·1	<·01
competitive–co-operative	5·5	5·9	5·6	6·0	0·3	n.s.
destructive–productive	2·8	4·8	3·0	4·3	28·7	<·001
obstructive–helpful	3·8	5·7	3·9	5·5	19·9	<·001
masterful–subservient	6·1	6·0	5·7	5·9	0·0	n.s.

Figure 9.2 Mean ratings and statistical comparisons of 'the union case' and 'the management case' in 'B. M. Workshops' for two validating groups

1 = outcome between 70% and 80%.
2 = 80%.
3 = outcome between 80% and $82\frac{1}{2}$% (including $82\frac{1}{2}$%).
4 = outcome between $82\frac{1}{2}$% and 85%.
5 = outcome of 85%.
6 = outcome between 85% and 95%.
7 = outcome of 95% or above.

Outcomes were scored according to the rules described in Chapter 8.

RESULTS

Outcomes of negotiations

Outcomes of the negotiations are shown in Figures 9.3 and 9.4. Separate analyses were conducted of data from CG and ICG conditions. Unless otherwise stated, differences between treatments were tested by calculating the relevant values of the Mann–Whitney *U* statistic on differences between the mean ranks.

	Face-to-face			Telephone			
	Male	*Female*	*All*	*Male*	*Female*	*All*	
Knowledge	4·8	4·7	4·7	3·5	4·0	3·7	4·2
No knowledge	3·5	5·0	4·3	4·5	3·8	4·2	4·2
			4·5			4·0	

Figure 9.3 Mean outcomes of negotiations in Experiment III: incompatible goal conditions (in scale points)

When goals were incompatible the difference between F and T groups was in the *predicted direction only* in NK male-male groups, and even there the effect was not statistically reliable. There were no statistically reliable differences between male-male and female-female dyads in any of the four experimental treatments (Kruskal–Wallis $H = 9\cdot2$, *d.f.* = 7, *p* = n.s.).

On the other hand, when goals were compatible, union negotiators *did* achieve higher outcomes in T groups than in F groups (as can be seen from Figure 9.4), although the difference between treatments was not statistically reliable. However, this trend disguised an interaction between medium of communication and knowledge of opponent's minimum goal: in NK treatments union negotiators achieved higher outcomes in T groups than in F groups, but in K treatments they achieved the reverse. The same interaction, although not statistically significant, was present in both male-male groups

	Face-to-face			Telephone			
	Male	*Female*	*All*	*Male*	*Female*	*All*	
Knowledge	4·6	3·0	4·0	4·3	2·7	3·5	*3·8*
No knowledge	4·4	3·3	3·9	5·3	4·3	4·8	*4·3*
			3·9			4·2	

Figure 9.4 Mean outcomes of negotiations in Experiment III: compatible goal conditions (in scale points)

and female-female groups. Overall, union negotiators attained (non-significantly) higher outcomes in T groups than in F groups in both male-male and female-female dyads. There were no statistically significant differences between male-male and female-female dyads in any of the four experimental treatments (Kruskal–Wallis $H = ·47$, $d.f. = 7$, $p =$ n.s.).

Times to agreement

The times taken to reach agreement are presented in Figures 9.5 and 9.6. The shortest negotiation lasted thirteen minutes, but 48/61 cases used thirty minutes or more of the time available to them. Data from CG and ICG treatments were combined and Kruskal–Wallis analyses of variance computed for male-male and female-female dyads. For the male-male data a value of $H = 121·6$ was obtained, indicating that statistically significant differences existed between two or more of the eight experimental treatments ($d.f. = 7$, $p < ·001$). In fact, a significant value of H was obtained simply because subjects, not surprisingly, needed significantly less time ($p < ·025$) to reach agreement when their goals were compatible than when they were not. A nonsignificant value of $H = 12·1$ ($d.f. = 7$) was obtained from the female-female data.

Once again, there was no evidence to suggest that time to agreement was related to the value of the agreement obtained: when goals were compatible, r_s (male-male) $= ·17$ ($N = 16$) and r_s (female-female) $= ·05$ ($N = 13$); when goals

	Face-to-face			Telephone			
	Male	*Female*	*All*	*Male*	*Female*	*All*	
Knowledge	34·8	27·0	31·4	32·8	33·3	33·0	*32·2*
No knowledge	34·3	33·3	33·8	34·3	25·3	30·7	*32·1*
			32·7			31·6	

Figure 9.5 Mean time required to reach agreement in Experiment III: incompatible goal conditions (in minutes)

	Face-to-face			Telephone			
	Male	*Female*	*All*	*Male*	*Female*	*All*	
Knowledge	33·0	30·0	31·9	30·0	30·0	30·0	*31·1*
No knowledge	28·4	32·0	30·0	33·3	24·0	28·7	*29·5*
			30·9			*29·3*	

Figure 9.6 Mean time required to reach agreement in Experiment III: compatible goal conditions (in minutes)

were incompatible, r_s (male-male) $= -·02$ ($N = 18$) and r_s (female-female) $= -·23$ ($N = 14$). These values were small and not significantly different from zero.

Perceptions of opponent

Once negotiations had been completed, Mr Y was asked privately to rate Mr X and Mr X to rate Mr Y, in terms of the semantic differential scales shown in Figure 9.2. Separate analyses were conducted for X's ratings of Y (i.e. rating of the management negotiator by the union negotiator) and for Y's ratings of X (i.e. rating of the union negotiator by the management negotiator).

Generally, the perceptions of management negotiators were unaffected by the experimental treatments and determined almost entirely by the role that they were given to play. The perceptions of union negotiators, on the other hand, were affected by both role assignment and the independent variables of the experiment. Sixteen of the scales shown in Figure 9.2(A) provided a measure of other esteem. The scale explicit–implicit was not included; the measure of other esteem equalled the unweighted mean score obtained over the remaining scales. Medium of communication and compatibility of initial goals interacted to determine the esteem that X gave to Y, as shown in Figure 9.7. When goals were compatible X gave *less* esteem to Y in F groups than in T groups, but when goals were incompatible the reverse relationship applied. The interaction between formality and compatibility of goals was highly significant and also appeared at the level of some of the individual scales (e.g. sweet–sour, true–false, fair–unfair). In addition, when goals were compatible X saw Y as being harder, more emotional, more hostile and more obstructive in F groups than in T groups, but when goals were incompatible this relationship was reversed.

DISCUSSION

Experiments I and II, reported in Chapter 8, demonstrated that when male-male dyads were given incompatible goals and negotiated under conditions of incomplete-incomplete information, outcomes in favour of subjects given the

	FF/CG	T/CT	FF/ICG	T/ICT	F *ratio for interaction* (*FF/T × CG/ICG*)	p (*d.f. = 1,53*)
Other esteem	5·6	6·3	5·8	5·4	6·1	< ·02
Sweet	5·3	6·0	5·3	4·8	4·4	< ·04
Fair	5·8	7·3	6·3	5·6	4·3	< ·04
True	6·1	7·2	6·5	5·8	5·7	< ·02
Hard	4·8	4·0	4·6	5·3	4·2	< ·04
Emotional	3·7	3·2	3·1	4·6	4·4	< ·04
Hostile	3·6	2·5	2·9	4·3	10·2	< ·002
Obstructive	4·9	3·7	2·8	4·4	7·3	< ·01

Figure 9.7 Mean perceptions of management negotiators in four experimental treatments

stronger case were positively associated with formality in the system of communication used. In particular, subjects given the stronger case achieved higher outcomes in telephone/free groups than in face-to-face/free groups. A similar result was produced by the male-male ICG/NK dyads in Experiment III, but the difference between the treatments was not statistically reliable. Consequently, the findings of Experiments I and II were *not* reproduced in the data of Experiment III.

Several other (nonsignificant) trends in the data of Experiment III are worth comment, if only for the purposes of generating further hypotheses. It is clear that, in this experiment at least: (a) outcomes were more favourable to the union in T/CG/NK groups than in FF/CG/NK groups for both male-male and female-female dyads; and (b) the effect of information was to make outcomes more favourable to the union in FF groups than in T groups. In other words, the difference between FF and T outcomes was in the predicted direction when subjects negotiated under conditions of incomplete-incomplete information but in the opposite direction when they did not.

The most parsimonious interpretation of the data on person perception is that they reflected the findings that, treating the data as a whole, union negotiators achieved higher outcomes (and gave more esteem to their opponents) in FF/CG groups than in T/CG groups but, conversely, achieved higher outcomes (and gave more esteem to their opponents in T/ICG groups than in FF/ICG groups.

On the basis of these findings we would not be justified in extending the results of Experiments I and II beyond their original context. However, the handout describing the dispute at 'B. M. Workshops' differed from that describing the dispute at 'Demy Ltd' in two main respects: it not only described a different industrial context but also was (slightly) longer and dealt with a much more complicated dispute. It was felt that if subjects had been given more time to prepare for negotiation the predicted interaction between medium of communication and strength of case would have been obtained – at least in the ICG/NK treatment. Experiment IV was carried out to investigate this possibility. Some small changes were made in the instructions given to subjects, but, unless otherwise indicated, procedures were identical to those used in Experiment III.

Experiment IV

SUBJECTS

Subjects were forty male undergraduate students at the University of Hull.

PROCEDURE

Pairs of subjects, not previously acquainted with one another, were given thirty minutes independently to read the background to the dispute at 'B. M. Workshops'. After twenty minutes they were randomly allocated to roles as management or union representatives and given their negotiation assignments. Union representatives received the instructions used in Experiment III, namely:

'You are to take the role of Mr X, the AEF convenor, and you see your negotiating assignment as being to secure 95% of the total savings for distribution as bonus, and in line with this demand you would like a bonus of £4. 5. 6, to be paid during the first year (January–December 1970). You are very well aware of the fact that your members will be very dissatisfied with a settlement of less than 85% (and a corresponding first-year bonus of £3. 16. 6) and may regard you as having "sold out" to the management. You have a further ten minutes before negotiation with Mr Y begins.'

Management representatives received the following (modified) instructions:

'You are to take the role of Mr Y, the Personnel Manager of B. M. Services, and you see your negotiating assignment as being to secure a settlement of 70% of the total savings being distributed as bonus, and in line with this demand you would like a bonus of £3. 3. 0 to be paid during the first year (January–December 1970). You are very well aware of the fact that top management will be very dissatisfied with a settlement of more than 80% (and a corresponding first-year bonus of £3. 12. 0). You have a further ten minutes before negotiation with Mr X begins.'

(Each management representative was thus no longer told that he must not permit a strike to develop.) All subjects were assigned to the ICG/NK treatment and negotiated via face-to-face/free or telephone/free systems of communication.

RESULTS

As shown in Figure 9.8, union negotiators achieved significantly higher outcomes in telephone/free groups than in face-to-face/free groups ($U = 28.5$, $Z = 1.7$, $p < .05$, one-tailed test), thus confirming the results of Experiments I and II using different experimental materials. Furthermore, once again we can rule out the possibility that union victories were achieved against weak personality types because (a) the mean times to agreement were virtually identical in face-to-face and telephone groups, and (b) the correlation between the time taken and value of agreement obtained was extremely small and not significantly different from zero ($r_s = -.07$, $N = 20$).

Debriefing sessions revealed that 38/40 subjects perceived strength of case as intended by the experimenter.

DISCUSSION

Of the four experiments reported so far, two used the 'Demy Ltd' scenario and two the 'B. M. Workshops' scenario. In each case the subject given the stronger case in male-male groups obtained more favourable outcomes in the T/NK treatment than in the FF/NK treatment (and in 2/4 cases the obtained trends were statistically reliable). Apparently, the original findings reported in Experiments I and II were not restricted to the context of the 'Demy Ltd' negotiations.

However, the original findings of Experiments I and II were *reversed* in Experiment IV when subjects were given knowledge of their opponents' minimum goals (although in no case was the difference between FF/K and T/K treatments statistically reliable). It was decided to pursue this finding in the context of the 'Demy Ltd' scenario used in Experiment II. First, however, it was decided to investigate the effects of a slight change in the experimental materials given to subjects in Experiment II.

Union negotiators (given the stronger case) in Experiment II received some information which management negotiators did not. When assigned to roles they were asked to consider five additional points of information in support of their case; management negotiators were not given this information. But, since strength of case had been defined in terms of the nature of the information given to *both* subjects, it was important to investigate whether the effects obtained in Experiment II were due to *strength of case* or to *differences in the nature of the information given to the subjects concerned*. The latter possibility seemed unlikely in view of the results of Experiment IV (in which subjects were given *identical* information) but could not be dismissed lightly because, after all, the face-to-face *v.* telephone comparison was not

	Experiment IV			Experiment V			Experiment VI		
	FF/NK/ICG	T/NK/ICG	p	FF/NK/ICG	T/NK/ICG	p	FF/K/ICG	T/K/ICG	p
Mean outcomes of negotiations (scale points)	3·3	4·3	<·05	3·4	4·4	<·05	4·5	3·8	n.s.
Mean time to agreement (minutes)	30·8	29·6	n.s.	30·6	32·0	n.s.	29·8	30·4	n.s.

Figure 9.8 Outcomes of negotiations and times to agreement in Experiments IV to VI

statistically significant in Experiment I. Experiment V was designed to clarify this issue.

Experiment V

SUBJECTS

Subjects were thirty-two male undergraduate students at the University of Hull. Psychology students were excluded from participating in the experiment.

THE NEGOTIATION TASK

A revised version of the 'Demy Ltd' scenario used in Experiment II was employed. The only change made was to provide *both* subjects with the information previously given in instructions to union negotiators. The final section of the handout was therefore amended to read as follows.

The union's reaction to the Board's proposal

The Union objected strongly to the Board's proposal on seven main grounds:

1 The arguments used by the Board indicated a shameful lack of trust in the workpeople at Demy Ltd, particularly in view of the history of co-operation in this successful co-ownership company.
2 That the union had taken the initiative in proposing the change to a more desirable system of work organisation was in itself indicative of their sense of responsibility to the firm and inconsistent with the Board's implicit charge of opportunism and calculation.
3 The management representatives on the working party agreed that the working party could (and did) make a *conservative* estimate of the increase in productivity to be expected from the new proposals. It is only fair to let the workpeople, as well as the management, benefit from this.
4 Since the estimate was *agreed* to be conservative, the union were asking for the whole of the estimated savings to be consolidated onto the basic wage.
5 It should also be remembered that the union members generally lived five or six miles from the factory and had to provide their own transport. Dissatisfaction with this situation was likely to be aroused if the Board did not accept the working party's proposals.
6 In view of the unanimity of the working party the union could only suspect the Board's motives in refusing to grant this increase. Should this feeling grow, productivity would almost certainly *drop* now.
7 Until the last Board meeting it had been tacitly assumed that the whole (100%) of the savings would be consolidated.

On these grounds, and the fact that the working party's proposals were unanimously agreed by both the management and union representatives, the union stated that a figure of 70% was unacceptable. However, the union agreed that their convenor, Mr X, discuss the matter with Mr Y, the Personnel Manager, and that any agreement reached by them be binding on both sides.

Each management representative was given the following written instructions:

'You are to take the role of Mr Y, the Personnel Manager, and you see your assignment as being to see that 70% of the savings are consolidated onto the basic wage. You realise that the Board would be most unhappy with a figure of more than 80%.

'The accompanying document lists the cash-in-hand values of various settlement points. You have a further ten minutes before the negotiation begins.'

Each union representative was given the following written instructions:

'You are to take the role of Mr X, the union convenor, and you see your negotiating assignment as being to see that the whole (100%) of the savings are consolidated onto the basic wage. You realise that your members would be most unhappy with a figure of less than 90%.

'The accompanying document lists the cash-in-hand values of various settlement points. You have a further ten minutes before the negotiation begins.'

RESULTS

Union negotiators (given the stronger case) achieved higher outcomes in T/NK groups than in FF/NK groups, as shown in Figure 9.8, and this trend was statistically reliable ($p < ·05$). Outcomes in T groups took slightly longer to obtain than outcomes in FF groups, but this trend was not statistically significant, and time to agreement was not related to the value of agreement obtained ($r_s = ·04$, $N = 16$).

All the subjects appeared to perceive strength of case as intended by the experimenters.

DISCUSSION

Apparently, the effects reported in Experiment II were at least partly due to the manipulation of strength of case (although it may still be argued that the effects were reinforced by the additional information given to union negotiators). Furthermore, the effect of medium of communication persisted when each management negotiator (given the weaker case) was no longer told that he could not permit a strike to develop.

It was decided to use the same experimental materials to investigate the effects of knowledge (of other's resistance point) upon the outcomes of 'Demy Ltd' negotiations. On the basis of the findings of Experiment III it was expected that the side given the stronger case would obtain higher outcomes in face-to-face/free groups than in telephone/free groups, thus *reversing* the results obtained in Experiments I, II, IV and V. Experiment VI was undertaken to investigate this possibility.

Experiment VI

SUBJECTS

Subjects were thirty-two male undergraduate students at the University of Hull. Psychology students were excluded from participating in the experiment.

PROCEDURE

The procedures followed were identical to those used in Experiment V, except for the instructions given to the subjects. After five minutes of reading time, each management representative was given the following written instructions:

'You are to take the role of Mr Y, the Personnel Manager, and you see your assignment as being to ensure that 70% of the savings are consolidated onto the basic wage. You realise that the Board would be most unhappy with a figure of more than 80%. Mr X would be most happy to secure a settlement of 100% for his members, and they will be most unhappy if he settles for less than 90%.

'The accompanying document lists the cash-in-hand values of various settlement points. You have a further ten minutes before the negotiation begins.'

Each union representative was given the following written instructions:

'You are to take the role of Mr X, the union convenor, and you see your negotiating assignment as being to see that the whole (100%) of the savings are consolidated onto the basic wage. You realise that your members would be most unhappy with a figure of less than 90%. Mr Y would be most happy to secure a settlement of 70% and the Board will be most unhappy if he settles for more than 80%.

'The accompanying document lists the cash-in-hand values of various settlement points. You have a further ten minutes before the negotiation begins.'

RESULTS

Figure 9.8 shows that union negotiators achieved higher outcomes in FF/K groups than in T/K groups, as predicted, but the difference between the groups was not statistically reliable. The mean times to agreement were almost identical in the two treatments, as shown in Figure 9.8, and there was no relationship between the time taken and value of agreements obtained ($r_s = \cdot06$, $N = 16$).

DISCUSSION

While the difference between FF/K and T/K groups was not statistically significant, the direction of the difference confirmed the findings obtained in the IG conditions of Experiment III. We can conclude that the effect of giving subjects knowledge of their opponents' minimum goals was to *remove* the difference between FF and T groups and, if anything, to reverse the direction of the interaction between strength of case and formality of the system of communication used.

Experiments I to VI, however, involved only two media of communication; that is, all negotiations were conducted in either face-to-face or telephone groups. Consequently, while it was clear that strength of case and medium of communication interacted to determine the outcome of male-male negotiations conducted under conditions of incomplete-incomplete information and a negative settlement range, it was *not* clear that it was the *formality* of the medium of communication which produced these effects. After all, face-to-face and telephone media differ in at least two respects: not only is the telephone medium more *formal* than the face-to-face medium, but also the participants are *physically separated*. Experiment VII was an attempt to specify which was the more important variable by using face-to-face/free (FF), telephone/free (T) and television/free (TV) media of communication.

The TV medium is almost identical to the FF medium in terms of formality concerned and is identical to the T medium in terms of physical presence. Accordingly, it was expected that: (a) if an interaction between strength of case and *formality* was involved, the side with the stronger case would obtain higher outcomes in T groups than in TV or FF groups; but (b) if physical presence was the crucial variable, the side with the stronger case would obtain higher outcomes in both T groups and TV groups than in FF groups. In the first case, similar outcomes would be obtained in TV and FF groups; in the second case, similar outcomes would be obtained in TV and T groups.

Experiment VII[1]

SUBJECTS

Subjects were forty-eight male undergraduate students from the University of Hull. Psychology students were excluded from participating in the experiment.

THE NEGOTIATION TASK AND PROCEDURE

The scenario,[2] instructions and procedure were identical to those of Experiment II, except that subjects were assigned to roles after ten minutes of reading time (and given a total of twenty minutes of preparation time in all). Furthermore, since all TV groups were run with the co-operation of the Audio Visual Communication Centre at the University of Hull, the first sixteen pairs of subjects were assigned to the TV condition in order to fit in with production schedules. Otherwise pairs of subjects were alternately assigned to FF or T groups.

MEDIA OF COMMUNICATION

Subjects in F groups sat about three feet apart in an experimental booth in the Department of Psychology at the University of Hull. Subjects in T groups sat in separate booths and negotiated via the microphone/headphone combination used in Experiments IV to VI. The TV medium requires a rather more detailed description.

Subjects in TV groups were physically separated, and each sat facing a domestic TV receiver placed on a trolley directly in front of his desk. Subjects were filmed by studio TV cameras situated some fifteen feet in front of them and just above their own monitor screens. This arrangement did not, however, permit eye contact to be perceived by the subjects, since a subject would only be seen to be looking at his opponent when he was himself looking at the camera and his opponent was looking at the TV screen. Consequently, the TV medium was a little *more formal* than the FF medium. Subjects in TV groups spoke into microphones placed on the desk in front of them and heard their opponents through a free-standing loudspeaker located a little to one side of their monitor screens.

[1] This experiment was conducted as an undergraduate project by D. Brown, under the supervision of I. E. Morley.

[2] An experiment conducted a few months later using the same experimental materials confirmed that subjects perceived the union case as higher on each of the dimensions – (A), (B), (C) and (D) – used to assess strength of case in Experiment III (Stedman 1972).

RESULTS

Mean outcomes of negotiations are presented in Figure 9.9. Union negotiators (given the stronger case) achieved significantly higher outcomes in T groups than in FF groups ($p < .014$). Outcomes obtained by union negotiators in TV groups were intermediate between those obtained in FF groups and in T groups; however, whereas outcomes in TV groups were not significantly more favourable to the union than outcomes in FF groups, they were significantly less favourable than outcomes in T groups ($p < .05$).

	Face-to-face	Television	Telephone
	3*	6*	5*
	4*	4*	6*
	5*	4*	5
	6	4*	5
	4	4*	4
	3	3	7
	3	1	7
	2	6	4
Mean	3·8	4·0	5·4

*Denotes computed outcome

Figure 9.9 Outcomes of negotiations in three different media of communication: Experiment VII (in scale points)

DISCUSSION

The crucial question concerns the position of the TV groups. The TV condition was, as we have explained, *slightly* more formal than the FF condition. Consequently, if formality rather than physical presence was the crucial variable, outcomes in TV groups should have been *slightly* more favourable to the union than outcomes in FF groups, but considerably less favourable than outcomes in T groups. This was exactly the result obtained, and Brown's results therefore provided clear support for the view that it was formality rather than physical presence which interacted with strength of case in determining the outcomes of the negotiations described.

There is only one caveat which needs to be made. There were a surprising number of deadlocks in TV groups, and settlements were computed by taking the arithmetic mean of subjects' final offers in 5/8 cases. This raises the question of the validity of such a procedure. It should, however, be noted that the mean of the computed settlements was *higher* than that of the settlements actually obtained. Consequently, any deficiency in the averaging procedure would work *against* the hypothesis that formality was the crucial variable involved in differences between the FF and T media of communication.

It should also be noted that the difference between outcomes obtained in FF groups and those obtained in T groups replicated the findings of Experiments II and V.

The Generality of the Interaction Between Strength of Case and System of Communication Used

It is important to be clear about exactly what has been established so far and what has not. Seven experiments have been reported in which subjects were asked to take roles in laboratory simulations of industrial disputes. In each case subjects were *randomly* assigned to roles, and no attempt was made to ensure that a subject was given a role congruent with his general orientation to management or union. Strength of case was manipulated by the content of the experimental materials: more and better-quality arguments were (initially) made available to one negotiator than to the other. Six of the seven experiments (Experiments I, II, III, IV, V and VII) investigated the effects of medium of communication upon the outcomes of male-male negotiations conducted under conditions of incomplete-incomplete (NK) information and in the context of a negative (ICG) settlement range. *In every case* the side given the stronger case achieved higher outcomes in telephone/free (T) groups than in face-to-face/free (FF) groups, despite various changes in experimental procedures and in the content of the scenarios used. In four of the six experiments this trend was statistically reliable (Experiments II, IV, V and VII); in the other two it was not (Experiments I and III). However, Experiment I did provide reliable evidence that the side with the stronger case achieved higher outcomes in telephone/constrained groups than in face-to-face/free groups, and it seems that the trend would have been statistically significant in Experiment III if subjects had been given more time to prepare for negotiations.

It seems quite clear that under certain circumstances (NK, ICG, male-male dyads) there is an interaction between strength of case and medium of communication, such that the side with the stronger case achieves higher outcomes the more formal the medium of communication used. Furthermore, it seems likely that a similar interaction obtains when male-male subjects negotiate under conditions of incomplete-incomplete (NK) information within the context of a positive (CG) settlement range, although this is by no means well established. We may speculate that the trends in Experiment III would have been statistically significant if subjects had been given more time to prepare for negotiation.

CONFIRMATION BY SHORT

Results obtained by Short (1971a, 1974) have confirmed that the interaction between strength of case and medium of communication is sufficiently robust to survive changes in context and experimental procedure. In his studies, fifty-four male and six female civil servants were drawn from managerial training courses and formed into a total of twenty-four male-male and six male-female dyads. Three of the male-female dyads were assigned to each medium of communication. Most of the subjects had met their opponents but only during the training courses involved. The scenario used was a version of that given to subjects in Experiments III and IV (obtained from us), revised to keep pace with increases in the cost of living.

There were five major changes in procedure from those used in Experiments I to VII:

1 Subjects were (randomly) assigned to roles at the *beginning* of the experiment, so that each knew the case he/she would have to argue before he/she began reading the experimental materials.
2 Subjects were given as much preparation time as they felt was needed to assimilate the experimental materials. Apparently, twenty-five to thirty minutes were sufficient in the majority of cases.
3 *Subjects were allowed to set their own minimum goals.* They were simply instructed to maximise the payoff to their own side within the limits of the constraint that an agreement should be reached.
4 Subjects were informed that they could use as much negotiating time as they felt was necessary to deal with the issues raised by the dispute. In fact, all negotiations were stopped by the experimenter after forty minutes had elapsed, and 'settlements' were computed by taking the arithmetic means of subjects' final offers.
5 Outcomes were assessed in terms of the percentage of the savings distributed among the workforce.

Since no attempt was made to assess what subjects' minimum goals actually were, an ordinal scale of the type involved in Experiments I to VII could not be used. Subjects negotiated in face-to-face/free (FF) or telephone/free (T) groups. (Telephone groups actually negotiated by telephone rather than a microphone/headphone combination.)

Union negotiators secured higher outcomes in T/NK groups (mean = 85·8%) than in FF/NK groups (mean = 81·5%), and the difference between FF/NK and T/NK treatments was statistically reliable ($p < ·05$). However, negotiators apparently required more time to reach agreement in FF than in T groups: 14/15 pairs in the FF treatment reached agreements before the forty-minute 'guillotine' was applied, whereas only 9/15 pairs in the T treatment did so. Consequently, more settlements were computed for T pairs than for FF pairs, and once again this raised the question of the validity of the averaging operation involved. But if computed settlements were excluded from the analysis, union negotiators still obtained higher outcomes in T/NK groups (mean = 84·1%) than in FF/NK groups (mean = 81·6%). Consequently, even when data were excluded in this way, there was still some evidence that settlements in favour of the side with the stronger case were positively associated with formality in the medium of communication used (although the difference between T/NK and FF/NK treatments was no longer statistically reliable).

Concluding Comments

The original research hypothesis was stated as: *other things being equal, settlements in favour of the side with the stronger case will be positively associated with formality in the system of communication used.* Different negotiation situations may be described in terms of a number of dimensions, *one* of which is formality. A fairly simple experimental design, involving two-person negotiations conducted via different media of communication, was used precisely to keep other things equal (e.g. seating arrangements, presence of an audience, etc.), but the nature of the *ceteris paribus* clauses was not explored in any real detail. When other situational variables are involved some, presumably, will increase the size of the effect and others will decrease it. Some of these variables were considered; others were not.

For instance, it is clear that the effect no longer obtains when the information available to participants is changed in certain ways. Two of the seven experiments involved negotiations in which subjects were each given knowledge (K) of their opponents' minimum goals. In each case, the side with the stronger case obtained higher outcomes the more *informal* the medium of communication used, although the differences were not statistically reliable. Furthermore, it is not difficult to identify other relevant variables (e.g. seating arrangements, size of team, presence of an audience, etc.) although very little is known about the precise nature of the effects they involve. Here, we want to consider some of the variables inherent in the nature of the experimental paradigm we used.

There was in fact a great deal of variation in the outcomes obtained *within* the experimental treatments employed in Experiments I to VI. This may perhaps be explained by pointing out that different subjects face different types of conflict (Short 1971c, 1973). In any laboratory simulation of the RPD type at least two sorts of contributing factor are involved:

1 The conflict inherent in the nature of the agenda items to be discussed (Walton and McKersie 1965; Druckman and Zechmeister 1970).
2 The conflict between (a) a subject's personal attitudes (ideology, personal orientation, etc.) and beliefs (e.g. in the merits of the case he is required to argue), and (b) the attributes and beliefs he attributes to the role occupants (all of them) described in the experimental materials.

These factors may combine in rather complex ways, and, as Short (1971c) has pointed out, 'it is by no means clear that the effects of medium of communication should be similar for conflicts of essentially different natures' (p. 1). It is also not at all clear how such factors may affect the nature of the interaction between strength of case and formality in the system of communication used. These factors are worth further consideration.

In our experiments, while medium of communication sometimes affected the *value* of agreements obtained by the side with the stronger case, there was no evidence that these agreements were easier to obtain in one medium than the other. Considering Experiments I to VII as a whole, 13/76 face-to-face/free and 9/73 telephone/free groups failed to reach agreements. These proportions were not significantly different ($X^2 = \cdot62$, *d.f.* $= 1$, $p =$ n.s.). Furthermore, the mean times required to reach agreement were remarkably similar in the two treatments. There was no evidence to suggest that the time taken was related to the value of agreements obtained.

B

The Process of Negotiation

Introduction

In 1963 McGrath and Julian were able to say that research on negotiation had failed 'to investigate directly the negotiation process itself' (p. 119). In some respects this failure has been remedied; in others it has not. The process of bid and counterbid has been fairly extensively studied in distribution games and games of economic exchange (see Chapter 5), but very little is known about the more elaborate processes of verbal communication involved in experimental debates and 'social negotiations' (Walton and McKersie 1965) (see Chapter 6). We shall now present our own analyses of experimental debates (Chapter 11) and real life negotiations (Chapters 12 and 13).

The method of analysis used, which we call *Conference Process Analysis* (CPA), is described in detail in Chapter 10. It involves dividing transcripts of negotiations into units or 'acts', each conveying a 'point', 'proposition' or 'single thought'. Each unit is then described in terms of one and only one set of categories chosen from a given list. Briefly, each unit is coded in terms of three dimensions – mode, resource and referent – one category being attributed to it for each dimension. The *mode* dimension indicates how 'information' is being exchanged (offer, seek, etc.); the *resource* dimension indicates what sort of 'information' is being exchanged (procedure, settlement point, acknowledgement +, acknowledgement −, etc.); and the *referent* dimension indicates who is being explicitly talked about in that 'information' (person, party, opponent, etc.).

In many respects the procedures we followed were similar to those of Manheim (1960), Morris (1960), Landsberger (1955a) and Bales and Strodtbeck (1951), but the categories we used *were specially designed for use with negotiation (rather than problem-solving) groups*. We wish to emphasise the part played by CPA in elaborating the processes of interpersonal and interparty exchange identified by Douglas (1957, 1962) which have been discussed in Chapter 2.

Consider first the analysis of experimental debates. We have argued (in Chapter 7) that the outcome of a negotiation will be partially determined by the balance between interpersonal and interparty 'climates' in bargaining. Our programme of experimental research (which has been described in Chapters 8 and 9) was predicated upon the assumption that different systems of communication would affect this balance, thus producing different settlements in different experimental treatments. We showed that, in certain two-person negotiations of the RPD2 type, settlements in favour of the side with the stronger case were positively associated with formality in the communication system used. Our explanation of these findings was along the following lines: the more *formal* the system of communication the greater negotiators' concern with the interparty aspects of their relationship (and the greater the attention paid to the content of the verbal exchange); the more *informal* the system of communication the greater their concern with the interpersonal aspects of their relationship (and the greater the extent to which party goals were modified by personal considerations).

Chapter 11 presents a detailed analysis of the communications which led to different outcomes in the 'Demy Ltd' [RPD2] negotiations of Experiment II (described in Chapter 8). Differences between the systems of communication are elaborated and a more precise meaning is given to some of Douglas's ideas. We shall also consider whether there are any general characteristics associated with 'successful' performance, regardless of the system of communication used.

So far as real life negotiations are concerned, considerable theoretical interest attaches to *changes over time in the balance between the interpersonal and interparty forces involved*. According to Douglas, 'successful' negotiations go through *stages* which 'unsuccessful' negotiations do not. In particular, 'successful' groups are those in which negotiators initially emphasise the disagreement between the parties they represent before moving on to a problem-solving stage in which their personal relationships assume much more importance. From this point of view disagreement is seen as productive and likely to *generate* 'problem-solving' attempts to deal with the negotiation task.

In contrast, Landsberger (1955a) has suggested that negotiation success is determined by the extent to which groups pass through a series of problem-solving stages conceptualised in terms of Bales's (1950) 'Interaction Process Analysis' (IPA). 'Successful' groups, apparently, are those which deal *in turn* with problems of 'orientation', 'evaluation' and 'control'. They show a progressive increase in both positive and negative social-emotional behaviours from beginning to end of the negotiations. From this point of view disagreement *increases* as problems of control come to the fore, and, in general, conflict is seen to arise in response to the demands of coping with a problem-solving task.

Chapters 12 and 13 contain a detailed discussion of our own research on stages in the process of negotiation for agreement. Chapter 12 presents our analysis of two real life negotiations: one involving a Type 2 task, the other a Type 3 task (see Chapter 3). The former negotiation involved a single session, the latter three separate sessions. Two facts emerged very clearly: (a) neither negotiation followed the sequence identified by Landsberger in his research; and (b) *different phases were observed in different sessions of a negotiation*. The movement described by Douglas was characteristic of the first and final sessions of these disputes but was not otherwise observed. In fact, our analysis was consistent with Douglas's suggestion that 'successful' negotiations go through stages which 'unsuccessful' negotiations do not. The suggestion is made that the referent category '*other*' may provide an index of the progress being made. The suggestion is made very tentatively, but it is at least one illustration of the fact that CPA can be used to generate interesting research hypotheses. Chapter 13 attempts to integrate the findings from our experimental and field research. Some additional data are described and an elaborated version of Douglas's quasiprescriptive model is set out.

Chapter 10

Conference Process Analysis

There is a fairly extensive literature dealing with the problems involved in the systematic observation of interaction within (and between) groups (e.g. Bales 1950, 1970; Berelson 1952; Heyns and Zander 1954; Mishler and Waxler 1968; Weick 1968; Holsti 1969; Wiener 1971; Fisher 1974). Consequently, it is a fairly simple matter to establish that a number of category systems are available for the description of communication in problem-solving groups (e.g. Bales 1950; Crowell and Scheidel 1961; Borgatta and Crowther 1965; Fisher 1970; Morris 1970), family groups (e.g. Longabaugh 1963; Borke 1967; Mishler and Waxler 1968; Mark 1971) and a number of other groups of one sort or another (e.g. Thelen 1954; Longabaugh *el al*. 1966; Katz *et al*. 1969). There are also three systems of categories which have been designed explicitly for use with negotiation groups (Osterberg 1950; Julian and McGrath 1963; Rackham 1972). We shall not attempt to review this literature in detail, but we would like to indicate some of the ways in which it has influenced the development of Conference Process Analysis (CPA).

One point which emerges very clearly from a study of the literature is that any category system must contain *two sets of rules* (Morley 1973): one defining the basic units ('acts') to be described, and another defining the description ('categories') to be used. However, the first set of rules is rarely specified in any detail, and the second is often given in summary form. This makes it extremely difficult to use many of the systems outlined in the literature, unless one has been specially trained by the authors concerned.

The Division of Interaction into Basic Units ('Acts')

As Wiener (1971) has pointed out, the unit of analysis an investigator chooses is partly determined by the nature of the data that he expects to collect. The division rules detailed were predicated upon the assumption that one major source of data would be tape recordings and/or transcripts of the verbal communication in negotiation groups. Consequently, there were several alternative sorts of rule which could have been adopted:

1 A *temporal* unit, defined in terms of some arbitrary time interval (e.g. Berg 1967).

2 A *transactional* unit, defined in terms of an uninterrupted speech burst (e.g. Julian and McGrath 1963; Rackham 1972).
3 A *psychological* unit, defined in terms of the expression of a simple thought (e.g. Bales 1950; Crowell and Scheidel 1961).
4 A *categorical* unit, defined in terms of the system of categories to be used (e.g. Back 1961; Faucheux and Moscovici 1966; Katz *et al.* 1969).
5 A *hybrid* unit, defined in terms of a combination of elements of the above type (Fisher 1970; Wiener 1971).

The unit of analysis an investigator chooses is also determined by the sort of question that he is interested in answering. In our case it seemed desirable to choose a unit which allowed the estimation of a subject's proportional contribution to the debate. This ruled out transactional (2) and hybrid (5) units. A temporal unit (1) was ruled out because any arbitrary unit was likely to be extremely difficult to score. A categorical unit (4) was ruled out because (a) the categories to be used did not seem to demand this sort of unit, and (b) we wished to separate the process of division from the process of categorisation. Consequently, it was decided to use a 'psychological' unit (3).

But what constitutes the expression of a simple thought? According to traditional English grammars the answer is that a *sentence* does (e.g. Fries 1952; see Palmer 1971). From this point of view the problem of dividing speech into psychological units amounts to the problem of dividing speech into simple subject-predicate sentences or equivalent forms (Bales 1950; Auld and White 1956; Mishler and Waxler 1968). This is not a simple task. Auld and White have commented that 'although the sentence has been defined by grammarians for more than two thousand years, no one has ever demonstrated that speech can be reliably divided into sentences' (p. 273). Speech is rarely 'packaged' in neat subject-predicate form; it is often ungrammatical, contains false starts, and so on. Consequently, in the early stages of CPA one major source of disagreement was the nature of the units to be coded.

While neither formulation seemed entirely satisfactory in its own right, the work of Auld and White (1956) and Mishler and Waxler (1968) suggested to us that a useful set of rules could be formulated along these lines. The rules given by Auld and White defined too large a unit and those given by Mishler and Waxler defined too small a unit. For instance, Auld and White have defined the following communications as single units: 'That's uh . . . just a Biblical phrase that I uh heard maybe half a dozen times a year, just like I heard thousands of other Biblical phrases,' and 'And I think he asked me to read it, after he discussed it a little.' Each would be coded as two units in CPA. Mishler and Waxler have defined the following communications as involving two units: 'I think/(that) they're old enough to have a party,' and 'If they had planned this party in advance/(then) they wanted to have a good time,' and 'There is the fact/that the Boy Scouts are a group.' Each would be coded as a single unit in CPA. Nevertheless, Mishler and Waxler have provided a comprehensive summary of a number of interaction codes and made a major contribution to the problem of dividing transcript into units.

The rules we eventually adopted, which allowed transcripts to be divided into units with a high degree of interobserver reliability, are described in detail in Chapter 11.

The Choice of Interaction Codes: The Categories to be Used

Despite the fact that Bales's (1950) categories were designed for use with problem-solving groups, it will be convenient to begin with a description of his system of 'Interaction Process Analysis'. Accordingly, a summary of his IPA categories (showing the relationships between them) is given in Figure 10.1. Bales has given essentially a 'psychological' definition of the basic unit, despite his assertion that 'The unit to be scored is the smallest discriminable segment of verbal or non-verbal behaviour to which the observer . . . can assign a classification under conditions of continuous serial scoring' (p. 37). It is, however, clear that the unit is supposed to correspond to a 'complete simple

---

A	1	*shows solidarity:* raises other's status, gives help, reward.
	2	*shows tension release:* jokes, laughs, shows satisfaction.
	3	*agrees:* shows passive acceptance, understands, concurs, complies.
B	4	*gives suggestion:* direction, implying autonomy for other.
	5	*gives opinion:* evaluation, analysis, expresses feeling, wish.
	6	*gives orientation:* information, repetition, confirmation.
C	7	*asks for orientation:* information, etc.
	8	*asks for opinion:* evaluation, etc.
	9	*asks for suggestion:* direction, possible ways of action.
D	10	*disagrees:* shows passive rejection, withholds help.
	11	*shows tension:* asks for help, withdraws from field.
	12	*shows antagonism:* deflates other's status, defends or asserts self.

A = social-emotional area: positive 'reactions'
B = task area: attempted answers
C = task area: questions
D = social-emotional area: negative 'reactions'

6, 7 = problems of orientation
5, 8 = problems of evaluation
4, 9 = problems of control
3, 10 = problems of decision
2, 11 = problems of tension reduction
1, 12 = problems of reintegration

Figure 10.1 Summary statement of Bales's (1950) IPA categories

thought' and that Bales has simply not described in any detail the division rules to be used. Each unit is described in terms of one (and only one) of twelve possible categories, concerned with either 'task' or 'social-emotional' behaviour. Task behaviour may be 'given' (B) or 'asked for' (C); social-emotional behaviour may consist of 'positive reactions' (A) or 'negative reactions' (D).

However, Bales's groupings disguise a distinction between the *function* of the information being exchanged (to deal with problems of orientation, evaluation, control, etc.) and the *way* in which that information is made salient in the exchange (given, asked for, agreed with, disagreed with). This sort of distinction is central to those category systems which view social interaction as involving an exchange of resources (Longabaugh 1963; Longabaugh *et al.* 1966) and is preserved in CPA. CPA is thus one form of Longabaugh's 'Resource Process Analysis' (RPA) in which, broadly speaking, all acts are coded in terms of a *mode* dimension (indicating *how* information is being exchanged) and a *resource* dimension (indicating *what sort* of information is being exchanged).

Let us consider Bales's (1950) discussion of the 'problem-solving sequence' as a frame of reference for his observers (pp. 56–7). This sequence consists simply of a progression from initial acts ('questions'), through medial acts ('attempted answers') to terminal acts ('positive reactions', 'negative reactions'). It suggests the use of four modes: seek ('questions'), offer ('attempted answers'), accept ('positive reactions') and reject ('negative reactions'). However, whereas Bales has distinguished between different types of information (resources) which can be 'asked for' (categories 7–9) or 'given' (categories 4–6), he has not distinguished between the content of the information accepted (category 3) or rejected (category 10). This sort of operation is central to the organisation of CPA.

Longabaugh (1963) has contrasted the logic of RPA with that of IPA (pp. 324–5). Most other discussions of Bales's system have been concerned with the problems of obtaining agreement between different observers (e.g. Psathas 1961; Waxler and Mishler 1966) or of expanding the system without dramatically changing its basic organisation (e.g. Borgatta 1963; Borgatta and Crowther 1965; Bales 1970).

But CPA is not simply a version of Longabaugh's system which has been applied to negotiation groups rather than mother-child groups (Longabaugh 1963) or patient-patient groups (Longabaugh *et al.* 1966). While the categories used in CPA are organised according to his principles of RPA, they are applied to the same basic units as those of Bales's IPA. Longabaugh (1963) has defined the basic unit of his system as 'any coherent bit of behaviour by an actor which was judged by the observer to have the intent of acting as a stimulus for a response by a present other' (p. 329). Furthermore, he has argued that 'Although a sentence was a convenient unit for quantifying a social act it was felt that it was only a gross measure. Occasionally, it takes several sentences to present one coherent stimulus to another person' (p. 329). But no examples are given of how the categories are to be used, and we are therefore left with the worst sort of notional definition. It is perhaps not surprising that Longabaugh found that 'the chief cause of unreliability was act omission by one or the other of the observers' (p. 333). The 'psychological' unit preferred by Bales is rigorously defined in CPA.

It is also desirable (although not essential) that any system of categories should be *exhaustive* and *mutually exclusive*; that is, each act should be (a) coded, and (b) coded only once (Duncan 1972; Fisher 1974). Nearly all systems attempt to meet the first requirement. IPA (Bales) uses only the twelve categories shown in Figure 10.1 and adopts the division rule that 'meaningless' material is included as part of the following act. Both RPA (Longabaugh) and CPA (Morley and Stephenson) prefer to use the more straightforward procedure of including an 'unascertainable' category. Some systems attempt to meet the second requirement (Bales 1950); others do not (Longabaugh 1963; Julian and McGrath 1963). Julian and McGrath used double coding partly because they adopted a transactional definition of the basic unit. It is not clear whether they regarded the complete speech as a more *appropriate* unit of analysis or were simply avoiding the problem of providing a detailed specification of the division rules which (otherwise) would have had to be applied. However, if it is felt desirable to analyse sequences of acts – as has been suggested by Barker and Wright (1955), Wright (1967), Weick (1968), Morris (1970) and Fisher (1970) – it is very much more convenient to have categories which are mutually exclusive. This necessitates an extremely high agreement between observers on an *act-by-act* basis (Mishler and Waxler 1968). Techniques such as 'contiguity analysis' (Scheidel and Crowell 1964) can be applied providing that the categories used are mutually exclusive. The categories used in CPA have therefore been defined to be mutually exclusive.

There are other differences between IPA (Bales), RPA (Longabaugh) and CPA (Morley and Stephenson). The most important of these concerns the fact that, whereas IPA codes each act in terms of a single dimension and RPA codes each act in terms of two dimensions (mode and resource), CPA codes each act in terms of three dimensions (mode, resource and referent).

The third dimension was required to elaborate the distinction between interpersonal and interparty exchange. We were encouraged by the work of Grace and Tandy (1957), who have concluded from their study of delegate communication (see Chapter 6) that 'Frequent statements about other groups (infrequent self references) suggest greater tension within or upon the group' (p. 97). This sort of result seemed of considerable interest in the context of negotiation groups. Accordingly, a (quite considerably) modified version of Grace and Tandy's scale appears in CPA. Grace and Tandy used categories originally designed by Bugental (1948) for research in clinical psychology. Bugental's system was comprised of six categories (see Grace and Tandy 1957, p. 93):

1 *Self* ('statements of the "I am . . . type"').
2 *Self on self* ('statements in which the effect of one aspect of the self upon another aspect of the self is described').
3 *Self on not-self* ('describes the manner in which the self affects that which is not part of the self').
4 *Not-self on self* ('statements concerning the effects of others upon oneself').
5 *Not-self on not-self* ('statements in which one referent, other than the self, relates to another').
6 *Not-self* ('descriptions of referents not explicitly related to the self or to another referent').

In CPA the referent dimension is used to indicate who is being explicitly described in the information being exchanged and, furthermore, to make a distinction between Personal and Party considerations which is of considerable theoretical interest in the study of negotiation groups.

Mode		*Resource*		*Referent*
1 Offer	*Structuring Activity*		0	No Referent
2 Accept	1	Procedure	1	Self
3 Reject	*Outcome Activity*		2	Person
4 Seek	2	Settlement point (a) initial (b) new	3	Other
	3	Limits	4	Party
	4	Positive consequences of proposed outcomes	5	Opponent
	5	Negative consequences of proposed outcomes	6	Both persons
	6	Other statements about outcomes	7	Both parties
	Acknowledgement			
	7	Acknowledgement + (a) own and both sides, (b) other side		
	8	Acknowledgement − (a) own and both sides, (b) other side		
	Other Information			
	9	Information		

Figure 10.2 Conference Process Analysis: a list of categories used

A list of the categories used in CPA is shown in Figure 10.2. The categories are defined later, but we hope that already the reader will have an intuitive sense of how they are to be used. Some examples may help. A sentence like 'M: We can offer you 80% now,' would be coded as 1/2/4 (1 = offer, 2 = settlement point, 4 = party), and a sentence like 'M: £2 a week should boost the morale of the workers considerably,' would be coded as 1/4/5 (1 = offer, 4 = positive consequence of proposed outcome, 5 = opponent). Of course, very few sentences are as easy to code as this. But at this stage our concern is to illustrate the sort of coding involved in CPA rather than to detail precise rules for its use. These will be given later. Here, we hope that enough has been said to demonstrate two points:

G

1 The resources involved in CPA have a high face-validity; they seem to be the stuff of which negotiations are made. This is not accidental. Longabaugh (1963) has argued that 'a central task of the investigator is to decide what resources will be salient in a particular setting or experiment before he begins to collect his data' (p. 322). But if the investigator has few theoretical presuppositions he is quite likely to conclude that negotiations are composed of offers, counteroffers, threats, promises, arguments about consequences, contributions, wage rates, working conditions, etc. The categories included in CPA have been designed to preserve commonsense distinctions of this sort (Morley 1973). In fact, one of the distinctions we found it impossible to preserve was that between Bales's (1950) categories of orientation and evaluation.

2 The organisation of CPA allows the system to be expanded (or contracted) in a number of ways. For instance, resource category 1 might be expanded to distinguish between 'procedural structuring' and 'content structuring', as in Julian and McGrath's (1963) scheme. Similarly, resource category 3 might be expanded to distinguish between conditional offers (e.g. 'I'll concede on A if you'll concede on B') and unconditional offers (e.g. 'I've been instructed not to go beyond 80%'). And so on. Certain elaborations of this kind will be evident in Chapter 11.

The Current Status of CPA

Once again, it is interesting to compare CPA (Morley and Stephenson) with IPA (Bales). In his *Interaction Process Analysis* Bales (1950) has written: 'This work in its initial form should be regarded as a progress report designed primarily for other researchers in the field. It is a working manual, not a finished product. Most of the data presented can be regarded as only illustrative. In so far as the term "Interaction process analysis" is accepted by other workers, it should be taken to refer to a body of closely related but changing and developing methods' (p. ii). These comments apply equally well to CPA. Like IPA, CPA is a form of high inference coding which requires very considerable training of the observer and very considerable effort on his part. (A thirty-five minute transcript often takes a full day to code.)

A Detailed Description of CPA

To recapitulate, an act in CPA is a 'psychological' unit which conveys a *point*, *proposition* or *single thought*, as (for instance) in the simple sentence containing one explicit subject and one explicit predicate. The purpose of the division rules presented below is to show how more complex communications can be broken down into simpler and equivalent forms.

Consequently, these rules have a generality which extends far beyond that of the negotiation group.

Because CPA involves high inference coding it is assumed that, whenever possible, the observer will work from tape *plus* transcript of the relevant negotiations (Psathas 1961; Waxler and Mishler 1966; Mishler and Waxler 1968). Certainly, in its present form it would be ergonomically impossible to use CPA under conditions of continuous serial scoring. Typically, a transcript is completely divided into units, and the interaction codes are then applied. (A thirty-five minute negotiation can contain anything between 250 and 850 units.)

Some systems of observation require the observer to categorise behaviour in terms of its impact upon the group (e.g. Bales 1950); others require him to assess the intention of the speaker involved (e.g. Julian and McGrath 1963). Here, it was assumed (following Longabaugh 1963) that 'The action is coded neither on the basis of what meaning it has for the actor, irrespective of effect on target, nor is it coded solely on the basis of its presumed effect on the target, irrespective of what the actor had intended. Rather the judgement as to content is made on the basis of the meaning of the act for the . . . relationship as a relationship' (p. 324).

Rules for Dividing Transcripts into Units

1 SIMPLE SENTENCES

Simple sentences are those which contain a single explicit subject and a single explicit predicate. They are coded as separate acts: e.g.

The 70% increase is very generous/
I vote to move on to another point/
Demy Ltd is a co-ownership company/
We've been working on this old system for a quite a while/
I entirely agree with you/
I don't think we can predict anything at this stage/

It is important to note that the predicate of a basic unit must contain either an intransitive verb or a transitive verb plus its object (otherwise a point has not been made). Consequently, in contrast to Mishler and Waxler (1968) the following sentences would be coded as *one* unit:

Are we saying, 'Well that's your bloody problem'/?
The Board will be extremely dissatisfied if you go beyond 80%/
I think you'll agree that these figures are conservative/
I think the 70% increase is very generous/

2 INCOMPLETE SENTENCES

A variety of incomplete sentences may qualify as basic units.

2.1   Sentences with complete subject and incomplete predicate are coded as separate acts if the predicate is implied by the context: e.g.

> Are you going to start on this/*or shall I*/?
> I'm not quite sure what is going to happen/, *are you*/?

2.2   Sentences with incomplete subject and complete predicate are coded as separate acts if the subject is implied by the context: e.g.

> You don't have any midweek overtime/ *which is a real incentive*/
> This is an added concession on our part/ *which balances things again*/

2.3   Sentences with incomplete subject and incomplete predicate are coded as separate acts if both subject and predicate are implied by the context: e.g.

> It appears now that you're sort of going back on this after your recent Board meeting/ and trying to knock it down considerably/. *In fact, 70% of this value*/
> This is an increase of £2 per week for all chargehands/. *Grade A*/, *Grade 1A*/, *Grade B*/, *2A*/, etc./

2.4   Some incomplete sentences have both subject and predicate implied by 'parenthesis', vocal stress or temporal isolation: e.g.

> (1) I said/ (2) *as far as I was concerned*/ (1) I couldn't remember this document/
> It's not being forced upon him/. (Pause) *Is it*/?

On the other hand, structurally similar phrases may be coded as part of a larger unit if they serve mainly to clarify the sentence and are not emphasised in any special way: e.g.

> Yes/, that's true/. *So far as I'm concerned this is entirely something new*/
> *As far as I'm concerned I couldn't recall this document*/

2.5   Some incomplete sentences are given clear content by what Mishler and Waxler (1968) have called their 'generally accepted cultural meaning' (p. 343). Consequently, they are coded as separate acts: e.g.

> Good/ What/? See/? Yes/ No/ Remember/? Right/ Right/? OK/ Mm hm/

3 COMPOUND SENTENCES

It is extremely difficult to divide compound sentences into basic units. There seem to be exceptions to almost every rule. But coding the sentence as a compound sentence (one unit) is equally unsatisfactory. After a great deal of deliberation, the following guidelines are suggested.

3.1 When two or more clauses are linked by 'and', 'or', 'but', etc. each main clause is coded as a separate unit, because two or more *points* have clearly been made: e.g.

£1·30 is a considerable increase on £16·30/ and the chargehands obviously are not a majority in the working population of the factory/
Are you going to start on this/ or shall I/?
We realise that the workers are being co-operative/ but there's a limit to how co-operative they can be/
The working party came to certain findings/ which were then turned down by the Board at their meeting/
I think you'll agree that these were conservative figures/ which must weaken your position a bit/

This is relatively straightforward.

3.2 When one or more conditional clauses are linked to a main clause the position is less straightforward. In general, one unit is recorded when the conditional clause *precedes* the main clause, but two are recorded when it *follows* the main clause. The position taken here is that statements of the form 'If X, then Y' (etc.) make a single point because 'If X . . . ' is incomplete, implying that the (conditional) point has not yet been made. On the other hand, statements of the form 'Y, if X' constitute two units, because the main clause ('Y') stands as a unit in its own right and because the conditional clause ('If X . . .') is an incomplete sentence which takes its sense ('If X, then Y') from the context of the preceding unit ('Y'). A few examples may help to clarify the point. One unit is recorded in the following cases:

Even after the most extreme forms of intervention in the affairs of the union were over the hostility of the Board continued to be manifest/
As this is a completely new venture we must keep our costs down to the level of what we estimate will be the new costs/
If you refuse to give us 80% you'll have a strike on your hands/
I mean, if you say 'Well, that's your bloody problem,' you say it/
If we see it's been favourable we'll give you the full 100%/
If you come down to 85% I'll agree to a review after six months/
Despite the uncertainty you can afford to pay us 100%/
Although production has gone up it hasn't gone up far enough/

Two units are recorded in the following cases:

> Well I feel that it would not be paid/ because obviously the changeover to a new system is going to increase costs initially/
> I'll still have the bloody need/ whatever you do/
> We're going to get a loss of confidence in management/ if the 100% is cut down that drastically/
> I think it's reasonable to give it two years/ to see how it's going to work out/
> Tell us next week/, when you've had a get-together/

The rule that statements of the form 'If X, then Y' (etc.) are coded as one unit can be broken when contextual cues suggest that, because of special emphasis, the conditional clause has become a point in its own right. Here the observer really *needs* the tape recording to hear what was involved; the following was one example from the 'Demy Ltd' negotiations transcribed in Chapter 12:

> Supposing as a factory we decide to work through the bank holiday/, then, well, I mean all the circumstances we're talking about/

Similarly, the rule that statements of the form 'Y, then X' (etc.) are coded as two units can be broken when contextual cues indicate that only one point is involved: e.g.

> And Stan, and bring Stan into the rotation as far as the bank holidays are concerned/
> Everything was all right until you changed the work schedule/

4 INCOMPLETE SENTENCES WHICH ARE NOT CODED AS BASIC UNITS

An act must make a point in its own right. Many phrases are not coded as acts because they cannot stand alone in this way. Adjectival and adverbial clauses provide good examples of what we mean. The appropriate phrases are indicated in parentheses in the examples below. They do not constitute separate units: e.g.

> But can we get back to the point (where I am now)/?
> One of the solutions for me, in fact, is to cover that/, which is, in fact, to recruit someone on the understanding that he understands quite clearly (before he comes here) what duties we're going to require of him/
> We can only guarantee the increase (which we've been talking about) if we're given this extra efficiency/
> I'm thinking in terms of one day (in the course of the year)/
> We'll have to wait for the opportunity (which we talked about)/
> You have circumscribed me to such an extent (that I can't find a solution)/
> We've got to the point where they've had this document from John/ in

which it appears that in the course of the discussion (that took place at the time) they made the point that they want a few bank holidays/

5 FALSE STARTS AND INTERRUPTIONS

5.1 False starts are not coded as separate units unless the speaker clearly has changed his mind about what to say and decided to make a quite different point. Consequently, the following communications, in which the speaker is trying to decide exactly how to make his point, are coded as single units: e.g.

> You, well you say we don't care/
> We, we employ, we employ all kinds of people/
> I can't, couldn't recall this document/
> Are you now going back on your view that these increases, this 100% increase is an unfair increase/?
> You're getting, the thing is you're getting this on a plate/
> I am, as a last resort I can't go above 80%/

However, the following communications are split into two units because the first phrase stands alone as the preface to a point which has not been completed: e.g.

> I feel 90% would be more/ Well, we'll have to see what the figures are obviously on this/
> One obvious way would in fact be to/ You don't understand our point of view/
> So I would have thought/ You say you've got this trust in the workers/

5.2 When the speaker is interrupted by another person, the uncompleted point is coded as a separate unit. Interruptions are marked with an asterisk on the transcript: e.g.

> M:　　But then you pose us a problem/ because from within/ . . .
> U:*　　Well it's posed me a problem for the last five years/.

5.3 When a speaker is interrupted, but carries on to complete his point, only one unit is scored: e.g.

> M:　　It's necessary that someone should . . .
> U:*　　But/.
> M:　　stop behind at nights/.
> M:　　If you sit down, in fact, to detail this thing to the nth degree . . .
> U1:*　　Yeah/.
> U2:*　　Yeah/.
> M:　　you'll never succeed/.
> M:　　Look, let's sort of start/. One of the dangers of this, you see, is this/, that we start raising all kinds of hypothetical . . .
> U:*　　Yeah/.

M: questions/. All this will produce . . .
U:*   Nothing/.
M: is in fact nothing/.

6 OTHER CONVENTIONS USED

6.1   If one point is broken off and completed after another point has been placed in parentheses, so to speak, each point is coded as a separate unit: e.g.

M: (1) If we take on another electrician/ (2) or we do something/ (1) do we have the right to require, to require them to do it/?

U: (1) That's the one day you get a holiday/, (2) then you've . . .
M1:* (3) How, how . . .
U1: * (2) got to sit at home/.
M1:   (3) how are we supposed to cover now/?
M3:   (4) What you're . . .
U1:* (5) Ugh/.
M3:   (4) saying is that you don't want to be here on bank holidays/ (5) and that's why you don't want to be on standby/. (6) Well, if we did as Brian suggested/ (7) and left it to Bill/ (8) or possibly Stan/ (7) to find somebody/ (6) you just said you all want to be away/.

M: (1) And if it looks as though it's going to be a success/, (2) if people react to it favourably/, (3) if the workers do bear their responsibilities without checking them/, (1) and so then we'll review the situation after that time/.

6.2   All quotations are broken into separate points and coded as separate units: e.g.

M: (1) It says here that 'The Board now claimed that, although the working party contained representatives of management, the proposed increase could not be accepted without further discussion/. (2) The financial effects of the new proposals could not/ (3) they claimed/ (2) be predicted with sufficient accuracy/.'

Definitions of Categories Used

Transcripts are divided into acts (points of information), and each act is coded in terms of three major dimensions:

1 The *mode* dimension indicates *how* information is exchanged in group interaction.

2 The *resource* dimension indicates the *function* of the information being exchanged.

3 The *referent* dimension indicates who is being (explicitly) *talked about* in that information.

We shall now define the categories used and then present samples of typescript to illustrate how the system is used.

1 THE MODE DIMENSION

Four modes of offer, accept, reject and seek were suggested by Bales's (1950) idea of a 'problem-solving sequence'. Their definition is best accomplished by example.

Category 1: Offer. The great majority of behaviour in negotiations consists of offers of one sort or another. Each of the units detailed below is coded as 'offers': e.g.

We thought 70% was quite a reasonable figure/
That's all we're asking for/
You've got to bear these sort of things in mind/
I would say now that we've got to reach agreement on the exact percentage/
You did admit that they'd be prepared to go above 70%/
85% is a straight split/
I don't think we can predict anything at this stage/
Somewhere there has got to be some form of coverage/
We have never wanted to do it/
If you think conceding 20% is losing face, I would have thought that to have brought the management up by 10% would have outweighed that/
There's people who do not like sort of giving up the chance of working overtime on a Saturday and a Sunday/ and their midweek overtime/ and we're giving up, we're giving these concessions to you/

Category 2: Accept. Each of the units italicised below is coded as 'accepts': e.g.

U: So I think we are justified in claiming the 100%/.
M: *I would agree that in the time if things go as they should do, then this would be a good thing for both company – and the workers/.*
U: That requires a direct yes or no/.
M: *That's true/.*
M: How would you suggest then that we deal with this now/ as a company/? I mean, you're part of the community in this respect/.
U: *Yeah/. Yeah/.*

U: I would say now that we've got to reach agreement on the exact percentage/.
M: *Yes/.*
M: We have to think of this before lashing out on 85%/.
U: *Well yes/. I entirely agree with you/.*

Category 3: Reject. Each of the acts italicised below is coded as 'rejects': e.g.

M: I think there's no possibility of agreement this direction/.
U: *Yes/ there is/.*
U: Are you now going back on your view that these increases, this 100% increase is an unfair increase/?
M: *Oh no/, certainly not/, by no means/.*
M: I suggest that we move on to the next item/.
U: *That's not what we agreed/.*
M: How about 80%/?
U: *No/.*

Category 4: Seek. Each of the following acts is coded as 'seeks': e.g.

Which issue do you consider most important/?
What do you think about that/?
Would this be acceptable/?
You reckon that's too far/?
Could you explain/?
Could you give me a few details of how you warrant the immediate 100% payment of the £2·50 increase/?
Where is that/?
Can we get on to some other point/?

2 THE RESOURCE DIMENSION

A resource is defined as something or some category of behaviour which an individual is able to offer, seek, accept or reject in an interaction. Most of the analyses in this book have involved the use of nine resource categories.

Structuring activity

Category 1: Procedure. Category 1 contains all units which define or set limits to the way in which negotiations shall be conducted; it includes any commands, injunctions or authoritative directions relating to such conduct: e.g.

I vote now to move on to another point/
Let's discuss it/
But think about that as a proposition/
Shall we leave it there/?
Let us try and get some figure out of this/
Look at the figures shown in Table 1/
Let's talk about the leading chargehands/
There are two issues really over which we need to argue/

Outcome activity

Category 2: Settlement point. Category 2 contains all units (unconditionally) offering, accepting, rejecting or seeking statements of a Party's current position. The restriction is placed, however, that reference must be made to a *specific* settlement point: e.g.

You want £2·50 per worker per week basic increase/?
We are willing to offer 70% of the proposed increase/
How about £1·50/ plus a review after six months/?

A further distinction may be made between (a) initial, and (b) newly proposed settlement points.

Category 3: Limits. Category 3 contains all units which relate to the form an agreement might take. It includes statements of resistance points, instructions given, etc. It also includes conditional statements of the form 'I'll concede on A if you'll concede on B,' and 'I'll go to 80% if you'll go to 90%,' etc.: e.g.

Of course, we are prepared to give an increase in wage/
I've been told that my Board will be extremely dissatisfied if I go beyond 80%/
As a last resort I just can't go above 80%/
I'll drop to 80%/*but only if we can agree a productivity bonus*/
I just can't go any further than this/
There are no other options open to me/

Category 4: Positive consequences of proposed outcomes. Category 4 contains all units referring to the advantages of accepting the outcomes described by categories 2 and 3: e.g.

If we agree on 85% I'm sure productivity will go up/
It would be a safer way of doing things/
You know, I would have thought that you'd have saved face/

If he's given the chance to organise his work his job satisfaction will increase/
You will benefit enormously from the reorganisation/

Category 5: Negative consequences of proposed outcomes. Category 5 contains all units referring to the disadvantages of accepting the outcomes described by categories 2 and 3: e.g.

Unless you give us 85% there'll be a strike/
To give only 70% makes it seem that you don't trust the workers/
It's difficult to know how people are going to react/
If you're not prepared to offer more than 70% productivity is likely to go down/

Category 6: Other statements about outcomes. Category 6 contains all other statements about outcomes or the consequences of outcomes: e.g.

Well, it's a question of about 30p/
80% is what/? £2 per worker per week/

Acknowledgement

Category 7: Acknowledgement +. Category 7 includes all statements implying praise, congratulation or recognition of a contribution which has been made: e.g.

That's a good point/
Demy Ltd has a long tradition of co-operation between management and union/
I have listened patiently to your arguments/
We're giving these concessions to you/
We have done a lot of work/ and have initiated these proposals/
My figure of 90% is a drop from 100%/
A further distinction may be made between those acts which imply praise of (a) own or both sides, and (b) other side.

Category 8: Acknowledgement −. Category 8 contains all units making derogatory statements, sarcastic comments and statements of censure or blame. It also contains leading questions which, if answered in the affirmative, would leave the respondent open to censure: e.g.

Well, the estimate of the increase in productivity must surely have taken into account that possibly a very small minority of the workers would shirk their work/

The way it seems to be working out is that we've done all the work/ *and you're making a damn sight more out of it than we are*/
You should have these figures for us to see/
I'm to blame on that one/
The Board are being quite unreasonable on this/

A further distinction may be made between those acts which imply criticism of (a) own or both sides and (b) other side.

Other information

Category 9: Information. Category 9 contains all other statements of fact or opinion: e.g.

This is why we suggested the 70% for a year/
The working party had equal representation of management and union/
The company is paying its way quite well at the moment/
What percentage of your workers would you say were doing more than five hours overtime a week/?
Well, I think I can see your point there/
It's the only document which we've got at the moment/

3 THE REFERENT DIMENSION

The referent dimension is *only* scored when the attitudes or behaviours of some Person or Party involved in the dispute are *explicitly* described in a given act. Consequently, some acts have referents whereas some do not.

Category 1: Self. Category 1 is scored whenever a negotiator explicitly describes his own attitudes or behaviour: e.g.

Now I feel that this is fair/
I'm sorry/
I shall carry on/
Well, if everybody had an equal share then I would not be complaining/
I'm not saying this will occur/
I think that, well I'm prepared to drop to 95% of the increase/

However, it is important to note that category 1 is *not* scored in those cases whereby a negotiator describes the behaviour of some other Person or Party in the guise of an opinion statement: e.g.

I think your offer is a very reasonable one/ (category 5: opponent)
I do feel that we are making a fair offer/ (category 4: party)

I don't think you can accept the situation/ (category 3: other)
I can see your difficulties on this/ (category 3: other)
I think you've been made quite a very good, well a very good offer/
(category 5: opponent)

Category 2: Person. Category 2 is scored whenever a negotiator explicitly describes the attitudes or behaviour of some other Person or Persons within the negotiation group on his own side: e.g.

As Jack here just said/
I'll say it again/ *but Bill has said it all before/*

Category 3: Person. Category 3 is scored whenever a negotiator explicitly describes the attitudes or behaviour of some other Person or Persons on the opposing side: e.g.

It's very kind of you to make these gestures/. I can see you've got trouble with the workers/
I'm sure you agree with me on this/
I think you were slightly wrong there/
You said so yourself/

Category 4: Party. Category 4 is scored whenever a negotiator explicitly describes the attitudes or behaviour of the organisation he represents or of members of his organisation not present in the group: e.g.

U: To the working man £2 is a considerable increase/.
U: I think you'll find every worker is fully aware of the problems/.
U: I can't help feeling that the people I represent are likely to come out of this the worst/.
U: I admit there are workers who shirk/.
M: As this is a completely new venture, we must keep our costs down to the level of what we estimate will be the new costs/.
M: Our offer is very generous/.
M: If the firm's productivity, if we can increase our productivity then we will/.
M: Overtime is very very expensive to the company/.

Category 5: Opponent. Category 5 is scored whenever a negotiator explicitly describes the attitudes or behaviour of an organisation (involved in the dispute) which he does not represent or of members of an opposing organisation not present in the group.

U: And it really is your job to sort these things out/.
U: You benefit out of this more than we do/.

U: I mean, you're getting an increase in productivity out of this/.
U: You pay 6% to your shareholders/.
M: We appreciate your making this gesture/.
M: But there are a certain number of your workers, no doubt, who don't really understand the system of shares/.
M: A leading chargehand will get an increase of £2·50/.
M: A certain number of people work a lot of overtime/.

Category 6: Both persons. Category 6 is scored when the negotiator explicitly describes the attitudes or behaviour of Persons from both sides within the negotiation group: e.g.

Well we must deal with this together/
Shall we leave this till later/?
I mean we've got to try and reach a figure on this/
We agreed earlier that we'd backdate the agreement/
We both are going to have to put in a great deal of extra work over this/

Category 7: Both parties. Category 7 is scored when the negotiator explicitly describes the attitudes or behaviour of the Parties to the negotiation: e.g.

There's been a long history of co-operation between management and workers/
This involves us all as a company/
We both make something out of it/
We all have shares in the company/
This goes not only for workers; it goes for management as well/

Category 0: No referent. Not all acts have referents. A referent is not scored unless the attitudes or behaviour of some Person or Party involved in the negotiation (or dispute) is explicitly described. Thus, the following acts do *not* have a referent and are assigned a code of 0:

That's fair comment/
How about vacation pay/?
There are certain unknown factors, unknown quantities, which balance it the other way/
This is 100%/
But it's 78%/ plus the dividend on the shares/
The government doesn't really come into this/
This is all a matter of profits and loss obviously/

Other Coding Conventions

1   Reported speech is broken into units according to division rule (6.2). The referent is then determined by the sense of the introductory remarks: e.g.

It says here that 'The workers might abuse the new system (category 0)/. The proposals involve new responsibilities for all (category 0)/'
In this document you say the increases in productivity cannot be predicted (category 3)/

2 When an act does not complete a point, mode, resource and referent are each coded 'O'.

CPA Decision Sequence

We suggest the following decision sequence for categorising acts according to mode, resource, and referent.

	Question	*Answer = Yes*	*Answer = No*
Mode			
Q.1	Is it seeking?	SEEK	Read Q.2
Q.2	Is it rejecting?	REJECT	Read Q.3
Q.3	Is it accepting?	ACCEPT	OFFER
Resource			
Q.1	Is the act intended to be uncomplimentary to any opposing person or party involved in the negotiation?	ACKNOWLEDGEMENT − (Other side)	Read Q.2
Q.2	Is the act intended to be uncomplimentary to any other persons or parties involved in the negotiation?	ACKNOWLEDGEMENT − (Own or both sides).	Read Q.3
Q.3	Is the act intended to be complimentary to any opposing person or party involved in the negotiation?	ACKNOWLEDGEMENT + (Other side)	Read Q.4
Q.4	Is the act intended to be complimentary to any other persons or parties involved in the negotiation?	ACKNOWLEDGEMENT + (Own or both sides).	Read Q.5
Q.5	Does the act convey a directive, proposal or suggestion about what the group should do or decide?	Read Q.6	Read Q.9
Q.6	Does the directive, proposal or suggestion concern OUTCOME activity?	Read Q.7	PROCEDURE
Q.7	Does the outcome refer to an initial settlement point?	INITIAL SETTLEMENT POINT	Read Q.8
Q.8	Does the outcome refer to a new settlement point?	NEW SETTLEMENT POINT	LIMITS

Q.9	Is the act otherwise concerned with OUTCOME activity?	Read Q.10		INFORMATION
Q.10	Does the act describe negative consequence of outcomes?	NEGATIVE CONSEQUENCE OF OUTCOMES		Read Q.11
Q.11	Does the act describe positive consequences of outcomes?	POSITIVE CONSEQUENCES OF OUTCOMES		ANY OTHER STATEMENT ABOUT OUTCOMES

Referent

Q.1	Does the act contain a statement particularly referring to some other person, persons, or party on the opposite side to the speaker?	Read Q.2		Read Q.3
Q.2	Does the statement refer to a person or sub-group of persons in the opposing negotiating team?	OTHER		OPPONENT
Q.3	Does the act contain a statement particularly referring to some other person, persons or party on the same side as the speaker?	Read Q.4		Read Q.5
Q.4	Does the statement refer to a person or sub-group of persons in the same negotiating team as the speaker?	PERSON		PARTY
Q.5	Does the act contain a statement referring jointly to persons on both sides or to both parties?	Read Q.6		Read Q.7
Q.6	Does the statement refer to a sub-group of persons on both sides?	BOTH PERSONS		BOTH PARTIES
Q.7	Does the act contain any reference to the speaker himself?	SELF		NO REFERENT

Sample Transcripts

The following examples taken from two-person experimental negotiations may help to illustrate how the system has been used.

EXAMPLE A

U: (1) The working party did comprise equal numbers of management and union (1/9/6)/ (2) and they did agree to the proposals (1/9/6)/. (3) It was beneficial from your point of view that it did increase efficiency (1/4/5)/, (4) reduced overtime (1/4/0)/, (5) and placed more responsibilities on the workers (1/4/4)/, (6) which you did make a point of (1/9/5)/. (7) And now you seem to be denying this responsibility (1/8/5)/ (8) or at least denying that the workers will accept this responsibility (1/8/4)/.

M: (9) Well not precisely (3/8/0)/. (10) Our objection stands, is based on the fact that when people, when they're faced with new situations/ (11) and changes (1/9/0)/ (12) and so on (1/9/0)/ (10) they're not predictable (1/9/5)/. (13) This goes not only for workers; it goes for management as well (1/9/7)/. (14) It involves responsibilities/, (15) quite heavy responsibilities (1/9/0)/ (14) for all concerned (1/9/7)/, (16) and we feel that this thing would best be done gradually (1/3/4)/ (17) rather than with one blow (1/3/0)/. (18) This is why we suggested the 70% (1/6/3)/ (19) and see how it goes (1/6/0)/, (20) see how people react (1/6/5)/ (21) and if it looks as if it's going to be a success/, (22) if people do react to it favourably (1/3/5)/, (23) if people react the workers do bear their responsibilities without checking them (1/3/5)/ (21) then we'll review the situation after that time (1/3/4)/. (24) Well if we see it's been favourable then we'll give you the full 100% (1/3/4)/.

EXAMPLE B

U: (1) Well, I agree this travel concession is quite a head start, you know (1/7/1)/. (2) I'll give you that (1/7/1)/. (3) We only differ on 2/6 either way (1/6/6)/. (4) It isn't very much (1/6/0)/.

M: (5) Well it would be a pity to see any major issue develop over such a small amount (1/6/0)/. (6) Anything so radical as a strike over 2/6 would be a blot on the ledger (1/6/0)/.

U: (7) Well, it would be difficult to move very much from this figure (1/3/0)/. (8) I mean we've shifted a fair bit in coming down (1/7/4)/. (9) Well I think we'll be shifting a bit too much in coming down to 80% (1/3/4)/.

M: (10) You reckon that's too far (4/3/5)/?

U: (11) A bit too far (1/3/0)/. (12) If only from the point of view of face (1/5/0)/.

EXAMPLE C

M: (1) It's not a very large firm (1/9/0)/, (2) not excessively so at any rate (1/9/0)/. (3) Can we get on to some other point (4/1/6)/? (4) We're going round in circles at the moment (1/8/6)/. (5) I'm willing now 75% (1/2/1)/. (6) I feel this is as far as I can go (1/3/1)/. (7) As you know, I'm responsible to other people (1/9/1)/. (8) This is as far as we can go without seeing off this trial period (1/3/4)/. (9) It's not that we don't trust you (1/9/3)/ (10) or the majority of the members of your union (1/9/5)/, (11) but I do not feel that it is unreasonable to try out the system (1/6/1)/. (12) After all, it's only this short period, relatively, that we're asking you to go down to this 75% level (1/6/4)/.

U: (13) Oh true (2/6/0)/, (14) but this trial period I think I must object to

(3/3/1)/, (15) because we the union (0/0/0)/. (16) I admit there is only one of us (1/9/4)/, (17) there's only one union (1/9/4)/. (18) And I think you're very lucky in that there's only one union (1/7/5)/, (19) even though I say it myself (1/7/1)/. (20) Because let us, if we look around us we see disputes where there are three or four different unions involved (1/9/7)/. (21) And nobody knows quite who wants that (1/9/0)/. (22) So I think you're very lucky (1/7/5)/. (23) And I think it is something that the union itself went into this (1/7/4)/ (24) on its own (1/7/4)/. (25) We drew up the proposals (1/7/4)/ (26) and we made the suggestions (1/7/4)/. (27) I think we are justified in claiming the full increase (1/7/4)/.

M: (28) We appreciate your making this gesture (2/7/5)/ (29) and coming forward with the initial proposals (2/7/5)/. (30) This is much appreciated (1/7/0)/. (31) But we still have this problem of whether all your workers are responsible (1/8/5)/. (32) I know you as one would not try to take advantage of the situation (1/7/3)/, (33) but you must admit that it's human nature to try and make as much money as possible (1/8/3)/. (34) We all know this (1/8/7)/.

EXAMPLE D

M: (1) We're quite willing to if productivity can be increased to a sufficient rate to even raise these pay scales in due time (1/3/4)/.

U: (2) Oh yes (2/3/0)/, (3) but a year is too long at this minimum of 78% (3/2/0)/, (4) when we/, (5) as I said (1/7/1)/, (4) assumed tacitly for the whole of this session that we'd get the whole 100% of the savings consolidated to us (1/6/4)/. (6) And 78% is, well, it's too low really quite honestly (3/2/0)/. (7) I can't go back and say, 'We've got 78% on a year's trial' (3/2/1)/. (8) I mean, this doesn't really put much trust in the people I represent (1/8/4)/. (9) Does it (4/8/0)/?

M: (10) I can see your difficulties on this (1/7/2)/ (11) and I hope that *you* can see mine (1/9/2)/. (12) But it's 78% (1/2/0)/ plus the dividend on the shares (1/2/0)/.

EXAMPLE E

U: (1) Let us try and get some figure out of this (1/1/6)/. (2) I mean, we don't have much longer (1/9/6)/. (3) Can I call on you to give me another quote (4/2/3)/? (4) I think I've told you that your 78% is quite unjustified (1/8/3)/.

M: (5) I am, as a last resort I'm, I just can't go above 80% (1/2/1)/. (6) This is really the outside (1/3/0)/.

U: (7) 80% (1/9/0)/. (8) Well, if we were to make it a realistic figure of, say (0/0/0)/, (9) if I'm asking 90 I think possibly if I were to ask you for 84% (1/2/3)/, (10) I don't think that would be unrealistic (1/7/1)/.

M: (11) It's very kind of you to make these gestures (1/7/3)/. (12) I can see you've got trouble with the workers in trying to (1/7/3)/. (13) I suppose really at the outside we just can't go above 82% (1/2/4)/. (14) It doesn't seem much (1/6/0)/, (15) as I was quibbling about 5/– before (1/6/1)/. (16) I know this isn't much (1/6/1)/. (17) I just can't go any further than this (1/3/1)/.

U: (18) I can't really go back with this (3/2/1)/.

The Reliability of CPA

CPA contains two sets of rules: a set for dividing transcripts into acts, and another for assigning categories to the units obtained. Observers have few problems applying the first set of rules reliably. In a typical instance, three observers divided the transcript of an experimental negotiation into acts: of the 466 units coded by one observer (Morley), 433 (92·9%) were coded by another observer (Stephenson) and 448 (96·1%) by the third observer. It is clear that the division rules can be applied with a high degree of reliability.

A number of reliability studies of the category assignment have now been performed on different experimental and field data. All have produced reasonably satisfactory outcomes. Three will be reported here.

CONSISTENCY OF A SINGLE OBSERVER

A transcript from Experiment I, coded initially in August 1973, was recoded by the same observer in June 1974 (Morley 1974). Of the 263 acts recoded at time 1: (a) 259 (98·5%) were coded as having the same *mode* at time 2; (b) 207 (78·7%) were coded as having the same *resource* at time 2; and 223 (84·8%) were coded as having the same *referent* at time 2. Another similar analysis of a transcript from the experimental data, obtained by Stephenson, Ayling and Rutter (1976) (in press, and quoted in Chapter 11), gave the following results: mode, 96·1%; resource, 95·7%; and referent, 93·1%. The comparison for Morley's data between the overall percentages of categories ascribed at times 1 and 2 (portrayed in Figure 10.3) indicated what is customarily found using the system: that there is high agreement between *overall* profiles obtained on two separate occasions.

CONSISTENCY OF TWO OBSERVERS

Hogg (1976) has reported the results of an experiment using Bass's (1966) experimental materials and involving both face-to-face and telephone negotiations. A trained graduate coder (TGC) was employed to apply CPA to all the transcripts of the negotiations; he subsequently recoded one of these negotiations some months later, as described before in (a). It was also coded once independently by Hogg (MRAH). Figure 10.4(a) gives the percentage

Dimension and Category	Time 1 (August 1973)	Time 2 (June 1974)
Mode	%	%
1 Offer	82·9	82·5
2 Accept	7·6	8·0
3 Reject	1·9	1·9
4 Seek	7·6	7·6
Resource		
0 Not ascertainable	7·6	8·0
1 Procedure	3·0	3·4
2 Settlement point	4·6	5·7
3 Limits	13·7	15·2
4 Positive consequences of proposed outcomes	5·3	7·2
5 Negative consequences of proposed outcomes	1·9	1·9
6 Other statements about outcomes	4·2	12·9
7 Acknowledgement +	8·8	8·4
8 Acknowledgement −	3·0	3·0
9 Information	47·9	33·8
Referent		
0 No referent	39·5	41·0
1 Self	9·8	9·1
2 Other	4·2	4·6
3 Party	27·0	24·3
4 Opponent	12·6	13·7
5 Both persons	3·8	3·8
6 Both parties	3·0	3·4

Figure 10.3 Consistency of a single observer: CPA profiles obtained at times 1 and 2 (after Morley 1974)

agreements and reliability coefficients calculated on an act-by-act basis for modes, resources and referents separately. Column A shows the comparison between the coding of the trained graduate coder at time 1 (TGC 1) and time 2 (TGC 2); column B shows the comparison between Hogg's coding (MRAH) and that of the trained graduate coder at time 1 (TGC 1); and column C shows the comparison between Hogg's coding (MRAH) and that of the trained graduate coder at time 2 (TGC 2). It can be seen that the ranking for reliability was in the order mode > referent > resource, as with Morley's (1974) data. The reliability coefficients were moderately satisfactory for both the mode and referent categories but unacceptably low for the resource categories. Fortunately, inspection of the results indicates that most of the confusion occurred between different categories of outcome. 'Limits', for example, were confused with 'new settlement points' and 'new settlement points' with 'initial settlement points'. The remaining confusion, as in Morley's study, invariably involved the 'information' and various 'outcome' categories.

In a further experimental study (Hogg 1976) undergraduate students played the part of representatives of one or other student faction campaigning for a particular method of degree assessment. Participants were selected according

	A Percentage Agreement	r	B Percentage Agreement	r	C Percentage Agreement	r
(a) First experiment						
Mode	94·4	·882	89·7	·786	92·7	·828
Resource	71·9	·667	67·5	·619	69·9	·645
Referent	90·1	·842	86·8	·795	87·4	·803
(b) Second experiment						
Mode	96·1	·916	93·0	·849	94·7	·882
Resource	82·3	·716	74·7	·651	74·4	·658
Referent	92·7	·868	92·1	·859	91·0	·836

A = 2 codings by TGC
B = TGC 1st coding and MRAH coding
C = TGC 2nd coding and MRAH coding

Figure 10.4 Consistency of a single observer and of two observers: percentage agreement and reliability coefficients obtained for act-by-act CPA codings of experimental face-to-face two-person industrial negotiations (Hogg 1976)

to their attitudes, such that their opinions matched their role. Negotiations lasted about twenty-five minutes. The coding procedure followed in Hogg's first experiment was repeated, with results as portrayed in Figure 10.4(b). It can be seen that, although the pattern of results confirmed the earlier findings, the coefficients were uniformly higher. The resource categories continued to

	Resource Categories	0	1	2	3	4	5	6	7	8	9
0	Not coded	9·8									0·4
1	Initial settlement point		1·0	0·3	0·4						0·4
2	New settlement point			5·4	3·6		0·2	0·1			0·5
3	Limits				8·1	0·4	1·0	0·1			4·2
4	Positive consequences of outcomes					5·0					1·0
5	Negative consequences of outcomes						5·6				8·6
6	Procedure							1·3			0·9
7	Acknowledgement +								0·2		0·4
8	Acknowledgement −									0	0·0
9	Information										41·3

Figure 10.5 Mean percentage agreements in three pairs of CPA codings of transcript of undergraduate negotiation (Hogg 1976)

be the most difficult to score. Once again the outcome and information categories were hardest to distinguish.

Figure 10.5 summarises the combined results from the three pairs of codings of the second experiment. It is evident that 'limits' and 'negative consequences of outcomes' were most frequently confused by the coders. The coders agreed on the 'limits' category on $8 \cdot 1\%$ of occasions but disagreed on $9 \cdot 7\%$ (i.e. $0 \cdot 4\% + 3 \cdot 6\% + 0 \cdot 4\% + 1 \cdot 0\% + 0 \cdot 1\% + 4 \cdot 2\%$). 'Negative consequences' were in harmony on $5 \cdot 6\%$ of occasions and in conflict on $9 \cdot 8\%$. 'Limits' shared the confusion almost equally between 'new settlement points' and 'information', whereas 'negative consequences' were confused predominantly with 'information'. Results for these two categories taken separately must obviously be treated cautiously. In addition, for certain purposes there would seem to be good reason to combine categories 2 and 3 (i.e. 'new settlement points' and 'limits').

Chapter 11

The Analysis of Experimental Negotiations Conducted via Different Systems of Communication

In this chapter we shall present the results of using Conference Process Analysis (CPA) to analyse the 'Demy Ltd' negotiations of Experiment II, in which union negotiators were given the stronger case in a laboratory Type 2 task. They obtained higher outcomes in telephone groups than in face-to-face groups ($p < \cdot01$) but failed to achieve higher outcomes in constrained groups than in free groups (see Figure 8.2). (While it is clear that the side with the stronger case generally achieved higher outcomes in constrained groups than in free groups – see p. 152 – there is some evidence that in this case the effect was slightly reversed. The mean scale values obtained were identical in the free and constrained treatments. However, outcomes in free negotiations had higher mean ranks than those in constrained negotiations. The value of U in the Mann–Whitney test was not statistically reliable.)

The Effects of Medium of Communication

'DEMY LTD' NEGOTIATIONS

Chapter 7 has outlined specific predictions about the mechanisms involved (pp. 133–5). Briefly, we argued that one effect of formality would be to *depersonalise* the negotiation situation. We therefore expected certain CPA categories to be distributed differently in face-to-face and telephone groups. In particular, we expected face-to-face negotiation groups to manifest (a) relatively less disagreement than telephone groups, (b) relatively more praise for opponent, (c) relatively less blame for opponent, (d) relatively more explicit references to self and/or other, and (e) relatively fewer references to party and/or opponent. In other words, we predicted face-to-face and telephone negotiations to differ along dimensions of (a) mode: reject, (b) resource: acknowledgement + and acknowledgement −, and (c) referent: self, other, party and opponent.

Figure 11.1 gives the CPA data for Experiment II. (In this case differences between treatments were tested for statistical significance by calculating the relevant values of the Mann–Whitney U statistic. For convenience, mean values are shown in the Figure. Unless otherwise stated, the direction of an effect is the same whether the mean or the mean rank of the scores concerned is considered.) Only one of the predicted differences was statistically significant:

	Union				Management			
	FF/F	FF/C	T/F	T/C	FF/F	FF/C	T/F	T/C
Total acts	54·1	47·8	47·7	51·7	45·9	52·2	52·3	48·3
Mode								
Unclassified	0·1	0·2	0·0	0·1	0·0	0·1	0·0	0·0
Offer	45·0	41·3	36·2	47·2	36·0	44·0	42·5	41·2
Accept	3·2	2·7	4·2	2·7	3·0	3·8	4·1	3·7
Reject	3·0	0·8	2·3	0·7	3·2	1·2	3·2	0·7
Seek	2·8	2·9	5·1	1·0	4·0	3·1	2·7	2·4
Resource								
Unclassified	5·5	3·6	6·8	4·5	6·1	5·2	6·3	4·5
Settlement point	4·1	2·9	4·6	1·0	4·6	3·0	4·6	1·8
Limits	2·3	3·9	2·2	3·8	4·1	8·7	5·7	6·9
Positive consequences of outcomes	6·8	3·9	3·1	1·6	2·8	2·6	3·4	5·9
Negative consequences of outcomes	4·3	2·3	4·0	6·2	2·3	1·3	4·4	2·2
Other statements about outcomes	2·0	3·6	1·7	1·9	2·2	3·8	3·1	3·6
Procedure	1·4	1·3	1·1	2·1	1·2	1·5	1·1	2·0
Acknowledgement +	6·0	4·9	6·6	5·1	5·0	3·7	7·0	2·3
Acknowledgement −	5·0	2·2	4·3	4·0	2·6	0·8	2·4	1·9
Information	16·7	19·4	13·5	21·8	15·1	21·9	14·2	17·3
Referent								
No referent	13·8	16·6	14·8	15·0	14·3	18·4	15·6	16·9
Person	5·1	5·7	7·1	3·3	4·7	6·6	6·1	5·3
Other	2·3	2·2	2·6	2·8	3·4	2·5	2·6	4·0
Party	15·4	14·9	12·0	18·8	12·5	11·6	13·9	7·4
Opponent	12·6	5·3	8·0	8·2	7·7	8·2	10·5	12·6
Both persons	1·7	1·1	0·6	1·2	2·6	2·4	2·4	0·9
Both parties	3·2	2·2	2·7	2·6	0·8	2·6	1·4	1·2

FF = face-to-face   F = free to interrupt
T = telephone   C = constrained

Figure 11.1 Distribution of CPA categories in 'Demy Ltd' negotiation (Experiment II) (in percentage of total number of acts given by each pair)

management negotiators made smaller use of references to opponent (referent: opponent) in face-to-face groups (mean $= 7.9\%$) than in telephone groups (mean $= 11.5\%$) ($p < .02$). Otherwise, the direction of the predicted effects was sometimes confirmed and sometimes not. The most striking feature of the data is that the differences between the media were extremely small so far as the above dimensions were concerned.

Apparently, increasing the formality of the medium of communication used did not in Experiment II depersonalise the process of the negotiations involved. The messages may of course have had a different impact in the two situations, but if the concept of depersonalisation is to have any predictive value it must refer to differences in the types of communications transmitted rather than in the impact of communications received. We shall present evidence showing that absence of visual cues (as in telephone negotiations) may depersonalise other conversations, but we must seek an explanation for the results of Experiment II by considering other aspects of the negotiators' behaviour. Broadly speaking, we must consider whether different types of argument were used in face-to-face and telephone groups.

Relative participation of the negotiators did not vary between media. There was no greater tendency for management or union representatives to contribute more in one circumstance than in the other. The use of the different *mode* categories was not significantly affected by medium, nor by management/union role. *Resource* categories, however, were differently distributed in face-to-face and telephone groups, although the effect was not the same for management as for union subjects. In face-to-face groups union negotiators made proportionately more references to the positive consequences of outcomes than their management opponents (union mean $= 5.3\%$, management mean $= 2.7\%$), whereas in telephone groups they made proportionately fewer such references (union mean $= 2.4\%$, management mean $= 4.7\%$). This interaction was statistically reliable ($p < .028$). Furthermore, it is clear that the interaction was due to changes in the behaviour of the union ($p = .038$) rather than the management negotiators (p = n.s.).

To summarise: medium of communication did affect the process of the 'Demy Ltd' experimental negotiations. However, very few of the differences observed were statistically reliable, and in general the effects obtained were disappointingly small. It would seem that if personal considerations do affect the outcomes of such negotiations they are introduced by nonverbal cues of one sort or another.

FURTHER EVIDENCE

While there is little evidence that absence of visual communication acted to depersonalise the 'Demy Ltd' negotiations of Experiment II, other research confirms that our initial suggestions do have some foundation. Rutter and

Stephenson (in press) have shown that participants interrupted more frequently when face-to-face than when communicating via an audio link. They have suggested that the main advantage of visual communication is the increased potential for spontaneity which it permits, because the participants may interrupt more frequently without threatening the continuity of the interaction. Wilson (1974) has shown that greater disagreement occurred between President Nixon and his aides when conversations were conducted by telephone than when they took place face-to-face. The use of the telephone channel served to increase anonymity and to decrease the intimacy of the conversations. Short (1973) has demonstrated that argument between people leads to greater opinion change in audio encounters than in face-to-face encounters, for they are not distracted from detailed argument by irrelevant information of a personal kind. The information may be verbal or nonverbal, but the merits of the case are more likely to prevail in audio encounters than when debate occurs face-to-face. However, the most direct evidence in support of our initial proposals comes from a study by Stephenson, Ayling and Rutter (1976; in press). Their results will be described in some detail.

THE STUDY OF STEPHENSON, AYLING AND RUTTER

Randomly selected students from the University of Nottingham were asked to complete a questionnaire about union–management relations. The questionnaire was developed from Campbell (1960) and included items on the role of unions in industrial strife, questions of management prerogative and efficiency, the unions' right to strike, etc. Twelve male-male pairs and twelve female-female pairs were formed on the basis of the scores, in such a way that one member of the pair held broadly pro-union views and the other broadly pro-management views. It was ensured that members of a pair were strangers and did not meet until the experimental session. Pairs were randomly assigned to either the face-to-face or audio condition, with the constraint that each condition should include six male and six female pairs. Subjects assigned to the face-to-face condition sat at adjacent sides of a rectangular table, and those assigned to the audio condition sat in physically separate rooms and communicated by microphone-headphone units fitted to the head. Each pair was allocated two questionnaire items on which the subjects held opposing views consistent with their overall persuasions, and the task was to spend fifteen minutes discussing either or both items. In the audio condition, one subject was randomly assigned to start the discussion. All twenty-four conversations were tape recorded and were terminated by the experimenter after fifteen minutes. Verbatim transcripts were made from the tape recordings and were checked by one of the authors before being typed. The task was not therefore a formal negotiation task, although the subjects were made aware of their differences and required to discuss them. In terms of the formal classification of experimental paradigms, it approximated most closely to the substitute debate. As subjects were less constrained in this situation than in the situations we have previously employed, and reported here, a consequent increase in the salience of media effects on interaction was expected.

CPA was used to describe the content of the debates. The twenty-four scripts were coded by Ayling, and the script coded first was recoded after completion of the remaining twenty-three. The two codings were highly congruent on an act-by-act basis, with correlations of ·8 or more for the mode, resource and referent dimensions taken separately.

The effects of medium of communication (face-to-face v. audio), sex and role (management v. union) on the process of argument were investigated by computing the proportion of acts allocated to each CPA category. Differences between treatments were assessed (taking each mode, resource and referent category separately) by means of the appropriate analysis of variance (Myers 1972, pp. 242–53). Furthermore, all combinations of mode: offer and mode: accept with resource: information and each referent category were subsequently analysed separately employing two-way analyses of variance, with medium of communication and role the independent variables.

Once again, specific predictions were made about the depersonalising effects of the absence of visual communication. In terms of CPA it was predicted that depersonalisation would be manifested by (at least): increased blame for opponent, less praise for opponent, fewer 'self' references, more 'party' references, and increased disagreement. As shown in Figure 11.2(a), all of these predictions were upheld but only two were statistically significant at an acceptable level. There was less praise for opponent ($F = 4\cdot61, d.f. = 1, 20, p < \cdot05$) and were more 'own party' references ($F = 5\cdot10, d.f. = 1, 20, p < \cdot05$) in the audio condition.

Several other differences in behaviour emerged which were interpreted to 'testify to a preoccupation with the issues in the audio condition, compared to face-to-face exchange' (see Figure 11.2(b)). Briefly, more offers of information were exchanged in audio groups than in face-to-face groups ($F = 4\cdot76, d.f. = 1, 20, p < \cdot05$). Union representatives also made more offers of information about opponent (i.e. management) in audio groups ($F = 6\cdot32, d.f. = 1, 20, p < \cdot025$), although management representatives did not. More acts were incomplete in the face-to-face than in the audio condition (supporting the formal analysis of speech reported in Rutter and Stephenson (in press) and revealing the greater spontaneity of face-to-face discussions).

Three interactions between medium of communication and role of participants are also germane to the present discussion (see Figures 11.2(c) and 11.3): management representatives were more likely to offer in the face-to-face condition, whereas union representatives were more likely to do so in the audio condition ($F = 8\cdot98, d.f. = 1, 20, p < \cdot01$); more management acts were coded as information in the face-to-face condition, whereas more union acts were so coded in the audio condition ($F = 9\cdot77, d.f. = 1, 20, p < \cdot01$); and

	Face-to-face	*Telephone*	p
(a) Depersonalisation			
Blame for opponent	2·00	2·17	n.s.
Praise for opponent	0·92	0·25	<·05
'Self' references	7·58	7·25	n.s.
'Party' references	7·67	11·17	<·05
'Rejects' (disagreement)	0·67	1·08	n.s.
(b) Other Effects of Medium			
Outcome	1·75	1·25	n.s.
Offers of information	48·56	55·53	<·05
'Union' offers of information			
about opponent's party	1·60	3·10	<·025
(c) Management–Union Differences			
Own party	2·07	7·51	<·001
Opponent's party	8·26	2·57	<·001
Criticise opponent	1·69	0·56	<·01
Praise opponent	0·50	0·22	<·01
Praise own/both sides	0·19	0·62	<·025
Criticise own/both sides	0·24	0·58	<·025

*Figures represent the mean percentage of all units allocated to CPA categories, averaged across the management–union variable.

Figure 11.2 Means* of CPA categories (after Stephenson, Ayling and Rutter, 1976)

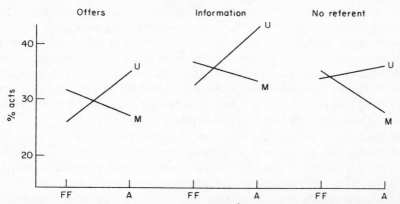

Figure 11.3 The effects of management/union role and medium of communication on three CPA variables (FF = face-to-face condition, A = audio condition, U = union representatives, M = management representatives) (after Stephenson, Ayling and Rutter 1976)

more union acts had no referent in the audio condition, whereas more management acts had none in the face-to-face condition ($F = 6·02$, $d.f. = 1$, 20, $p < ·025$). In addition, more 'both party' references were made by management representatives in the face-to-face condition and by union representatives in the audio condition ($F = 10·00$, $d.f. = 1$, 20, $p < ·01$), although the absolute frequency of these categories was very small.

How may these interactions of role with medium of communication be explained? Two related factors are important to the interpretation. First, union negotiators probably felt more *confident in their role* than management negotiators. Stephenson, Ayling and Rutter experienced great difficulty in obtaining students committed to management and hostile to the unions. This probably indicates that students in the union role were more likely to have had the courage of their convictions. There were in fact large differences in CPA referent categories between the sides, indicating that the debates focused on the attitudes and behaviour of the unions (see Figure 11.2(c)). For example, large differences occurred in the referent categories 'own party' and 'opponent's party'. The union representatives referred more frequently to 'own party' ($F = 41·84$, $d.f. = 1$, 20, $p < ·001$) and the management more frequently to 'opponent's party' ($F = 32·91$, $d.f. = 1$, 20, $p < ·001$). The remaining differences clarify the picture, demonstrating that the different emphases on 'own' or 'other party' were embodied largely in affective statements of one kind or another. Management representatives repeatedly commented both more 'critically' and 'favourably' on their opponents than did union representatives ($F = 13·62$, $d.f. = 1$, 20, $p < ·01$ and $F = 11·25$, $d.f. = 1$, 20, $p < ·01$ respectively). The union representatives, on the other hand, responded predictably with greater 'praise' and 'criticism' for 'own or both sides' ($F = 7·77$, $d.f. = 1$, 20, $p < ·025$ and $F = 7·27$, $d.f. = 1$, 20, $p < ·025$ respectively). Overall, the picture is clear: union behaviour and attitudes were the main subject of discussion, with management criticising the unions but acknowledging their contribution to industrial relations, and the unions perhaps acknowledging faults but vigorously defending the cause. We know that the party with the stronger case tends to excel by telephone where, we have suggested, the representative can press home his advantage without being made aware of the other's loss of face. Perhaps a similar effect occurred here. The union representatives, with their supposedly morally superior views, were being more aggressive and determined in the audio condition than in the more embarrassing face-to-face condition.

Second, we can assume that there were *differences in social class background* between the two groups which might have contributed to this interaction. Personal differences in appearance and manner, which reflect differences in social background, education and attitudes, are more likely to become apparent and salient when the participants can see each other. By and large, it is likely that those subjects whose sympathies were predominantly with management were from backgrounds of higher socio-economic status than were those whose allegiance was to the unions. The established tendency for higher status persons to assume leadership was perhaps more readily elicited in the face-to-face than in the audio condition because of the nonverbal cues arising from appearance and manner. When they were interacting face-to-face, this would have reinforced the tendency (a) for the union representatives to lose their grip somewhat, and (b) for the management representatives to make more offers than the union representatives and to inform over a wider range of circumstances and events beyond the immediate issues.

An interesting further finding emerged in an analysis of what might be called *'responsiveness'*. Stephenson, Ayling and Rutter measured responsiveness by examining the transition from one speaker to the next and calculating the extent to which the new speaker was responding directly to what had gone (immediately) before. For example, if he responded to mode: offer with mode: reject, to resource: outome with resource: outome, and to referent: own party with referent: own party, the transition would contribute a score of $+3$ to an overall measure of responsiveness (offer–reject $= 1$, outcome–outcome $= 1$, own party–own party $= 1$). Six other mode–mode transitions; four other resource–resource transitions, and fourteen other referent–referent transitions could contribute to the total score in the same way. It must be admitted that this definition of responsiveness is rather arbitrary and the analyses presented should be treated with a good deal of caution. Nevertheless, it seems that responsiveness was not directly affected by medium: participants were no more or less likely to respond directly to one another in the absence of visual communication. However, the correlation between the responsiveness of the participants did vary in that in the audio condition there was a large negative correlation ($-\cdot8$). In other words, in the audio condition one person (more often the union representative) tended to initiate new topics and new ideas and so was low on responsiveness, while the other tended to respond to these initiations and so was high on the measure. In the face-to-face condition the correlation was also negative ($-\cdot2$), but not significantly so, and was significantly less ($p < \cdot05$) than the correlation in the audio condition.

DISCUSSION

The differences in behaviour produced by Stephenson, Ayling and Rutter's (1976) manipulation of medium of communication were consistent with the results of our analysis of 'Demy Ltd' negotiations (Morley and Stephenson 1970b). In addition, several new and provocative findings have emerged from their study. Apparently, CPA can detect differences in behaviour of the predicted sort, and the failure to find face-to-face/audio differences in Experiment II cannot be attributed to the inadequacy of the category system *per se*. Rather, we are inclined to suggest that differences between the two situations were due to the differences in the tasks used. We used a formal negotiation task in Experiment II, whereas Stephenson, Ayling and Rutter did not. Furthermore, the latter authors gave subjects greater freedom to control the content of the 'agenda' than did the former. The implication is that in Experiment II the task was so highly structured that the expected behavioural differences could not emerge.

We shall now move on to consider behavioural differences between negotiations in free and constrained experimental treatments. It should be remembered that this manipulation did not produce statistically reliable effects upon the outcomes of the negotiations in Experiment II. The mean scale values obtained were identical in the two treatments. However, comparison of the mean ranks assigned to outcomes suggests that, in this case, the side with the stronger case obtained slightly more favourable settlements in free negotiations than in constrained negotiations. (This does not, of course, reflect the general trend in the data from Experiments I and II combined.)

The Effects of Freedom to Interrupt: 'Demy Ltd' Negotiations

In Experiment II we had expected that the effect of increasing formality (by restricting freedom to interrupt) would be to depersonalise negotiations in the constrained groups. However, only two of the relevant comparisons were statistically significant, and these showed greater depersonalisation in free groups than in constrained groups. Results are shown in Figure 11.1. Both union ($p = \cdot002$) and management ($p = \cdot002$) negotiators placed relatively greater emphasis on rejection in free groups than in constrained groups. Furthermore, management negotiators made proportionately greater use of 'acknowledgement $+$' ($p = \cdot05$) and 'acknowledgement $-$' ($p < \cdot064$) in free groups than in constrained groups (although the latter trend was not statistically significant at the 5% level of confidence). The tendency for management negotiators to make more 'party' references in free groups than in constrained groups also approached statistical significance ($p = \cdot082$). Other comparisons were sometimes in the predicted direction and sometimes not. Once again, we must conclude that the effect of formality was not to depersonalise the exchange of communications involved in these negotiation groups.

While formality did not affect the relative participation of union and management negotiators, in general it is clear that subjects followed different strategies in free and constrained groups. By and large, different trends were shown by union and management negotiators. *Union* negotiators ask relatively more questions when negotiation was free than when it was constrained ($p = \cdot028$), made relatively more offers of specific settlement points ($p = \cdot002$), and placed relatively fewer limits on the type of settlement they were prepared to consider ($p = \cdot02$). Union negotiators also made proportionately more use of 'information' in free groups than in constrained groups, although this trend was not statistically reliable ($p = \cdot064$). *Management* negotiators made relatively more offers of specific settlement points in free groups than in constrained groups ($p = \cdot05$). Three other management trends approached statistical significance: management negotiators made proportionately less use of 'limits' ($p < \cdot064$) and 'information' ($p = \cdot064$) in free groups than in constrained groups; they also made proportionately more statements about the negative consequences of outcomes ($p < \cdot082$).

A Further Consideration of the Effects of Formality

We manipulated formality in two ways in our programme of experimental research: (a) we varied the medium of communication and examined the effects of strength of case on outcomes in face-to-face, television and telephone groups; and (b) we varied negotiators' freedom to interrupt one another. In Chapter 7 we suggested that settlements in favour of the side with the stronger case would be positively associated with formality in the system of communication used – and that the same explanation would apply however formality was manipulated. Our experimental findings, summarised in Figure 11.4, cast some doubt on that earlier analysis.

In general, the verbal behaviour of the negotiators was remarkably similar in the face-to-face and telephone groups of Experiment II. In particular, there was no evidence to suggest that the absence of visual cues depersonalised the verbal exchange in telephone groups. While it is clear that formality can depersonalise telephone conversations (Stephenson, Ayling and Rutter, 1976; in press), it seems unlikely that the Experiment II analysis results can be explained in the same way. Many more differences in the distribution of CPA categories were obtained in comparisons between free and constrained groups

	Effects of Medium of Communication		*Effects of Freedom to Interrupt*	
	Face-to-face groups	*Telephone groups*	*Free groups*	*Constrained groups*
Union-high	Positive consequences of outcomes		Reject Seek Settlement point	Limits
Management-high		Opponent	Reject Acknowledgement + Settlement point	

Figure 11.4 Summary of significant differences between different systems of communication in 'Demy Ltd' negotiations of Experiment II

(and in addition a number of effects were significant at the 10% level of confidence). There was no evidence that restricting subjects' freedom to interrupt depersonalised negotiations in the constrained groups. Indeed, negotiations in free groups were in certain respects more depersonalised than negotiations in constrained groups. This latter finding is interesting in view of the failure to obtain differences in outcomes in the two systems of communication. The concept of depersonalisation may still have some value in explaining the differences between outcomes in the free and constrained conditions of Experiment I.

These findings suggest the possibility of distinguishing between two types of formality: formality in the medium/channel of communication ('channel formality'), and formality in the procedures/conventions employed ('conventional formality'). Apparently, variations in channel formality have the same effects on the outcomes of experimental negotiations as variations in conventional formality – but perhaps for different reasons. We shall return to this question in Chapter 13, but it is important to note that any firm conclusions must rest on the analysis of additional data.

'Successful' and 'Unsuccessful' Negotiations

Union negotiators achieved higher outcomes in telephone groups than in face-to-face groups, but *within* each treatment a range of settlements covering four scale points was obtained. It was therefore decided to divide negotiations within each treatment into two groups: those providing settlements relatively favourable to the union, and those providing settlements relatively unfavourable to it. Fortunately, it was possible to do this in such a way that two of the four negotiations within each group were free and two were constrained. For the purpose of analysis we assumed that groups whose outcomes reflected strength of case were more 'successful' than those whose outcomes favoured no one side or favoured the management side. (Other methods of assessing negotiation success have been discussed in Chapter 3.) It was then possible to compare differences between 'successful' and 'unsuccessful' groups.

There were few general characteristics of negotiation success which obtained, whichever system of communication was used. Neither side predominated, and there were no differences characteristic of both union and management negotiators. Management negotiators, however, asked fewer questions ($p < \cdot 05$) and made relatively more explicit references to 'self' ($p < \cdot 028$) in successful than in unsuccessful groups. No other statistically reliable effects were obtained.

This analysis was of course exploratory. It is likely that a great deal of data is required in order to answer questions of this sort (Bartos 1966, 1970). Nevertheless, it is interesting to compare our results with those of McGrath and Julian (1963) who also tried to characterise the behaviour of successful groups. To recapitulate: McGrath and Julian found that successful groups were those which resolved their problems of content structuring in time to prepare written contracts. Our definition of success differed from that used by McGrath and Julian, and the negotiations differed in type. 'Structuring' activity played little part in any of our groups. No doubt the pattern of behaviour which leads to effective performance in one situation need not do so in another.

Differences between successful and unsuccessful groups will be discussed in more detail in Chapters 12 and 13.

Chapter 12

The Analysis of Stages in Real Life Negotiations

Several authors have suggested that 'successful' negotiations go through stages which 'unsuccessful' negotiations do not. We do not ourselves have enough case material to follow Landsberger (1955a) and compare the former with the latter. Instead, we shall present an analysis of two quite different negotiations which took place in two quite different industrial contexts. Transcripts of each negotiation will be presented in the text.

Two methods of analysis were employed: (a) CPA was used to describe the content of the negotiations concerned; and (b) Douglas's (1962) procedure was adopted of asking judges, working from unlabelled transcripts, to identify the party responsible for each uninterrupted speech burst. There were significant differences in the judges' ability to perform this task when transcripts were taken from different stages of the two negotiations.

Analysis of the first negotiation showed that success was not obtained by conforming to the phase sequence identified by Bales and Strodtbeck (1951) and Landsberger (1955a). Analysis of the second negotiation confirmed that the groups we observed had little in common with Bales's (1950) problem-solving groups and showed that different phases were observed in different sessions at the bargaining table.

An Informal Negotiation in a Co-ownership Company: 'Demy Ltd'

BACKGROUND TO THE NEGOTIATION

On 24 January 1969 we interviewed three electricians who had participated in an informal Type 2 negotiation with management representatives some two weeks earlier. The negotiation had occurred almost spontaneously. 'We asked for a meeting in the morning and they came in the afternoon.' Its informality reflected the (agreed) absence of union activity in what was a highly successful co-ownership company.

The cause of the dispute was the callout procedure for electrical fitters. In particular, the electricians objected to their having to be available on all bank holidays. Their request was to be relieved entirely of this irksome responsibility and was expressed forcefully by the leading spokesman, U1, in reply to the question: 'Is this merely an attempt on your part to negotiate some price for this external to the agreement?' asked by the chief management spokesman, M1:

'No . . . we don't want to do it in any case. We just want bank holidays as bank holidays. We simply want the time off. We don't, we won't accept it. We don't want to accept it for £10 a day. We don't want money for it. We don't want money for it. We don't want to do it. We never have wanted to do it, and we thought it was about time. We've been doing it now for about five years, and we thought it was about time we made a stand.'

The stand was effective. After forty-five minutes of tough debate the electricians agreed to consider the principal management proposal: to increase the number of electrical staff by one and to rotate responsibility for electrical coverage at bank holidays between the available staff.

The second meeting was briefer and even less formal than the first. 'I went home that night, and . . . I went home and got some paper out, and wrote down things, then came back, and we had a chat in the morning, and we resolved you know, something which was agreeable to them . . . I think it was the second time, and he just rang down and we all trooped up, didn't we . . . We had another meeting after the one you taped which came up with the proposals which are actually in force now.' These final proposals went slightly beyond those tentatively agreed in the first meeting. The principle of rotation was accepted, but a day off in lieu was agreed whether or not the electrician on standby was called out. The dispute was settled, satisfactorily to both sides we gathered.

The complete transcript of the first main discussion is reproduced in full below because we wish to use this case study for a further test of the efficacy of CPA in the description of behaviour in negotiations. In particular, we wish to examine the ability of CPA to highlight the important contrasting roles of interpersonal and interparty exchange in negotiations, a task in which previous category systems have failed.

THE ELECTRICIANS' INFORMAL NEGOTIATION

M1:   As I understand it, with reading this document which we've produced, it seems to me that there are two issues really over which we need to argue.

U: Yes.

M1:   Don't we agree?

?:   Yeah.

M1:*   The one has to do with the specifically detailing conditions where, or rather, what we will do in the event of extensive working hours. That is, that we agree time off the next day, which we readily agree to

*= interruption cutting short the previous speaker.

	concede. The second one, in fact, has to do with the wish that you have to exclude from the callout system the statutory emoluments.
U:	Yes.
M1:	Now it is on this one I think perhaps it is worth spending attentions because obviously this will be the biggest crunch point.
U:	Yes.
M1:	Because this is in fact a departure from the previous field. Now let me say. So far, what I have done: I asked in fact Stan, I asked Bill U. to comment on this.
U:	Yes . . .
M1:	And he said as far, as far as they were concerned this was really the bone of contention. As far as they were concerned. In as much as they had to be calculated. Bill felt that this is something we ought to be planning to do. Stan said, well desirably one ought to do it. Or at least, or at least. Or to put it another way, somebody had to do it. Right?
U:	Yes.
M1:	So if we can begin at that point, and what has been said there. Can you sort of? Would you like to explain yourself what you're after? Or, or what?
U1:	Well I say, can I go back to the beginning?
M1:	Yes.
U1:	Er, when we had this meeting with Mr, Mr Smith.
M1:	Last week?
U1:	Yes. At that meeting we specifically said, er we didn't want to do a callout on a bank holiday, and he took that down as noted. Well there was no minutes taken at the meeting whatsoever.
M1:	This was all they said about it?
U1:	Yes. The fitters was there, and we were there. Then came out the original callout procedure, which has never been altered on paper. And it said 365 days per year, and we kicked up then that we did not agree to this, 'cos it said there 'as agreed by us'. We kicked up then, us fitters, that this had never been agreed on.
M1:	When was this now? This was way back, was it?
U1:	Yes. This was the very original . . .
M1:*	?
U1:	(continues) callout procedure.
M1:	This is 1963. 5th June. This is just after I came here. As I came here, as I came here in March 18th. So this, in fact, April–May, three months after I came here.
U1:	Yes.
M1:	I wasn't involved in this at all. You had these discussions. But since this time we've had various agreements, or rather talks.
U1:	Yes.

M1:   In which we have in fact discussed pay in relation to your commitment in work.

U1:   Yes. I say we've always done the bank holiday . . .

M1:*   Well, as far as I'm concerned . . .

U1:*   (continues simultaneously) but we've never wanted to do it.

M1:*   (continues simultaneously) I can't, couldn't recall this document. Number one. And certainly it's never been brought up in the discussions which we have had together.

U1:   Well, it's the only document which we've got.

M1:   Right. Would you agree that's true?

?:   Yes.

M1:   Yes, that's true. So far as I'm concerned this is entirely something new. I didn't know this document's existence. Number one. Perhaps I ought to have done, but I haven't been here long enough for it to register.

?:   Yeah.

M1:   And so you've got me over a barrel on this, because I didn't . . .

U1:*   Well that's the original . . .

M1:*   (continues) know of it.

U1:*   (continues) and this is what we took. And this is what we should like as the amendment.

M1:   Yeah. Well, OK. So now, as far as I'm concerned, to date – in our discussion to date – I understood – and there is no reason for me to suppose otherwise – that bank holidays were in fact . . .

U1:   Unacceptable . . .

M1:*   Yeah.

U1:*   (continues) to us.

M1:   Right? Yes. Because in fact it was done, it was never thought of as not being done, and therefore it was reasonable to think this from my point of view, this now is something new as far as I'm concerned.

U1:   Yeah.

M1:   And certainly as far as we are concerned.

U1:   Yeah.

M1:   That is, the four of us, or five of us in the talk. So you've now come back now the full circle back to where you began.

U1:   Yes.

M1:   Now, could I ask one or two things?

U1:   Yes.

M1:   This, this turnup: I mean, it is an embarrassment to us, in fact, not to have covered. This is manifestly obvious, because somewhere there has got to be some form of coverage. Two questions I could ask. The first is: Is this merely an attempt on your part to negotiate some price for this external to the agreement. . . ?

U1:   No.

M1:   Or not to do that at all?

U1:   No, we do not. We won't accept. We don't want to do it in any case. We just want bank holidays as bank holidays. We simply want the time off. We don't, we won't accept it. We don't want to accept it for £10 a day.

M1:   ?

U1:*   We don't want money for it. We don't want money for it. We don't want to do it. We never have wanted to do it, and we thought it was about time. We've been doing it now for about five years, and we thought it was about time we made a stand.

M1:   How would you suggest then that we deal with this now, as a company? I mean, you're part of the community in this respect.

U1:   Yeah. Yeah. Well, unless you want . . .

U2:*   On what as. I just wondered if you could have a certain person. That is, if something did happen, we should, you know.

?:   ?

U2:   It seems ridiculous if you've got, the plant has got to close down. Naturally there might be an odd thing that can happen. Now you've got to have coverage. But since. I mean, you take Christmas, if you have a holiday, holiday Christmas Day.

M1:   Well could we go?

U2:   I just wondered if you could have a certain person, say, on these holidays that you could say if there is something happening one Saturday or on a bank holiday you get in touch with him. And try and get one of the electricians. Instead of one electrician being on call, perhaps, if this is agreeable with the other two.

M1:   Yes, but let's, now let's get back to the case in point. We've got so far, Bill, to the point where they have had this document from John, which was about three months after I got here, in which it appears that in the course of the discussions that took place at the time they made the point that they want a few bank holidays. But in fact the document itself set out in fact certain requirements. I said, as far as I was personally concerned, I couldn't recall this document, as it was just after I came here. And certainly in all the discussions we've had to date it has never been an issue that that the question of this was at stake.

M2:   Do you remember we, we reviewed this on their request, about what, about eighteen months ago, when, when in fact you got a slight increase in money?

M1:*   No.

M2:   Do you remember, when we had a meeting down at the bottom end of the laboratories?

U1:*   ? We haven't had a slight increase.

M2:*   Well, you were expected to do less for your money then, let's put it this way.

M3:	No, we also agreed that we would pay you when you came in at weekends.
M2:	That's what I mean.
?:	Yes.
M2:	That's what I mean.
M1:	I say bank holidays were never brought up by you . . .
?:*	?
M1:*	(continues) never brought up by you, nor was I aware of them.
?:	?
M1:	Now let's quote from you. What we have is this.
?:	We had a session on bank holidays once in your office.
M1:	This, this issue wasn't raised.
?:	?
M1:	Bank holiday as such wasn't brought up, and, and I've got a pretty good memory you know for recent events, in the last three years or more. What they say now is they don't want to work bank holidays, you see, at all. So I can extend what we've said. So what I, at this point, want to do. I say, 'Well OK, how, in fact, do they suggest that we cover the need possibly to have electrical work done during this time?' I mean, you know, have you got any suggestions? Or any . . .
U2:	Well it's not insulation work. I mean, you know . . .
M1:*	No, no, that's not the point at issue.
U2:	Well, as I've just said, I'm not disagreeing with you. You have one man that you can contact, say, on management, if. I don't know how you're going to work it out, but if you could contact him, and if he wants an electrician, he should be on the 'phone. Then 'phone round and see if he can get someone in.
M1:	If they can't get one?
U2:	Well, you're bound to get somebody.
M1:	No, no, no. Let's sort of be practical about this. Let's suppose now.
U1:	The idea of not wanting to work is so that we can go out. That's the idea.
M1:	Exactly . . .
U1:*	Yeah.
M1:	(continues) exactly, exactly.
U1:*	That's the one day you get er a holiday, then you've . . .
M1:*	How, how . . .
U1:*	(continues) got to sit at home.
M1:	(continues) how are we supposed to cover now? I mean already we've run things at Christmas time.
U1:	Mm.
M1:	Now, in the past (pause). We run sweepstakes, for example. A variety of things are in fact going on.
U3:	Well, I don't think Christmas is too bad really. It's not.

U:	Have you been called out over Christmas?

U: ?

M2:   None of you have been called out over Christmas.

U: We're not going anywhere.

U: ?

U: ?

M2:   All right, you're not going anywhere.

M1:   No. But I'm saying in fact that one. It's manifestly there are occasions when we have to run things. The why I'm asking is: How in fact can we cover this, at all, if in fact? I mean, I take your point you see. One of the purposes, in fact, of having this up is that you were not called in for any reason. Therefore you can't really suddenly say, 'Well you can try your luck,' because this violates the principle just as much in fact as being committed to callout, because the issue is you don't want to be disturbed on that particular day.

U1:* Yes.

M1:   For any reason. Now, this leaves us holding the baby in fact. We have in fact possibly to do something. But how are we to do this? How in fact are we to cover this? Can you suggest to me some way out? Or, in fact, are we saying, 'Well that's your bloody problem?' (Very long pause) And if you feel that, then, then let's say so. I mean, if you say, 'Well that's your bloody problem,' you say it.

U1:   Yes, we. We can say it, but we still come back to the same em . . .

M1:* No. No. No. Because it seems to me I can't make you come in. But we have a problem in fact to cover certain eventualities, and it seems to me that we, we will not be able to do so. For . . .

U1:* I say ex . . .

M1:   (continues) the very reason that we can't call on you . . .

U1:* For, for the . . .

M1:   (continues) for any reason.

U1:   For the whole five years now we, we've covered every single day . . .

M1:* Yes, I . . .

U1:   (continues) and all . . .

M1:* I . . .

U1:   (continues) we're asking is for five days in a year . . .

M1:* Yes, I agree.

U1:   (continues) each year . . .

M1:* I agree.

U1:   (continues) to have off, so if we all wanted to go out somewhere that day we can all bugger off somewhere, without no fear we . . .

U2:* . . . the holiday.

U1:   I've got to stay in. I've got to stay in. I'm sorry, missus, I can't take you and the kids out. It's a lovely day but I've got to stay in.

M2:	But this only happens to a third of the five days, not to all of the five days of the bank holiday.
U1:	But bank holiday is when my wife wants to go out.
U:	Yes.
M1:	You . . .
M2:*	You're not, you're not kept in for all of the five of them are you, at the moment?
U2:	No, but . . .
U:*	A third.
U2:	(continues) it doesn't work that way. There's no callout rota. There's no special way of arranging it. It comes to the holiday and two people say, well . . .
M2:	?
U2:	?
M1:	Well, what, what, what the situation, however we skirt around it is, is that we have got to find some means of having electrical coverage outside of the people that we employ. That's what we're saying. (Long pause)
M3:	You see, Brian, if you say . . .
M1:*	That's what it amounts to, isn't it?
M3:	(continues) if you say . . .
U1:	?
M1:	That's my problem. And if I can't bloody well solve it, then that's that then.
M3:	What you're . . .
U1:*	?
M3:	(continues) saying is that you don't want to be here on bank holidays, and that's why you don't want to be on standby. Well, if we did as Brian suggested and left it to Bill, or possibly Stan, to find somebody – you just said you all want to be away.
M2:	Yeah (agreeing with M3).
M3:	Then (pause) we couldn't find somebody.
M1:	You wouldn't find anybody.
M3:	How often have you been called out on, on bank holiday?
U2:	That's not it, not it.
U1:*	It's not so much the being called out. You . . .
U2:*	We can . . .
U1:	(continues) you, you say . . .
U2:*	You can, you can say, 'Well you don't get called out at all.' Well then, you don't have anybody, and then . . .
U:*	. . . really.
U2:	(continues) you can have on calling out . . .
U1:*	I can imagine if I was on call, and the wife said, 'Well, we'll go down to Wellingborough Zoo' We'll go down Wellingborough Zoo. It's a

nice day. The kids love the Zoo. We go down there about four or five times a year. I go down to the Zoo. Something stops at X's, and they want somebody quick. I can imagine them. What's going to happen? What if they had to hunt round Wellingborough Zoo for me?

M1:   Right, the position is this.

U1:*   I can imagine what trouble I'd be in the following day.

U: Yes. Yes.

M3:   What?

U2:   The only thing is, I've never said bank holiday's different for the other people.

U1:   Huh! Huh!

M1:   Well, you, you pose in fact really an impossible . . .

U:*   Nobody. . . ?

M1:   What you're saying is, 'This is your problem'.

U1:   Well we felt it was impossible at the beginning.

?:   Yes.

M1:   All right.

U1:*   But we still agreed, we done it for the last five years.

M1:*   All right, all right. But we're still in the same mess, when the company . . .

?:   That's clever that is.

M1:   What?

?:   This.

?:   I'd never thought of that.

U2:   We've always had bank holidays different to the other people.

M3:   But how would that change the situation?

?:   No.

U1:   No.

M1:   It wouldn't.

U2:   No, you ignore it (agreeing with M1).

M3:   But how, how would it change it?

?:   But bank holidays, bank holidays . . .

?:   . . . to this very minute.

M3:   How would it change it?

U2:   Well it's. I should. If the person's on callout now . . .

?:   ?

?:   ?

M3:   Whenever you . . .

?:   ?

M3:   (continues) whenever you three lads are not going to be here there's one of you that's got to be on standby.

U2:   Fair enough. If the person is on standby, he hasn't a day off. Because for one, for that being bank holiday, he can't go anywhere. He's stuck here, isn't he?

M2:	So stagger them. So stagger them.
U2:	Er, I don't know what you're saying.
U1:	You mean. . . ?
?:	?
U1:	You mean, if I'm on call Christmas Day, then you're on call Boxing Day? You have a day off from doing, I have a day off from doing?
M2:	Yeah.
U1:	No, I don't want anything out of it. I just don't want to do it.
U:	No (agreeing with U1).
U1:	I don't want money for it. I don't want a day off in lieu for it. I just don't want to do it, bank holidays.
M1:	But then you pose us a problem, because from within . . .
U1:*	Well it's posed me a problem for the last five years.
M1:*	Yes, well this doesn't help us, Brian, does it? The fact of the matter is that, as. We, we employ, we employ all kinds of people, right?
U1:	Yeah.
M1:	For certain specific functions. And from within ourselves we try to cover all the needs that we've got. I'll still have the bloody need, whatever you do.
U1:	Yeah.
M1:	But then I'm lumbered with it. I can't find a solution.
U1:	Well, here's one solution. Pay Stan for doing the bank holidays. He'll do 'em if he's paid for doing 'em. (Pause)
?:	That's fair enough. (Pause)
M2:	Right. That's it. If the regulars won't do it, Stan'll have to do it. ? ? Isn't it?
U1:	You see we never, if we'd agreed to it in the very first – we didn't – we wouldn't have had a leg to stand on. But, on the very first meeting, we, we said we do not want to do it 365 days. We want to do it 365 days minus the bank holidays on it, then come out a bit of paper with the bank holidays on it.
U:	But we kicked up.
U1:	We kicked up there and then. But we didn't know nothing about it. The fitters kicked up there and then as well.
M3:	At this first meeting, Brian, where you say. The X meeting?
U1:	Yeah. Yes.
M3:	Before our time then. At least mine, anyway. What arrangements did you arrive at then for covering this, the er bank holidays?
U1:	Well, it was in the air. It was just passed down and forgotten.
M3:	Well, presumably there was a need, just the same as there is a need now, to have some kind of cover.
U1:*	But before we found something out.
U2:*	Sort something out.
M1:	Tell you. If we take on another electrician, or we do something

	(pause), er, do we have the right to require them to do it, if they come in on that understanding?
U1:	If they come in on the understanding that they will be on call with us for 365 days a year, and they accept that . . .
U2:*	They share the burden of the callup.
U1:	Not necessarily.
M1:*	Now suppose we recruit an electrician, and say, 'Well now, part of your job will be in fact to cover these days.'
U1:	What, bank holidays? Oh, the guys wouldn't think that's fair.
M1:	We'll ask the recruit.
U1:	No, no, no, no. For us to sit at home, go, to go out there five days and leave Joe Soap in for work.
M1:*	Well, how can we do this then? What you're telling me now, I can't . . .
U1:*	No, I'm sorry, but if you done that, I shall have to say well I'll. See I shall have to do one of the bank holidays, and that's it.
M1:	Well, I er . . .
U1:	?
?:	?

(General laughter)

M2:*	You don't want to do it, and you don't want anybody else to do it!
M1:	And you won't let anybody . . .
M2:*	(simultaneously) That's what it boils down to.
M1:*	(continues simultaneously) else do it.
U1:	No. I think it's totally unfair that anybody should be asked to do the complete fill at bank holidays.
M2:	Well, you, you think it's unfair that you should be asked to do a share of them too! So you don't want to share and you don't want anybody to do it at all. This is what you're saying. Isn't it?
U1:	I'm not obliged to make a decree . . .
M2:	What, what do you think, if the bank holidays were taken as separate days, on a rota, so that the bank holidays were not a part of the existing rota, so that you couldn't stand a chance in one year of doing, say, three bank holidays? But it would, would be laid down say a year in advance that you did fifty . . .
U1:*	There, there, you see, Bill.
M2:*	(continues)?
U1:	What happens when you come bank holidays?
U2:*	Taking it in turns . . .
U1:*	If I was on bank holiday I would have said, 'Well look, I did the last bank holiday'.
M2:	All right.
M3:	What you're saying really, Brian, is that it's not a bank holiday when you're on standby.

M2:	It is.
M:	(simultaneously) ?
M:	(simultaneously) ?
U:	(simultaneously) How can it be a bank holiday?
U:	(simultaneously) ?
M3:*	Well, fair enough, I, I er understand that point of view . . .
U2:*	?
M3:*	(continuing) that the choice . . .
U3:*	The trouble is, every one of us is on every bank holiday.
U1:*	?
U2:	It's always Friday, Saturday, Sunday. I know it doesn't seem . . .
U1:*	(simultaneously) ?
M1:*	(simultaneously) ? You do one each.
U?:	Yeah.
M3:	?
U2:	Yeah, I mean but you could organise that. But I . . .
U?:*	?
M2:	This is, this is what I was meaning. You could do er one complete bank holiday each.
U:	Oh no.
M2:	You would know you wouldn't be on call Christmas. You would know you wouldn't be on call Easter. And you would know you wouldn't be on call August.
U?:	How're you going to . . .
U2:	Yeah, but this is. It's far better how we. If we're gonna do it, it's far better how we're doing it now. Y'see not one day, part it, say Christmas . . .
?:*	?
U2:*	(continues) has . . .
?:*	?
U2:*	(continues) has er three days.
?:*	?
U2:	Yes, because I er, I don't want to do three days at Christmas.
M2:	No, 'cos it's a chance in a million you getting called out.
U1:	I know, but you've still got to be here. ? ?
U2:*	It's all the same . . .
U1:*	(continues) ?
U2:*	(continues) whether it's a chance in six million. I mean, I been saying to myself all. It's chancy that I'm on being called out.
U:	? I agree. ?
M1:*	But can we get back to the point where I am now? Where what you're saying is, 'You have a problem.' Right? I want to be free. One of the solutions for me, in fact, is to cover that, which is, in fact, to recruit someone on the understanding that he understands quite

clearly before he comes here what duties we're going to require of him.

U1:*   Yes.

M1:*   You tell me this is unacceptable to you because you . . .

U1:*   No.

M1:*   (continues) feel . . .

U1:*   No, we don't want that.

M1:   What? You would feel you'd have to come in?

U1:   Yeah.

M1:   But this . . .

U1:*   ?

M1:*   (continues) just puts us back to square one, doesn't it? Because what you're saying is that I would in some way then probably be coercing you by pressure, if you like. Er by creating a situation in which you couldn't resist the fairness of the situation to get involved again. Now, OK, we'll say, 'Right, this is unfair.' OK? 'I ought not to do this.' So, in fact now, back to square one. I have no solution. You have circumscribed me to such an extent that I can't find a solution because not only are you going to say I have a right to determine, but you will not have me create a set of circumstances which in any way makes me feel I ought to help.

U1:   Well, I mean, I'm sorry, but if you did have, did get somebody in, and he wants to do all the bank holidays, I'd just say, 'Well Jack,' or whatever your name is, 'I'll do one of them for you. Save you doing all five.'

M1:   Yeah. Yes, but . . .

U1:*   But I don't think it's fair, not not for anyone to have to do all five.

U: No (agreeing with U1).

M1:   But how do you know? What if he accepts it?

U2:   But on the other hand you could say . . .

U: (simultaneously) ?

U: (simultaneously) ?

M1:*   He is. It's a condition of work. It's not a question of force. It's not being forced upon him. (Pause) Is it? (Long pause)

M3:   The other thing, of course, if we agree to another electrician the incidence of your other standbys would be . . .

U:*   ? ?

M3:   (continues) would be reduced.

(Laughter)

U1:   Is this all hypothetical? Or are you thinking about doing that? I mean, is it?

M1:*   No, I'm just asking you see. What I know. Why I've got to be careful with you people you see. That in fact that you don't manoeuvre me into a situation while I'm still bollocksed.

U1:	Yeah.
M1:	Because you see basically you don't care actually, what actually in the situation, you see, t'do about these five days. I mean, that's my problem.
U2:	Oh we do. Oh we do.
M1:	And what I'm saying is that if I'm gonna do this, I've got to find a way out of this. Now I don't want to pressurise anybody into it, as long as I know what's going to happen when I do something. One obvious way out would in fact be to recruit somebody else. But, presumably, hiring both people, now fairly frequently. So, fair enough, it would be quite reasonable to make a case that we ought to increase the number to four, for example. And then, one chap comes on and says, 'Well, this is the situation, the existing si'. I will tell them that.
U2:	Yeah. Mm.
M1:	The existing people will not do bank holidays. And, and this is something that you would have to do.
U:	Yeah.
M1:	I mean, I wouldn't sort of clear cover the situation at all. I would make it perfectly clear . . .
?:*	?
M1:*	(continues) to the individual what he was accepting.
U1:*	Yeah. Mm.
M1:	And why. And if he then accepted I'd have to offer it in that way.
U1:	You, well you say we don't care. Well we do care, with due respect, 'cos we've done it for five years.
M1:	Yes, but . . .
U2:*	Yes, but you can understand our point of view.
M1:	Yes, but it doesn't resolve the problem.
U2:	I know it doesn't resolve the problem.
M1:	For me: I have a problem to deal with. We've got to have a cover . . .
U1:*	We can . . .
M1:*	(continues) and that is that.
U1:*	(continues) keep saying to ourselves, 'We'll probably lose bank holidays. We're sick and tired of them and do nothing about it'.
M1:	Well it seems to me at this particular point actually that all we can do is say well, as for that, that is the situation. We're not going to do bank holidays. We'll have to try and resolve, find some way, either along the lines of recruiting someone who will have to do the bank holidays – or examine some means of doing it.
M3:	You're saying that because you're on standby you don't really have that day as a holiday. It's not a holiday.
U2:	It's not.
?:*	It's not. Well?

M3:   Supposing we said that you have the holiday at some other time.

U2:   That's what I'm just saying. At some acceptable time.

?:   It's just because of his research duties.

U1:   Oh, I don't want time off for it. I don't want money for it. I just don't want to do it (pause), bank holidays.

M1:   Do the rest of you feel this way as well? I mean, Brian obviously feels very strongly about this matter.

U3:   We don't want to make a scene.

M1:   No. I just wondered you know, if you felt the same way.

U3:*   We did.

M1:   I mean precisely the same way.

U3:   Before we came here. Before four o'clock anyway.

M1:   I mean, you know, because this is fair enough, I mean, you know: this is what it's all about isn't it? Your saying what you think and feel.

U2:   Well, let's say, well (pause). I, I'm not sure. (Very long pause) Yes it's (pause). You talk us into something and . . .

M1:   I'm not talking anybody into it at all. You, you have a right to determine what you do. After all, it's a free country isn't it? I mean the obligations that you accept are those which you accept. I've still got a problem, whatever you do, which is, in fact, to ensure that if we get a breakdown that somebody is available. I mean, this I've got to do. And it isn't a question of whether we shut the place and lock it. There are times when things have got to be working, and that's all there is to it. And I can't escape this at all. I mean if we. For example, if we decided to work, for example, right? Supposing as a factory we decide to work through the bank holiday – then we're lumbered, well, I mean all the circumstances we're talking about . . .

U2:   But this also happens if the factory's shut down completely.

M1:   Well yes, it could do certainly. It could do, but it's particularly important that you could get a failure of some kind, if something was left on. There are all the kinds of things that can actually happen, but er, well er, I mean, well you know. Can I accept now, at this particular point, there is, that you are in agreement that this outcome, there is no other alternative as far as the rest of you is concerned? That's it? There are no other options open?

U1:   Well, I'll, I'll say we, we don't want paying for it.

M1:   No, no, no, no. I know. I mean . . .

U1:   Stan, Stan would do the five days if were paid a remuneration for it.

U2:   You don't know till you've asked him.

M2:   What you're saying is that you want to opt. You are, in fact, opting out you know.

U1:   Yeah, we, we never opted in. We had it thrown. We had this bit put in. We never even accepted it there and then, so it's not a case of

	opting out of doing it. We've done it for the last five years because, 'cos we done it, and that you know we didn't want to do it. We've never wanted to do it.
M2:	And do you two feel the same way?
U1:	We've done it the last five years.
U2:	And when it comes to bank holiday I don't want to do it, as naturally I don't.
M2:	I'm not saying what you want to do. You, you know you might not want to come to work for five days a week. I'm, I'm saying, 'What are you prepared to do?'
U2:	Well, see if we can find a solution somehow around it.
M3:	Well what proposed solutions have we got to consider?
U2:	You were saying . . .
M2:*	?
U2:*	(continues) have a day off in lieu.
M3:	I can understand what you're saying really is that when you're sitting beside the 'phone it's not a holiday, and you've not really had a holiday.
U2:	?
M3:	?
U2:	I accept this.
M3:	?
U2:*	And the other two don't. And that lays it on to me. Well if it lays it on to me . . .
M3:*	?
U2:*	(continues) I'm not going to do it, because that means I'm going to be committed to the four bank holidays.
U1:	Yeah.
M1:	Yeah. Well, unless we recruit somebody else.
U2:	Well that's still only two of you, and you still get in it, ain't you?
M1:	Yes. Agreed, agreed. Well, I mean, this is what I'm asking. I mean it's quite obvious isn't it, there has to be virtually two of you to agree to this. If we take someone else on as we – well I can say we have thought it, I've thought, established – as well, in view of the number of people we do employ. But it needs at least two. But I mean, I don't want to force this on anyone. I mean, I'm just asking you, 'What is the situation?' Is the option in fact that time off is somehow a proposition, or isn't it?
U2:	Well, can we have a little time to stew on this, and see what we feel, really feel, among ourselves?
M1:*	Yes.
U2:	(to own side) What do you think?
U3:	Let's discuss it and see if . . .
U2:	What do you say?

U: ?

M1:   No, no. I don't want anybody to . . . (Interruption) What we've got is a problem. I can't solve it alone. It does, in fact, concern you. It concerns all of us. You know, if we compare this lookout with. Well it is in fact a matter of mutual concern. There's no agreeing . . .

U1:*   ?

M1:   We can't pretend it isn't.

U2:   But you can see our point of view?

M1:   Yeah, I can. But what I'm asking is, 'Is there any way out of the dilemma?' You know, I can't impose solutions of this kind. I'm trying to find a way which meets most people's needs if it can, if, if it is humanly possible.

U2:   That's why I . . .

M1:*   The fact is there is a problem there and we can work around it, but we, you know it's going to be there.

U2:   Well now, I see it, you see . . .

U3:*   The trouble about the system you can slip out of anything.

U2:   This is, this is. . . ?

U3:   The trouble about the system you can slip out of anything.

U2:   ? This is your problem, not any conventional problem. You say well . . .

M1:*   That's it (agreeing with U2).

U2:   This is how I. . . ?

U: . . . puts it . . .

U3:   But even I have a conscience about it, putting him on the spot then. But unless we put you on the spot, we'll never be rid of it. We'll be, we'll never get a solution, we'll be stuck on this for ever more until we drop dead.

U2:   Y'see this is what, how I feel. Say on a bank holiday I'm at home and I'm on call. Now I've got to stop in that vicinity. Now I can see . . . the wife can see other . . . The family can come round, round and say, 'Look we're going, would you like to come?' and I can say 'No.' Well come the following day when it's back to work, I'm back to work with the others and the wife will say we haven't had a bank holiday, you see. That's how I feel personally.

U1:   Sometimes I've actually be fished out the pub, or . . .

M1:*   Yeah.

U1:*   (continues) on Easter Monday, and that was it, about quarter past nine.

M1:   Er, you see, if we take on another person there'll be four here; with Stan as well, there's be five.

?:*   Yeah.

M1:*   If we had five, for example, would it be a proposition, share between five ways? Cover one bank holiday in the course of a year, and go

along and rotate them. Is that a proposition? And bring Stan to . . .
who'll get this establishment, as it seems now we ought to do, to
form the shop. And Stan, and bring Stan into the rotation as far as
the bank holidays are concerned. And it will be one day in five and
rotate them around.

U:*	Much more people in it, it won't be so bad, but if there's three of us . . .
M1:	I mean, will you think about that?
U2:	Well, as I say . . .
U1:*	?
M1:	You know it will mean one day in the year.
?:	Yeah. We're talking in individual terms, we shall be talking of . . .
M1:*	But think about it first.
U2:	If we can . . .
U1:	Yeah, yeah.
M1:	Don't answer now.
U2:	No.
M1:	I mean, tell us next week, when you've had a get-together . . .
U2:*	?
M1:*	(continues) and think about it. What?
U2:	I said, 'Part of our problem it's yours.'
M1:	But think about that as, as a proposition. But make certain in your own mind that you know, know, have decided, and come back. I think that's the best way is to leave it at that, and have a think, which is only fair if you want to think and talk, and not just decide separately.
?:*	No.
M1:*	It's separately that you get agreement. Otherwise if one is out then he becomes an ostracised by the others and you know he feels guilty. It's important really that you all come to the same decision.
U2:	Well say if one is out, it means the three . . .
M1:	It's a very difficult situation for the one and for the two because eventually they resent him and he resents the implication that he ought to be one of the two, to make three.
U2:	Yeah.
M1:	It's important really that you agree, you know. It's very important. Between yourselves it's important.
U?:*	?
M1:	Agree to agree. Shall we leave it there? You come back next week, and let us know what you think.
U2:	Just one more thing. What do you class as a callout? That's what we want.
M1:	A callout?
U2:	Now, when we first had the meeting, when this was first (pause), it

was for first aid to the plant. That was working – if there was a breakdown – right – you come out – get it going – go home – and that's it. Now that was classed as a callout. Now, since, I mean all this installation work – polymer – we've been brought out say just for disconnecting . . .

M1:* No. No.

U2:* (continues) things or reconnecting things for the sake of fitters that's been working. Now to me I don't class that as a callout. I don't class that as a callout. I mean, you know, there's work to be done, you know they might as well get somebody in you know on overtime and get this work done. But it's been left to fetch the callout man. It's so easy, you see.

M1: What do you think, Bill? I'm not aware of the details.

M2: Well, myself, I think this appeals to the argument that I sometimes hear from the fitters, as to what is incidental to overtime, you know. As far as I am concerned, if we want you at a specific time, then that is a callout.

?: ?

M2: If we want you out of hours then that is a callout.

U?: ?

U1: There was a long period when all of us three were fetched out on this. We hadn't been having any overtime. There hadn't been any callouts. But they came in doing overtime. They came in Saturday morning. They'll knock on the door. 'I want this disconnecting.' You come out here, you disconnect, don't get paid. You've disconnected something so that the bloke can carry on working and get paid for it.

M2:* This is not, no (pause). This is not . . .

U1:* ?

M2:* This might have happened.

U?:* ?

M2:* No. Not on a Saturday morning. On a Saturday morning. No.

U1: This happened to us. This happened to us.

M2: Not disconnecting something so that you can carry on their business.

U2: Oh, come off it.

M2:* Now if it's a breakdown . . .

U?:* ?

M2:* (continues) if it's a breakdown . . .

U1: Oh yes, if it's a breakdown . . .

U2:* Oh, yeah.

U1:* (continues) we must come out and do it.

M2: This is not the usual run of things . . .

U1:* But I know . . .

M2:*	(continues) and you know it doesn't regularly happen.
U1:	He's been called out, and he's been called out.
U?:	I've (pause) I've . . .
U2:	I've been called out twice.
M2:*	Now be fair . . .
U2:*	?
U1:*	?
M2:*	(continues) it hasn't happened very often.
U2:	It hasn't happened very often, but it has happened, you see. And I just wanted to know.
M2:*	?
U1:*	. . . to come out and do it. To be quite honest . . .
U2:*	Well I would do! If there's a knock on the door I think.
M2:*	Oh yes. I would accept that you should feel obliged, but the only thing I would say is . . .
U1:*	Well?
M2:*	(continues) that on a Saturday morning if that happens like that and it's work, that is either my mistake or Stan's mistake for not planning and asking you to come in and do it. Then in fact you should get paid for this, because you get paid for coming in on Saturday morning, don't you? .
U2:*	This happened on a Sunday morning as well. (Long pause)
M1:	Er . . .
M2:*	Yeah, I accept this as a fair point.
M1:*	(continues) expressing an opinion, I would say that if through lack, I think I would agree with that. The intention of callout in my mind was first aid.
U2:*	First aid.
M1:*	First aid (pause). This I would agree, yeah, mm . . .
M2:*	But I mean (disagreeing with M1) . . .
M1:*	(continues) for however long it takes, in fact . . .
U1:*	Mm (agreeing with M1).
M1:*	(continues) it is immaterial . . .
M2:*	If . . .
M1:*	(continues) ?
M2:*	(continues) it's necessary that someone should . . .
M1:*	But . . .
M2:*	(continues) stop behind at nights on incidental or full-time basis; even if it's on a capital point, to get something finished that we want done, fair enough . . .
U1:	That's incidental.
U2:*	That's incidental overtime. That ain't callout.
U1:	?
U2:	This is what we're talking about. No . . .

M1:*	. . . callout. The fact is they've already left the place. I would, that if in fact for the reasons that we've stated you're brought in for work, really that is the failure of planning, or something of (pause) then I would agree that to be overtime.
M2:	This is fair enough. I accept this.
M1:	That would be my opinion.
U2:*	But as it is now, say if there's a job to be carried on . . .
M1:*	Yes, but you see, one of the difficulties that I face in this – I'm quite sure we've talked a good deal about this – if you sit down, in fact if any sat with me, grievances between us, to detail this thing to the *n*th degree . . .
U1:*	Yeah.
U2:*	Yeah.
M1:*	(continues) you'll never succeed.
U2:	Yeah.
M1:	You always in the end have to to rely upon the fact that if the situation comes up, in which you feel that in some way he's twisted the interpretation or the understanding, the only thing really that can be done is for you to bring it up and for us to discuss it.
U2:*	Yeah.
M1:*	And we agree on an interpretation, and (pause) then we've solved that one particular precedent.
U2:	One particular problem, yeah.
M1:	But I think in a sense it's better to have a general idea of what we're trying to do, and to knock the ones on the head as they come up, rather than to say, 'Let's work out a bloody Magna Carta here . . . '
U2:*	Yeah, yeah.
M1:*	(continues) and dream up every possible eventuality that's going to occur.'
U2:	Yeah.
M1:	Because you spend all your time thinking about hypothetical circumstances that may never come about. I think that you, you know it's a pity you didn't bring this up before, because I would have said then that this was overtime, not in fact, er not in, not callout . . .
M2:*	This is not a regular occurrence though.
M1:*	(continues) you know.
U2:*	(disagrees)
M1:*	But even so, it was not your intention . . .
M2:*	I've just said, I accept the . . .
M1:*	Not your intention.
M2:*	(continues) fact, you know.
U1:	I said a few weeks ago, er, this happened to me: It was getting on for five o'clock. At, at er (pause) I put the motor back on the new

	polyester, and they said they want it reconnecting and it would be ready about seven. Right? Now, we was in the shop. Stan came down and he says, 'Now, who's on call?' he said. 'Brian, you've got to come back and reconnect this up.'
M2:	Yes.
U1:	Well, he said to me – I didn't like that for a start. He could have said, 'Oh Brian, being as you're on call, OK come back.' I'd have said, 'You're on.' But he says, 'You've got to come back and reconnect this when they want you.' I go home. I sit at home. The 'phone rings. I pick it up. It's Ian on the 'phone. He says, 'Can you come out?' I said, 'Well Ian, I've only got me moped,' I says, and being as it's classed as a callout, because it was in my opinion because Stan had told me I'd got to go when I was called, I said, 'Can you come and fetch me?' A little while after – twenty minutes after – Stan himself calls up. He takes me over here. I reconnect it back up, and he takes me home. Well, don't you think that's a waste of labour?
M2:	Yes, I do.
M3:	I agree with you now.
M1:	I agree with that entirely.
M2:	Yes.
M1:	I agree that was wrong.
M2:	Well, in my opinion you should have gone, come out on your moped. That was my opinion. And if you like to talk about . . .
U1:*	(comments angrily) I classed it as a callout.
M2:*	(continues) another circumstance similar, that occurred only a fortnight ago when commission polyester – when it was your callout night again – and they said – we wanted to check the direction of rotation of the pumps in the switch room, and you couldn't stop, and it was twelve minutes past five!
U1:*	Just a minute. I, I can explain.
M2:*	I was there myself!
U1:	I went up there, they says, 'We're not ready for it'.
M2:*	No.
U1:	I says, 'Well, can we give it a try?' and we couldn't see which way it was going. I said, 'I've got to go'.
M2:*	Can't we straighten here?
U1:*	I said, 'I've got to go.' See me little child was ill. The wife couldn't go out. I said, 'I've got a lot of shopping to do.' I had. I had to leave here at five. I rushed, I rushed all the way round the town, and I got back in home about five to six, and that's when the 'phone. The wife said they'd rung, and they were coming for me.
M1:	The phone . . .
M2:	. . . but it was twelve minutes past six, and if you'd stopped twelve minutes you could have done the job, because I was there myself.

U1:*	If I hadn't er (pause). If hain't had a hell of a lot of shopping I'd have stopped, but really . . .
M1:*	Yeah.
U1:*	(continues) couldn't somebody else have stopped?
U2:	No one was out.
M2:	Well surely if, if, if it's inconvenient for you, you can ask one of these two. I mean, don't you think this is the way to do it? If you're down as a man on the job . . .
U1:*	I had to (pause) at the time. Now look, Stan, I must go at five. I got a lot of shopping to do . . .
M1:*	Look.
U1:*	(continues) and I had to get it done.
M1:*	Look, look, let's, let's, let's not lose sight of what we're trying to do.
U1:*	There's chance in a million that . . .
M1:	What I was saying is this: as far as we're concerned, in every situation there is in fact reasonable agreement in fact.
U1:	Yes.
U2:	Yes.
M1:	In this particular context if we, we knew roughly in fact what the intentions are. I'm quite sure of this, that everyone of us in fact participating knows roughly what we intend.
?:	Yeah.
M1:*	And we all know when the intention strays, what actually happens – strays from the intention. If that is the case, then I think that all that can actually happen then is that the matter is raised, and is dealt with as quickly as possible, in a, by just having, discussing the thing on its own merits.
U2:	Yeah.
M1:	And er, I would suggest that if this arises again on a question of interpretation of the thing, this is all we can do. You know, I mean there's no other solution for this but in fact to raise it and discuss it.
U1:	Yes.
M1:	Eh (pause) ah . . .
U2:	Ah (pause) sorry, you . . .
M1:	Go on.
U2:	You wouldn't expect Brian to come out on his moped on that, surely?
M1:	Yes, but . . .
U1:	?
U2:*	You won't get me out on call.
?:	What about me?
M1:	Look, let's sort of start (pause). One of the dangers of this, you see is this (pause) that we start raising all kinds of hypothetical . . .
U2:*	Yeah.
M1:*	(continues) questions. All this will produce . . .

U2:*	Nothing.
M1:*	(continues) is in fact nothing, because it will foster a series of propositions in which you will prejudge the situation as to what's going to happen, and this kind of thing, and it's crookedly profitless in fact to pursue them you know. You have to wait until the moment, and as you point in your case if the circumstances aren't known the motives in fact can't be determined. Right?
U1:	Yes. I just had to get home at that moment.
M1:*	As I say, but unless they're known, they can't be done.
U1:	First time the kid's been ill since he was born.
M1:	Can we go back to the point where we agree that what you do now is to think about the proposition made?
U1:	Yes.
M1:	That in fact we are thinking about, to increase the establishment, electrical wise. I'm thinking in terms of one day in the course of the year . . .
U2:*	Yeah.
M1:*	(continues) rotating.
U1:	?
U2:	?
M1:*	And let's get to the crunch of the matter.
U2:*	It's the . . .
M1:*	This would mean that if it's Christmas time, for example, it's once in five years. If it's a bank holiday in the summer, it's once in five years. That's the order of magnitude of which we speak . . .
U2:*	Yeah.
M1:*	(continues) in terms of the dislocation, to put it in perspective. So if you would think about this, but, please agree . . .
U2:*	Yeah.
M1:*	(continues) among yourselves. OK? And then when you're ready, please let us know next week when you want to talk.
U2:	Erm, stores.
U1:	There's that other on the paper as well.
U2:	What's that?
U1:	About not taking out the twelve till five.
M2:	About what?
U1:	?
M3:	Pardon?
M2:	About what?
U2:	You mean er (pause). You've already said that though.
U3:	You said we agreed on that.
U1:	?
U2:	What if we get called out after twelve?
M2:	?

U1:   ?
M2:   I say it's never been argued really.
M1:   Well we have done it.
M2:   It's never been argued really.
M1:   No, we, we don't disagree with that at all.
U3:   It's just a matter of arranging what time . . .
U1:   Yeah, er, there's one other thing. Being called out, we need keys . . .
U2:*   Yeah.
U1:*   (continues) to get into places.
U2:   Stores.
U1:   Now we've found out today that the storekeeper's had the keys
          changed on his store (pause) stores. He says – he said to us – his
          actual words was, 'I'm having so much stuff pinched out of it I'm
          changing the locks.' Well, who else is having the lock? Because,
          because we said, 'Are we having the lock?' and he said, 'No.' I said,
          'Well, how do we get to our stores?' He said, 'You use the side door
          round the side'. Well, the side door's a hell of a job to open, and if we
          open them, the stuff's bursting at the seams so you've got to . . .
M2:   (laughs) We'll get you a key.
M1:   We'll get you a key. OK? We'll get you a key for that, yes.
U1:   We'll get a key for that?
M1:   Yes.
U1:   Make it soon, because of . . .
M1:*   OK, we'll . . .
M2:*   If you're not accommodated you just see the shift fitter. It's dead easy.
U1:   Oh, yeah, yeah, and I can tell him . . .
M2:   ?
U2:   ?
(General laughter)
M2:   I didn't even know he'd changed the lock, to be honest.
U1:   ?
U2:   His words to me, he accused me of leaving the door open when he
          wasn't there, that's what he did.
M2:   Well, let's face it, he's got a problem . . .
U1:   Yeah, yeah.
U2:   Yeah, yeah.
M2:   You're not the only one with a problem.
M1:   Well furthermore, I'm glad to say . . .
U2:   ?
U1:   ?
M2:   (laughs)
M1:   That's it. OK?
U1:   Yeah.
U2:   Yeah.

Role identifiability

Douglas (1957, 1962) has claimed that the identifiability of speakers as individuals and as affiliated to management or union varies in different stages of negotiation. We decided to test the notion directly in the present instance by asking judges, working from unlabelled transcripts of the negotiation, to identify the party (management or union) responsible for each uninterrupted speech burst. Twenty judges were employed in one of two experimental conditions. Half were given pages of the transcript in *random* order; the remaining ten were given pages in their correct order.

There were no differences in the accuracy of diagnosis between those judges working through the transcript in random order and those progressing from page one to the end in true sequence. Nor were there significant differences between judges in their diagnostic ability. *There were, however, significant differences in the ability of the judges to identify speakers' roles at different stages of the negotiation.* In particular, when the transcript was divided into three equal parts by length there were significant differences between role identifiability in the three phases. Figure 12.1(a) shows the relative number of errors made by judges in each phase of the negotiation, and Figure 12.1(b) shows the results of variance analysis on the data. The main effect of phases was highly significant ($p < \cdot001$).

We can therefore be very confident that the fewest errors are made in the middle phase of negotiations of this sort. Inspection of the transcript indicates that during the middle phase the electricians were stating their case most vehemently; their party affiliation was quite evident. In the first phase, by way of contrast, there was an attempt by both sides to establish the facts of the situation, and roles were confused. In the final phase, confusion of roles occurred as both sides enjoyed the relief that came from having apparently resolved their differences.

Analysis by CPA categories

What light did analysis in terms of CPA categories throw on the course of interactions in this negotiation? Figure 12.2 presents analyses of the data according to the distribution of categories of mode, resource and referent dimensions, considered separately, across the three phases of the negotiation. The distribution of mode categories was nowhere statistically significant, but interesting effects of phases did occur among the resource and referent categories. Moreover, the significant differences occurred in those innovatory categories of CPA designed specifically to reflect the distinctive character of exchange in negotiations: the *outcome* categories of the resource dimension and the *person/party* dichotomies of the referent dimension.

(a) Judges' Error Scores for the Three Phases of Negotiation (*in %*)

	Phase 1	Phase 2	Phase 3
Sequential	29·17	18·08	18·33
page presentation	28·00	12·33	19·17
	25·58	15·17	25·00
	11·92	8·83	31·08
	21·42	26·75	28·83
	34·00	27·50	33·58
	26·08	12·50	9·42
	34·83	20·58	28·92
	33·25	23·50	22·67
	22·58	17·50	22·92
Random	36·33	28·83	32·58
page presentation	27·83	11·92	30·25
	23·08	25·42	24·00
	25·75	16·50	23·00
	28·83	18·75	25·25
	18·17	12·00	20·67
	22·83	15·08	23·67
	21·67	17·50	19·67
	22·67	30·08	19·08
	18·85	17·25	21·17
Means	25·63	18·80	23·96

(b) Analysis of Variance on Error Scores

		SS	d.f.	VE	F	d.f.	p
A	Random *v.* Sequential presentation	294·832	1	294·832	0·032	18	n.s.
B	Phases (3 × 12 pages)	72928·126	2	36464·063	9·861	36	< ·001
AC		3714·543	2	1857·272	0·502	36	n.s.
S	Judges	$1·664 \times 10^5$	18	9247·173			
S × C		$1·331 \times 10^5$	36	3697·833			

Figure 12.1 Role identifiability of speakers in electricians' informal negotiation

The latter indicate clearly why role identifiability was so high in the middle phase of the negotiation. Figure 12.3 shows that here there was a dramatic increase in reference to persons on the *other* side, i.e. explicit statements about those in the opposition and present in the room: e.g. 'what you're really saying, Brian, is that it's not a bank holiday when you're on standby'; 'you tell me this is unacceptable to you'; 'you have circumscribed me to such an extent that I can't find a solution'; 'you, well you say we don't care'; and 'you were saying have a day off in lieu'. The argument in the middle phase was truly under way, and battle was joined, making the party and opposition roles quite salient in the interaction. References to own party, however, started high and remain high until the final phase, where they almost disappeared. In that phase the negotiators were more 'interchangeable' as they began to discuss personal problems and issues arising independently of their stance on the side of management or workforce.

	Grand Mean	Phase 1	Phase 2	Phase 3	F	d.f.	p
Mode							
Offer	68·0	67·2	64·4	72·4	1·23	2,12	0·326
Accept	9·5	10·8	8·4	9·2	0·35	2,12	n.s.
Reject	2·6	2·6	3·5	1·8	0·36	2,12	n.s.
Seek	9·7	10·5	11·7	6·8	1·98	2,12	0·181
Unclassified	10·2	8·9	11·9	9·8	0·45	2,12	n.s.
TOTAL	100·0	100·0	99·9	100·0			
Resource							
Initial settlement point	2·0	4·3	1·8	0·0	8·92	2,12	0·004
New settlement point	8·9	7·2	9·4	10·2	0·26	2,12	n.s.
Limits	18·2	22·8	23·4	8·3	5·32	2,12	0·022
Positive consequences of outcomes	1·8	0·8	1·3	1·5	0·19	2,12	n.s.
Negative consequences of outcomes	2·7	3·1	4·1	1·0	1·18	2,12	0·340
Procedure	1·1	0·8	0·5	2·0	1·11	2,12	0·361
Acknowledgement + (own side/both sides)	0·1	0·3	0·0	0·0	1·00	2,12	0·397
Acknowledgement + (other side)	0·1	0·0	0·3	0·0	1·00	2,12	0·397
Acknowledgement − (own side/both sides)	0·5	0·5	0·5	0·5	0·00	2,12	n.s.
Acknowledgement − (other side)	1·1	0·3	2·5	0·5	2·21	2,12	0·152
Information	48·0	43·2	39·5	61·3	2·22	2,12	0·151
Unclassified	16·1	16·9	16·8	14·6	0·18	2,12	n.s.
TOTAL	100·6	100·2	100·1	99·9			
Referent							
Self	14·5	12·6	14·8	16·2	0·22	2,12	n.s.
Person	1·2	1·0	1·0	1·5	0·14	2,12	n.s.
Other	9·1	6·7	13·8	6·8	6·64	2,12	0·011
Party	9·2	14·1	11·2	2·3	6·04	2,12	0·015
Opponent	0·6	1·8	0·0	0·0	2·03	2,12	0·174
Both persons	2·8	3·1	2·0	3·2	0·26	2,12	n.s.
Unclassified	62·6	60·8	57·1	70·0	2·06	2,12	0·170
TOTAL	100·0	100·1	99·9	100·0			

Figure 12.2 CPA categorisation of acts by phases in electricians' informal negotiation (in percentages)

The distribution of the outcome categories reinforced the picture of movement from interparty to interpersonal exchange as the negotiation proceeded. Initial settlement points decreased ($p = ·004$) as new settlement points increased (not significantly). Most striking was the reduction in 'limits' with time ($p = ·022$), i.e. in the number of statements expressing attitudes or facts serving to constrain the final settlement in one way or another: e.g. 'have you been called out over Christmas?'; 'we've always had bank holidays different to the other people'; 'whenever you three lads are not going to be here there's one of you that's got to be on standby'; and 'if he then accepted I'd have to offer it in that way'. Clearly, the use of 'limits' to compel agreement with one's proposals was a salient technique, at least in this negotiation, and in this instance it was especially characteristic of the behaviour of management. The essence of the technique was to suggest that the facts of the situation were such as to *necessitate* settlement on the lines proposed.

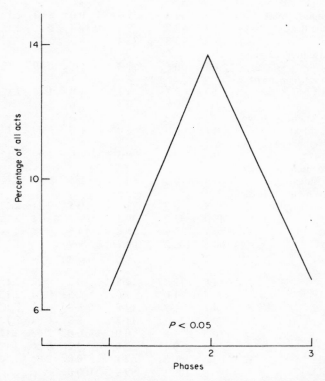

Figure 12.3 Use of CPA category referent: other in electricians' informal negotiation

The course of positive and negative affect did not appear to have much significance in this negotiation. Negotiators differed little in their acceptance or rejection of the opposition's statements as the negotiation proceeded from start to finish. Straightforward praise or criticism of the opposition was negligible. Altogether there was little evidence that the so-called 'socioemotional behaviours' increased with time in response to difficulties encountered with the problems, as the analysis of Bales and Strodtbeck (1951) would suggest.

A Three-Session Wage Negotiation

BACKGROUND TO THE NEGOTIATION

An opportunity was given to observe a wage negotiation on a Type 3 task in a small local food-manufacturing plant. The negotiation lasted three afternoons within the space of three weeks (17 May 1973 to 6 June 1973). There were seven main issues raised by the shop stewards at the plant. Principal among these were demands for: a supplementary payment in addition to the nationally negotiated increase; an increase of 10% on shift allowances; an additional 2p per hour on all job evaluation rates; a noncontributory pension scheme; and four weeks' holiday a year.

The first meeting followed very much the pattern of 'establishing the bargaining range' described by Douglas (1957, 1962). Each of the seven items was described fully and responded to in turn by the management team. On five issues the union claims met with outright rejection (partly on the grounds that they contravened current government legislation), but management did agree to consider the remaining two items and to take further advice. The meeting was adjourned in this state of clearly understood deadlock, and the date for the next meeting was cordially agreed.

The positions of the parties had not really altered at the next meeting one week later. The management repeated their fundamental objections to the five unacceptable union claims but offered compromise proposals on the remaining two issues. In addition, they pointed to some confusion in the union ranks about precisely whom the shop stewards were representing. The stewards agreed to adjourn in order to consult with their district union organiser on the proposals and points raised by the management team. The district organiser suggested that the stewards should modify their claims, principally to concentrate on issues which offered realistic chances of success and would not be the cause of interunion dispute. His advice was given in detail and took tactical considerations carefully into account.

The final session was highly productive. Wage increases within the guidelines of government policy were negotiated with relative ease, and significant concessions on other items were obtained from the management. The meeting was adjourned amid a certain degree of goodwill, to enable the agreed package to be presented to the female shop stewards. Their agreement was obtained.

Stephenson, Kniveton and Morley (in preparation) have described the results of an analysis of this three-session wage negotiation in terms of both the identifiability of speakers and CPA categories. The observer (BHK) attended all three afternoon sessions (and the union caucus) and recorded the content of the interaction in 'shorthand' form on a moving paper tape. This 'transcript' was later typed, and time values for each speech were indicated on the typescript. The transcript was then coded by our trained graduate coder.

I

Circumstances did not permit the tape recording of the meeting (for a discussion of the methodological problems this deficiency poses see Shaw, Fischer and Kelley 1973). Extracts from each of the three transcripts are reproduced later to illustrate the sort of data obtained.

CHARACTERISTIC BEHAVIOUR IN NEGOTIATION GROUPS

This negotiation gave us the opportunity to examine the process of negotiation in rather more detail. In social psychology, knowledge of group process comes primarily from the study of problem-solving groups, in which the information required for the solution of the problem is the main object of discussion. It provides a common interest and focus, a rallying point for all the participants. In negotiation groups, by contrast, what is given is a conflict of interest between the parties which serves not to unify but to divide the participants into two or more factions. Whereas problem-solving groups make decisions on the basis of evidence, negotiation groups must determine between decisions that have already been made. The task is very different, and this makes it unlikely that conclusions about an appropriate process for problem-solving groups are applicable to negotiation groups.

If Bales and Strodtbeck (1951) are correct, the performance of certain problem-solving tasks proceeds through a series of three stages. The tasks are those in which 'it may be assumed that the functional problems of *orientation*, *evaluation* and *control* are each to a major degree unsolved at the beginning of observation and are solved in some degree during the period of observation' (p. 627). (They have provided examples of eight-man academic groups planning a thesis, four-man groups planning a Christmas party, and five-man groups of beginners planning the first move of a chess game.) The stages are those in which the problems of orientation, evaluation and control are dealt with *in turn*. Bales and Strodtbeck's results are portrayed in Figure 12.4.

Socio-emotional problems and behaviours are said to be a byproduct of dealing with the issues. Both positive and negative socio-emotional behaviours are supposed to *increase progressively* from the first through the second to the third phase of the problem-solving process. This characteristic of successful problem-solving groups is really rather different from that feature which has been said to characterise successful negotiation groups. In negotiation groups, conflict is particularly likely to be characteristic of the *first* phase of the negotiation, rather than something which gradually builds up in the course of the interaction (it should be remembered that Bales's (1950) negative social-emotional categories include disagreement as well as antagonism).

Conflict is the essential precursor of negotiation groups and is encountered at the outset. The opening stages of negotiation groups are frequently said to be characterised by hard-hitting aggressive tactics on the part of negotiators on both sides. Rather than gathering information relevant to the solution of the problem, the sides adopt positions which on the face of it render the solution impossible to achieve. We have already quoted Douglas (1957), who has asserted that 'the principals strive for a convincing demonstration that they are impossibly at loggerheads, taking up solid, adamant postures in defence of which they marshal an elaborate factual exposé' (p. 73). The information presented is geared to the justification of a divisive position, not to the solution of a common problem. It is not until much later that negotiators as *individuals* try to ascertain how their parties' divergent interests

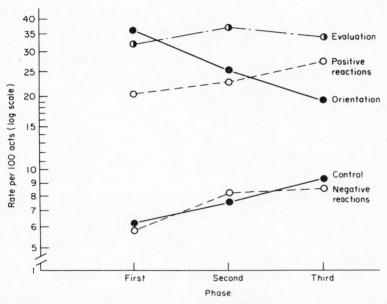

Figure 12.4 Phases in the performance of a problem-solving task (Bales and Strodtbeck 1951)

may be reconciled in a formula which pays due respect to both sides. At this point they act less as representatives and more as individuals, trying to find a solution to the problem which their respective parties have engineered for them. Thus, *the principal difference between problem-solving and negotiation groups is that, whereas in problem-solving groups coping with the task leads to conflict, in negotiation groups conflict yields to coping with the task.* Douglas (1962) has produced some evidence for this distinctive character of the negotiation group. She has claimed that negotiators are less identifiable in terms of their party role, on the management or union side, in the middle phase of prolonged negotiations. The implication of this is that in the first phase of negotiation negotiators are emphasising interparty conflict, whereas later they are coming to grips as individuals with the problems that this conflict creates for them.

EXTRACT FROM THE FIRST MEETING

From phase 1

Secs	Group member[1]	
102	3	As the shop stewards met yesterday there was quite a bit spoken about people leaving to get higher rewards and hence we are going for a higher award. We are aware that there is government legislation which we do not agree with. We will put in this claim knowing it will be above Phase 2 but hoping it will be operated after Phase 2 is over.
18	4	All we are here to do is to discuss from within Phase 2.
72	5	Put it this way. The union want to negotiate an amount to be paid whenever we can have it. You are talking about shift rates up 10%. What do you mean?
13	3	That after the Phase 2 shift rates will go up.
21	5	Now, you are advocating a figure which is an across-the-board figure, or does it apply to each grade?
17	3	Yes, it will be across the board but on each grade.
12	(Silence)	
15	3	Ah, we have taken that one. Have you any answer?
26	5	The point of the answer is that we cannot pay £3·33 but we can pay the difference.
21	4	This is presupposing the company wants to discuss an outside issue.
35	5	Basically this is outside Stage 2. Your request is outside the NJIC as the discussion is only concerned with Phase 2.
45	3	I disagree with this statement. I agree that the full figure is outside the NJIC but inside the £3·50 we are asking for.
45	5	You will note that a letter we have, at the end of paragraph 12 this is only operative for Phase 2. This means that local negotiations are not accepted.
35	3	I disagree with you. Local negotiations have always been available. This is why this firm is above the NJIC wage.
37	5	Obviously you have an advantage over me. We are a party to the NJIC and it specifically eliminates local participation.
50	3	I cannot see anywhere where it says we can negotiate locally. Referring to your comment re we having local negotiations, I remember that there was something . . .
24	5	I must assure you that if we stick to the paragraph of the NJIC we should not negotiate.

[1]Union representatives = 1, 2 and 3; management representatives = 4, 5, 6 and 7.

Secs	Group member	
44	3	But I should assure you the rules are meant to be bent. I think we cannot give you an answer here.
29	4	It's only when you read this slowly you see that the work residual means you negotiate locally for the 4%.
5	1	I agree.
11	5	But I think that the union is asking for more.
22	3	We are putting forward a claim for the difference between the residual amount and over-rate.
34	4	If you were to include the 30p which is the residual and asking for £3·00 to bring it in local line . . .
21	2	Mr A. can see for himself we used to have many applicants for jobs but we don't have now.
18	5	We are aware of the problem but we are aware of the law of the land.
25	3	I hope, Mr A., that we are aware of the law of the land and that is why we have come to you now.
5	5	I appreciate that.
14	3	The thing is people are leaving this plant.
11	4	I don't think we can follow that now.
12	3	Oh no, we cannot comment now.
11	1	It's obvious.
10	3	The Personnel Officer is here.

From phase 2

Secs	Group member	
64	3	I disagree that on item 4 they have defeated us already. Item 4 is our pension scheme. Mr B. says between you and us. I want to ask whether you are going to give the workers free pension.
26	5	I think I can answer this. The company is not going to give you a noncontributory pension scheme.
15	3	A straightforward no? No discussion or argument?
26	5	We are going to discuss this with all the shop stewards. It is costing us a lot anyway.
17	4	Are you talking about a contributory scheme or a noncontributory one?
4	5	No, a contributory scheme.
21	3	There are subtle differences about the pension scheme from the old one.
35	4	One of the drawbacks of a free scheme is that if you leave before the end of the scheme you get nothing.
13	1	But you do get the state scheme.
12	5	It is in the employees' scheme.

Secs	Group member	
20	3	If employers are good enough to give a free scheme there should be no such problem.
12	5	As far as we are concerned the answer is no.
68	3	We might as well go on to item 5. Item 4 on the NJIC letter covers the customary holidays. The customary holidays will be paid on the basis of statutory holidays as soon as possible. Can we have it now, as usually we are a forerunner of the NJIC?
95	5	The law says that we interpret that assuming Phase 3 allows in the light of the NJIC ruling. Unless we reduce another payment we cannot come in and pay this before the NJIC. What it would do is that it would only affect one bank holiday. We would have to reduce the 4% on the basic rate.
25	3	At the same time we have an item to sort out. New Year's Day.
19	5	That is something which has gone to the government. Regarding May Day and New Year's Day.
21	1	I think the Breweries have got it.
8	5	They are not in our NJIC.
16	3	I'm glad you said that. There are fifteen different NJIC groups.
13	5	No, we are represented in the Food Manufacturers' group.
17	3	That only includes Food, Drink and Tobacco.
15	5	I'm prepared to keep you up to date.
18	3	You're prepared to batter us to death with that little group.
36	5	The point is that it is our rule. You're making a formal request for New Year's Day to be granted off in 1974 and after?
4	3	Yes.
25	5	The only thing I can say is that it is something which affects other people.
28	3	I object to this. In one breath you say you are independent and in the next you're saying it affects other people.
2	5	No.
19	3	I object to this if changing the holidays in the factory are separate from these other issues.
42	5	That is not my understanding. We are regarding New Year's Day. We will consider it favourably. My view is that we should have it.
33	3	I'll have a stronger argument on the next issue. It is a result of differing holiday arrangements in the factory.
14	5	Can you enlighten me?
23	3	The electricians have had two weeks as a result of their NJIC and have come into line.
12	4	Nationally or here?

Secs	Group member	
12	3	Yes, nationally, and I would force your hand.
30	5	And yet you just said you agree here. We would have to look into this.
29	3	The management is not very forthright nor capable with your answers.
20	5	We were prepared for certain things maybe you will not bring up.
40	3	You mean hope that we will forget.
8	4	Is that what you think?
12	2	The point is that most places have New Year's Day off.
10	3	Not just outside the town?
16	5	All I'm going to say is we are going to offer favourable consideration to this.
14	3	I don't like this, I have to keep talking.

From phase 3

17	3	I think you are out of order to introduce a pension scheme.
68	5	Under its rules the trustees can alter it without notice. It is a result of the pressures from your agencies. In Devon they were legally required to wind up the scheme. The conventional scheme has been improved so that it is better or at least equal to this scheme.
3	3	Is it?
27	5	We would like to discuss it with you as a group. We would like to enlighten you.
34	3	Put it in layman's language. We are being asked to sign a form saying that they can do what they like.
32	5	No, you are being asked to sign that this money may be transferred from the X pension scheme.
8	3	That rules out all A, B and C.
24	5	No, it does not. Read the paper sent to Don.
10	3	Yes, but we have no option.
10	1	What if someone does not agree?
16	5	The condition is that they must as a condition of employment.
25	3	It's a condition of the X scheme. Do you include working floor personnel?
14	4	I think I remember that it means everyone.
12	5	That's out of date. We used to have two schemes.
14	4	It says now everyone who works here.
7	3	It's out of date.

Secs	Group member	
27	5	Don, to assist you in understanding this it is essential you have the book. You will see there are improvements.
18	3	I can see that. This one is the same. We pay more.
59	5	Take the hypothetical figures. He explains details of the scheme.
12	3	But the females had the chance to join or not.
11	4	The females always had the option.
15	5	You will know of a case of a long term sickness?
8	1, 2	Oh yes, there are two cases.
13	5	There are two and maybe more.
17	3	You are talking about a percentage which is very low.
8	2	It's an insurance.
29	5	It's cheaper to have your own insurance. It would cost you more on your own.
40	3	It would be cheaper for me to get it under national aid than to lose $\frac{1}{2}\%$ of my wages to pay for your scheme. This scheme means that it does not pay to work overtime.
15	4	The scheme is not to finance this latest scheme.
23	3	All the money goes into a kitty, and don't tell me Mr C. doesn't spend it.
19	5	You will find that the pension money is separate from Cavendish.
22	3	I'm saying that Mr C. is on the committee which runs the pension fund.
16	4	He's using his expertise to help our pensions.
18	2	Pension schemes are restricted.
18	5	There will be a meeting which will give outline about the scheme.
21	4	I think we will endeavour to answer as many questions as possible.
19	3	I asked a question at the last meeting and am still waiting for an answer.
5	4	What was the question?
18	3	It refers to a person on a high grade of pay who is off sick.
3	4	Yes.
13	2	It is answered in the new scheme.
15	3	I have dealt now within the new scheme.
37	5	I can assure you that, having been at a meeting regarding pensions, the people who run it know the scheme backwards.
10	3	OK, seems as though . . .
13	5	OK, you have mistrust as a result of previous events.
14	4	People have mistrust of previous events.

Secs	Group member	
12	5	Can we arrange the next meeting?
7	4	Unless you're on holiday.
5	1	Wednesday, Sam?
12	3	Here's me losing money to come here.
27	5	I was told that the day best suited to your work was Thursday.
24	3	Part of the reason for wanting stewards was that they have devious minds.
11	5	I saw the slight glint in your eye.
5	4	When's it to be?
5	5	Wednesday.
9	2	I'll have a word with Fred.
7	3	Either Wednesday or Thursday.
13	4	Let's make it Wednesday at 10.30 a.m. again.

EXTRACT FROM THE SECOND MEETING

From phase 1

17	6	The point is the company don't want to negotiate for the foreseeable future.
13	3	We want something hard and fast now.
11	6	How can we sensibly agree on a figure?
15	3	We want something now.
10	5	We want to negotiate within the JIC.
47	3	You are members within the factory who don't want to recognise the JIC? A precedent has been set in this factory with negotiating outside the JIC.
13	5	Always taking JIC as a guideline.
19	3	No, I can quote you of examples where you set an exception.
8	6	That's the only instance.
17	3	No, there is an example of where there was agreement above NJIC.
5	4	That was 2p an hour?
73	3	Yes, that was 2p. It was negotiated with me and Mr G. concerning the privileges of females and he gave us 1p an hour while we are talking. This it was accepted under two provisos. Item 1 was that it should be sorted out and then there should be more negotiation on this and the management have not come on to this.
92	5	This is separate item to the one we are dealing with. I should make it clear that the company has an attitude and the

Secs	Group member	
		company is going to look at the whole situation. At this time we are not prepared to negotiate outside Phase 2 but we are prepared to look at it at the time when Phase 2 is over.
13	3	I'm sorry with your answer.
12	5	We are prepared to negotiate at the end.
27	3	You notice that at the end of Phase 2 you go back to NJIC.
16	5	We are prepared to negotiate at the end regardless of the NJIC.
28	3	You will promise you will negotiate at the end of Phase 2? Outside Phase 2?
10	4	You mean, we will look at the situation?
16	6	Can we say that we are clear. We . . .
35	4	We are prepared to consider the situation at the end of Phase 2 regardless of the JIC. How far have you got?
23	3	In the situation that after reading that you are only prepared to consider not negotiate.
11	5	That's right, we are prepared to consider it.
14	3	I want to say you will promise to negotiate.
7	5	Let's look at the other points.
10	3	It gives you a stranglehold.
6	5	Let's move on.
19	3	Still on item 1. Have you any propositions?
21	4	We are proposing that each grade is adjusted by £1·00 plus 4%.
13	3	Thank you for your proposition.
12	6	Are you prepared to make a counterproposal?
20	3	We made a proposal last time to say we would get it over the board.
18	4	You will remember last time you negotiated on the differential.
9	3	We negotiated for a flat wage increase.
12	4	All right, the company considering it in a different manner.
7	6	I don't see there is any difference.
41	3	The difference is causing difficulties between the men, as under Phase 2 we would prefer a flat wage award. The government scheme, Mr D., was with the aid of helping the lower paid.
22	4	I think what we are to do is to negotiate a flat rate and see a reduction of the differential.
23	3	I don't think we can do it. The grade levels will remain the same.
15	2	A flat increase on the differential will be same.

Secs	Group member	
10	6	Not on a per cent basis.
8	3	Item 2 will deal with it.
6	6	Item 3 you mean.
6	4	We altered it.
14	3	My feeling is that we should get a proposal from the management.
31	4	The union has asked for it to go across the board. If you will accept an . . . of the differential.
16	3	We are not prepared to accept that.
6	5	We cannot do that.
12	3	Yes you can, if there is less than 100 workers.
23	4	No you cannot, if applied to one person. The method of report varies.
4	3	So what?
10	4	You are asking the company to break the law?
11	3	Yes.

From phase 2

19	3	Have you got the details then? It is basically up 2p.
64	4	That would mean it would go up. If one does an across-the-board one. We are prepared to agree to an across-the-board increase but would not accept that this could alter the situation with the differential between grade rate and that at this stage we would accept a reduction.
14	6	These your words at this stage.
41	3	I said that I would not let you negotiate with other sections of the factory. I'll have to talk to my colleagues.
14	4	That's not the impression I got from other sources.
13	3	In other words we have factions in this factory.
33	4	Well not even the other proposals will give them 17p over NJIC but I believe you are asking us to . . .
22	3	As the government said, right across the board from Prime Minister to cleaner.
47	4	We have had approaches from unions. You ought to get together and decide on your grouping. The government is quite happy for us to negotiate in any grouping.
17	3	Might I say that the management cursed this grouping.
12	5	We are prepared to negotiate with any grouping.
30	4	We have been approached by the engineers and builders. It is not our job to tell you how to negotiate.
21	3	I was not at this meeting and therefore we need to negotiate.

Secs	Group member	
19	5	Seems this meeting should cease until you decide.
27	3	We need not cease. We have your proposition. We are not satisfied. My colleagues will support me.
8	4	That is across the grades.
8	6	Or alternatively, through the grades.
6	1	That is £1·88.
18	3	I thought the management would have got these figures.
15	5	They did not have time to get the accounts.
18	3	We had the same thing last week. We said we would not get far before we started.
8	6	We agree on the principle.
31	4	Following your comments, do you want to arrange a meeting with your stewards to arrange a meeting?
37	3	I will also be blunt and say you are talking to three members of the TUC and we have no power to negotiate on their behalf.
7	4	That's what I say.
45	3	I would say now that if we wanted to go to it the three representatives of the engineering, building and electricians would say they wanted to negotiate but would be outvoted.
13	6	Has this been discussed?
11	1	They said they had been in contact.
2	4	No.
19	1	I was led to believe they had.
12	2	The electricians is on a different shift system.
7	4	That was done last June.
9	1	They've been in contact.
8	6	Not before that meeting.
32	4	The only thing we can do to assist is to ask them whether they are prepared to accept an across-the-board. There is very little we can do.
15	3	Except that you have trouble on your hands from the process workers.
24	4	Whereas in the past you have been willing to accept that building workers have more increase, now you are not.
12	2	That was before free bargaining.

From phase 3

28	3	I still think we have a good case. You have rejected this but I feel we have a good case.
14	1	We had a lot of absenteeism last year.
16	6	A lot of the engineers' people had extra holidays at that time.

Secs	Group member	
16	4	The engineers simply take it off their three weeks' holiday.
18	1	I've seen agreement and it definitely gave it to them.
51	3	Can we make it clear? Item 6 is rejected but the management will consider it. Now item 7. Fourth week holiday. This will be accepted once NJIC has negotiated it.
12	1	Is there a meeting this year?
10	4	It's up to you to chase them.
28	3	I can assure you that he will or he'll have a lot of members. Item 6.
36	5	We are prepared to offer when NJIC does, subject to some conditions.
20	6	Cannot we talk about it and give Don a typewritten list?
134	5	That the workers are willing to do other work when there is no work available. In the event of production failure that rests in strike action in our factory, in supplier's factory, railway and transport services and other associated industries. The . . . of the period of guarantee should . . . action be suspended. The guarantee will not operate.
10	4	Let him get over the page.
10	3	You're looking over my shoulder.
46	4	That's during a period of sickness the work will carry on and this does not apply to part-time employees. There are one or two in the filling room.
8	3	I'm aware of that.
22	5	On the question of part-time employees. This starts at the 1st March.
20	6	Not temporary but permanent. It's just that we do not employ any more.
75	3	All in your statements are the normal parts of the guaranteed week and I feel they have to be accepted by our members. I don't think it will be any problem. I have been speaking a lot. I don't know whether you will appreciate Mr E. is the Senior Shop Steward.
6	6	What are you to do?
29	4	You can do two things: either we can adjourn or you can ring up your district organiser.
19	6	You need to do something as we have to see these others.
32	3	I agree with you that we must contact Mr F. and if necessary let Mr F. take over negotiations with the management.
34	4	Would you underline to him that the management will negotiate with any group which is acceptable to all members? We would like you as unions to sort this out yourselves.

EXTRACT FROM THE THIRD MEETING

From phase 1

Secs	Group member	
13	5	You went away to discuss the group problems.
37	3	We had word with Mr F. He says we should let electricians and engineers continue to negotiate for themselves. We are not wanting to get into an interunion fight.
2	4	OK.
82	3	In any union conflict that leaves us with the proposal the management put it in on grades. That leaves me with the problem of how the management will implement this. As a consequence of reading the bill I see it says that the total will not exceed an increase above 4% on the total. To average out across the scales would be a big job.
4	7	Should I say . . . ?
4	4	Please do.
150	7	Harry is hoping to have the figures for your group worked out by 10.30 this morning. We worked it out on the basis of a flat week plus the good service including overtime. This has been worked out for all employees who have been thère for the previous year. The grade total has been added and divided to give a total figure. To ensure the rates were correct the old rates had been taken and adjusted for the 1p increase. We can only take nine months of that increase on account.
5	3	Till June.
19	7	As I say, Harry is going to make them available to you.
16	3	I understand again that incidentals are excluded?
3	7	Yes.
6	3	Can I ask the situation about the holidays?
22	7	Yes, we are taking three weeks and it includes overtime for the three weeks.
6	3	For the forty-hour week?
8	7	Yes, these have been included.
9	5	When you're taking money from . . .
5	7	From June.
6	5	From last Friday.
43	7	Yes, any other point in favour is that we have not checked each individual and seen whether they've had an increase in the year. It will make little difference.
13	3	You'll be OK with the Phase 2?
20	7	We cannot see the way to increase this amount.

Secs	Group member	
19	5	That will be the average increase for everyone?
4	7	Yes.
7	5	But the grades are different.
11	7	But the unions wanted a flat rate.
9	4	Over each individual's earnings.
20	7	But we could not have taken it for every individual because it's too complex.
15	5	So you're taking everyone on the books yesterday?
12	7	No, it's based on the total pay.
16	1	If they are here five weeks it will be five fifty-seconds?
7	7	Yes, five fifty-seconds.
19	3	The other thing is I can see difficulties going over the grades.
15	7	You said you wanted it across the board.
5	3	Not sure now.
9	5	I think that's better.
11	4	You want to include all people.
20	3	We now don't want an across-the-board increase. No.
14	7	Basically across the board or for each grade.
8	4	You will have the figures?
21	7	Yes, but there will be a delay while we make sure it will be weighted.
28	3	If you do that it will be a wider step below each pair. It will erode the job evaluation.
29	5	Depending how many are in the group. If we are doing it on each grade it's just 4% on each grade.
10	7	It only makes a small difference but.
15	3	It will make a big difference depending on shift levels.
4	2	And overtime.
6	3	Shifts etc.
15	7	I think if we do it on grades we can put up shift rates.
17	5	You cannot put shift up as well.
6	7	Oh yes.
12	5	So you can increase the shift and the good service twice?
3	7	Yes.
9	3	Oh yes, I've checked this.
27	7	What we could do is increase both across the group and a flat rate increase across the board.
9	4	You're not going to get it done.
11	7	The problem is the holidays the same as, Don.
9	1	We can get back pay.
24	7	So get two increases a variable one so everyone gets a fair crack of the whip.

Secs	Group member	
7	1	It depends.
20	3	We are trustful of the management that an increase will be on June 1st.
10	4	I thought of it.
21	7	We thought you would want to see the figures.
11	1	This figure will be down by 10.30.
8	7	It could be a few minutes late.
17	5	This gives everyone the same increase?
4	7	Yes.
8	3	This is the idea of the government scheme.
12	7	Would you like to have a few minutes to discuss it?

From phase 2

30	5	Don should realise that about the pension scheme there has been lots of negotiations previously. It was official.
40	3	Yes I knew. You two won't understand but I realised as I had an opportunity to be there.
8	4	Next point, Don.
51	3	Average pay and New Year's Day. Seems it might be legislated and also the four weeks' holiday. The company is not prepared to commit yourself. You're not prepared to consider it regardless of the JIC.
33	4	I think we must emphasise that we will accept the JIC as a guideline and I don't see why we cannot discuss these matters again?
6	7	I don't see why not.
10	3	The point is it won't debar negotiations later.
3	4	No.
42	3	We were supposed to have some negotiations about the guaranteed working week. Our union officer has not sent a letter so we don't have an alternative proposition.
12	7	Can you tell us the grounds for your objection?
86	3	The thing is that the word 'reasonable' in the text in item A is negotiable. Item B about in our factory, we have already said that we have agreements within the factory which would mean that a strike by one group would debar another group from having a guaranteed week.
64	7	As far as the management is concerned we cannot guarantee work if certain aspects are not controlled. It could be that as a result of strikes certain members are not able to do their

Secs	Group member	
		proper jobs. It's because I don't think they would be prepared to move.
12	3	As I say, we have not got our counterproposals.
14	7	Quite. That is our objective.
44	3	Clause B, item 2. Supplier's factory. Once again this would mean that a strike in the Siberian salt mines would affect us.
15	2	The thing is we would stop with no supplies.
5	7	It could be.
5	4	Let's hear Don.
9	7	You distrust clause B?
31	3	Yes, I distrust clause B. While we trust this management at this factory but this management is responsible to Cavendish.
22	4	True to say if we were not supplied, we would have to change.
15	5	But when we run out of cartons we would find alternative work.
31	7	I feel sure if we didn't give you work as a result of some stoppage or other then there would be a strike.
54	3	Oh yes, it's just tumbled. Now rail and transport. Once again you put it in and I don't see much point. We have our own transport. We had strikes as a result of the rail stoppage and it did not affect us.
13	5	It is only if it disrupts production.
19	3	But it's unlikely. You put it in and there seems no point.
12	7	You wanted a guaranteed week.
10	3	These are comments not necessarily ours.
4	7	Yes.
23	3	And other associated industries. Cavendish is a big organisation and 'associated industries' covers a lot.
9	4	Not salt mines in Siberia though!
10	3	Even if Pirelli stops making tyres.
6	4	We'd buy Dunlop.
4	3	Yes but . . .
10	5	All of them could happen.
31	3	When we were talking with Mr F. who did promise to give us some information . . .
8	7	I was keeping quiet.
21	3	We contacted Mr F. but did not find him. I could . . .
6	4	Carry on with item D.
41	3	Item D. I cannot see why a form of guaranteed week should not apply to part-time employees. It should apply for them.

Secs	Group member	
20	7	You are saying that if they do twenty hours regularly they should be guaranteed it.
10	4	You want less than a guarantee.
10	3	They should get a per cent.
18	7	The only one we are waiting for is the item from Mr F. on item B.
15	3	Item B and C.
16	7	The situation is we broadly accept A. B and C you will have a counterproposal?
2	3	Yes.
26	7	Do you feel that part-timers should be included in some form? There is not much we can do about B and C.
19	4	No, wait until we get the literature. Any other points?
7	3	No, we are waiting for the figures.
19	4	One point we should make is that we should give all we can within Phase 2.
70	3	Thank you, Mr D. I think from the discussion it can be seen that you are doing what you can.

From phase 3

72	H[1]	I came to a figure of 254 and the wage to go against that was x and 4% was 17 x's. Total divided by the number employed was for a week on an hourly basis, is £0·71 per hour anywhere near?
6	3	Slightly out.
6	H	Divided the year by four.
12	7	You include the foremen and first-aiders.
4	3	And holiday pay.
57	H	This includes shifts etc. No, but on the figures upstairs that's in order. Not to miss anyone we used the top interrogation list. I have no objection to seeing if you have not.
4	1	No.
17	7	We should make sure individual names are crossed out.
10	3	Before we say, are the females included?
11	H	They are in on fifty-three weeks not fifty.
16	7	I was under the idea that you wanted it across the board.
34	H	We could do it but it is time again. If you want it by Thursday it must be in by Monday.
13	7	Should we leave these two together?

[1]H = Accountant called in to advise the meeting.

Secs	Group member	
23	1	Would it raise it much if the females are brought in?
26	7	Why not give someone a ring to bring the machine down?
5	4	What about?
8	7	To bring females into line.
22	3	It must be straightforward with men is that, what is going through my mind is that the females . . .
13	1	Get another 50p in December.
21		(General chat)
8	7	It is an adjustment.
12	1	We can negotiate for an adjustment.
16	3	The agreement was reached in December. It was arranged before.
14	5	The $\frac{1}{2}$ is the difference that came last December.
19	7	For me it would be better to leave it, as it is for them to get it in December.
30	3	I hope you don't think we are being difficult but we are here as representatives of female as well as male and want to protect their interests.
6	1	Down at the bottom . . .
7	4, 7	(Mumble).
17	1, 6	(Mumble).
19	4, 5, 7	(Mumble).
20	1	If you gave the males the 4% you could bring the females up by $\frac{1}{3}$.
42	7	Then they could not get their chunk in December.
12	3	Had an interesting conversation while Harry's been away.
9	7	He's been fiddling the books!
23	H	It's £1·70 with the women and £1·88 all round.
27	3	That's what they will get in December anyway.
7	5	Is the . . . on?
13	H	All the lot.
13	7	The women will drop 18p and men up 10p.
8	3	In December they will get an increase.
16	7	They will get 50p.
18	4	Can we re-meet this afternoon?
20	3	It's just a case of saying which way it will go.
13	7	If you want to have a further meeting?
12	4	I can come away from my meeting.
37	3	I think that we should not decide yet without the females' discussing it. We can get the female stewards in here.
5	4	Thank you.
6	3	Fair enough.

THE ANALYSIS

Role identifiability

Fifteen judges assessed the identifiability of speakers in terms of their allegiance to the management or union. The three transcripts were presented to the judges in random order. For purposes of statistical analysis each transcript was divided into three 'phases', each phase containing eight 'bits', each bit consisting of an equal number of CPA acts. Figure 12.5(a) gives the means of error scores for the three phases in each session. The *session* means showed a statistically significant increase in errors from session 1 to session 3. This indicated that as the negotiation proceeded from one session to the next, the contributions of the participants were less distinguishable one from another. The participants were increasingly 'interchangeable'. The main effect for *phases* was only marginally significant but interesting to the extent that it

(a) *Judges' Mean Error Scores for the Three Phases of Each Session of the Negotiation (in %)*

	Phase			
	1	*2*	*3*	*Session means*
Session 1	35·65	23·33	27·18	28·72
Session 2	25·30	34·79	36·27	32·12
Session 3	34·34	28·47	37·99	33·60
Phase means	31·76	28·86	33·81	31·48 = Grand mean

(b) *Analysis of Variance on Error Scores*

		SS	d.f.	VE	F	d.f.	p
Judges	A	25208·251	14	1800·589			
Sessions	B	4508·669	2	2254·334	4·544	28	< ·05
Phases	C	4455·005	2	2227·502	4·173	28	< ·10
Bits	D	6853·986	7	979·141	2·453	98	< ·05
	AB	13890·840	28	496·101			
	AC	14945·630	28	533·773			
	AD	39110·325	98	399·085			
	BC	19116·368	4	4779·092	7·084	56	< ·01
	BD	20949·375	14	1496·384	3·355	196	< ·01
	CD	10222·149	14	730·153	1·498	196	< ·10
	ABC	37780·211	56	674·647			
	ABD	87417·861	196	446·010			
	ACD	95543·243	196	487·466			
	BCD	48143·189	28	1719·400	4·287	392	< ·01
	ABCD	$1·572 \times 10^5$	392	401·051			
	TOTAL	$5·854 \times 10^5$	1079				

Figure 12.5 Role identifiability of speakers in three-session wage negotiation

duplicated the results from the previous Type 2 task (i.e. the electricians' informal negotiation). The reduction of errors in the second phase was in fact statistically significant in the electricians' negotiation, indicating that the main interparty confrontation occurred in the middle phase of that single negotiating session.

However, the most striking feature of the three-session negotiation results, as Figure 12.5(b) indicates, was the interaction between sessions and phases. The overall phase effect was mainly characteristic of the first and final negotiating sessions. Session 2 produced a progressive increase of errors from phase 1 to phase 3. It must be concluded that *the structure of a single session will undoubtedly vary according to its place in the overall negotiation.*

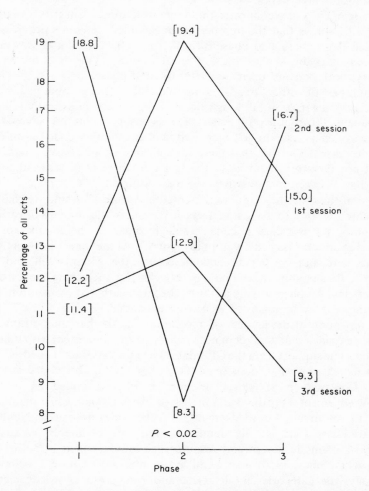

Figure 12.6 Use of CPA category referent: other in three-session wage negotiation

Analysis by CPA categories

The CPA data confirmed the importance of the referent category 'other'. Analysis of variance of the proportion of acts coded as 'other' showed a significant sessions/phases interaction, portrayed graphically in Figure 12.6. The phase effect identified in the electricians' negotiation appeared in sessions 1 and 3 but was reversed in session 2. Given that session 2 was adjourned at the request of the union and that session 3 ended in agreement, it is tempting to suggest that the 'other' category provides an index of the progress being made in negotiation. Subsequent research may or may not support this (very tentative) conclusion, but it is at least clear that CPA is capable of generating interesting research hypotheses.

The use of CPA also confirmed that there were some main effects of phase. Figure 12.7 shows that the number of 'unclassified' referents progressively increased from phase 1 to phase 3 (in fact the effect of phases was in this instance remarkably similar to the effect of sessions). The use of the referent category 'both persons' decreased after the first phase.

A number of other trends confirmed the findings obtained in the electricians' negotiation (although none of these were statistically reliable). Once again, the number of acts coded as resource: limits decreased, the number coded as referent: self increased, and the number coded as referent: party decreased. The fact that there were clear sessions/phases interactions should not therefore blind us to the fact that there were some important similarities between phases, whenever they occurred.

Some of the other findings are presented in Figure 12.7, and we shall pay particular attention to the main effects of *sessions* in the analyses of variance. There was, for instance, a considerable increase in the number of acts containing an 'unclassified' referent in session 3. At the same time there was a decrease in the number of acts coded in terms of the referents 'self' and 'both persons'. Presumably these findings reflected an increasing emphasis on interpersonal problem solving as the negotiation gathered momentum. If so, our analysis may be regarded as having expanded Douglas's (1957, 1962) characterisation of the process of 'reconnoitering the bargaining range'.

Douglas's idea that conflict in negotiation groups *diminishes* with time also received some support from the CPA data. The number of acts coded as mode: accept increased over sessions ($p < \cdot06$), while the number coded as mode: reject decreased ($p < \cdot06$). The number of acts coded as resource: acknowledgement + (other side) increased over sessions, while the number coded as resource: acknowledgement − (other side) decreased. Neither of these trends was statistically significant. They are of interest because the categories of mode: accept and resource: acknowledgement + (other side) define what Bales (1950) would call 'positive social-emotional' behaviour. Similarly, the categories mode: reject and resource: acknowledgement − (other side) define what Bales would call 'negative social-emotional

	Grand Mean	Session 1	Session 2	Session 3	F	d.f.	p	Phase 1	Phase 2	Phase 3	F	d.f.	p
Mode													
Offer	79·2	78·0	80·1	79·5	0·39	2,27	n.s.	79·5	78·0	80·1	0·35	2,27	n.s.
Accept	3·9	3·3	2·5	6·0	3·20	2,27	0·056	4·6	3·8	3·5	0·34	2,27	n.s.
Reject	3·6	5·0	4·6	1·2	3·20	2,27	0·056	4·8	4·5	1·6	2·27	2,27	0·123
Seek	11·8	13·3	11·8	10·2	0·79	2,27	n.s.	10·7	12·6	12·1	0·32	2,27	n.s.
Unclassified	1·5	0·4	0·9	3·1	1·61	2,27	0·219	0·5	1·2	2·7	1·05	2,27	0·364
TOTAL	100·0	100·0	99·9	100·0				100·0	100·1	100·0			
Resource													
Initial settlement point	5·4	2·8	9·3	4·3	3·09	2,27	0·062	6·3	3·1	7·0	1·17	2,27	0·327
New settlement point	1·6	2·4	0·0	2·4	3·88	2,27	0·033	1·3	2·7	0·8	2·06	2,27	0·147
Limits	30·2	32·0	29·4	29·0	0·12	2,27	n.s.	32·4	33·6	24·5	1·14	2,27	0·333
Positive consequences of outcomes	1·1	2·2	0·7	0·2	2·44	2,27	0·106	0·2	1·0	2·0	1·85	2,27	0·177
Negative consequences of outcomes	1·5	1·3	0·7	2·4	0·99	2,27	n.s.	1·2	1·6	1·6	0·08	2,27	n.s.
Procedure	7·8	2·2	9·0	12·1	4·26	2,27	0·025	8·6	6·1	8·7	0·37	2,27	n.s.
Acknowledgement + (own side/both sides)	0·1	0·2	0·0	0·0	1·00	2,27	n.s.	0·2	0·0	0·0	1·00	2,27	n.s.
Acknowledgement + (other side)	0·8	0·4	0·7	1·2	0·97	2,27	n.s.	0·8	0·5	0·9	0·97	2,27	n.s.
Acknowledgement − (own side/both sides)	0·3	0·2	0·2	0·5	0·45	2,27	n.s.	0·5	0·2	0·2	0·29	2,27	n.s.
Acknowledgement − (other side)	0·9	1·3	1·2	0·2	1·72	2,27	0·199	0·2	0·8	1·7	2·75	2,27	0·082
Acknowledgement + (outside party)	0·1	0·0	0·2	0·0	1·00	2,27	n.s.	0·0	0·0	0·2	1·00	2,27	n.s.
Information	47·7	53·3	46·8	42·9	0·74	2,27	n.s.	46·0	48·3	48·7	0·56	2,27	n.s.
Unclassified	2·8	1·7	1·9	4·8	2·31	2,27	0·119	2·4	2·3	3·6	0·45	2,27	n.s.
TOTAL	100·3	100·0	100·1	100·0				100·1	100·2	99·9			
Referent													
Self	10·2	12·6	9·7	8·3	3·39	2,27	0·049	7·7	12·7	10·3	4·37	2,27	0·023
Person	13·4	10·9	13·9	15·2	1·09	2,27	0·351	15·4	13·4	11·2	1·01	2,27	0·378
Other	13·8	15·6	14·6	11·2	2·62	2,27	0·091	14·1	13·5	13·7	0·05	2,27	n.s.
Party	6·5	10·2	5·8	3·6	2·85	2,27	0·075	8·4	5·9	5·3	0·66	2,27	n.s.
Opponent	3·7	4·1	4·9	2·1	1·93	2,27	0·165	3·9	5·0	2·2	1·94	2,27	0·164
Both persons	3·8	2·0	6·5	2·9	6·27	2,27	0·006	5·9	2·6	2·9	3·70	2,27	0·038
Both parties	0·8	1·5	0·5	0·5	1·97	2,27	0·159	1·2	0·8	0·4	0·81	2,27	n.s.
Unclassified	47·9	43·1	44·2	56·2	7·24	2,27	0·003	43·4	46·1	54·1	4·27	2,27	0·025
TOTAL	100·1	100·0	100·1	100·0				100·0	100·0	100·1			

Figure 12.7 CPA categorisation of acts by sessions in three-session wage negotiation (in percentages)

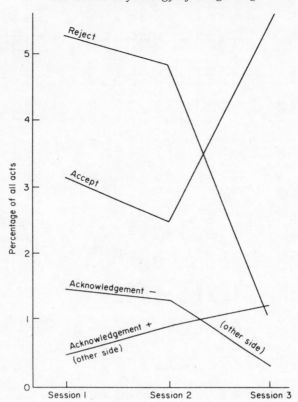

Figure 12.8 Distribution of two mode (reject and accept) and two resource (acknowledgement + (other side) and acknowledgement − (other side)) CPA categories in three-session wage negotiation

behaviour'. Figure 12.8 shows that, whereas positive social-emotional behaviour did indeed increase with time (in line with Bales and Strodtbeck's (1951) data), negative social-emotional behaviour did not. This gradual decrease in criticism ran quite contrary to the pattern of behaviour predicted by results from problem-solving groups. Once more we are forced to recognise the distinctive character of negotiation groups.

Bales and Strodtbeck's data also show a progressive increase in the amount of communication dealing with problems of *control*. Here it is interesting to note that, while there were some changes in individual categories over time, the amount of time spent on the 'outcome' categories as a whole was remarkably steady over the three sessions. This finding is portrayed in Figure 12.9.

Figure 12.9 also shows a steady increase in the use of the coding resource: procedure. At the same time there was a steady decrease in the use of resource:

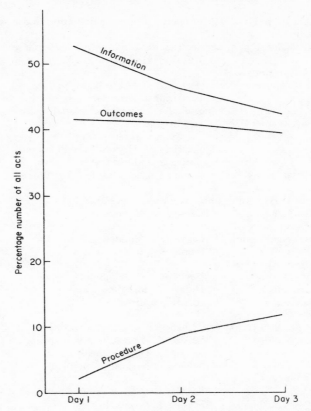

Figure 12.9 Distribution of three resource (outcomes, information and procedure) CPA categories in three-session wage negotiation

information. If anything, we would have assumed an emphasis on procedural issues to be prominent in the early rather than the late stages of debate. Examination of the transcript indicates that the high level of procedure reflected an increasingly businesslike approach. A certain sense of urgency characterised the endpoint of discussion. It remains to be seen whether this increasing incidence of procedure is a general feature of the negotiating process. Our interpretation is that it is yet another indication of the increasingly problem-solving orientation of negotiators as they partially shed their role as representatives and come to grips with the issues.

The Movement from Interparty to Interpersonal Exchange

Figure 12.10 presents a summary of the movement through phases and sessions which characterised the two negotiations. By and large, the pattern of behaviour recommended by Douglas (1957, 1962) seems to have been

(a) MAIN EFFECTS OF PHASE (electricians' informal negotiation and 3-session wage
     negotiation)
     Role identifiability   electricians': Highest in middle phase
                                     3-session: Highest in middle phase

     CPA resource categories
        initial settlement point   electricians': Decrease with phase
        limits   electricians': Decrease with final phase
                                     3-session: Decrease with final phase

     CPA referent categories
        self   3-session: Increase with phase
        other   electricians': Highest in middle phase
        party   electricians': Decrease with phase
        both persons   3-session: Decrease after first phase

(b) MAIN EFFECTS OF SESSION (3-session wage negotiation)
     Role identifiability   Decrease with session
     CPA resource categories
        new settlement point   Decrease in middle session
        procedure   Increase with session
     CPA referent categories
        self   Decrease with session
        both persons   Highest in middle session
        unclassified   Increase with session

(c) SESSIONS PHASES INTERACTION (3-session wage negotiation)
     Role identifiability   Session 1: Highest in middle phase
                                     Session 2: Decrease with phase
                                     Session 3: Highest in middle phase

     CPA referent categories
        other   Session 1: Highest in middle phase
                                     Session 2: Lowest in middle phase
                                     Session 3: Highest in middle phase

Figure 12.10 Summary of statistically significant changes in negotiators' behaviour by phase and
by session

followed in the electricians' callout dispute and in sessions 1 and 3 of the three-
session wage negotiation. Changes in the distribution of the referent
categories of CPA confirmed the shift from interparty (Douglas's stage 1) to
interpersonal (Douglas's stage 2) phases of the negotiation: references to 'self'
increased from the first to the final phase, while references to 'party' decreased;
references to 'other' were highest in the middle phase. Furthermore, changes
in the distribution of the CPA resource categories confirmed the shift from the
stage of 'reconnoitering the bargaining range' (Douglas's stage 2) to the stage
of 'decision-making crisis' (Douglas's stage 3): the use of 'limits' showed a
marked decline in the final phase of negotiation, and there was some evidence
that concern with 'information' and/or 'procedure' showed a corresponding
increase. It is also interesting to note that the proportion of acts without an

explicit referent (referent: unclassified) showed a final phase increase in each of the negotiations (although neither trend was statistically reliable).

Douglas's finding that identifiability of negotiators is highest in the initial stages of negotiation was not confirmed by our analysis. The level of identifiability remained relatively high throughout, but participants were most readily identified when references to 'other' were at a maximum in the second phase. It may be significant that the one exception to this rule was provided by session 2 of the three-session wage negotiation – which was adjourned at the union's request. There, judges' errors increased over phases and references to 'other' were at a minimum in the second phase.

We shall return to these findings in Chapter 13.

Chapter 13

Stages in Negotiation:
A Quasiprescriptive Model

The time has now come to put together the information we have obtained in an attempt to characterise the behaviour of negotiators in successive phases of a negotiation. Our observations of the behaviour of the individual members of a negotiation group have suggested, with previous work, that behaviour characteristically changes in time. From an initial period of exposition of his own group's position and criticism of the stance adopted by his opponent, the negotiator progresses to a more relaxed discussion of the difficulties of obtaining agreement, then to a positively conciliatory period of decision making. Explanation of this movement in purely psychological terms may yield highly misleading results. Douglas (1962) reflected on the observation of her recordings in the opening stages of negotiations by clinical psychologists, and was moved to comment,

'Some of the most misleading interpretations of the behaviour during this first stage have been contributed by psychologists. Having gone into this field with the idea that a negotiating conference is merely another example of the small, autonomous problem-solving group which has engaged so much social science attention in recent years, they have pointed to the donnybrook of outbursts and denunciations as evidence of anxiety, hostility, and aggression as clinicians are accustomed to dealing with these. In their haste to extrapolate in a straight line from clinical observation of troubled persons to relationships between modern-day power-aggregates, they have mistaken purposive social action for individual *re*-action' (pp. 15–16).

Douglas was inclined to minimise the role of individual personalities, suggesting that a negotiator 'more nearly resembles his opposite number in the conference room than himself outside the conference room' (p. 159). We may agree with Douglas that participants in a negotiation are to some degree self-consciously playing a part in a drama and that the existing relationship between the groups ensures that the script is at least partly dictated in advance. The *drama* of the process may be captured if we consider the characteristics of the total group as it moves from its representation of initially divisive positions to the concluding statement of agreed policy. In the first phase the balance of power is determined, and the principal direction which the final outcome must take is thereby decided. The sides weigh up their chances and adjust their goals in the light of the arguments presented. Demands and the ability to enforce them by whatever appropriate means are the crux of the discussion at this stage.

The first phase may be anticipated more or less accurately by those acquainted with the parties and their prior dealings. Even so, even at that stage individual variation may be important. Negotiators may vary, for example, in their commitment to the representative role, and their expository and critical skills may be subject to even greater variation. There is perhaps even more room for individual variation at the later stages, in skills and in perceptions of appropriate behaviour. Both individual and group standpoints are necessary if the complexity of the process is to be conveyed.

How has our analysis of real life negotiations clarified the issues raised by the experimental work? What picture of the negotiation process has been suggested by the results from both aspects of our work? There was one principal theme in both the experimental and field work we conducted: the critical role played by the interpersonal relationship between the participants. This constitutes, in Plön's (1975) words, 'the social-psychological aspect par excellence of "negotiation" '. The experimental work has demonstrated that variations in channel formality (which manipulates the number of cues available to participants) may affect the outcome of a negotiation. In other words, outcomes of negotiation may be determined, at least in part, by the *accessibility* of the other, or others (Stephenson 1975). The analysis of the real negotiations has indicated that the *identifiability* of the other is a salient marker of progress in negotiation. We shall discuss each of these findings in turn, before considering the relationships between them.

Accessibility of the Other

There is a tendency in the literature on industrial relations, international relations and other areas of intergroup activity to speak of relations between the 'sides' as somehow abstracted from the interaction of the members. The 'power relationship' between the 'sides' is somehow supposed to determine strategy and hence the outcomes of negotiations, independently of the decision by representatives to exploit, exaggerate, misperceive, minimise or otherwise interpret or use this power relationship in negotiations. This political exaggeration is opposed by an equally inappropriate exclusive reliance on economic factors, in which, for example, labour is seen to be purchased at the market price according to well-established laws of supply and demand.

Such political and economic models of bargaining have dominated the theory of industrial relations, although the scene is rapidly changing (Bain and Clegg 1974, Brotherton and Stephenson 1975). In the work of experimental psychologists these biases are also apparent. The predominance of political and economic models is aptly illustrated in the emphasis on matrix gaming situations on the one hand and bilateral monopoly situations on the other. The paradigm has been the situation of 'interaction between two individuals, considered as the all-purpose matrix for gaining knowledge of economic processes – which are reduced to nothing but price-bargaining – and political processes reduced to nothing but questions of the choice of tactics' (Plön 1975).

A recent paper by Brown and Terry (1975) accepts the need to explore the influence of the *personal relationship* between negotiators on the outcomes of negotiations. Nevertheless, they have found it necessary to warn of the danger of placing too great an emphasis on this 'bargaining relationship': 'just as diplomats tidy up the outcome of a battle rather than fight it themselves, the bargaining relationship should always be seen as subordinate to the ongoing power relationship between management and workforce' (p. 10). Why is the 'bargaining relationship' even of such limited importance? What does it *do* to the process of negotiation?

The relationship between the individual negotiators may be described on two main dimensions which are not necessarily of equal importance. Walton and McKersie (1965) have emphasised the effects that *liking* may have on mutual influence, trust and the desire to co-operate. By implication they have also stressed the important role that a negotiator's *knowledge* of the other person may play in rendering his behaviour and interactions predictable and hence, in principle, controllable. Both knowledge of the other and liking for him are affected by what we have termed *accessibility*. Accessibility may be determined, as in our experiments, by the formality of the communication system or the frequency of interaction. However, we have emphasised the effect that accessibility has on the *'affective'* relationship between the negotiators: certain tactics and behaviours are rendered less acceptable in the more 'accessible' circumstances. Brown and Terry, on the contrary, have emphasised the *'cognitive'* component of the relationship between individual negotiators:

'We shall define the bargaining relationship that exists between two opposing negotiators as the extent to which they are able to make each other aware of the constraints under which they operate and the likely reactions by one organisation to actions by the other. We thus see the concept primarily in terms of information flows . . . we would describe a bargaining relationship as "high" when the two protagonists are able to communicate changes in their bargaining positions rapidly and thus have a high degree of certainty about likely outcomes from fresh developments' (p. 8).

While useful for purposes of analysis, it is doubtful that the affective and cognitive aspects of the personal relationship can be so readily separated in practice. Human nature being what it is, a 'high' bargaining relationship is likely to increase liking, which in turn will influence the willingness of negotiators to be 'high' one with another. Nevertheless we can accept Brown and Terry's argument that at least for professional negotiators 'it is primarily a reciprocal business relationship between the opposing roles of negotiators, and if it should gain affective overtones, they are very secondary (and possibly damaging)' (p. 9). Indeed, the 'possibly damaging' effects of the interpersonal relationship have been illustrated by our results, which showed inappropriately equal outcomes following distinctly unequal inputs in the less formal conditions. It is interesting to note in this respect that the relationship between formality and strength of case disappeared when subjects had knowledge of opponent's minimum goals – as would occur in what Brown and Terry have termed a 'high' bargaining relationship.

Identifiability of the Other

One inevitable danger in a continuing interpersonal relationship between opposed negotiators is the possibility of misunderstanding with their respective principals. A 'high' relationship between negotiators may with some justice be viewed with suspicion by other members of the representatives' parties. In the context of such a relationship, negotiators may well be better able to arrive at an informed estimate of relative bargaining strengths and hence the appropriateness of different proposals, but acting on this information presents problems. Reasonable action by an informed person may seem truly unreasonable to the uninformed. The understandable fear is created that negotiators by virtue of their personal relationships with opponents may somehow neglect their duties, by putting the preservation of their personal relationship before the interests of their constituents. Brown and Terry (1975) have stated 'that the bargaining relationship is an inevitable part of the collective bargaining process, and that, inherent in it, is the danger that the negotiator may become isolated from his organization' (p. 10).

Fear of the 'sell-out' is an obsessive theme in industrial bargaining and other bargaining relationships, and it brings home again the fundamental dilemma for the negotiator: how to reconcile the demands of his role as representative with the requirement that agreement presently be obtained. Increasingly, there are those who believe that any form of negotiation is in some sense a 'betrayal', since successful negotiation invariably involves compromise. Such constricted views of essential interests bypass the needs of the professional, who must perforce negotiate in order to survive. In practice, how does he cope?

It is certain that in negotiations the obligation to do full justice to party's position is frequently paramount. The representative is an advocate and will not be lightly forgiven if the strength of party's case is not made evident. Whether or not he may appear to perform any other task in negotiations is variable. In extreme circumstances the personal relationship must perforce go underground, to perform its conciliatory work away from the gaze of suspicious constituents (Stephenson 1971b). More typically, we venture to suggest, the 'bargaining relationship' progressively takes charge as negotiations proceed from the formal expositions of differences to a discussion of how the issues may be resolved. This is indexed by the decreasing identifiability and, we may surmise, the increasing 'interchangeability' of negotiators from opposing sides. It is as if the movement towards an interpersonal discussion is facilitated by an effective presentation of interparty conflict.

How may the importance of the initial presentations be judged? Douglas (1962) has advocated the representative role in the first stage of a negotiation primarily to ensure that full justice is done to party's position *before* agreement is reached. There must be bloody noses to prove that a fight has indeed occurred:

'For local colour there are forensic fireworks and dogmatic pronouncements. There is a great show of muscles – verbal, of course (with the promise of other kinds to come) – augmented by lengthy statements about firm positions which everyone knows will eventually give way, though the principals continue stoutly to deny this. There are vehement demands and counter-demands, arguments and counter-arguments. Each side shows prodigious zeal for exposing and discrediting its opposite, and sooner or later there almost invariably comes from each side a conscious, studied, hard-hitting critique of the other. These attacks are typically vigorous and spirited; not infrequently they are also derisive and venomous' (p. 15).

This more or less stage-managed battle is not, however, the whole story. The first stage of a negotiation does more than demonstrate the gladiatorial skill of the contestants. Just as importantly, and certainly paradoxically, by emphasising disagreement it *directly* facilitates the subsequent movement towards agreement. As we have noted earlier, the extent to which one side initially differentiates itself from the other may affect how concessions are subsequently exchanged. Pruitt (1969) has argued that negotiators must 'reach an agreement about the exchange rate for their concessions before they can move towards agreement' (p. 44). It is for such reasons that Douglas (1962) has asserted that 'the net effect of Phase 1 is not essentially negative but positive' and 'To a not inconsiderable extent what is settled for in the end will reflect the determination about original positions which the principals have imparted and detected in this first stage' (p. 21). We may say that in this first stage the protagonists are assessing the form of the parties with respect to the particular course on which the present contest will take place. 'Strength of position' is shrewdly assessed from a consideration of the *merits* of the arguments and the *power* of party to inflict damage on opponent in the event of failure to agree.

In this respect it is instructive to refer to some observations made of the shop stewards' meeting with their local district organiser following the second session in the three-session wage negotiation described in Chapter 12. The presentation of case by both sides had resulted in deadlock. The union case had been severely damaged when the management had correctly pointed out that certain important aspects of the claim were prohibited by the terms of Phase 2 of the government's policy for prices and incomes. This *weakness* was confirmed by the district organiser who, moreover, pointed out that the stewards were *powerless* to compensate for this inadequacy. Militancy was out of the question 'because your industry is not of national importance'. Subsequent bargaining in this case took into account the respective position strengths of the parties that had emerged in the course of those early sessions.

Accessibility, Identifiability, and Strength of Case

As we have seen, interparty exchanges may be evaluated in terms not only of their dramatic impact but also of their effectiveness in eliciting a clear portrayal of the relative strengths of the parties. The importance of this process must not be underestimated. Where the relative merits of the positions of the two sides are similarly perceived, progress towards an equitable outcome may be achieved. The experimental work described in Chapters 8 and 9 has illustrated this point. In the more formal circumstances outcomes reflected strength of case in the two contending parties; that is, outcomes were more equitable. We have argued that by increasing formality we decrease accessibility. This is self-evident given the absence of channels of communication which would otherwise be available. Again, we have argued that formality encourages an emphasis on interparty exchange in a number of different ways: it decreases sensitivity to the others' feelings, it directs attention to the issues involved, and it means that personal reciprocity is eschewed. Undeniably this leads to the expectation that *formality will be positively correlated with identifiability*. While negotiators become progressively less identifiable with time, we may nevertheless expect negotiators in formal conditions to be more identifiable in terms of party affiliations than their counterparts in less formal settings. If this hypothesis was confirmed it would provide further support for the suggestion that *one principal function of the first stage of negotiation (in which identifiability is high) is to establish the strength of case of the parties concerned.*

We investigated this possibility using transcripts from (a) Experiment II, and (b) the work of Stephenson, Ayling and Rutter (1976) (reported in Chapter 11). In the first case, speeches were selected randomly from the four conditions of Experiment II. The judgements of twenty people indicated that identifiability was significantly better by telephone than face-to-face. Figure 13.1(a) shows a summary of the findings. Only 20·3% of speeches were judged erroneously by telephone, whereas 29·0% were incorrect face-to-face ($F = 27·31$, *d.f.* $= 1,560$, $p < ·001$). Most interestingly, the free *v.* con-

(a) *Experiment II*

	Face-to-face	Telephone	Mean
Free	25·27	20·69	22·98
Constrained	32·68	19·91	26·30
Mean	28·98	20·30	

(b) Experiment by Stephenson. Ayling and Rutter 1976

Face-to-face	Telephone
40·8	33·6

Figure 13.1 Role identifiability of speakers: judges' error scores (as percentage of number of speeches) in two experimental situations (average of 20 judges)

strained comparison showed a significant effect in the reverse direction, again suggesting a distinction between 'channel formality' and 'conventional formality'; there were 23·0% errors in the less formal (free) conditions and 26·3% errors in the more formal (constrained) condition ($F = 3·99$, $d.f. = 1,560$, $p < ·05$). Moreover, a significant interaction occurred between medium of communication and freedom to interrupt. Fewer errors were made in face-to-face/free groups than in face-to-face/constrained groups, but more errors were made in telephone/free groups than in telephone/constrained groups. As Figure 13.1(a) makes quite clear, the effect of the 'constraint' was located almost entirely in the face-to-face groups. This is especially interesting in view of the fact that 'constraint' had the effect of *increasing* the length of speeches in the face-to-face conditions. One might have thought that increased utterance length would enhance identifiability. This was not the case, and the result casts doubt on any suggestion that differences in identifiability at different stages in a negotiation (or via different media) may be merely an artefact of speech length.

The analysis of transcripts from the Stephenson, Ayling and Rutter (1976) experiment also showed a marked and statistically significant effect of medium on identifiability. Pages were taken randomly from transcripts of all the dyadic discussions, and speeches were given to twenty judges as before. An error score was calculated for each page of transcript. Pages from face-to-face discussions produced an average of 40·8% errors, whereas those from telephone discussions produced an average of 33·6% errors (see Figure 13.1(b)).

The relationship between medium of communication and identifiability has been clearly established by these two sets of data. (In neither case was there a statistically significant effect of judges, alone or interacting with other factors.)

A Quasiprescriptive Model of Behaviour in Negotiation Groups

We are now in a position to extend Douglas's (1957, 1962) ideas. Figure 13.2

| | Characteristics of Negotiation Group | | Characteristics of Individuals | | |
	Main requirement	Most salient feature	Main requirement	Most salient behaviour	Overall Characterisation
Stage I	To establish criteria for appropriate settlement point	Power relationship Strength of case	To fulfil role as representative	Role-oriented: exposition and criticism	Distributive bargaining
Stage II	To explore range of solutions which satisfy above criteria	Interpersonal 'bargaining' relationship	To establish working relationship	Problem-oriented: proposing and evaluating	Problem solving
Stage III	To agree on most appropriate settlement point	Historical relationship	To satisfy own group and negotiation group demands	Reality-oriented: checking, assessing and implementing	Decision making and action

Figure 13.2 Description of stages in negotiation groups: I

presents a summary statement of those changes in behaviour which seem common to Douglas's (1962) cases and our own.

Negotiations start with a period of hard *distributive bargaining* in which the feasibility of demands is assessed. It is decided, implicitly no doubt, who will have to concede most in the subsequent moves towards agreement. Both strength of case and the power relationship between the parties are important at this stage. In the electricians' informal negotiation the electricians' arguments against the prevailing arrangements were unassailed. It rapidly became transparently clear that proposals which substantially modified the present arrangements in their favour were required. It remained only for an appropriate set of proposals to emerge.

The 'movement towards agreement' constitutes a period of *problem solving*. Proposals are made and evaluated in the light of the opening exchanges. The major effort of the management in the middle phase of the electricians' negotiation was directed towards ensuring that the electricians' representatives themselves contributed to this problem-solving exercise. In other words, the interpersonal bargaining relationship came to the fore when proposals were required which met the criteria established in the first phase.

Proposals must finally be adopted for trial. Consequently, there follows a period of *decision making and action* in which the implications of possible settlement points are thoroughly explored. The criterion of consistency with the previous pattern of relationships between the parties is important in this respect. In the electricians' negotiation the chief management negotiator (M1) presented alternative proposals. The proposal most favourable to the

	Identifiability of negotiators	*Use of CPA categories*	*Characterisation*

Stage I→ Stage II	Increases	Referent: self–increases
		Referent:
		  other–increases
		Referent:
		  party–decreases
			Increasing emphasis on interpersonal rather than interparty aspects of relationship

Stage II→ Stage III	Decreases	Resource:
		  limits–decreases
		Resource: procedure
		  and/or resource:
		  information–increase(s)
		Referent: self–increases
		Referent
		  other–decreases
		Referent
		  party–decreases	

Figure 13.3 Description of stages in negotiation groups: II

electricians suggested that the company employ an additional individual who would be specially contracted to cover all bank holidays. M1 no doubt felt free to make such a proposal because it contravened the traditionally egalitarian relationship within the company. He could safely anticipate rejection, despite the fact that this particular proposal fully met the demands of the men (in contrast to the other proposals, which did not).

So far so good, but the findings reported in Chapter 12 can now be used further to extend Douglas's analysis. The most relevant results are summarised in Figure 13.3. It remains to be seen how many of these findings are likely to be general. Our conclusions about the structure of the negotiation process rely on very few observations, and it is not clear how the cases presented have differed from those of Landsberger (1955a) who obtained very different results. No doubt part of the difference relates to the fact that Landsberger studied sessions in which third parties were introduced to mediate negotiations which had already broken down – but such issues need not concern us here. The claim we wish to make is rather modest. We believe that our research has provided some support for Douglas's ideas and allowed a more precise characterisation to be made of the interpersonal and interparty climates she has described.

References

Abelson, R. P. (1968), 'Simulation of social behaviour', in Lindzey, G. and Aronson, E. (eds), *Handbook of Social Psychology*, vol. 2 (Reading, Mass.: Addison–Wesley) pp. 274–356.

Adams, J. S. (1965), 'Inequality in social exchange', in Berkowitz, L. (ed.), *Advances in Experimental Social Psychology,* vol. 2 (New York: Academic Press) pp. 267–99.

Alexander, C. N. Jr and Weil, H. G. (1969), 'Players, persons, and purposes: situational meaning and the Prisoner's Dilemma Game', *Sociometry, 32,* 121–44.

Angell, R. C., Dunham, V. S. and Singer, J. D. (1964), 'Social values and foreign policy attitudes of Soviet and American elites', *Journal of Conflict Resolution, 8,* 329–41.

Argyle, M. (1969a), Talk delivered to Social Psychology Research Seminar (Nottingham: Department of Psychology, University of Nottingham, 4 March).

Argyle, M. (1969b), *Social Interaction* (London: Methuen).

Auld, F. Jr and White, Alice M. (1956), 'Rules for dividing interviews into sentences', *Journal of Psychology, 42,* 273–81.

Back, K. W. (1961), 'Power, influence and pattern of communication', in Petrullo, L. and Bass, B. M. (eds), *Leadership and Interpersonal Behaviour* (New York: Holt) pp. 137–64.

Bain, G. S. and Clegg, H. A. (1974), 'A strategy for industrial relations research in Great Britain', *British Journal of Industrial Relations, 12,* 91–113.

Bales, R. F. (1950), *Interaction Process Analysis: A Method for the Study of Small Groups* (Reading, Mass.: Addison–Wesley).

Bales, R. F. (1970), *Personality and Interpersonal Behaviour* (New York: Holt, Rinehart and Winston).

Bales, R. F. and Strodtbeck, F. L. (1951), 'Phases in group problem-solving', *Journal of Abnormal and Social Psychology, 46,* 485–95.

Balke, W. M., Hammond, K. R. and Meyer, G. D. (1972), *Application of Judgment Theory and Interactive Computer Graphics Technology to Labor–Management Negotiation: An Example*, Report No. 145, Program of Research on Human Judgment and Social Interaction (Boulder, Institute of Behavioural Science, University of Colorado).

Barker, R. G. and Wright, H. F. (1955), *Midwest and Its Children* (Evanston, Ill.: Row Peterson).

Baron, R. A., Byrne, D. and Griffitt, W. (1974), *Social Psychology: Understanding Human Interaction* (Boston, Mass.: Allyn and Bacon).

Bartos, O. J. (1966), 'Concession-making in experimental negotiations', in Berger, J., Zelditch, M. Jr and Anderson, B. (eds), *Sociological Theories in Progress,* vol. 1 (Boston, Mass.: Houghton–Mifflin) pp. 3–28.

Bartos, O. J. (1967), 'How predictable are negotiations?', *Journal of Conflict Resolution, 11,* 481–96.

Bartos, O. J. (1970), 'Determinants and consequences of toughness', in Swingle, P. (ed.), *The Structure of Conflict* (New York: Academic Press) pp. 45–68.

Bass, B. M. (1966), 'Effects on the subsequent performance of negotiators of studying issues or planning strategies alone or in groups', *Psychological Monographs: General and Applied, 80*, whole no. 614, 1–31.

Bass, B. M. (1967), *A Program of Exercises for Management and Organizational Psychology* (Pittsburgh: MDA).

Bass, B. M. and Dunteman, G. (1963), 'Biases in the overevaluation of one's own group, its allies and opponents', *Journal of Conflict Resolution, 7*, 16–20.

Bass, B. M., Vaughan, J. A. and Cox, C. (1968), English version of Bass, B. M. (1967) 'Exercise negotiations', Exercise 9 in *A Programme of Exercises for Management and Organizational Psychology*. English version marketed by European Research Group on Management (ERGOM), Vaarstraat 22/4B, Louvain, Belgium.

Bem, D. J. (1965), 'An experimental analysis of self persuasion', *Journal of Experimental Social Psychology, 1*, 199–218.

Bem, D. J. (1967), 'Self-perception: an alternative explanation of cognitive dissonance phenomena', *Psychological Review, 74*, 183–200.

Bem, D. J. (1968), 'The epistemological status of interpersonal simulations: a reply to Jones *et al.*', *Journal of Experimental Social Psychology, 4*, 270–4.

Bem, D. J. (1972), 'Self-perception theory', in Berkowitz, L. (ed.), *Advances in Experimental Social Psychology*, vol. 6 (New York: Academic Press) pp. 1–62.

Benson, O. (1962), 'Simulation of international relations and diplomacy', in Borko, H. (ed.), *Computer Applications in the Behavioural Science* (Englewood Cliffs, NJ: Prentice–Hall).

Benton, A. A. and Druckman, D. (1974), 'Constituents' bargaining orientation and intergroup negotiations', *Journal of Applied Social Psychology, 4*, 141–50.

Berelson, B. (1952), *Content Analysis in Communication Research* (New York: Free Press).

Berg, D. M. (1967), 'A descriptive analysis of the distribution and duration of themes discussed by task-oriented small groups', *Speech Monographs, 34*, 172–5.

Bernard, Jessie (1965), 'Some current conceptualizations in the field of conflict', *American Journal of Sociology, 70*, 442–54.

Bishop, R. L. (1964), 'A Zeuthen–Hicks theory of bargaining,' *Econometrica, 32*, 410–17.

Blake, R. R. and Mouton, Jane S. (1961a), 'Comprehension of own and outgroup positions under intergroup competition', *Journal of Conflict Resolution, 3*, 304–10.

Blake, R. R. and Mouton, Jane S. (1961b), 'Heroes and traitors: two patterns of representing groups in a competitive situation', *International Journal of Sociometry*.

Blake, R. R. and Mouton, Jane S. (1961c), 'Perceived characteristics of elected representatives', *Journal of Abnormal and Social Psychology, 62*, 693–5.

Blake, R. R. and Mouton, Jane S. (1961d), 'Competition, communication and conformity', in Berg, I. A. and Bass, B. M. (eds), *Conformity and Deviation* (New York: Harper Bros) pp. 199–299.

Blake, R. R. and Mouton, Jane S. (1961e), 'Loyalty of representatives to ingroup positions during intergroup conflict', *Sociometry, 24*, 177–84.

Blake, R. R. and Mouton, Jane S. (1962), 'The intergroup dynamics of win–lose conflict and problem-solving collaboration in union–management relations', in Sherif, M. (ed.), *Intergroup Relations and Leadership* (New York: John Wiley and Sons) pp. 95–140.

Bonham, M. G. (1971), 'Simulating international disarmament negotiations', *Journal of Conflict Resolution, 15*, 299–315.

Borah, L. A. Jr (1963), 'The effects of threat in bargaining: critical and experimental analysis', *Journal of Abnormal and Social Psychology, 66*, 37–44.

Borgatta, E. F. (1963), 'A new systematic observation system: behaviour scores system (BSs system)', *Journal of Psychological Studies, 14*, 24–44.

Borgatta, E. F. and Crowther, Betty (1965), *A Workbook for the Study of Social Interaction Processes* (Chicago: Rand McNally).

Borke, Helene (1967), 'The communication of intent: a systematic approach to the observation of family interaction', *Human Relations, 20*, 13–28.

Boulding, K. E. (1956), *The Image* (Ann Arbor, Mich.: University of Michigan Press).

Boulding, K. E. (1964), 'Toward a theory of peace', in Fisher, R. (ed.), *International Conflict and Behavioural Science* (New York: Basic Books) pp. 70–87.

Boulding, K. E. (1968), 'The learning and reality-testing process in the international system', in Farrell, J. C. and Smith, A. P. (eds), *Image and Reality in World Politics* (New York: Columbia University Press) pp. 1–15.

Brody, R. A. (1969), 'The study of international politics qua science: the emphasis on methods and techniques', in Knorr, K. and Rosenau, J. N. (eds), *Contending Approaches to International Politics* (Princeton, NJ: Princeton University Press). pp. 110–28.

Brotherton, C. J. and Stephenson, G. M. (1975), 'Psychology in the system of industrial relations', *Industrial Relations Journal, 6*, no. 3, 42–50.

Bronfenbrenner, U. (1961), 'The mirror-image in Soviet–American relations: a social psychologist's report', *Journal of Social Issues*, Vol. 17, 45–56.

Brown, D. (1972), 'A study into the effects of different communication channels on the outcomes of bargaining', unpublished research paper submitted towards the degree of B.Sc. (Hull: Department of Psychology, University of Hull).

Brown, E. H. P. (1964), 'Bargaining', in Gould, J. and Kolb, W. L. (eds), *A Dictionary of the Social Sciences* (Glencoe: Free Press) pp. 50–1.

Brown, L. and Hammond, K. R. (1968), *A Supra-Linguistic Method for Reducing Intra-Group Conflict*, Report No. 108, Program for Cognitive Processes (Boulder, Institute of Behavioural Science, University of Colorado).

Brown, W. (1973), *Piecework Bargaining* (London: Heinemann Educational).

Brown, W. and Terry, M. (1975), 'The importance of continuity to an understanding of bargaining', paper presented at a symposium on 'Psychology and Industrial Relations' (Nottingham: Annual Conference of the British Psychological Society, April).

Bugental, J. F. T. (1948), *An Investigation of the Relationship of the Conceptual Matrix to the Self-Concept*, Ph.D. thesis (Columbus, Ohio: Ohio State University).

Campbell, D. T. (1965), 'Ethnocentric and other altruistic motives', in Levine, D. (ed.), *Nebraska Symposium on Motivation*, vol. 13 (Lincoln, Neb.: University of Nebraska Press) pp. 283–311.

Campbell, R. J. (1960), *Originality in Group Productivity, III: Partisan Commitment and Productive Independence in a Collective Bargaining Situation*, Office of Naval Research Contract Nonr – 495(15) (NR 170–396) (Columbus, Ohio: Ohio State University Research Foundation).

Chalmers, W. E. and Cormick, G. W. (eds) (1971), *Racial Conflict and Negotiations: Perspectives and First Case Studies* (Ann Arbor, Mich.: Institute of Labor and Industrial Relations, University of Michigan – Wayne State University and the National Center for Dispute Settlement of the American Arbitration Association).

Chapanis, A. (1973), 'The communication of factual information through various channels', *Information Storage and Retrieval, 9*, 215–31.

Chapanis, A., Ochsman, R., Parrish, R. and Weeks, G. (1972), 'Studies in interactive communication: the effects of four communication modes on the behaviour of teams during cooperative problem-solving', *Human Factors, 14*, 487–509.

Chertkoff, J. M. and Conley, Melinda (1967), 'Opening offer and frequency of concession as bargaining strategies', *Journal of Personality and Social Psychology, 7*, 181–5.

Coddington, A. (1968), *Theories of the Bargaining Process* (London: George Allen and Unwin).

Cohen, J. (1951), 'The technique of role reversal: a preliminary note', *Occupational Psychology, 25,* 64–6.

Coplin, W. (1966), 'International simulation and contemporary theories of international relations', *American Political Science Review, 60,* 562–78.

Cross, J. G. (1965), 'A theory of the bargaining process', *American Economic Review, 55,* 67–94.

Cross, J. G. (1969), *The Economics of Bargaining* (New York: Basic Books).

Crow, W. J. (1963), 'A study of strategic doctrines using the internation simulation', *Journal of Conflict Resolution, 7,* 580–9.

Crowell, Laura and Scheidel, T. M. (1961), 'Categories for analysis of idea development in discussion groups', *Journal of Social Psychology, 54,* 155–268.

Daniels, V. (1967), 'Communication, incentive, and structural variables in interpersonal exchange and negotiation', *Journal of Experimental Social Psychology, 3,* 47–74.

Dashiell, J. F. (1935), 'Experimental studies of the influence of social situations on the behaviour of individual human adults', in Murchison, C. (ed.), *Handbook of Social Psychology* (Worcester, Mass.: Clark University Press) pp. 109–58.

Davis, J. A. (1969), *Group Performance* (Reading, Mass.: Addison–Wesley).

Deutsch, M. (1958), 'Trust and suspicion', *Journal of Conflict Resolution, 2,* 265–79.

Deutsch, M. (1962), 'Psychological alternatives to war', *Journal of Social Issues, 18,* 97–119.

Deutsch, M., (1973), *The Resolution of Conflict: Constructive and Destructive Processes* (New Haven, Conn., and London: Yale University Press).

Deutsch, M. and Krauss, R. M. (1960), 'The effects of threat upon interpersonal bargaining', *Journal of Abnormal and Social Psychology, 61,* 181–9.

Deutsch, M. and Krauss, R. M. (1962), 'Studies of interpersonal bargaining', *Journal of Conflict Resolution, 6,* 57–76.

Douglas, Ann (1957), 'The peaceful settlement of industrial and inter-group disputes', *Journal of Conflict Resolution, 1,* 69–81.

Douglas, Ann (1962), *Industrial Peacemaking* (New York: Columbia University Press).

Druckman, D. (1967), 'Dogmatism, pre-negotiation experience, and simulated group representation as determinants of dyadic behaviour in a bargaining situation', *Journal of Personality and Social Psychology, 6,* 279–90.

Druckman, D. (1968), 'Prenegotiation experience and dyadic conflict resolution in a bargaining situation', *Journal of Experimental Social Psychology, 4,* 367–83.

Druckman, D., Solomon, D. and Zechmeister, K. (1972), 'Effects of representational role obligations on the process of children's distribution of resources', *Sociometry, 35,* 387–410.

Druckman, D. and Zechmeister, K. (1970), 'Conflict of interest and value dissensus', *Human Relations, 23,* 431–8.

Druckman, D., Zechmeister, K. and Solomon, D. (1972), 'Determinants of bargaining behaviour in a bilateral monopoly situation: opponent's concession rate and relative defensibility', *Behavioural Science, 17,* 514–31.

Duncan, K. D. (1972), 'Strategies for analysis of the task', in Hartley, J. (ed), *Strategies for Programmed Instruction: An Educational Technology* (London: Butterworth) pp. 19–81.

Dutton, J. E. and Walton, R. E. (1966), 'Interdepartmental conflict and cooperation: two contrasting studies', *Human Organization, 25,* 207–20.

Edgeworth, F. Y. (1881), *Mathematical Psychics* (London: C. Kegan Paul).

Etzioni, A. (1969), 'Social psychological aspects of international relations', in Lindzey,

G. and Aronson, E. (eds), *Handbook of Social Psychology*, vol. V (New York: Addison–Wesley) ch. 43, pp. 538–601.

Evan, W. M. and MacDougall, J. A. (1967), 'Interorganizational conflict: a labor–management bargaining experiment', *Journal of Conflict Resolution, 11*, 398–413.

Evans, G. W. and Crumbaugh, C. M. (1966), 'Effects of Prisoner's Dilemma format on cooperative behaviour', *Journal of Personality and Social Psychology, 3*, 486–8.

Faucheux, D. and Moscovici, S. (1966), 'A contribution to the psycho sociology of language', an invited paper to the symposium 34 on 'Methodological Problems in Social Psychology' (Moscow: International Congress of Psychology, 4–11 August).

Feigenbaum, E. A. and Feldman, J. (eds) (1963), *Computers and Thought* (New York: McGraw–Hill).

Fiedler, F. E. (1967), *A Theory of Leadership Effectiveness* (New York: McGraw–Hill).

Fink, C. F. (1968), 'Some conceptual difficulties in the theory of social conflict', *Journal of Conflict Resolution, 12*, 412–61.

Fischer, C. S. (1970), 'The effect of threats in an incomplete information game', *Sociometry, 32*, 301–14.

Fisher, B. A. (1970), 'Decision-emergence: phases in group decision-making', *Speech Monographs, 37*, 53–66.

Fisher, B. A. (1974), *Small Group Decision Making: Communication and the Group Process* (New York: McGraw–Hill).

Fisher, R. (1964), 'Fractionating conflict', in Fisher, R. (ed.), *International Conflict and Behavioural Science* (New York: Basic Books) pp. 91–109.

Fisher, R. (1969), *Basic Negotiating Strategy: International Conflict for Beginners* (London: Allen Lane).

Flack, M. J. (1972), 'The objectives and purposes of instruction in diplomacy', in Simpson, S. (ed.), *Instruction in Diplomacy: The Liberal Arts Approach*, Monograph 13 (Philadelphia: American Academy of Political and Social Sciences) pp. 77–87.

Flanders, A. (1968), 'Collective bargaining: a theoretical analysis', *British Journal of Industrial Relations, 6*, 1–26. Reprinted in Flanders, A. (ed.) (1969) *Collective Bargaining* (Harmondsworth: Penguin Books) pp. 11–41.

Foa, U. G., Mitchell, T. R. and Fiedler, F. E. (1971), 'Differentiation matching', *Behavioural Science, 16*, 130–42.

Foldes, L. (1964), 'A determinate model of bilateral monopoly', *Economica, 122*, 117–31.

Frank, J. D. (1968), *Sanity and Survival* (London: Barrie and Rockliff, Cresset Press).

Frey, R. L. Jr and Adams, J. S. (1972), 'The negotiator's dilemma: simultaneous in-group and out-group conflict', *Journal of Experimental Social Psychology, 8*, 331–46.

Fries, C. C. (1952), *The Structure of English* (New York: Harcourt, Brace).

Froman, L. A. Jr (1967), *The Congressional Process* (Boston, Mass.: Little Brown).

Froman, L. A. Jr and Cohen, M. D. (1969), 'Threats and bargaining efficiency', *Behavioural Science, 14*, 147–53.

Froman, L. A. Jr and Cohen, M. D. (1970), 'Compromise and logroll: comparing the efficiency of two bargaining processes', *Behavioural Science, 15*, 180–3.

Gallo, P. S. Jr (1966), 'Effects of increased incentives upon the use of threat in bargaining', *Journal of Personality and Social Psychology, 4*, 14–20.

Gallo, P. S. Jr and McClintock, C. G. (1965), 'Cooperative and competitive behaviour in mixed-motive games', *Journal of Conflict Resolution, 9*, 68–78.

Galtung, J. (1959), 'Pacifism from a sociological point of view', *Journal of Conflict Resolution, 3*, 67–84.

Golombiewski, R. T. (1962), *The Small Group: An Analysis of Research Concepts and Operations* (Chicago and London: University of Chicago Press).

Gouldner, A. W. (1960), 'The norm of reciprocity: a preliminary statement', *American Sociological Review, 25,* 161–78.

Grace, H. A. and Tandy, Margaret Jane (1957), 'Delegate communication as an index of group tension', *Journal of Social Psychology, 45,* 93–7.

Gruder, C. L. (1970), 'Social power in interpersonal negotiation', in Swingle, P. (ed.), *The Structure of Conflict* (New York: Academic Press.) pp. 111–54.

Gruder, C. L. (1971), 'Relations with opponent and partner in mixed-motive bargaining', *Journal of Conflict Resolution, 15,* 403–15.

Gruder, C. L. and Rosen, N. (1971), 'Effects of intragroup relations on intergroup bargaining', *International Journal of Group Tensions, 1,* 301–17.

Guetzkow, H. (ed.) (1962), *Simulation in Social Science: Readings* (Englewood Cliffs, NJ: Prentice-Hall).

Guetzkow, H. (1968), 'Some correspondences between simulations and "realities" in international relations', in Kaplan, M. A. (ed.), *New Approaches to International Relations* (New York: St Martin's Press). pp. 202–69.

Guetzkow, H. and Gyr, J. (1954), 'An analysis of conflict in decision-making groups', *Human Relations, 7,* 367–81.

Guetzkow, H. *et al.* (1963), *Simulation in International Relations: Developments for Research and Teaching* (Englewood Cliffs, NJ: Prentice–Hall).

Haggard, W. (1970), *The Hardliners* (London: Cassell).

Hammond, K. R. and Boyle, P. J. (1971), 'Quasi-rationality, quarrels and new conceptions of feedback', *Bulletin of the British Psychological Society, 24,* 103–13.

Hammond, K. R. and Summers, D. A. (1972), 'Cognitive control', *Psychological Review, 79,* 58–67.

Hammond, K. R., Todd, F. J., Wilkins, Marilyn and Mitchell, T. O. (1966), 'Cognitive conflict between persons: application of the "lens model" paradigm', *Journal of Experimental Social Psychology, 2,* 343–60.

Harbison, F. H. and Coleman, J. R. (1951), *Goals and Strategy in Collective Bargaining* (New York: Harper).

Harsanyi, J. C. (1956), 'Approaches to the bargaining problem before and after the theory of games', *Econometrica, 24,* 144–57.

Harsanyi, J. C. (1962), 'Bargaining in ignorance of the opponent's utility function', *Journal of Conflict Resolution, 6,* 29–38.

Hartmann, F. H. (ed.) (1952), *Readings in International Relations* (New York: McGraw–Hill).

Harvey, O. J. (1956), 'An experimental investigation of negative and positive relations between small groups through judgmental indices', *Sociometry, 19,* 201–9.

Hatton, J. M. (1967), 'Reactions of negroes in a biracial bargaining situation', *Journal of Personality and Social Psychology, 7,* 301–6.

Hermann, C. F. (1967), 'Validation problems in games and simulations with special reference to models of international politics', *Behavioural Science, 12,* 216–31.

Hermann, Margaret G. and Kogan, N. (1968), 'Negotiation in leader and delegate groups', *Journal of Conflict Resolution, 12,* 332–44.

Heyns, R. W. and Zander, A. F. (1954), 'Observation of group behaviour', in Festinger, L. and Katz, D. (eds), *Research Methods in the Behavioural Sciences* (London: Staples Press) pp. 381–417.

Hill, N. (1954), *Contemporary World Politics* (New York: Harper).

Hoffmann, S. (1968), 'Perception, reality, and the Franco–American conflict', in Farrell, J. C. and Smith, A. P. (eds), *Image and Reality in World Politics* (New York: Columbia University Press) pp. 57–71.

Hogg, Maryon (1973), 'The effect on two-person negotiations of differing degrees of familiarity with the opponent's stated case', paper presented to the symposium on 'Experimental Studies of Negotiation Groups' (Canterbury: Annual Conference of the British Association for the Advancement of Science, 24 August).

Hogg, Maryon (1976), '*An experimental investigation of the efficacy of some procedural role requirements in simulated negotiations*', Ph.D. thesis (Nottingham: University of Nottingham).

Hoggat, A. C. and Balderston, F. E. (eds) (1963), *Symposium on Simulation Models* (Cincinatti, Ohio: S. W. Publishing).

Hollander, E. P. (1967), *Principles and Methods of Social Psychology* (New York: Oxford University Press).

Holmes, J. G., Throop, W. F. and Strickland, L. H. (1971), 'The effects of prenegotiation expectations on the distributive bargaining process', *Journal of Experimental Social Psychology*, 7, 582–99.

Holsti, O. R. (1969), *Content Analysis for the Social Sciences and Humanities* (Reading, Mass.: Addison-Wesley).

Homans, G. C. (1961), *Social Behaviour: Its Elementary Forms* (London: Routledge and Kegan Paul).

Horai, J. and Tedeschi, J. T. (1969), 'The effects of credibility and magnitude of punishment upon compliance to threats', *Journal of Personality and Social Psychology*, 12, 164–9.

Hornstein, H. A. (1965), 'The effects of different magnitudes of threats upon interpersonal bargaining', *Journal of Experimental Social Psychology*, 1, 282–93.

Iklé, F. C. (1964), *How Nations Negotiate* (New York: Harper and Row).

Iklé, F. C. and Leites, N. (1962), 'Political negotiation as a process of modifying utilities', *Journal of Conflict Resolution*, 6, 19–28.

Insko, C. A. and Schopler, J. (1972), *Experimental Social Psychology* (New York: Academic Press).

Janis, I. L. (1972), *Victims of Groupthink: A Psychological Study of Foreign-policy Decisions and Fiascos* (Boston, Mass.: Houghton-Mifflin).

Jensen, L. (1962), 'The postwar disarmament negotiations: a study in American–Soviet bargaining behaviour', unpublished doctoral dissertation (Ann Arbor, Mich.: University of Michigan).

Jensen, L. (1963), 'Soviet–American bargaining behaviour in the postwar disarmament negotiations', *Journal of Conflict Resolution*, 7, 522–41.

Jervis, A. S. (1970), *The Logic of Images in International Relations* (Princeton, NJ: Princeton University Press).

Johnson, D. W. (1967), 'Use of role reversal in intergroup competition', *Journal of Personality and Social Psychology*, 7, 135–41.

Johnson, D. W. and Dustin, R. (1970), 'The initiation of cooperation through role reversal', *Journal of Social Psychology*, 82, 193–203.

Johnson, D. W. and Lewicki, R. J. (1969), 'The initiation of superordinate goals', *Journal of Applied Behavioural Science*, 5, 9–24.

Johnson, H. L. and Cohen, A. M. (1967), 'Experiments in behavioural economics: Siegel and Fouraker revisited', *Behavioural Science*, 12, 353–72.

Julian, J. W. and McGrath, J. E. (1963), *The Influence of Leader and Member Behaviour on the Adjustment and Task Effectiveness of Negotiation Groups*, Technical Report No. 17, Office of the Surgeon General Contract DA–49–193–MD–2060 (Urbana, Ill.: Group Effectiveness Research Laboratory, University of Illinois).

Kahan, J. P. (1968), 'Effects of level of aspiration in an experimental bargaining situation', *Journal of Personality and Social Psychology*, 8, 154–9.

Kahn, A. (1972), 'Reactions to generosity or stinginess from an intelligent or stupid work partner: a test of equity theory in a direct exchange relationship', *Journal of Personality and Social Psychology*, 21, 116–23.

Kahn, A. S. and Kohls, J. W. (1972), 'Determinants of toughness in dyadic bargaining', *Sociometry, 35*, 305–15.

Karass, C. L. (1970), *The Negotiating Game* (New York and Cleveland, Ohio: World Publishing).

Katz, D. (1959), 'Consistent reactive participation of group members and reduction of inter-group conflict', *Journal of Conflict Resolution, 3*, 28–40.

Katz, E., Gurevitch, M., Danet, Brenda and Peled, Tsiyona (1969), 'Petitions and prayers: a method for the content analysis of persuasive appeals', *Social Forces, 47*, 447–63.

Kelley, H. H. (1964), 'Interaction process and the attainment of maximum joint profit', in Mersick, S. and Brayfield, A. H. (eds), *Decision and Choice* (New York: McGraw–Hill) pp. 240–50.

Kelley, H. H. (1965), 'Experimental studies of threats in interpersonal negotiations', *Journal of Conflict Resolution, 9*, 79–105.

Kelley, H. H. (1966), 'A classroom study of the dilemmas in interpersonal negotiations', in Archibald, Kathleen (ed.), *Strategic Interaction and Conflict* (Berkeley, Calif.: Institute of International Studies, University of California) pp. 49–73.

Kelley, H. H. and Schenitzki, D. P. (1972), 'Bargaining', in McClintock, C. G. (ed.), *Experimental Social Psychology* (New York: Holt, Rinehart and Winston) pp. 298–337.

Kelley, H. H. and Stahelski, A. J. (1970), 'Social interaction basis of cooperators' and competitors' beliefs about others', *Journal of Personality and Social Psychology, 16*, 66–91.

Kelley, H. H. and Thibaut, J. W. (1954), 'Experimental studies of group problem-solving and process', in Lindzey, G. (ed.), *Handbook of Social Psychology*, vol. II (Reading, Mass.: Addison–Wesley) pp. 735–85.

Kelley, H. H. and Thibaut, J. W. (1969), 'Group problem-solving', in Lindzey, G. and Aronson, E. (eds), *Handbook of Social Psychology*, vol. 4 (Reading, Mass.: Addison–Wesley) pp. 1–101.

Kelley, H. H., Beckman, Linda L. and Fischer, C. S. (1967), 'Negotiating the division of a reward under incomplete information', *Journal of Experimental Social Psychology, 3*, 361–98.

Kelley, H. H., Shure, G. H., Deutsch, M., Faucheux, C., Lanzetta, J. T., Moscovici, S., Nuttin, J. M. Jr, Rabbie, J. M. and Thibaut, J. W. (1970), 'A comparative experimental study of negotiation behaviour', *Journal of Personality and Social Psychology, 16*, 411–38.

Kelley, J. G., Ferson, J. E. and Holtzman, W. H. (1958), 'The measurement of attitudes toward the Negro in the South', *Journal of Abnormal and Social Psychology, 48*, 305–17.

Kerr, C. (1954), 'Industrial conflict and its mediation', *American Journal of Sociology, 60*, 230–45.

Kingston, N. (1970), 'Management research', *Management Abstracts, 10*, 32–5.

Klimoski, R. J. (1972), 'The effects of intragroup forces on intergroup conflict resolution', *Organizational Behaviour and Human Performance, 8*, 363–83.

Klimoski, R. J. and Ash, R. A. (1974), 'Accountability and negotiator behaviour', *Organizational Behaviour and Human Performance, 11*, 409–25.

Kogan, N., Lamm, H. and Trommsdorff, G. (1972), 'Negotiation constraints in the risk-taking domain: effects of being observed by partners of higher or lower status', *Journal of Personality and Social Psychology, 23*, 143–56.

Komorita, S. S. and Brenner, Arline R. (1968), 'Bargaining and concession-making under bilateral monopoly', *Journal of Personality and Social Psychology, 9*, 15–20.

Komorita, S. S. and Barnes, M. (1969), 'Effects of pressures to reach agreement in bargaining', *Journal of Personality and Social Psychology, 13*, 245–52.

Krauss, R. M. and Deutsch, M. (1966), 'Communication in interpersonal bargaining', *Journal of Personality and Social Psychology, 4*, 572–7.

Lall, A. S. (1966), *Modern International Negotiation: Principles and Practice* (New York: Columbia University Press).

Lamm, H. (1973), 'Intragroup effects on intergroup negotiations', *European Journal of Social Psychology, 3*, 179–92.

Lamm, H. (1975), 'Some recent research on negotiation behaviour', paper presented at the European Association of Experimental Social Psychology Conference (Bielefeld, West Germany, April).

Lamm, H. and Kogan, N. (1970), 'Risk taking in the context of intergroup negotiation', *European Journal of Social Psychology, 6*, 351–63.

Landsberger, H. A. (1955a), 'Interaction process analysis of mediation of labour–management disputes', *Journal of Abnormal and Social Psychology, 57*, 552–8.

Landsberger, H. A. (1955b), 'Interaction process analysis of professional behaviour: a study of labor mediators in twelve labor–management disputes', *American Sociological Review, 20*, 566–75.

Lawler, E. F. III (1968), 'Equity theory as a predictor of productivity and work quality', *Psychological Bulletin, 70*, 596–610.

Levine, R. A. and Campbell, D. T. (1972), *Ethnocentrism: Theories of Conflict, Ethnic Attitudes and Group Behaviour* (New York: John Wiley and Sons).

Liebert, R. M., Smith, W. P., Hill, J. H. and Keiffer, Miriam (1968), 'The effects of information and magnitude of initial offer on interpersonal negotiation', *Journal of Experimental Social Psychology, 4*, 431–41.

Lifshitz, Michaela N. (1971), 'Internal–external locus of control and negotiation', in Pepinsky, H. B. and Patton, M. J. (eds), *The Psychological Experiment: A Practical Accomplishment* (New York: Pergamon Press) ch. 5, pp. 89–111.

Longabaugh, R. (1963), 'A category system for coding interpersonal behaviour as social exchange', *Sociometry, 26*, 319–44.

Longabaugh, R., Eldred, S. H., Bell, N. W. and Sherman, L. J. (1966), 'The interactional world of the chronic schizophrenic patient', *Psychiatry, 29*, 78–99.

Luce, R. D. and Raiffa, H. (1957), *Games and Decisions* (New York: John Wiley and Sons).

McClintock, C. G. (1972), 'Game behaviour and social motivation in interpersonal settings', in McClintock, C. G. (ed.), *Experimental Social Psychology* (New York: Holt, Rinehart and Winston) pp. 271–97.

McClintock, C. G. and McNeel, S. P. (1966), 'Reward and score feedback as determinants of cooperative and competitive game behaviour', *Journal of Personality and Social Psychology, 4*, 606–13.

McGrath, J. E. (1966), 'A social psychological approach to the study of negotiation', in Bowers, R. (ed.), *Studies on Behaviour in Organizations: A Research Symposium* (Athens, Georgia: University of Georgia Press) pp. 101–34.

McGrath, J. E. and Julian, J. W. (1962), *Negotiation and Conflict: An Experimental Study*, Technical Report No. 16, SGO Contract MD 2060 and USPHS Contract M–1774 (Urbana, Ill.: Group Effectiveness Research Laboratory, University of Illinois).

McGrath, J. E. and Julian, J. W. (1963), 'Interaction process and task outcomes in experimentally created negotiation groups', *Journal of Psychological Studies, 14*, 117–38.

McGregor, D. (1967) (eds McGregor, Caroline and Bennis, W. G.) *The Professional Manager* (New York: McGraw–Hill).

Macmillan, H. (1969), *Tides of Fortune* (London: Macmillan).

Manheim, H. C. (1960), 'Intergroup interaction as related to status and leadership differences between groups', *Sociometry, 23*, 415–27.

Mark, R. A. (1971), 'Coding communication at the relationship level', *Journal of Communication, 21*, 221–32.

Messé, L. A. (1971), 'Equity in bilateral bargaining', *Journal of Personality and Social Psychology, 17*, 287–91.

Messick, D. M. and McClintock, C. G. (1968), 'Motivational bases of choice in experimental games', *Journal of Experimental Social Psychology, 4*, 1–25.

Miller, J. M. (1972), *Interpersonal Understanding: Laboratory and Field Investigations*, Report No. 136, Program of Research on Human Judgment and Social Interaction (Boulder, Institute of Behavioural Science, University of Colorado).

Mishler, E. G. and Waxler, Nancy E. (1968), *Interaction in Families: An Experimental Study of Family Processes and Schizophrenia* (New York: John Wiley and Sons).

Morgan, W. R. and Sawyer, J. (1967), 'Bargaining, expectations and the preference for equality over equity', *Journal of Personality and Social Psychology, 6*, 139–49.

Morgenstern, O. (1949), 'The theory of games', *Scientific American*, May, 86–9.

Morley, I. E. (1973), 'Social interaction in experimental negotiations', paper presented to a symposium on 'Experimental Studies of Negotiation Groups' (Canterbury: Annual Conference of the British Association for the Advancement of Science, 21 August).

Morley, I. E. (1974), *Social Interaction in Experimental Negotiations*, Ph.D. thesis (Nottingham: University of Nottingham).

Morley, I. E. and Stephenson, G. M. (1969), 'Interpersonal and interparty exchange: a laboratory simulation of an industrial negotiation at the plant level', *British Journal of Psychology, 60*, 543–5.

Morley, I. E. and Stephenson, G. M. (1970a), 'Formality in experimental negotiations: a validation study', *British Journal of Psychology, 61*, 383–4.

Morley, I. E. and Stephenson, G. M. (1970b), 'Strength of case, communication systems, and the outcomes of simulated negotiations: some social psychological aspects of bargaining', *Industrial Relations Journal, 1*, 19–20.

Morris, C. G. (1970), 'Changes in group interaction during problem-solving', *Journal of Social Psychology, 81*, 157–65.

Murdoch, P. (1967), 'The development of contractual norms in a dyad', *Journal of Personality and Social Psychology, 6*, 206–11.

Myers, J. L. (1972), *Fundamentals of Experimental Design* (Boston, Mass.: Allyn and Bacon).

Nash, J. F. (1950), 'The bargaining problem', *Econometrica, 18*, 155–62.

Neal, F. W. (1964), 'Diplomacy', in Gould, J. and Kolb, W. L. (eds), *A Dictionary of the Social Sciences* (Glencoe: Free Press) pp. 201–2.

Nemeth, Charlan (1970), 'Bargaining and reciprocity', *Psychological Bulletin, 74*, 297–308.

Nemeth, Charlan (1972), 'A critical analysis of research utilizing the Prisoner's Dilemma paradigm for the study of bargaining', in Berkowitz, L. (ed.), *Advances in Experimental Social Psychology*, vol. 6 (New York: Academic Press) pp. 203–34.

Neumann, J. von and Morgenstern, O. (1964), *Theory of Games and Economic Behaviour* (New York: John Wiley and Sons).

Newell, A., Shaw, J. C. and Simon, H. A. (1963), 'Chess playing programs and the problem of complexity', in Feigenbaum, E. A. and Feldman, J. (eds), *Computers and Thought* (New York: McGraw–Hill) pp. 39–70.

Nicholson, H. (1954), *The Evolution of Diplomatic Method* (New York: Macmillan).

Nicholson, M. (1970), *Conflict Analysis* (London: English Universities Press).

Niemela, P., Honka-Hallila, S. and Jarvikoski, A. (1969), 'A study in intergroup perception stereotype', *Journal of Peace Research*, 57–64.

Nogee, J. L. (1963), 'Propaganda and negotiation: the case of the ten-nation disarmament committee', *Journal of Conflict Resolution, 7*, 510–21.

Oppenheim, A. N. and Bayley, J. C. R. (1970), 'Productivity and conflict', *Proceedings of the International Peace Research Association, 3rd General Conference* (Essen: Netherlands: Van Gorcum).

Orwant, Carol J. and Orwant, J. E. (1970), 'A comparison of interpreted and abstract versions of mixed-motive games', *Journal of Conflict Resolution, 14*, 91–7.

Osgood, C. E. (1960a), 'A case for graduated unilateral disengagement', *Bulletin of the Atomic Scientists, 16*, 127–31.

Osgood, C. E. (1960b), *Graduated Reciprocation in Tension Reduction: A Key to Initiative in Foreign Policy* (Urbana, Ill.: Institute of Communications Research, University of Illinois).

Oskamp, S. (1971), 'Effects of programmed strategies on cooperation, in the Prisoner's Dilemma and other mixed-motive games', *Journal of Conflict Resolution, 15*, 225–59.

Oskamp, S. and Perlman, D. (1965), 'Factors affecting cooperation in a Prisoner's Dilemma Game', *Journal of Conflict Resolution, 9*, 359–74.

Osterberg, W. H. (1950), 'A method for the study of bargaining conferences', *Personnel Psychology, 3*, 169–78.

Palmer, F. (1971), *Grammar* (Harmondsworth: Penguin Books).

Parsons, T. (1951), *The Social System* (New York: Free Press of Glencoe).

Patchen, M. (1970), 'Models of cooperation and conflict: a critical review', *Journal of Conflict Resolution, 14*, 389–407.

Pen, J. (1952), 'A general theory of bargaining', *American Economic Review, 42*, 24–42.

Peston, M. and Coddington, A. (1967), *The Elementary Ideas of Game Theory*, CAS Occasional Paper No. 6 (London: HMSO).

Peters, E. (1955), *Strategy and Tactics in Labour Negotiations* (New London, Conn.: National Foreman's Institute).

Pilisuk, M. and Rapoport, A. (1964), 'Stepwise disarmament and sudden obstruction in a two-person game: a research tool', *Journal of Conflict Resolution, 8*, 36–49.

Pilisuk, M. and Skolnick, P. (1968), 'Inducing trust: a test of the Osgood Proposal', *Journal of Personality and Social Psychology, 8*, 121–33.

Pilisuk, M., Potter, P., Rapoport, A. and Winter, J. A. (1965), 'War hawks and peace doves: alternate resolutions of experimental conflicts', *Journal of Conflict Resolution, 9*, 491–508.

Pilisuk, M., Winter, J. A., Chapman, R. and Haas, N. (1967), 'Honesty, deceit and timing in the display of intentions', *Behavioural Science, 12*, 205–15.

Plischke, E. (1972), 'The optimum scope for instruction in diplomacy', in Simpson, S. (ed.) *Instruction in Diplomacy: The Liberal Arts Approach*, Monograph 13 (Philadelphia: American Academy of Political and Social Science) pp. 1–25.

Plön, M. (1975), 'On the meaning of the notion of conflict and its study in social psychology', *European Journal of Social Psychology, 4*, 389–436.

Podell, J. E. and Knapp, W. M. (1969), 'The effect of mediation on the perceived firmness of the opponent', *Journal of Conflict Resolution, 13*, 511–20.

Pondy, L. R. (1967), 'Organizational conflict: concepts and models', *Administrative Science Quarterly, 12*, 296–320.

Porat, A. M. (1969), *Planning and Role Assignment in the Study of Conflict Resolution: A Study of Two Countries*, Technical Report No. 28 (Rochester, NY; Management Research Center of the College of Business Administration, University of Rochester).

Porat, A. M. (1970), 'Cross-cultural differences in resolving union–management conflict through negotiations', *Journal of Applied Psychology, 54*, 441–51.

Pritchard, R. D. (1969), 'Equity theory: a review and critique', *Organizational Behaviour and Human Performance, 4*, 176–211.

Pruitt, D. G. (1967), 'Reward structure and cooperation: the decomposed Prisoner's Dilemma Game', *Journal of Personality and Social Psychology, 7*, 21–7.

Pruitt, D. G. (1969), 'Indirect communication in the search for agreement in negotiation', in *Indirect Communication in Negotiation Project*, Working Paper II 1 (Buffalo, NY: Center for International Conflict Studies, State University of New York).

Pruitt, D. G. (1970), 'Motivational processes in the decomposed Prisoner's Dilemma Game', *Journal of Personality and Social Psychology, 14*, 227–38.

Pruitt, D. G. and Drews, Julie Latane (1969), 'The effect of time pressure, time elapsed, and the opponent's concession rate on behaviour in negotiation', *Journal of Experimental Social Psychology, 5*, 43–60.

Pruitt, D. G. and Johnson, D. F. (1970), 'Mediation as an aid to face saving in negotiation', *Journal of Personality and Social Psychology, 14*, 239–46.

Psathas, G. (1961), 'Alternative modes for scoring interaction process analysis', *Journal of Social Psychology, 53*, 97–103.

Rabbie, J. M. and Horwitz, M. (1969), 'The arousal of ingroup–outgroup bias by a chance win or loss', *Journal of Personality and Social Psychology, 13*, 269–77.

Rabbie, J. M. and Wilkens, G. (1971), 'Intergroup competition and its effect on intragroup and intergroup relations', *European Journal of Social Psychology, 1*, 215–34.

Rackham, N. (1972), 'Developing negotiating skill', *Industrial and Commercial Training, 4*, 266–75.

Rapoport, A. (1960), *Fights, Games and Debates* (Ann Arbor, Mich.: University of Michigan Press).

Rapoport, A. (1963), 'Formal games as probing tools for investigating behaviour motivated by trust and suspicion', *Journal of Conflict Resolution, 7*, 570–759.

Rapoport, A. (1964), *Strategy and Conscience* (New York: Harper and Row).

Rapoport, A. (1967), 'Games which simulate deterrence and disarmament', *Peace Research Reviews, 1*, whole no. 4.

Rapoport, A. (1968), 'Editor's introduction', in Rapoport, A. (ed.), *Clausewitz On War* (Harmondsworth: Penguin Books) pp. 11–80.

Rapoport, A. (1970), 'Conflict resolution in the light of game theory and beyond', in Swingle, P. (ed.), *The Structure of Conflict* (New York: Academic Press) pp. 1–43.

Rapoport, A. and Chammah, A. M. (1965), *Prisoner's Dilemma: A Study in Conflict and Cooperation* (Ann Arbor, Mich.: University of Michigan Press).

Rapoport, A. and Chammah, A. M. (1966), 'The game of Chicken', *American Behavioural Scientists, 10*, 10–14, 23–8.

Rapoport, A. and Orwant, Carol J. (1962), 'Experimental games: a review', *Behavioural Science, 7*, 1–37.

Raven, G. H. and Kruglanski, A. (1970), 'Conflict and power', in Swingle, P. (ed.), *The Structure of Conflict* (New York: Academic Press) pp. 69–109.

Rehmus, C. M. (1965), 'The mediation of industrial conflict: a note on the literature', *Journal of Conflict Resolution, 9*, 118–26.

Rosnow, R. L. and Robinson, E. J. (eds) (1967), *Experiments in Persuasion* (New York: Academic Press).

Rutter, D. R. and Stephenson, G. M. (in press), 'The role of visual communication in synchronising conversation', *European Journal of Social Psychology*.

Sampson, E. E. (1969), 'Studies of status congruence', in Berkowitz, L. (ed.), *Advances in Experimental Social Psychology*, vol. 4 (New York: Academic Press) pp. 225–70.

Sawyer, J. and Guetzkow, H. (1965), 'Bargaining and negotiation in international relations', in Kelman, H. C. (ed.), *International Behaviour and Social Psychological*

Analysis (New York: Holt, Rinehart and Winston) pp. 466–520.

Scheidel, T. M. and Crowell, Laura (1964), 'Idea development in small discussion groups', *Quarterly Journal of Speech, 50*, 140–5.

Schelling, T. C. (1960), *The Strategy of Conflict* (New York: Harvard University Press). Reissued as Oxford University Press paperback (1968). References are to OUP edn.

Schelling, T. C. (1966), *Arms and Influence* (New Haven, Conn.: Yale University Press).

Schenitzki, D. P. (1962), *Bargaining, Group Decision-Making and the Attainment of Maximum Joint Outcome*, doctoral dissertation (University of Minnesota). Cited in Kelley, H. H. and Schenitzki, D. P. (1972) 'Bargaining', in McClintock, C. G. (ed.), *Experimental Social Psychology* (New York: Holt, Rinehart and Winston) pp. 298–337.

Schlenker, B. R., Bonoma, T., Tedeschi, J. T. and Pivnick, W. P. (1970), 'Compliance to threats as a function of the wording of the threat and the exploitativeness of the threatener', *Sociometry, 33*, 394–408.

Scodel, A., Minas, J. S., Ratoosh, P. and Lipetz, M. (1959), 'Some descriptive aspects of two-person non-zero-sum games', *Journal of Conflict Resolution, 3*, 114–19.

Secord, P. F. and Backman, C. W. (1974), *Social Psychology* (New York: McGraw–Hill).

Sermat, V. (1970), 'Is game behaviour related to behaviour in other interpersonal situations?', *Journal of Personality and Social Psychology, 16*, 92–109.

Shaw, J. I., Fischer, C. S. and Kelley, H. H. (1973), 'Decision-making by third parties in settling disputes', *Journal of Applied Social Psychology, 3*, 197–218.

Sherif, M. (1967), *Group Conflict and Cooperation* (London: Routledge and Kegan Paul).

Sherif, M. and Sherif, Carolyn W. (1953), *Groups in Harmony and Tension* (New York: Harper and Row).

Sherif, M. and Sherif, Carolyn W. (1969), *Social Psychology* (New York: Harper and Row).

Sherif, M., Harvey, O. J., White, B. J., Hood, W. R. and Sherif, Carolyn W. (1961), *Intergroup Conflict and Cooperation: The Robbers' Cave: Experiment* (Norman, Okla.: Institute of Group Relations, University of Oklahoma).

Shomer, R. W., Davis, Alice H. and Kelley, H. H. (1965), 'Threats and the development of coordination: further studies of the Deutsch–Krauss trucking game', *Journal of Personality and Social Psychology, 4*, 119–26.

Short, J. A. (1971a), *Bargaining and Negotiation: An Exploratory Study,* Ref. E/71605/SH (London: Communication Studies Group, Joint Unit for Planning Research, 172 Tottenham Court Rd, W1P 0BS).

Short, J. A. (1971b), *Cooperation and Competition in an Experimental Bargaining Game Conducted Over Two Media*, Ref. E/71160/SH (London: Communication Studies Group, Joint Unit for Planning Research, 172 Tottenham Court Rd, W1P 0BS).

Short, J. A. (1971c), *Conflicts of Interest and Conflicts of Opinion in an Experimental Bargaining Game Conducted Over Three Media*, Ref. E/71245/SH (London: Communication Studies Group, Joint Unit for Planning Research, 172 Tottenham Court Rd, W1P 0BS).

Short, J. A. (1973), *The Effects of Medium of Communication on Persuasion, Bargaining, and Perceptions of the Other*, Ref. E/73100/SH (London: Communication Studies Group, Joint Unit for Planning Research, 172 Tottenham Court Rd, W1P 0BS).

Short, J. A. (1974), 'Effects of medium of communication on experimental negotiation', *Human Relations, 27*, 225–34.

Shure, G. H. and Meeker, R. J. (1968), 'Bargaining processes in experimental territorial conflict situations', *Peace Research Society: Papers, 11, The Budapest Conference*, 109–22.

Shure, G. H., Meeker, R. J. and Hansford, E. A. (1965), 'The effectiveness of pacifist strategies in bargaining games', *Journal of Conflict Resolution, 9*, 106–17.

Shurtleff, W. (1949), 'Union–Management relations: cooperation or conflict?', *Personnel Journal, 27*, 383–6.

Siegel, S. and Fouraker, L. E. (1960), *Bargaining and Group Decision Making* (New York: McGraw–Hill).

Simpson, S. (ed.) (1972), *Instruction in Diplomacy: The Liberal Arts Approach*, Monograph 13 (Philadelphia: American Academy of Political and Social Sciences).

Sinaiko, H. W. (1963), *Teleconferencing: Preliminary Experiments*, Research Paper P–108 (Institute for Defense Analyses, Research and Engineering Support Division).

Singer, J. D. (1958), 'Threat perception and the armament-tensions dilemma', *Journal of Conflict Resolution, 2*, 90–105.

Singer, J. D. (1965), *Human Behaviour and International Politics* (Chicago: Rand McNally).

Smith, D. H. (1969), 'Communication and negotiation outcome', *Journal of Communication, 19*, 248–56.

Smith, D. H. (1971), 'Communication, minimum disposition, and negotiation', in Pepinsky, H. B. and Patton, M. J. (eds), *The Psychological Experiment: A Practical Accomplishment* (New York: Pergamon Press) ch. 7, pp. 131–48.

Smith, P. B. (1974), *Groups Within Organizations* (New York: Harper and Row).

Smith, W. P. and Leginski, W. A. (1970), 'Magnitude and precision of primitive power in bargaining strategy', *Journal of Experimental Social Psychology, 6*, 57–76.

Snyder, R. C. (1963), 'Some perspectives on the use of experimental techniques in the study of international relations', in Guetzkow, H. *et al.*, *Simulations in International Relations: Developments for Research and Teaching* (Englewood Cliffs, NJ: Prentice–Hall) pp. 1–23.

Spanier, J. W. and Nogee, J. L. (1962), *The Politics of Disarmament: A Study in Soviet–American Gamesmanship* (New York: Praeger).

Stagner, R. (1948), 'Psychological aspects of industrial conflict: 1. perception', *Personnel Psychology, 1*, 131–43.

Stagner, R. (1967), *Psychological Aspects of International Conflict* (Belmont, Calif.: Brooks/Cole Publishing).

Stedman, Jane (1972), 'Introducing a mediator into a negotiation situation: an exploratory study', unpublished research report submitted towards the degree of B.Sc. (Department of Psychology, University of Hull).

Stephenson, G. M. (1971a), 'The experimental study of negotiating', paper presented to a symposium on 'Negotiating Behaviour', (Durham: British Psychological Society, Social Psychology Section Annual Conference, University of Durham, 25 September).

Stephenson, G. M. (1971b), 'Inter-group relations and negotiating behaviour', in Warr, P. B. (ed.) *Psychology at Work* (Harmondsworth: Penguin Books) pp. 347–73.

Stephenson, G. M. (1973), 'Experimental studies of negotiation groups', introduction to a symposium on 'Experimental Studies of Negotiation Groups' (Canterbury: Annual Conference of the British Association for the Advancement of Science, 21 August).

Stephenson, G. M. (1975), 'Experimental work on negotiation groups', paper presented to the British Psychological Society, Social Psychology Section Annual Conference (Nottingham: University of Nottingham, 7 April).

Stephenson, G. M., Ayling, K. and Rutter, D. R. (1976) (in press), 'The role of visual communication in social exchange', *British Journal of Social and Clinical Psychology*.

Stephenson, G. M., Kniveton, B. H. and Morley, I. E., 'Interpersonal and interparty processes in negotiation groups: an industrial case study', unpublished research paper, Department of Psychology, University of Nottingham.

Stephenson, G. M., Skinner, M. and Brotherton, C. J. 'Group participation and intergroup relations: an experimental study of negotiation groups', (1976) *European Journal of Social Psychology*, 6, (1), pp. 51–70.

Stephenson, G. M. and White, J. H. (1970), 'Privilege, deprivation and children's moral behaviour: an experimental clarification of the role of investments', *Journal of Experimental Social Psychology*, 6, 167–76.

Stevens, C. M. (1963), *Strategy and Collective Bargaining Negotiation* (New York: McGraw–Hill).

Stotland, E. and Canon, L. K. (1972), *Social Psychology: A Cognitive Approach* (Philadelphia: W. B. Saunders).

Strachey, J. (1962), *On the Prevention of War* (London: Macmillan).

Swingle, P. G. (1967), 'The effects of the win–lose difference upon cooperative responding in a "dangerous" game', *Journal of Conflict Resolution, 11*, 214–22.

Swingle, P. G. (1970a), 'Dangerous games', in Swingle, P. (ed.), *The Structure of Conflict* (New York: Academic Press) pp. 235–76.

Swingle, P. G. (ed.) (1970b), *The Structure of Conflict* (New York: Academic Press).

Tedeschi, J. T. (1970), 'Threats and promises', in Swingle, P. (ed.), *The Structure of Conflict* (New York: Academic Press) pp. 155–91.

Terhune, K. W. (1968), 'Motives, situation, and interpersonal conflict within Prisoner's Dilemma', *Journal of Personality and Social Psychology, 8*, no. 3, part 2 (Monograph Supplement).

Terhune, K. W. (1970), 'The effects of personality in cooperation and conflict', in Swingle, P. (ed.), *The Structure of Conflict* (New York: Academic Press) pp. 193–234.

Thelen, H. A. (1954), *Dynamics of Groups at Work* (Chicago: University of Chicago Press).

Thibaut, J. W. (1968), 'The development of contractual norms in bargaining: replication and variation', *Journal of Conflict Resolution, 12*, 102–12.

Thibaut, J. W. and Faucheux, C. (1965), 'The development of contractual norms in a bargaining situation under two types of stress', *Journal of Experimental Social Psychology, 1*, 89–102.

Thibaut, J. W. and Gruder, C. L. (1969), 'The formation of contractual agreements between parties of unequal power', *Journal of Personality and Social Psychology, 11*, 59–65.

Tjosvold, D. (1974), 'Threat as a low power person's strategy in bargaining: social face and tangible outcomes', *International Journal of Group Tensions, 4*, 494–510.

Tomkins, S. and Messick, S. (eds) (1963), *Computer Simulation of Personality* (New York: John Wiley and Sons).

Turner, J. (1972), 'Social comparison and social identity: some prospects for intergroup behaviour', paper presented at European Association of Experimental Social Psychology Small Group Meeting on 'Experimental Studies of Intergroup Relations' (Bristol: Department of Psychology, University of Bristol, 5 February).

Vidmar, N. (1971), 'Effects of representational roles and mediators on negotiation effectiveness', *Journal of Personality and Social Psychology, 17*, no. 1, 48–58.

Vidmar, N. and McGrath, J. E. (1965), *Role Assignment and Attitudinal Commitment as Factors in Negotiation*, Technical Report No. 3, AFOSR Contract AF49 (638)–1291 (Urbana, Ill.: Department of Psychology, University of Illinois).

Vidmar, N. and McGrath, J. E. (1967), *Role Structure, Leadership and Negotiation Effectiveness*, Technical Report No. 6, AFOSR Contract AF49 (638)–1291 (Urbana, Ill.: Department of Psychology, University of Illinois).

Vidmar, N. and McGrath, J. E. (1970), 'Forces affecting success in negotiation groups', *Behavioural Science, 14*, 154–63.

Vitz, P. and Kite, W. R. (1970), 'Factors affecting conflict and negotiation within an alliance', *Journal of Experimental Social Psychology, 6*, 233–47.

Walker, K. (1962), 'Executives and union leaders' perceptions of each other's attitudes to industrial relations: the influence of stereotypes', *Human Relations, 15*, 183–95.

Wallach, M. A. and Kogan, N. (1959), 'Sex differences and judgement processes', *Journal of Personality, 27*, 555–64.

Walton, R. E. (1969), *Interpersonal Peacemaking: Confrontations and Third-Party Consultation* (Reading, Mass.: Addison–Wesley).

Walton, R. E. and McKersie, R. B. (1965), *A Behavioural Theory of Labor Negotiations: An Analysis of a Social Interaction System* (New York: McGraw–Hill).

Walton, R. E. and McKersie, R. B. (1966), 'Behavioural dilemmas in mixed-motive decision-making', *Behavioural Science, 11*, 370–84.

Waxler, Nancy E. and Mishler, E. G. (1966), 'Scoring and reliability problems in interaction process analysis: a methodological note', *Sociometry, 29*, 28–40.

Weick, K. E. (1966), 'The concept of equity in the perception of pay', *Administrative Science Quarterly, 11*, 414–39.

Weick, K. E. (1968), 'Systematic observational methods', in Lindzey, G. and Aronson, E. (eds), *The Handbook of Social Psychology*, vol. II (Reading, Mass.: Addison–Wesley) pp. 357–451.

Weick, K. E. and Nesset, B. (1968), 'Preferences among forms of equity', *Organizational Behaviour and Human Organization, 3*, 400–16.

White, R. K. (1970), *Nobody Wanted War: Misperception in Vietnam and Other Wars* (New York: Doubleday).

Whitehead, A. N. (1953), *Science and the Modern World* (Cambridge: Cambridge University Press).

Wiener, R. S. P. (1971), 'Methodological difficulties associated with the observation of local government committee meetings', *Bulletin of the British Psychological Society, 24*, 31–4.

Wiener, Y. (1970), 'The effects of "task" and "ego-oriented" performance on two kinds of overcompensation inequity', *Organizational Behaviour and Human Performance, 5*, 191–208.

Wilcox, P. (1971), 'To negotiate or not to negotiate: toward a definition of a Black position', in Chalmers, W. E. and Cormick, G. W. (eds), *Racial Conflict and Negotiations: Perspectives and First Case Studies* (Ann Arbor, Mich.: Institute of Labor and Industrial Relations, University of Michigan–Wayne State University and the National Center for Dispute Settlement of the American Arbitration Association) pp. 26–70.

Williams, R. J. Jr (1947), *The Reduction of Intergroup Tensions*, No. 57 (New York: Social Science Research Council).

Wilson, A. (1970), *War Gaming* (Harmondsworth: Penguin Books).

Wilson, C. (1974), *Watergate Words: A Naturalistic Study of Media and Communication*, Ref. E/74240/CW (London: Communications Study Group, Joint Unit for Planning Research, 172 Tottenham Court Rd, W1P 0BS).

Wodehouse, P. G. (1974), *Aunts Aren't Gentlemen* (London: Barrie and Jenkins).

Wright, H. F. (1967), *Recording and Analyzing Child Behaviour* (New York, Evanston, Ill., and London: Harper and Row).

Wrightsman, L. S., O'Connor, J. and Baker, N. J. (eds) (1972), *Cooperation and*

Competition: Readings on Mixed-Motive Games (Belmont, Calif.: Brooks/Cole Publishing).

Wrightsman, L. S. *et al.* (1972), *Social Psychology in the Seventies* (Monterey, Calif.: Brooks/Cole Publishing).

Wyer, R. S. (1969), 'Prediction of behaviour in two-person games', *Journal of Personality and Social Psychology, 13*, 222–38.

Zeuthen, F. (1930), *Problems of Monopoly and Economic Welfare* (London: Routledge and Sons).

Zinnes, D. (1966), 'A comparison of hostile behaviour of decision-makers in simulated and historical data', *World Politics, 18*, 474–502.

Author Index

Subject Index